An Unlikely Socialist

AN UNLIKELY SOCIALIST

Henry Hyde Champion
and the Women He Loved

Sandra Burchill

First Published in 2022 by Echo Books

Echo Books is an imprint of Superscript Publishing Pty Ltd,
ABN 76 644 812 395

Registered Office: Suite 401, 140 Bourke St, Melbourne, VIC, 3000
www.echobooks.com.au

Copyright © 2022 Sandra Burchill

ISBN: 9781922603111 (paperback)

Contents

Introduction	7
Destined to Serve: Champion's Early Years (1859–1882)	14
Activism: Learning to be an Agitator (1882–1890)	24
His Place in History	52
One of the People: Juliet Bennett (1855–1886)	96
Salvation and Socialism: Margaret Elise Harkness (1854–1923)	114
Love in a Warm Climate: Adelaide Hogg (1854–1930)	166
A Mild Affection: Elsie Belle Goldstein (1870–1953)	226
A Guilty Secret: Katharine Susannah Prichard (1883–1969)	270
A Remembrance	333
Endnotes	336
Acknowledgements	350
Bibliography	351
Index	362

Introduction

HENRY HYDE CHAMPION (1859–1928) has been labelled variously as 'one of the idle class', 'an agitator' and 'a swell socialist' and even today he mystifies anyone looking at his life and legacy. One Australian newspaper identified him as 'something of a puzzle to many folks' and many variants of 'puzzle' are repeatedly used when discussing him. People were suspicious because here was 'a man of birth, education and social position' and 'at the same time a Socialist, of the most militant type'. Champion's friend Herbert Brookes (a financial supporter of his political campaign in Melbourne) saw 'some strange trait in his character which did not commend him to his fellow citizens' even though 'he would have wittingly taken risks and made sacrifices' to assist them.[1]

His political involvement is significant. A founding member of the Social Democratic Federation in England (1884), he incited the London Trafalgar Riots (1886), was a central figure in the Great London Dock Strike (1889) and, as an early advocate of a party for the working class, his efforts would culminate in the founding of the Independent Labour Party (1892). In Australia, he secured the ire of the trade union movement when involved in the early stages of the Maritime Strike (1890). Whether his historical importance can be accurately gauged or not, the balance tips towards recognition of his earnest commitment to political, labour and social issues, including concern for the advancement of women. There has been a general omission of his narrative in any accounts until recently, although he was surrounded by historically important people.

A Royal Artillery Officer educated at Woolwich and a gentleman from an aristocratic family with a proud historical connection to Scottish nobility, his London friends called him 'patrician'. He astounded his family and associates by throwing up his commission in the British Army to champion the working class, driven by a belief that socialism had the economic, political and social answers as well as the tools for systemic change. Socialism provided Champion with a way to realise this vision of freeing people from injustice, poverty and despair through the creation of a new party that had the interests of male and female workers as paramount.

Throughout history there exists a love-hate relationship for 'conviction' politicians who assert fundamental values or ideas rather than seeking compromise or consensus. Champion often seemed to stand alone, collecting enemies from both sides of the social divide and even across countries. Close contemporaries often used the words 'sincere', 'straightforward', 'honest' and talked of his 'courage', 'modesty' and 'self-sacrifice'; others saw him as 'autocratic', 'treacherous', 'unscrupulous', 'a coward', 'embittered' and saw his aspirations as shallow, believing behind them lay a personal desire for success and glory. In any case, he was widely regarded as an 'agitator', even a dangerous troublemaker.

Oscar Wilde's article, 'The Soul of Man Under Socialism', in February 1890, defined agitators as 'interfering, meddling people, who come down to some perfectly contented class of the community, and sow the seeds of discontent amongst them', to assist in an 'advance towards civilization'. In today's terms Champion would be called a disruptor because he effectively changed the status quo. By changing people's thinking and behaviour, disruption leads to the creation of something new, so Champion can be regarded as an innovator, shown specifically in his compelling assertion that a political machine was needed for the working class in the shape of an Independent Labour Party. By concentrating on an eight-hour day and working conditions, his small party of protest was transformed into one capable of being elected to government. Driven by a political purpose and aided by his many publishing ventures, he helped create an effective profile for socialists, one that fuelled change. He was also generous, helping many socialists burst into print, proofing and editing his friends' work as they explored their radical ideas. Without Champion's editorial assistance, John Burns, Tom Mann, Ben Tillett and Clementina Black could not have found their way into well-regarded journals where they reached a wide and diverse audience.

At an Old Bailey trial after the Trafalgar Square Riots in 1886, his close friend John Burns pointed to him as 'one of the idle classes' who chose the cause of workers. Too radical for the establishment, too unpredictable for the radicals, he was a double-edged sword and an outlier. Sometimes, the profile overtook the man, as in the case of 'Tory gold' when the Social Democratic Federation took money from a rich radical socialist for electoral expenses. Associated with Champion's name, this phrase was 'a standing joke' and 'a comic myth' for socialists such as Robert Blatchford. However, the term took on a life of its own and became a rolling historical cliché still used in politics over 135 years later. Rumours abounded about his wild ambition for his own advancement, some fuelled by Frederick Rolfe's fictitious presentation in *Hadrian the Seventh* about his role as 'commander-in-chief' for 'a Social Revolution'. Many echoed and embroidered fiction, labelling him H.M. Hyndman's 'lieutenant'. Herbert Brookes noted that insiders believed Hyndman and Champion had revolutionary plans to make Hyndman 'president' of 'a Peoples' Republic' and Champion 'head of the military'.

One notable impulse was Champion's love of poking a hornet's nest, a recklessness that was unsettling to friends and infuriating to enemies. His hard-hitting and brutal journalism made life-long enemies, attracted numerous libel suits and sometimes engendered vitriolic rage. When tempered by the inevitable march of time and history that diminished the intensity of old disputes, socialist recollections and reminiscences of Champion were of a person intensely committed to socialism, with the courage of his convictions. One contemporary historian of socialism in Great Britain recognised Champion had been left out of labour history:

> And if Champion has been pushed out of the scene, it is partly because he left England for Australia; and partly because, indifferent to fame, he was ambitious rather to get things done than to have the credit for the accomplished fact.[2]

In some ways Champion may have been responsible for his own enigmatic reputation. Walter Murdoch recognised this when he mentioned Champion's 'modesty' and took issue with his account of the London Dock Strike in 1889: 'You suppress your own personality so completely that critics a hundred years hence won't believe you wrote it. You leave out just what I want to know'.[3] The well-known maxim, 'a great deal of good is accomplished if a person doesn't care who receives the credit', was apparent in Champion who operated on the principles of service, duty and self-restraint.

After Champion's death on 30 April 1928 important objects went missing. His infantry swords (inherited from his father) disappeared. His service medal, struck in 1881 with Queen Victoria's profile from his time in Afghanistan with 5th Battery, 8th Brigade, and carried in his breast pocket during World War One, vanished. Like many soldiers and writers of the time, Champion also possessed diaries from his time in India, England and Australia, along with personal papers, letters from friends and relatives and precious manuscripts, such as the original 'revolutionary' poem by William Morris in his possession in 1896 when the latter died. None of these survived. Records and paperwork of Australian publishing ventures including the *Book Lover*, the Book Lovers' Library and the Australasian Authors' Agency were also destroyed.

Although Champion corresponded constantly with many literary and political authors and often released sections from these letters to the journal *Book Lover* and newspapers (*Socialist* and *Age*), few of these letters remain. The exception is correspondence from Champion to his close friend, Morley Roberts, written primarily between April 1896 and December 1910 (and sporadically during the early 1920s). Because Champion's letters were self-reflective and honest in their stream of consciousness, they illustrate his emotional interior and the landscape of love affairs. Together with Champion's interviews about events in his life for *Trident*, as well as newspaper articles, these primary sources provide essential information about a man scarcely mentioned in memoirs by friends and contemporaries. Diaries and letters from people like Bernard Shaw and Beatrice Potter, still exist today though these were written as individual records and precious keepsakes from a time that allowed secrets, when no-one envisaged the breaking of shorthand codes, access to the internet, library databases or correspondence sold to collectors.

After the Trafalgar Riots and the London Dock Strike propelled him to fame, Champion claimed to be the 'hero of no fewer than *seven* novels'.[4] This was no idle boast for he was a recognisable character in novels including Mrs Humphry Ward's *Marcella* (1894), Clementina Black's *An Agitator* (1894), Morley Roberts's *Maurice Quain* (1897), Margaret Harkness's two books, *Captain Lobe: A Story of the Salvation Army* (1889) and *George Eastmont: Wanderer* (1905), Frederick Rolfe's *Hadrian the Seventh* (1904) and Alfred Buchanan's *Bubble Reputation: A Story of Modern Life* (1906); perhaps even J.S. Fletcher's *Daniel Quayne: A Morality* (1907). He was also George Blake in his own book, *The Root of the Matter* (1895) and, many decades after his death, Katharine Susannah Prichard's newspaper editor in *Subtle Flame* (1967). In addition, he featured in *Studies in the Psychology of Sex* (1897–1910) where Havelock Ellis described Champion as a married 'man of letters' (History VI), joining subjects such as Olive Schreiner (History IX), Eleanor Marx (History X), Edward Aveling (History V), Edward Carpenter (History VII) and Beatrice Potter (History II).

At the turn of last century Ellis put on record Champion's 'mental and emotional interest in passion' rather than merely physical attraction for a woman. With his father absent in India for many years of his childhood, Champion was surrounded mostly by females, including his mother, three sisters, maternal aunts, cousins and a governess. When older he met a variety of women of different ages and interests, insisting 'the human race has been given, metaphorically speaking, two legs on which to advance; and it will never do so satisfactorily whilst one of its legs is tied up in a sling and it is forced as a consequence to hobble along on crutches'.[5] To Champion, women's rights were essential to the broader battle against injustice and oppression.

Ernest Belfort Bax, a member of the Democratic Federation, wrote in his 1918 memoirs that Champion was 'a fanatical Feminist' because of Australian 'family ties'. This observation pointed to Champion's sister-in-law, Vida Goldstein, a central figure in the suffragette movement. However, it ignored Champion's belief in universal suffrage, as stated in the first issue of *Justice* in 1884, as well as his early advocacy of August Bebel's theories on socialism and the 'Woman Question'. For Champion the term 'New Woman' was sculpted not only as an early image of suffragettes demanding the vote but for all women's rights. With sparkling wit, he argued against men using 'the intentions of nature', requesting from opponents an original, unrevised, 'authenticated copy' of these principles, writing: 'The New Woman has searched far and wide for an authoritative exposition of the laws of nature as she has always felt a certain difficulty about attempting to repeal a law until she knew what that law was'.[6]

Champion's book *The Root of the Matter* (1895) included a chapter 'of special value' to people curious about the Woman Question and equal rights. The centenary of Representation of the People Act 1918, recently marked in Great Britain and Ireland, is a reminder of the long struggle involved in the vote for women (at least in those days for women over 30 who held £5 of property). Champion's open admiration in August 1895 of Mary Wollstonecraft who 'hurled a thunderbolt into English conservatism' by writing *A Vindication of the Rights of Woman* (1792) made him a staunch supporter of the fledging women's movement in Australia. (Today, Wollstonecraft and her work are honoured in Newington Green with her words: 'I do not wish women to have power over men; but over themselves'.)

Clear evidence emerges that Champion had at least four major female relationships: a marriage with an English woman, Juliet Bennett, arguably one of George Bernard Shaw's inspirations for Eliza Doolittle; a close relationship with English journalist, novelist and social reformer, Margaret Harkness; a secret affair pursued with a wealthy, married, children's author in Australia, Adelaide Hogg; and a second marriage to Elsie Goldstein, a graduate of Melbourne University and sister to suffragette and social activist, Vida Goldstein. During Champion's last marriage, there is also substantial evidence of another clandestine affair with a young Australian writer, Katharine Susannah Prichard.

Champion was regarded as an outsider, someone who was not accepted by the working poor but who longed 'to become one of them; living as they live, suffering as they suffer'; marriage to Juliet would shore up his credentials with 'the People'. Maggie, a writer, social reformer and also an outsider, was inspired by Champion to work for Keir Hardie's election, to fight for dock workers during the London

Dock Strike and to travel to Australia; she would fight against her more romantic feelings for Champion and later write a novel about a labour leader using him as a model for her protagonist. Champion's intense and disastrous seven-year obsession with Adelaide Hogg, a married woman he wanted to rescue, 'gutted' him emotionally; he finally broke off the painful affair. A second marriage to Elsie Belle Goldstein established a stable domestic life that reinvigorated Champion and he seemed to have found genuine happiness. Only months after his marriage, his thoughtful words and gentle encouragement to a schoolgirl writer would lead (10 years later) to a lengthy secret friendship and affair. An unlikely socialist, with devotion to the ideals of service, duty, and self-sacrifice, would harbour other romantic ideas.

Writing is never a static process and new narratives are possible by taking a fresh look at old interpretations and sources. While a focus on a central personality has the potential to diminish other characters, Champion's life is a natural scaffold for the study of a number of women whose disparate stories perhaps would not be told. These women, in turn, highlight aspects of his life through their own stories, helping shape our perspective of a complicated and committed man with a vision for a better future.

Destined to Serve

Champion's Early Years (1859–1882)

The past is never dead. It's not even past.
(William Faulkner, *Requiem for a Nun*)

Henry Hyde Champion, or Harry to his family, was born on 22 January 1859 in Poona (Pune) in India in the aftermath of the Sepoy mutiny when his father was 600 miles away chasing the remnants of the Indian Rebellion at Mungrowlee (Mungaoli). James Hyde Champion was largely absent throughout Harry's early years in India where he served as Assistant Adjutant-General to General Sir John Michel and saw action in Rajghor, Mungrowlee, Sindwaho, Kurai and Mhow. A total of five children were born to James and his wife Henrietta in the East Indies: Anne Beatrice in 1857, nearly two years before Harry, then Charles Stuart the following year, Mary Leslie in 1862 and Louisa Elizabeth in 1863. A last child, Arthur Duncan was conceived by their father on a visit to England and born in 1865 when Harry was six. Around the end of 1863, Harry's father decided to move his family back to London where he became a visitor who returned only on army leave.

The family spent their June 1869 holiday at their country house in Buckden without their father, who was still stationed in India as a Colonel. Buckden was a special place for Harry's paternal grandmother. Elizabeth's brother, Adam Urquhart, had married the daughter of Edward Maltby, the Vicar of St Mary's church in Buckden; Maltby was later appointed Bishop of Chichester during Cardinal Manning's time as Archdeacon of Chichester.[7] The eldest boys, Harry and Charles, visited their six Duff cousins for a summer holiday at Hatton Castle in Turriff where they were encouraged to wander the halls and estate, roam the vast parklands, woods and lochs. The fifteenth century castle was Harry's favourite place as a young boy and he fondly remembered being in 'disgrace' after he was thrown into one of the Lakes of Hatton by three Duffs.[8] While their governess was picking up the two boys from the railway station, a catastrophic accident killed Charles, then only nine years old. Miss Amelia Murray had taken Annie Beatrice with her to collect them from the Peterborough station, conveniently situated on the East Coast Main line between Edinburgh and London. Half an hour after boarding, the train arrived at the small neighbouring parish of Offord and the children crossed the rail lines while Amelia was busy with luggage. Unaware of an express train coming around the bend, Charles was hit by the engine and his little body was thrown under the front of the train in full view of his two terrified siblings who narrowly escaped the same fate. There was a funeral in September and an inquest in Huntingdonshire, with a full investigation reported by the Cambridge press. Determined a tragic accident, the inquest apportioned no blame although a severe lack of staff and no telegraph ability was criticised for lengthy delays in summoning assistance.[9] While Harry never spoke of his brother's death in public the accident must have been a formative experience for a child aged ten. In a heartbreaking moment of inattention, Harry and Annie were witnesses to the full horror.

Exactly how the death of her son affected Henrietta is unclear. In the census of April 1871 when Harry was 12, his father was briefly home and the governess was still with them. As a schoolboy at Marlborough, Champion recalled being taken, 'as a visitor only', to a private mental asylum for luncheon where he listened to patients who bought bonds issued to support Arthur Orton's highly published claims to an inheritance, as a long-lost son in the Tichborne case.[10] A close relative temporarily struggling with issues seems likely for it was highly unusual for a student to be taken to such an institution. Barrister and writer Herman Merivale described his 'death-in-life' experience at one expensive, private asylum, Ticehurst, following his breakdown after a close relative died in *My Experiences in a Lunatic Asylum by a Sane Patient* (1879). An increasingly disconnected and damaged mother, together with a largely absent father, may have led to an emotionless comment to Morley Roberts on 26 October 1896: 'My Father and Mother have both died'. When Henrietta died in her seventies at Tower House on Avenue Road in Leicester, he also wrote that a father 'often knows but little of his children, and as they grow up is more or less a stranger to them'.[11] Harry's father never had a chance to know his own father who was shot disarming a drunk sentry in the Caribbean at Fort Charlotte when he was a baby; after which James Hyde was sent to the Edinburgh Academy at age 10 and, six years later, to the East India Company Military Seminary at Addiscombe. The pattern of absent fathers was the norm.

As an avid reader Harry retreated into a solitary and imaginative world of daring feats and dashing heroes. He read eagerly with an eye for excitement selecting the novels of Lord Lytton such as *Ernest Maltravers*, its sequel *Alice*, and adventure stories of a chivalrous highway man during the French Revolution, *Paul Clifford*. He took a special adolescent delight in James Grant's novels, especially *The Romance of War, or The Highlanders in Spain* (1845) whose central character was an impoverished laird's son marching with the 78th Highlanders at the Waterloo and Peninsular campaigns, with battles and skirmishes depicted and strategy explained. At twelve, Grant's novels were part of a 'long debauch, ending in a week of such book-drunkenness' where Harry abandoned his allocated household chores and duties and, as a consequence, the book was banned at home. A runaway Boston sailor, in the service of the family, became a steadfast friend who provided the cover for a small boy to continue his delightfully illicit reading.[12] The retainer played the concertina at the local Mechanics' Institute's dances and the 'martial strains' of his music were entwined with Harry's reading of Napoleonic wars. While the family believed Harry to be supervised and enjoying the local dances, he was next door in the men's dressing room eagerly reading one of his precious books loaned from the Free Library.

Seeking to steer his pre-teen son's enjoyment away from dare-devil heroes towards classic novels, Harry's father chose William Thackeray whom he met in Wiesbaden, West Germany after the Crimean War.[13] Thackeray often stayed at Wiesbaden, a town on the Rhine famous for over two dozen hot springs where visitors could take the waters and where he wrote *The Newcomes*, a story of a Colonel based in India who marries his cousin. *The Virginians* was also an ideal introduction and centred on twin brothers, Harry and George Warrington, born to an aristocratic British family descended from the Normans and fighting on opposite sides in the American War of Independence.

Three years after the tragic death of his little brother, Harry was a quiet teenager off to boarding school in Wiltshire. For the next four years (1872–76) he was educated at Marlborough College where his housemaster was Augustus Henry Beesly, a Greek and Roman historian, translator of Euripides and author of *Danton, and Other Verses* (1896). He remembered Beesly affectionately and would go on to correspond with him until his death; he felt indebted to him for his love of literature and the written word, for the enthusiasm and intellectual curiosity Beesly engendered. However, a couple of other schoolboys regarded Beesly in similar fashion as those enduring 'the swish of the cane' in Kipling's *Stalky & Co.*

Harry's classical education included the study of Robert Browning's Greek translations but his love of Browning's poetry began in earnest as a young lieutenant when he picked up two volumes in Gibraltar on the way to India.[14] His study of French made Harry a fluent speaker and later he translated *Scènes de la Vie de Bohème* by Parisian journalist Henri Murger into English as *Bohemian Life* (1895) using his pseudonym 'Leslie Orde'.[15] Leslie was a family name and 'Orde' suggested gold coin, a reference to 'Tory gold'.

At Marlborough, fellow students were Horatio Kitchener, Robert Percival Bodley Frost, Dion Boucicault Junior, Anthony Hope [Hawkins], Charles Llewellyn Davies and brother Arthur, the father of the boys who inspired *Peter Pan*, Richard Twopenny and several sons of Sir William Stawell, Chief Justice of Victoria. Anthony Hope was described as an 'inert and uninteresting' schoolboy who developed into a successful and popular author, although Harry too was a 'grave, shy, and reserved' youth. Harry's final academic report was dismissive of his overall results and brutally frank in assessing university as a pointless waste of time. Principal Frederic Farrar predicted 'his pupil would come to no good' because of his 'masterly faculty for doing nothing'.[16]

Harry decided on a structured military career, joining generations of his family who had seen military service. His father paid for an expert instructor as coach for the entry examinations and everyone was surprised in August 1876 when Harry excelled in Greek and Latin in open competition for admission to the Woolwich Military Academy where General Sir John Ayde was governor. A fellow cadet (later Major-General Sir Charles Edward Callwell) in his *Stray Recollections* (1923) noted Harry's popularity with other cadets, his ability to think effectively and his status as the 'most intellectual member' of their intake. As a young boy with a head full of adventurous dreams of William the Conqueror, the Crusades, Lairds and Chiefs, Harry embraced this military career pathway. His grandfather and father were successful officers who both married Scottish aristocracy, the Urquhart seats located at Meldrum House, Craigston Castle and Hatton Castle in Aberdeenshire, where cousins often intermarried to entwine their families over centuries. Harry's paternal grandfather, John Carey Champion, was a Captain in the 21st Regiment of Royal North British (Scots) Fusiliers and Sandhurst graduate. On 19 September 1813 he married Elizabeth Herries Urquhart who was one of eight children born to William Urquhart, Laird of Craigston Castle, after his second marriage to Margaret ('Peggy') Ogilvie on 27 December 1780. Their son, James Hyde Champion, Harry's father, married Henrietta Susan Urquhart on 4 December 1855 at St Matthew's church in Meldrum, Scotland. A friend from his youth Henrietta was one of fifteen children of Beauchamp Colclough Urquhart and with their marriage the house of Meldrum and Byth was united with the Urquharts of Craigston.

Knowledge of heraldry, as Thackeray wrote in *The Virginians*, was an essential part of the education of many noble families and at an early age Harry was aware of his ancestry as landed gentry. As one of the oldest families in Scotland, their lineage was traced back to one of the first Hereditary Sheriffs after the Conquest, William Urquhart of Cromarty. Elizabeth Herries Urquhart's father sold the Cromarty estate (on the Black Isle of the Cromarty Firth near Inverness) but retained Craigston. Harry felt the historical charm to an earlier clan chief Sir Thomas Urquhart of Cromarty who took part in the Royalist uprising for Charles II, and David Urquhart, a Scottish diplomat in Istanbul and friend of King William IV, Jeremy Bentham and Karl Marx. David Urquhart was part of the Meldrum house, a 'younger son' of another branch who owned Craigston Castle and so both Meldrum and Craigston branches had Sir Thomas Urquhart as their ancestor. When the branch was reduced to one Catholic priest after Lieutenant Colonel Francis Urquhart died in 1915, the debt-riddled Craigston estate was left to the Church; in fact, it passed from Arthur (Father Jerome) to another younger brother, Michael, to his son Bruce Urquhart, the latter an Indian-born conservationist, educational planner and bohemian, a lover of painters and writers.[17]

Harry's graduation in 1878 guaranteed him a commission in the Royal Artillery where he followed in the footsteps of his cousin who was friend and role model. While Harry was home on school holidays, Beauchamp Duff, 'the last of Kitchener's men', spent weekends at their Marylebone home while training at Woolwich. As a new lieutenant aged 19, Harry found himself posted to Plymouth in Devon, before he sailed to India via the Suez where he later recalled buying wares over the side of the ship from 'picturesque' Aden locals who 'paddled' off with both money and goods.

In India Harry followed a study routine similar to his Woolwich entry examination and secured the coaching services of two native language teachers in Bombay (Mumbai). Although it was not necessary for normal duties, he ambitiously studied two Hindustani languages for six weeks, sixteen hours a day in two rotations, in order to sit both a 'higher' and 'lower' examination for appointment to the Bombay Arsenal. Harry's study paid off in both money and elevation to second-in-command where at just 21 he was paid the substantial wage of £700 a year plus his normal army pay.[18] Later, his language skills were put to further use during the London Dock Strike when he conversed in Hindustani with Indian sailors serving on British ships about their conditions of employment.

Following the Cavagnari massacre in Afghanistan, Harry returned to Kirkee military base at Poona to his old unit, 5th Battery, 8th Brigade where his mountain battery was ordered to Lahore for travel to Kandahar to support the 2nd Mountain Battery.[19] Troops travelled quickly to the north-west frontier by marching over the Western Ghats in late July and then through the Bolan Pass. Their mule trains were loaded with supplies, ammunition and light guns that could be easily dismantled and carried on the backs of animals. Five Indian drivers from northern India who enlisted as cavalry found their responsibilities also included looking after 'hybrid and unclean' mules and, as an interpreter between the Indian and English-speaking troops, Harry explained their refusal to carry out duties on religious grounds. They were still sentenced to 50 lashes by a cat-o'-nine tails and at dawn Harry watched their brutal punishment. The vision of the flogging stayed with him and acted as an impetus for his later opposition to corporal and capital punishment. Later one of the drivers murdered the sergeant major responsible for their recruitment and was hung at Quetta. Recounting the unhappy tale, he pointed to 300 million people who were 'badly misgoverned' and even years later found the resulting tragedy difficult to explain.[20] He also spoke of a British invasion, the long Afghani memory and their hatred of those who imposed a 'puppet' leader upon them, writing cynically of a typical Kipling reader who 'generally fancies he knows all about the native question, to say nothing of re-organising the British army in India', acknowledging he could never work out such a complex country.[21]

Through difficult terrain and summer's blazing heat, men and animals travelled more than a hundred miles overland to Quetta, at that time part of Northern India and now in Pakistan. They wound their way quickly to the Khojak Pass not knowing when the battle for Kandahar would occur but realizing it was imminent, winter snows ensuring war fighting soon would be impossible. Travelling fast with little artillery or wheeled transport, General Roberts led a forced march of over 300 miles from Kabul to Kandahar to relieve the British garrison, envisaging troops from India as essential for battle. Harry briefly glimpsed Roberts, together with part of his division, after the battle as they marched back to Quetta on 9 September. He watched the 'thin and ragged line' of weary Scottish soldiers appear on the plain and vividly remembered the sight and sound as he rode his horse up the Khojak Pass in early morning darkness to meet Roberts and the 92nd and 72nd Highlanders: 'The skirling of the pipes could be heard through the winding passes for some time before one's eyes fell upon the tattered, war-worn veterans'.[22] Beauchamp Duff was with Roberts in Kabul and Lieutenant Thomas Bedford Urquhart was part of the

72nd Highlander regiment, telling his eight-year-old nephew 'many a story that sank deep in the mind' when home on leave. Later, after discovering a blind piper from the 92nd Highlanders in Aberdeen, Harry corresponded with Lord Roberts and received an immediate reply detailing arrangements for the Afghan War veteran's admission to care.[23]

The glorious tales of army battles and derring-do that had coloured Harry's childhood, turned out to be a long gruelling August march to Quetta only to discover the battle was over. Harry joined many who saw war as months of boredom punctuated by moments of sheer terror, echoing this sentiment to Morley Roberts on 3 October 1899 when he wrote about the possibility of becoming a Boer war correspondent for the *Age*: 'I've been through one campaign & I know it is but a ha'penny worth of excitement to an intolerable deal of marking time & incredible discomfort'.[24] The respite at Quetta was accompanied by typhoid, which raged for thirteen days and brought Harry close to death. The high fever affected the young lieutenant's health, inflaming and weakening his heart muscles and leaving him open in the long term to heart disease as well as neurological complications and perhaps infertility. After he was capable of being moved, he was invalided home to London to recover and lived with both his parents and siblings at 17 Harewood Square, Marylebone.

In summer 1881 Harry visited Passy on the Right Bank in Paris spending six weeks with his sixteen-year-old brother who was now finished school at Sherborne. Arthur was studying French in preparation for his own army examinations where language was a pre-requisite for joining the 21st Lancers; later Aide-de-Camp to the Governor of Trinidad and Tobago Arthur fought at Omdurman in the Sudan where he marched with Winston Churchill in 1898. Presumably Harry used his time in Paris to assist his younger brother and it was here, through a French artilleryman, that Harry met Victor Hugo.[25] Hugo spent many years in exile on the Channel Island of Guernsey where a branch of the Champions resided and dedicated *Les Travailleurs de la Mer* (1866) to 'this corner of old Norman land'; here he also wrote *Les Misérables* (1862).

A year's convalescence meant Harry saw a lot of his old Marlborough class-mate Percy Frost who, like Harry, was living with his mother and sisters in central London. Employed as a clerk for the West India Merchants Office, Percy was familiar with the East End of London where his uncle, Charles Henry Bromby, was headmaster of Stepney Grammar School. Percy took his 22-year-old friend to show him an existence far removed from fashionable London. Harry was shocked at the living conditions and poverty and recalled to Walter Murdoch: 'It appalled me. What I saw in London during those few weeks completely changed the course of my life'.[26] He later referred to the city as 'the great sink through which flowed in times of depression the vast mass of British misery and destitution'.[27] Many years before, Percy Bysshe Shelley captured London in an evocative image of a monstrous sea that 'vomits its wrecks' and continues wolf-like to devour and bay for more. Around the Tower Hamlets in the East End lived many unskilled workers and Charles Booth, a social researcher, estimated it was home to at least 10,000 casual, poorly paid dock labourers. The newly constructed £4 million Tilbury docks served the East and West India Dock Company's operations, with Tilbury pubs known as the 'shipping office' because workers often received their pay there.

Before Harry returned to military duty, he and Percy sailed to Boston, with the intention of visiting the American Civil War battlefields around Massachusetts, New York, Pennsylvania, Virginia and Georgia. In an interview nearly a decade later, he reported similarities between New York and Melbourne as both 'Mammon-worshipping places', scorning the reverence for material wealth by 'land-jobbers, and "boom" creators posing as popular leaders'. Although little is known about their wanders through this part of America, their route took them to Cumberland County in the Tennessee 'backwoods'.[28] Somewhere on the east coast of America, Harry picked up a small gold alarm clock that he kept on his mantlepiece in Gray's Inn Place, London. This clock featured in the writing of two friends – Margaret Harkness placed it on George's mantlepiece in *George Eastmont: Wanderer* and Bernard Shaw on the flower girl's mantlepiece over an empty fireplace in *Pygmalion*. During their American travels they immersed themselves in Henry George's pamphlet *The Irish Land Question* and his book *Progress and*

Poverty so it was no surprise ideas of land nationalism and taxation were central to Harry's first public speech, delivered in the open air at Peckham Rye Park late in 1881 to assert freedom of speech originally guaranteed by an Act of Parliament in 1872.[29] In the recollections of unionist James MacDonald, newly arrived in London from Edinburgh, Harry also delivered a nervous lecture to a meeting at 49 Tottenham Street where working men were vocal in their opposition to his open admiration of Henry George.

On return to Woolwich at the beginning of 1882, Harry was placed on light duties for a few months as he eased back into the army, retiring in the afternoons to his room where he smoked up to eight pipes of tobacco a day while reading and studying Adam Smith, John Stuart Mill, David Ricardo and Karl Marx. Woolwich housed the Garrison Theatre in an old church in the Royal Artillery barracks where Harry's love of theatre was sparked as he watched with amusement and admiration A.C. Daniell strutting the boards.[30] After a short respite, Harry was posted to Portsmouth as adjutant to Lieutenant Colonel W.R. Llewellyn, who held him in high regard from his time in India. He declined a posting as ADC to General Thomas Steele, commander of troops in Ireland.[31] Subsequently, his reasons for leaving the army in September 1882 were recorded:

> He disagreed with the policy of the Egyptian campaign and thought it was a thousand pities that England should have interfered to bolster up the Khedive Government. At that time intelligence came to hand of the success of the battle of Tel-el-Kebir, and as that was practically the close of operations he sent in his papers, though begged not to do so by his fellow officers, who said he had a good record.[32]

The whole direction of his life changed when he became a socialist.

Activism

Learning to be an Agitator (1882–1890)

*'What I saw in London during those few weeks
completely changed the course of my life.'*
(*Trident*, June 1908)

The year following Harry's departure from the British Army he found his calling, discovered his political voice and sought exciting new opportunities with a variety of associations advocating change. He was known formally as H.H. Champion in his publishing and speaking ventures, 'HH' by new friends like James (Jem) MacDonald, or simply 'Champion'. Before handing in his army commission, he and Percy Frost attended John C. Foulger's Progressive Association which met on Sunday nights at Islington Hall where they were brought into contact with a circle of people with radical ideas. Throughout 1882 a variety of lectures included Champion's 'Poets of the Revolution' and James Leigh Joynes's 'Adventures in Ireland'.[33] Champion chaired many discussions at these meetings, even as late as July 1885.

Champion first met Henry S. Salt, brother-in-law to Joynes, at an 'assemblage' of Eton masters headed by Edward Lyttelton. According to Salt, Joynes was forced to resign as teacher there after writing about his adventures with Henry George in Ireland and recalled Champion and Frost invited him to 'a complimentary dinner' after his resignation.[34] Champion, Frost and Joynes were also present in November 1882 at a Holborn Town Hall meeting where Hyndman claimed socialists gained 'a knot of very clever enthusiastic young men'.[35] Hyndman was the driving force for the creation of a socialist organisation as early as June 1881 after a meeting at the Westminster Palace Hotel in January, chaired by Joseph Cowen, that sought an alliance between workingmen's clubs.[36]

While living in Old Waterloo Road, Lambeth, Champion set up a window cleaning business with James MacDonald from the Marylebone Democratic Society and John (Jack) Edward Williams from the Rose Street Club in Soho, their enterprise turned into a very successful business by a subsequent owner.[37] Believing his son probably needed a more reliable occupation than cleaning windows, Champion's father gave him £2,000 to invest in a publishing house, Kegan Paul & Co, printers of *Progress and Poverty* (1881) by Henry George and the *Adventures of a Tourist in Ireland* (1882) by Joynes. Later, Champion recalled Charles Kegan Paul's warning that publishing was 'not the ready road to wealth that many people think it'. Within three months of working in the office at 1 Paternoster Row, Champion withdrew his investment in favour of a new enterprise to further his aspirations. With the original sum, plus an additional £2,000 provided by his father, he became a partner with Foulger in Modern Press and later admitted to spending the whole of his £4,000 within seven years on publishing propaganda, journals, pamphlets and books until the printing press ceased in 1889.[38]

Champion's pace was frenetic. As he explored various options, he became a frequent speaker at street corners around in Stepney. Reverend George Sale Reaney of the Stepney Meeting House Congregational Church admitted hearing Champion speak many times and inviting him to his church hall at the end of 1883 for a debate on emigration before an audience of working men, believing he was actively searching for a solution. Hyndman recalled Arnold White and Jack Williams also debating socialism at Reaney's Congregational Church Hall, the former running for the Mile End constituency in 1886 and the latter a branch secretary for the Democratic Federation.[39] Greatly worried about the poor, Reaney saw the East End as 'the drift of London, the human refuse of the whole land'.

Only eighteen months after first reading Henry George, Champion was on a committee with Alfred Russel Wallace to organise his lecturing tour. By then Cardinal Manning had read *Progress and Poverty* and wanted a meeting with the author.[40] In June 1883 at 14 Paternoster Row, Modern Press commenced publishing the *Christian Socialist*, a title derived from the founder of Christian Socialism, Frederick D.

Maurice, and Charles Kingsley. The newly formed Land Reform Union was used as a platform to spread Henry George's ideas with an objective of restoring land to the people with Champion treasurer and Frost secretary. A former student of Frederick Maurice at Cambridge and later a Fabian, Reverend Stewart Headlam, together with Sydney Oliver were two other founders of the Land Reform Union. At a committee meeting after its April 1883 formation, Champion told members of a potential member, Bernard Shaw, who joined and promptly recruited Sidney Webb.[41]

Champion was unmarried and living with his parents and sisters at Harewood Square in Marylebone, and Frost resided close by with his wealthy mother (widow of Reverend John Dixon Frost of Winchmore Hill). Bernard Shaw and his mother had moved from Fitzroy to Marylebone and were invited to Mrs Elizabeth Frost's home at 30 Woburn Place in Russell Square for high tea one spring afternoon in 1883. In Victorian London, upper-class women regularly held soirees or 'at-homes' and Shaw met Oscar Wilde during one such occasion at Lady Wilde's house. Within walking distance of the British Museum, the area was also the meeting place for 'the Socialists of Russell Square' in Clementina Black's novel *An Agitator* (1894), which provided a brief glimpse of Bernard Shaw, a proponent of Dr Gustav Jaeger's theories on rational clothing. Champion told an interviewer that Shaw entertained him with his wit, keeping him in hysterical laughter for the whole visit. He was also amused to record his first meeting with Shaw whose 'boots were in holes and his trousers ragged' and 'his income as a literary journalist was just 7/6 per annum'. Agreeing to read Shaw's manuscripts written in his 'tiny, cramped handwriting', Champion published two of his 'delightful whimsical' writings.[42]

The Unsocial Socialist, was serialised from March to December 1884 in *To-Day* which prompted William Morris to seek out a meeting with Shaw. *Cashel Byron's Profession* was also serialised in *To-Day* between 1885–86 and became Shaw's first novel to be published by Modern Press in February 1886. Champion was a 'devotee' although he recalled his friend's 'horrible habit' of proof revision where he changed words at the start of a paragraph so a compositor was forced to re-set each section as a whole.[43] Shaw noted in his preface to *Cashel Byron's*

Profession Champion's love of pugilism although he was not the only socialist in his circle who enjoyed the sport. Modern Press went on to publish Shaw's new edition of Laurence Gronlund's *The Co-operative Commonwealth in Its Outlines: an Exposition of Modern Socialism*, offering Shaw a paltry £5 in 1884 for a rewrite that irritated Shaw because of the time he spent editing. Later, Shaw would appoint Champion as his theatrical agent for plays performed in Australia.

Modern Press also printed the first political pamphlet for the Democratic Federation, *Socialism Made Plain*, their manifesto including 'stepping stones' for an eight-hour day and public work for the unemployed. At one stage 50,000 copies were in circulation and William Morris, a member of the Democratic Federation since 13 January 1883, was directed on 11 July to send 100 copies (signed by each Executive Committee member) to Reverend William Sharman who was vice president of the Highland Land Law Reform League.

According to Champion, he first met William Morris on 'Whit Monday' 14 May 1883 at a room underneath the Palace Chambers on 9 Bridge Street, Westminster when he and Frost first joined the Democratic Federation. As honorary secretary he signed the first official card to make Morris the treasurer, while Belfort Bax, Eleanor Marx and Aveling were present.[44] The card Morris designed featured an oak tree decoration symbolising knowledge, strength and wisdom while on the reverse were three words: 'Educate, Agitate, Organise'. In a letter on 22 June 1883 to C.E. Maurice (son of Frederick Maurice and husband of Octavia Hill's sister) Morris explained his decision to join England's 'only active Socialist organization' although he had been told it was 'a sort of Tory drag to take the scent off the fox'. Since the aims were obviously socialism and land nationalisation, Morris believed it was 'one of those curious lies for which no one seems responsible, but which stick very tight to the object they are thrown at'.[45] Three names, Hyndman, Champion and Morris, were on the Executive Committee of the Democratic Federation as reported in *Justice* until the organisation was renamed the Social Democratic Federation (SDF). By 26 August Morris thought Hyndman was 'inclined to intrigue and the making of a party',[46] an accusation often levelled at Champion.

Morris was passionate about artistic work centred on the days of chivalry, knightly journeys and quest allegories from Arthurian tales as well as Trojan heroes from the *Odyssey*. All of these medieval and classical tales were studied by Champion in his classical education at Marlborough and this reinforced his appreciation of Morris's creative work, arts and crafts, book illustration and design. As exemplified in the 'toil-worn craftsman' in Ward's *Marcella*, Morris was the embodiment of tension between the ideal of manly labour and the aesthetic beauty of his hand-crafted pieces of furniture and architectural delights. He became a favourite designer chosen by many wealthy people, including Australians, who decorated and furnished their nineteenth century homes. Champion often visited Morris at Kelmscott House where the stables of his eighteenth-century residence were later altered for a lecture hall for the Hammersmith Socialist League. Morris advocated art, education and freedom for all, not a select few, and Maggie Harkness recalled Keir Hardie and Cunninghame Graham asking him to write an ode about the eight-hour day issue; he replied that he would pen one on six because 'A man must have time to enjoy his life'.[47] Champion wrote fondly that Morris was a 'genius' but 'a very poor speaker' who during questions after a lecture 'would get into a towering rage, spluttering with fury and shaking head and fist at the unlucky proselyte who usually was sincerely anxious to clear up some difficulty'.[48]

Praised as one of the best days of his life, Champion rowed with friends in June 1884 up the Thames from Great Marlow (near Merton Abbey) and around Bisham Abbey where Percy Bysshe Shelley wrote *The Revolt of Islam* (1818). Friends included Morris, Shaw, Bax, Joynes, Andreas Scheu (executive member of the Democratic Federation) and artist Cyril R. Hallward (illustrator of Fergus Hume's *When I lived in Bohemia*). This 'golden afternoon' was full of joy with everyone 'in school-humour'. Because Bax and Shaw were 'incapables at the oar', they walked and towed the boat. They lunched at the bridge at Marlow at a way-side inn and ended at the ruins of the Cistercian Abbey at Medmenham in Buckinghamshire, frequented in a past century by the Hellfire Club, a secret society infamous for orgies.[49]

Secretary of Foulger's Progressive Association, Havelock Ellis, told of his first meeting with Champion and Frost in late October 1883, believing they were 'two amiable and noble-spirited young men'. Studying medicine at St Thomas's Hospital, Ellis was able to use many friends and associates, including those met in the Progressive Association and the SDF, as case studies for his *Studies in the Psychology of Sex* (1897–1910). Many Progressive Association attendees were interested in Thomas Davidson's Utopian ideas and on 24 October formed a new and adventurous organisation, 'The Fellowship of New Life'. Champion, Edward Pease and Percival Chubb were chosen for a committee to draft the organisation's aims and met in Champion's office at Modern Press on 15 November. Champion thought little of the title believing it was 'bumptious', 'over-pretentious and high-sounding' and within a few months developed an impatience with self-generating committees, indecision and discussions of spiritual foundations and urged action rather than talk. It was no surprise when he told Havelock Ellis he was not satisfied and would no longer attend but historians generally agree that the Fabian Society evolved from this group in January 1884.[50]

Fabians were no option for Champion as they took the position of influencers, their long-term goal to change opinions slowly through analysis, education and permutation, insufficient for a young man who wanted swift, decisive action and disliked endless compromise and vacillation. He was goal-oriented and firm in purpose. The Democratic Federation emphasised agitation, disruption and public demonstrations to convince others of the immediacy of social need. Active involvement in both the *Christian Socialist* and the Land Reform Union began to tail off as Champion and Frost moved enthusiastically to Democratic Socialism and distanced themselves from Henry George. Champion became more questioning, writing to ask George how land tax could benefit someone unemployed though willing to work, but received no reply.

The first issue of the Democratic Federation newspaper, *Justice: the Organ of Social Democracy*, hit London streets on 19 January 1884. Published by Modern Press in a ground floor building located in Sandland Street not far from Russell Square, production involved Champion, Morris, Shaw, Joynes, Salt, Hubert and Edith Bland and Helen Taylor (stepdaughter of John Stuart Mill). Edward Carpenter, poet and socialist, provided a generous financial gift of £300 to assist the weekly paper and if William Morris was an advocate of communal labour and beauty through craftsmanship, then Carpenter was an example of simple labour in the humble rural community near Sheffield. However, there was also a need for a further subsidy from Morris. Champion, Frost, Morris, Joynes, Hyndman, Williams and Harry Quelch put in long hours walking Ludgate Circus in Fleet Street with their placards to sell *Justice*.[51] Weeks after its launch, agitation by James MacDonald and Jack Williams in Blackburn produced a significant success for the Democratic Federation and resulted in the establishment of the first Lancashire branch during the cotton strike,[52] with membership subsequently increasing in the northern regions of Oldham, Rochdale, Salford and Bolton.

In the first issue of *Justice* Champion firmly stated his desire for universal suffrage and reforms in the political sphere and his contributions covered Henry George, trade unions and London government. A provocative series titled 'Letters to Revolutionary Agents' under the pseudonym 'Diogenes' dealt with such figures as Parnell, Chamberlain and Davitt, while in August he was particularly scathing about Wolseley's relief of General Gordon at Khartoum. Morris wrote a popular series of 'Chants for Socialists' with 'comrades' used as a celebratory address to revolutionary socialists in the old oral tradition of communal halls. A vegetarian tea-shop called the *Cyprus*, on the first floor overlooking Cheapside, was the meeting place and Shaw and Ellis noted they looked there for Champion, Hyndman and Foulger when they weren't at the Modern Press office.

Early in 1884 Champion subsidised a bid for Modern Press to publish the journal *To-Day: the Monthly Magazine of Scientific Socialism*, altering its grandiose subtitle from *A Monthly Gathering of Bold Thoughts* and installing Joynes and Bax as editors. After Bax's departure, Champion and Frost took the role. Champion introduced Ibsen to Britain after boldly proposing the publication of a translation of Ibsen's *Ghosts*, a controversial play dealing with issues of religion, venereal disease, incest and illegitimacy. That October, a series of letters from Havelock Ellis to South African author Olive Schreiner told of Champion being in favour of publication, even though Joynes was 'doubtful' and Frost 'strongly opposed'.[53] Eleanor Marx was asked to translate articles and write a regular feature, 'Record of the International Popular Movement' and under her influence Modern Press published F.A. Sorge's *Socialism and the Worker* (1884). In a letter on 21 July 1884 Eleanor Marx recorded her impressions of Champion as an apparatchik, 'just a tool of Hyndman's, albeit a talented and I think honest young man'.[54] Modern Press also published an English translation of August Bebel's *Woman in the Past, the Present and the Future* (1885) expanding on Bebel's earlier *Women and Socialism* (1879) to address the Woman Question; Eleanor later reviewed the translation in Morris's *Commonweal*.

When the Democratic Federation changed to the Social Democratic Federation (SDF) in August 1884, members elected to the Executive Council were recorded as Hyndman, Champion, Joynes, Morris, Burns, Bax, Aveling and Quelch, with three female members, Eleanor Marx, Matilda Hyndman and Amie Hicks. Champion called the group a 'little party of a dozen men and women'.[55] Champion was appointed secretary and Frost secretary of the 'Agitation Committee' for the East End and Clerkenwell. Champion gave the first address to a newly formed SDF branch in Clerkenwell in December[56] and secured new premises for meetings with a re-invigorated membership. He invited Lord William Barbazon to lecture at Clerkenwell after his article 'State-directed Emigration: its necessity' appeared in *Nineteenth Century* the month before, Hyndman calling it a truthful account. Remembering himself as 'a young man with more enthusiasm than discretion' when Champion later reviewed Richard Whiteing's novel *No. 5 John Street* for the *Book Lover*, he recognised Dan Chatterton (political orator and Chartist) as the novelist's 'half-crazed Jeremiah of the slums' and recalled Chatterton's response to the lecture.

> Gaunt, ragged, unshaven, almost blind, he stood, the embodiment of helpless, furious poverty, and shaking his palsied fist in Brabazon's face, denounced him and his efforts to plaster over social sores, winding up with a lurid imaginative account of the Uprising of the People and a procession in which the prominent feature would be the head of the noble lecturer on a pike.[57]

Clerkenwell also featured in *Oliver Twist*, while George Gissing's novel *The Nether World* described an 'Agora' filled with 'orators, swarmed with listeners, with disputants, with mockers, with indifferent loungers'.

Interviewed by Walter Murdoch, Bernard Shaw recalled Champion labouring 'like thirty thousand devils'[58] as he stumped the countryside, speaking up to ten times a week in various locations in England from street corners to workmen's clubs, in slum halls and public meetings, as he tried to convert people with almost religious fervour to new gospel of practical socialism. It was a battle for people's minds and, as a 'tub-thumper' and a 'stump-orator', Hyndman noted in his preface for Joseph Burgess, Champion excelled. He appealed to people who saw speeches as street theatre, with crowds amused and entertained by heckling, fighting and witty one-liners. In this arena his altruistic desire combined with a frenetic pace of speech writing, lecturing, publishing and organising.

Only four months after the SDF was established Morris and his supporters engaged in a robust disagreement and split from the SDF. The day before Christmas Eleanor Marx summed up Hyndman's 'disgraceful vilification of everyone' not devoted to the leader as the cause of the break away to the Socialist League.[59] Morris complained three days after Christmas in correspondence with John Carruthers that Hyndman was 'so overbearing that he has driven useful men into opposition to him, and then has attacked them as his enemies'. To his disappointment Morris was now in opposition 'to men like Mr Champion of whose singleness of purpose I neither had nor have the slightest doubt'. In a letter to Robert Thomas dated 1 January 1885 Morris discussed two main causes leading for the split: the attempt to expel journalist William J. Clarke for conversations with SDF Executive members inferring Hyndman was 'self-seeking'; and Hyndman's reading of a letter at a Glasgow branch meeting attacking Andreas Scheu in 'a treacherous manner' as 'disloyal' and 'an anarchist'. On the Executive of the Democratic Federation from 1883 and an SDF member Schue also wrote as 'Andrew Joy' for *Justice*. Finished with Hyndman's 'theatrical boasts, and warnings about immediate violent revolutions', Morris abandoned any attempt to control the simmering disquiet amongst members. Edward Carpenter visited Morris and

Hyndman early in January and was not sure about the splinter group, believing people were possibly conspiring and manipulating behind the scenes, although he too left the SDF and joined Morris in September.[60]

The departure of Morris and Carpenter meant subsidies to prop up the business were withdrawn. Hyndman ignored the Socialist League's manifesto issued on 13 January 1885 and signed by Morris, Aveling, Marx, Clarke, Bax, Mahon and four others. Reprinted in Tom Mann's memoirs, the manifesto told of members expelled or deemed 'unpopular' because they 'asserted their independence', attacks on two individuals (Clarke and Schue) and 'tyrannical' subservience. Hyndman recorded in his own memoirs another reason for the falling out, blaming 'the malignant lying of a despicable married woman, whom none of us knew well, on a purely domestic question' and wrote of holding letters in his pocket at the time, which he later burnt.[61] There is no record of what was in the letters, nobody ever stepped forward to challenge or explain Hyndman's assertion and so the woman's identity and her personal conflict remain a mystery. Why Hyndman thought her allegations led to the splintering of the organisation is incomprehensible. Champion may have also played a part in the decision of Edward Aveling and Eleanor Marx to leave the SDF after the charges that Aveling, as vice president of the National Secular Society, constantly borrowed money and never repaid this back to the organisation. According to Ellis in a letter on 6 September 1884, Champion stated that the SDF could not have a 'thief' as a member.[62] Forced to reply in writing in the *Justice* on 27 September, Aveling explained his money problems were the result of poverty and lack of 'business habits'. Only two months before, Eleanor admired Champion but now she had a strong dislike of both him and Hyndman.

Nonetheless, both the Social Democratic Federation and the Socialist League's free-speech protests were gaining serious momentum at this time and membership expanded. Agitation in the streets over five successive Sundays saw Jack Williams, John Fielding, Amie Hicks and Champion speaking at Dod Street Limehouse, not far from Polar and the Docks. When Morris spoke the following Sunday, 20 September 1885, Jack Williams, Hunter Watts, Charles Mowbray and Lewis Lyons were arrested. Williams was sent to Holloway Gaol and Modern Press would re-publish his account from the *Pall Mall Gazette* the following year. Champion remembered crowds growing from a few hundred to 5,000 and then 50,000 in a matter of a few weeks[63] and when Champion and Shaw went to the Socialist League the following day to hear details of Morris's arrest, there was obvious relief he wasn't convicted. During this time, the SDF, Socialist League and Radical Union formed the basis of the Free Speech Vigilance Committee, agreeing Committee-appointed speakers were to speak before others were permitted. Hyndman alleged Aveling broke that agreement at the demonstration on 27 September. Later, Aveling ignored instructions for Trafalgar Square and on 18 February 1886 Ellis reported that Champion was adamant he could not work with him.[64] Subsequently, a decision was made by the SDF to run Champion for county of Finsbury in the School Board election in October 1885, in addition to three other SDF members (Amie Hicks, Herbert Burrows and Harry Quelch). A personal problem meant Champion pulled out.

Admitting to having 'a little money at that time' to entice Tom Mann away from his engineering shop in Lambeth, Champion suggested Mann work on 'various socialistic schemes'.[65] Champion appointed Mann as treasurer for the election of John Burns to parliament, after a decision was made and announced in *Justice* on 3 October 1885 to run Burns as an SDF candidate for Nottingham West. The SDF would use a donation of £100 from 'a Radical capitalist'.

After SDF treasurer, Hunter Watts, wrote a letter to the *Pall Mall Gazette* on 4 December 1885 openly criticising the SDF Executive Council for accepting £340 for two SDF candidates without consulting other members, he unleashed a furore by accusing the Tories of trying to split the Liberal vote. Morris explained in a letter on 25 March 1886 that money was offered not only to Burns but to Jack Williams for Hampstead and John Fielding for Lambeth, although Morris believed the latter two had no possibility of winning. Morris also talked of Hyndman appearing 'to have lost his head', going to Joseph Chamberlain to tell him of socialist opposition to Liberal candidates and afterwards 'the whole thing got out' about Tory money, damaging Burns in the election.[66] (A decade later, Champion claimed to have observed the meeting between Joseph Chamberlain and 'one of the more erratic Socialists' [Hyndman] at the politician's home Highbury in Moor Green, Birmingham. Taking 'little or no part in the dialogue', he sketched a picture of Chamberlain as a cool-headed politician and a ready listener who argued for reforms of a practical nature as a Radical Liberal.)[67]

The term 'Tory gold' emanated from a statement in *Justice* that the Executive issued eight days after the allegation by Hunter Watts. Used as a catchy phrase to counter the accusation, it developed into a powerful slogan. These words ignited suspicion and took on a life of their own, becoming a useful tool for mischief and opposition. As Morris phrased it, when referring to accusations the Democratic Federation was Tory-inspired and Hyndman a Tory agent, these charges were designed to 'stick very tight to the object they are thrown at'. Socialists of the time scoffed and even Robert Blatchford in his autobiography commented, 'in political circles the idea that every man has his price seems a common obsession ... Tory gold was a standing joke amongst us: a comic myth'.[68] The phrase would become a lifelong slur used by enemies to discredit Champion, even though the SDF Executive openly sanctioned the payment. The *Labour Elector* and independent labour candidates associated with Champion would also be caught up in the scandal. Fanned by innuendo and direct smear, the aspersion also fuelled by Champion's stoic silence. In fact, his refusal to comment was not a tactical blunder but a deliberate decision to protect a friend.

Robert William Hudson was the 'Radical capitalist in Lancashire' (his soap factory located in Liverpool) and the source of financial assistance to SDF candidates although he was a Fabian at that time. His donation, used for John Burns to stand for the seat of Nottingham West, was provided 'principally out of the regard' he held for Champion.[69] Hudson's father, an apprentice to an apothecary and later a chemist, was the inventor of soap flakes and such a simple innovation saw demand skyrocket and exports expand. With his sudden wealth Robert Spear Hudson moved from a small house in West Bromwich and a shop in High Street, to a large house in Cheshire and a factory in Liverpool. Upon his death in August 1884, his son inherited a lucrative business, significant income and a newly restored home, and married in January 1886, Gerda Francesca, daughter of Irish surveyor Robert Johnson. Danesfield estate was purchased in 1897, Hudson was appointed High Sheriff of Buckinghamshire and restored the 12th Century Medmenham Abbey.[70]

Executive members of the SDF (and later the Independent Labour Party) knew of Hudson, his name loosely bandied around for twenty years before Joseph Burgess wrote his book pretending to disguise his identity by calling him 'Barlow'. An open admirer of Henry Broadhurst and Hyndman, Burgess claimed to have met Champion and Burns in a northern newspaper office – probably the *Cotton Factory Times* – when Burns was a candidate in the 1885 election. Burgess discussed allegations of bribery ('Tory gold') with them and agreed to accompany Champion on a three-hour train trip to visit the money's source. As 'another person's secret', Burgess gave an undertaking not to disclose the man's identity without permission. They visited 'a palatial edifice', a family home, Bache Hall near Chester, built from the proceeds of soap that Hudson had recently inherited. Here their host greeted Champion 'with an affection seldom evinced by grown men', their regard for each other described by Burgess as a true and trusted friendship of ancient Greeks, Damon and Pythias.

Burgess believed Hudson to be Champion's 'old university chum' and, while Hudson gained a BA (1880) and an MA (1885) from Cambridge, Champion did not attend university. They met each other after Champion's American travels, before he left the army. 'I was awfully annoyed when he threw up his commission in the army. It was a quixotic thing to do', Hudson told Burgess.[71] Champion spoke on Henry George at Cambridge, Eton and the Oxford Union and, with Irish uncles, cousins and stepmother, and an Irish father-in-law, Hudson was probably drawn to such debates on land reform. Though Hudson freely admitted to being a Fabian, he wanted to assist his friend in 'a career worthy of his abilities', to support him in forming a political party. However, because of the potential effect on business, Hudson did not want the public to know he was the source.[72]

Why did it take so long for Champion to see what those who had left the SDF and joined the Socialist League saw? From April 1886 he commenced a slow move away from Hyndman's autocratic and antagonistic influence, ceasing to be on the SDF Council, to lecture on their behalf or write for *Justice*. Essentially, he became quietly inactive in the SDF while still maintaining membership. With Modern Press increasingly under his control, Champion now published pamphlets on industrial problems with more direct appeal to the workers. His own *The Facts about the Unemployed: an Appeal and a Warning* (1886) addressed the eight-hour issue, explained Trafalgar Square's impact and issued a warning about ignoring causes of London's misery. At the same time, in his role as editor and publisher, he assisted Tom Mann in *What a Compulsory Eight-Hour Day Means* (1886) with attention drawn to the working conditions at the Bryant and May match factory.

Champion dated the start of the 'quarrel' to a celebratory dinner a few months following their trial for the Trafalgar Riots where he gave a speech that effectively led to his separation from the SDF. His words were apparently not liked by those in attendance because he maintained that socialists should achieve their aims either through 'violence or by parliamentary action' and he strongly advocated the latter. In August 1886 his article 'Street Fighting' asserted random agitation was not an effective political stratagem.[73] Favouring a parliamentary process, Champion stopped writing for *Justice* with his final article on 9 October 1886, although both he and Hyndman wrote letters as SDF members to the *Times* on 17 November about the administration of the Poor Law. Within a couple of months an internal battle was brewing and Mann's memoirs acknowledged parliamentary action was 'a bone of contention'. Hyndman himself attributed Champion's split from the SDF to his conversation with Champion at the latter's birthday dinner in late January:

> ... I believe I convinced him that we could not hope to succeed at once or for a very long time. Thereupon, with the usual exquisite illogicality of the human mind, he set to work to try to make twelve o'clock at eleven by carrying on an intrigue with the Tories in order to bring about some reforms in his own day [sic]. I daresay this was done with complete honesty; but the amusing part of the story is, as he himself will recognise should he read this, that he was carrying on his trade

with men whom I knew much better than he did, and who used his advances to them as an argument to me to give up Socialism altogether and join their party; seeing that the man I trusted most implicitly had so little faith in the movement that he wished to attain success for his cause in this roundabout way.[74]

Not only did Hyndman believe Champion's defection was used to secure Hyndman's political allegiance, he noted his loan of Voltaire's *Candide* had an 'injurious effect on Champion's mind'. It quickly became Hyndman's belief that the man he saw as his successor was now a rival and a traitor.

According to his diary entry of February 1887, Morris believed Champion intended to start a new paper that was no 'party journal' and he had financial support.[75] The backer was evidently Hudson and, next door to Modern Press (at 13 Paternoster Row) Champion commenced in May to print his own monthly journal, *Common Sense: For People With Brains and Hearts*. Featuring a front-plate with a light illuminating a divided city of east and west, poverty and wealth, the paper contained short inspirational pieces from thinkers such as Immanuel Kant, John Ruskin, Charles Kingsley, Herbert Spencer and Adam Smith. Champion had no patience with 'impractical visionaries', a term later used in the *Champion* newspaper, and wanted common sense. When Clementina Black's novel subsequently was released, she depicted him as separating from 'unpractical' socialists. Having lost £10 a week from the time *Justice* was first launched in January 1884, substantial money was now owed to Modern Press,[76] and they ceased publishing the paper the month after.

His title, *Common Sense*, was derived from an influential pamphlet of the same name published by Thomas Paine at the start of the American Revolution. This resonated with Champion who saw the socially transformative implications of well-delivered opinion and argument. He could not have foreseen that years of 'ignominy and abuse' suffered by Paine, would visit him also. Paine was relegated to a footnote in the early history of the American Revolution and Champion was similarly neglected in the early history of the Labour movement.

Returning to the company of Fabians, called 'the Micawber Club' by Hyndman after Dicken's poor but optimistic character in *David Copperfield*, Champion gave a series of four educational speeches on socialism at St James Hall Restaurant in Piccadilly in June 1887. He argued for an eight-hour day, a representative parliament, a graduated income tax structure, taxation of mining royalties, nationalised railways and free elementary education. He also joined Annie Besant's educational debating society, known as the Charing Cross Parliament, where on 8 July 1887 they appointed him prime minister of their mock government. *To-Day* in April 1888 later reported on a mock House of Lord's proceedings with Viscount Champion as Prime Minister of a new party.

Dismayed at the time and opportunity lost by organisational infighting, Champion became increasingly critical, desiring thoughtful disagreement not acrimonious debate and enmity. Played out for readers in both newspapers, *Common Sense* and *Justice*, the dispute centred on individual personalities and power struggles. After four years in the organisation, Champion systematically explained his decision to become inactive in the SDF, arguing vigorously against Hyndman's divisive and intransigent leadership and for a parliamentary route for the working class who required their own political apparatus. Highlighting personal attacks and accusations as part of the dysfunction damaging the SDF, Champion pointed the finger at Hyndman's leadership faults that failed to achieve practical change but focused merely on propaganda. He wrote of others including Carpenter, Bax, Shaw, Bland, Joynes and Salt who no longer wrote for *Justice*, complaining eloquently about all the issues William Morris had originally highlighted when he split from the SDF. These included suspicion of other socialist groups, assertion of corrupt motivations, disunity, and the irrelevancy of *Justice* as an educative newspaper.[77]

Although upset at his name being used, Joynes believed Champion's article demonstrated much common sense. The following month Herbert Burrows attacked Champion, accusing him of intrigues and attempting to sell the SDF. He understood it was a battle for people's hearts and minds with a key message in the *Common Sense* subtitle, *For*

People With Brains and Hearts. Champion's suggestion of honourable behaviour, balanced and truthful argument, and an attempt to forge a political weapon for workers was ignored by Hyndman.

Champion left London, staying with Hubert and Edith Bland at their home and later acknowledging Edith helped him in his time of trouble.[78] Champion had an invitation to speak on 'Socialism and Christianity' from Reverend John Llewellyn Davies, 'One of the most broad-minded and hard-working of the Anglican clergy in London'. On 6 October 1887 at a Church Congress at Wolverhampton, presided over by the Bishop of Lichfield, he pointed out that politicians spent £40,000 to regulate a 'stream' of traffic around the busy streets on Hyde Park Corner but wouldn't direct money to control a 'flood' of unemployed people whose journey ended at the workhouse or in 'suicide's grave'.[79] Hyndman believed this was a waste of time, as Champion wrote:

> I see *Justice*, in a paragraph which betrays the hand of Mr Hyndman, declares the tone of the Congress showed how hopeless it is to try 'to turn this great subsidised organisation of Mammonites and their hangers-on to some better use than acting as the mere chloroform agent of the upper classes'.[80]

Champion lectured around Birmingham, the *Commonweal* outlining his movements in the north and by December was in Aberdeen and Glasgow and noticeably absent from reports of increasing troubles around Trafalgar Square. He was not involved in the 'Bloody Sunday' demonstration held on 13 November 1887 where John Burns and Cunninghame Graham were arrested as they walked from the Hotel Metropole and the poet John Barlas was struck on the head by police truncheons. In fact, Champion claimed he told organisers 'nothing would induce' him to attend or speak at that demonstration.[81]

As he attracted people interested in an independent political party, Champion's power basis grew and he felt confident to put forward his own name in a South London by-election in Deptford in January 1888, although he withdrew a month later.[82] In March he closed *Common Sense* and founded in June a new paper called the *Labour Elector*, with

Maltman Barry as sub-editor and George Bateman as compositor. The title couldn't have been more explicit as a statement of Champion's political intention; this paper would support his parliamentary ambition for a new labour party and the first labour candidate would be Keir Hardie to whom he had been introduced by Cunninghame Graham MP.[83]

The *Labour Elector* immediately advocated for the East End match girls at Bryant and May, targeted by Modern Press two years before in *What a Compulsory Eight-Hour Day Means*. After Clementina Black presented a paper on female labour at a Fabian lecture on 15 June 1888, Champion spoke of the huge dividend reaped by shareholders while workers were refused a fair wage. To protest low wages paid to female employees, Champion moved a motion to boycott the manufacturer (seconded by Herbert Burrows) elevating the dispute to a famous industrial action by young women. When manufacturers demanded workers sign a statement refuting an article by Annie Besant in the *Link* on 'White Slavery in London' on 23 June, some refused. The factory dismissed one girl, then another two and work halted on 6 July. A strike fund was set up by Annie Besant, the Socialist League raised money through amateur theatricals and Charles Bradlaugh took the issue to parliament. Clementina Black's novel *An Agitator*, modelled on Champion, pointed to the exploitation: 'Think what it would mean to have your wife sitting up in her bed, finishing shirts or making matchboxes, before her baby was twenty-four hours old. I have seen that'. Distressingly, Champion also recalled visiting a woman assembling match boxes to pay for her baby's funeral, the dead body lying next to her on a shelf and boxes returned without payment because of a slight mark while rental for a single room was sixpence a day and she only earnt ninepence a day.[84]

The *Labour Elector* grew more influential in shaping public opinion as Champion took on other industrial issues. The North Metropolitan Tramways, whose employees' agreement was an impossible 112 hours work a week, were targeted by Champion in July 1888. At the Brunner-Mond chemical factory in Cheshire at Northwich, a second fatal accident within a short period led to an inquest that found the cause was excessive working hours. A Liberal MP for Cheshire, Sir John

Brunner, was one of the wealthiest chemical manufacturers in the country and he had helped establish the *Star* newspaper.[85] A challenge was issued in the *Labour Elector* in February 1889 for people to abandon that paper because it was printed by Brunner-Mond. Brunner's friend, Henry Broadhurst, leapt to his defence at the Trade Union Congress and was accused of holding shares in Brunner's company.

Tom Mann was asked by Champion to examine work practices for the *Labour Elector* as a factory labourer (under an alias 'Joe Miller') and his findings were reported from November 1888 to March 1889. Champion later spoke about workers at Brunner-Mond working daily shifts of 11–13 hours. One excessive shift of 19 hours caused some exhausted workers 'to fall into machinery' while over the course of years, overwork was the cause of the death of 35 men at this site.[86] Suddenly the *Labour Elector* changed from a monthly to a weekly, its subtitle changing to 'the Organ of Practical Socialism' with Cunninghame Graham and John Burns appointed to the editorial board. Burns was treasurer, Mann secretary and, with Ben Tillett, held positions on the paper's Committee of Management.[87] The sweating allegations by the *Labour Elector* forced Brunner to announce a massive libel suit for £5,000 damages in June 1889 but with rumours flying that Champion, Burns and Tillett were considering a strike at the chemical factory, Brunner-Mond introduced the long sought after eight-hour day for workers in October and allowed employees to start their own union.[88]

The gloves came off with the *Labour Elector's* success and the SDF started a stronger campaign, underpinned by Hyndman's resentful criticism of Champion in *Justice* on 20 October 1888. Titled 'Discipline and Distrust' he was scathing of Champion for being exploited by 'more unscrupulous intriguers' and of being used 'to discredit and injure our cause'. The next day, Hyndman wrote that Champion was an unfit member. Champion then directed criticism in the *Labour Elector* towards two specific people associated with Hyndman, his denunciation effectively ensuring his expulsion from the SDF. In the ensuing fight Hyndman saw two SDF members, Lewis Lyons and Adolphe Smith, subjected to 'blackguardly' censure.

The first accusation was against *Justice* staff member, Lewis

Lyons, son of German-Jewish parents and founder of the Working Tailors' Association, who Champion charged with appropriating money collected for victims of sweating after Lyons gave evidence to the House of Lord's Committee on Sweating.[89] Chaired by Lord Dunraven, the committee considered evidence from Ben Tillett, Arnold White, Clementina Black and Laura M. Lane (later Mrs Bogue Luffman), with Tillett later praising Dunraven in the *English Illustrated Magazine* for influencing the committee to extend investigations to the docks. Lewis Lyons received from Champion £50 damages (£800 was sought) and Hyndman hit back a month later, praising Lyons and labelling Beatrice Potter and Arnold White 'frauds' for their evidence. Champion's contribution to a chapter on socialism for White's book on over-population, commercial depression and social reform after the Trafalgar riots, *The Problems of a Great City*, had evidently displeased Hyndman after White requested Champion 'to state briefly his views on the Socialistic panacea of which he is so courageous and, it must be added so unselfish an advocate'. A member of the Mansion House Committee, Champion remembered White as 'the first man to rouse the conscience of England about the London dock-labourer'.[90]

A second member was Adolphe Smith who Ernest Belfort Bax later complained had not received due recognition 'for unostentatious and ungrudging work' performed for the SDF while others achieved 'kudos and public recognition'. He was a dangerous adversary remaining firmly in the background and Champion was not subtle when he wrote scathingly about Smith, born 1846 in Headingley, Yorkshire. 'Headingley' was often tacked onto his name and he reversed Smith from the end to the middle of his name, left it out, or abbreviated it to A.S. Headingley or Adolphe S. Headingley. Alluding to Robert Louis Stevenson's novel (the play performed two years later and linked to Jack the Ripper's Whitechapel murders), Champion called him 'Mr. Hyde-Jekyll Headingley-Smith' and accused Smith of assuming a number of 'Protean shapes' (a term for an actor with multiple parts). Champion claimed changing names allowed him to 'change principles for the sake of making money'. Champion was at his bristling best and particularly vehement when levelling accusations at Smith's 'slanderous lies' used 'against smaller men':

The telling of lies is an extremely dangerous occupation. Once embarked on it there is no turning back, for each lie, when found out or when in danger of being found out, has to be fortified with another, and that in its turn with yet another, and so on until the miserable wretch is hopelessly lost in the toils he spun for others.[91]

One of these alleged lies was against Maltman Barry, sub-editor of the *Labour Elector,* who Champion met around 1884. As a member of the General Council of the First International in 1871–1872, Barry supported Marx and Engels against reformists, including Adolphe Smith, who rebelled against the International's organisational principles. Barry was accused in *Justice* on 27 October 1888 of being 'a notorious agent of reaction' and a couple of days later Champion sought a meeting to garner the support of Eleanor Marx who was opposed to Smith because of her father's lengthy antagonism. However, on 30 October 1888 Eleanor called Champion 'v.[ery] able but utterly unscrupulous' and 'not a man to be too far trusted'.[92] After Smith arrived in June 1871 with French political refugees, the friction was seeded between him, and Marx and Engels. In the two men's eyes Smith was part of a group attacking the General Council in newspapers and a primary liaison between anarchist Paul Brousse and the newly formed SDF. Smith did publish several articles from March to June 1873 for the London *Examiner* on socialism in countries such as France, Belgium and Spain, using 'A.' as his identifier, and calling centralized governance 'despotism', in reference to the September 1871 Conference approving the General Council's resolutions and regulations.[93]

Champion alleged Smith's personal attacks included discrediting Karl Marx:

> Mr. 'Adolphe Smith Headingley' has, within the last few days, accused Karl Marx, the founder of the International, of 'being himself dishonest,' and has professed to give a number of instances to prove the truth of his accusation! Of course we do not propose to leave the matter here; we shall take certain steps, hereafter, to publicly convict Mr. 'Adolphe Smith Headingley' of this and other equally odious offences; but, in the meantime, we lift this corner of the screen which

hides his character from the public gaze, so that all may know what manner of man he is.[94]

Smith's appointment as a professional interpreter at multiple overseas International Congress meetings, did not sit well with those who saw his translations as slanted. Champion later claimed Smith used his pseudonym for his reports in the London *Times* that 'grossly misrepresented' Socialist Congresses and 'accused Karl Marx of being, during his term of exile in England, a spy in the pay of the German Government'.[95]

On arrival from France, Smith embarked on a series of lectures in London about the Paris Commune, sent Engels and Marx notice of his schedule, but abandoned his lectures as financially unviable because of lack of interest. As a result, Bax reported sarcastically, 'vowing vengeance in his wrath, the malignant Smith, as Engels declared, drew up and circulated the wicked manifesto attacking the Marxian policy', although Smith characterised his involvement as 'dictated by youthful enthusiasm'.[96] The accusations continued to fly with Hyndman insisting Barry and Champion were part of a 'little Marxist clique'.[97]

In the end, allegations that Champion betrayed Adolphe Smith through the publication of his dual identity and the attack on Lewis Lyons meant there was a rapid move to expel Champion from the SDF when a General Council meeting was convened, with *Justice* announcing his immediate expulsion. It was a political trap-door. To Hyndman, power was finite and a zero-sum game where one person's gain was another's loss. Champion, Hyndman's 'darling of the organisation', was now the enemy. This occurred within a very short time frame and suggested the SDF Executive moved with great speed, sending charges to a couple of branches to shape the motion. Allegations from three SDF members (Hyndman, Smith and Lyons) were used effectively in Champion's expulsion, although one charge stood out in both length and emotional outrage – Champion's revelation of Smith's pseudonyms. H.W. Lee's letter noted claims emanated from two or three SDF members and were based on three issues: Champion's actions over a few years (1887–1888) meant he was not 'a fit and proper person' to remain an SDF member; his article dismissive of leadership in the SDF in *Common Sense* (September 1887); and his naming of an SDF member 'Adolph Smith' as Adolphe Smith 'Headingley' in the *Labour Elector* (1 November 1888) was 'base', a 'betrayal' and 'treachery' by Champion who was 'a danger to all members' of the SDF.[98] The charges were sent around to unnamed branches for discussion and voting; and resolutions were passed on 6 November 1888 at the General Council meeting.

Labelling the meeting unconstitutional Champion announced his SDF resignation in the *Labour Elector* on the first day of December 1888. Surprisingly Adolphe Smith didn't go to court over Champion's claims even though these were considered dangerous. Expulsion was considered more damning. Though Champion's great sin was the exposure of Smith, SDF members used his two names interchangeably over the following years and, according to loyal followers of Hyndman, members often called him Smith, or Smith Headingley, to no great disadvantage and oddly without law suits. Champion's departure marked the date he was targeted by socialists, his friend Maggie Harkness wrote.[99] Words like betrayal, treachery and repudiation were attached to Champion's every ambitious move in the future. Tom Mann, John Burns, Keir Hardie and John Barlas continued the steady stream of people leaving the SDF. Meanwhile, the organisation would become increasingly dysfunctional.

In 1904 Frederick Rolfe (Baron Corvo) published *Hadrian the Seventh* pointing explicitly to suspicion, division, discord and rolling dissent amongst socialists. He knew his novel to be 'highly controversial, written from the inside with a scalpel' and 'deliciously libellous', for it contained some interesting observations about the person responsible for Champion's expulsion and denunciation by the SDF. A letter was sent by F. Lewis to an editor in London taking exception to Rolfe being called a 'sponger', recalling Rolfe 'had abnormal faults and eccentricities – vindictiveness against those who annoyed him very pronounced; but his many good qualities appear to be unknown'.[100] A schoolteacher and tutor in Oban in the early 1880s, Rolfe was confirmed by Cardinal Manning in 1886, studied for the priesthood in Rome before being dismissed in middle of 1890. He gained a position as a tutor at Seaton in September 1892 and then moved to Aberdeen where he was thrown out of lodgings for not paying rent.[101] Rolfe approached Champion at his apartment at 255 Union Street and, after hearing his woes, took him into his home and employed him for a couple of months at the *Aberdeen Standard* as his secretary and staff member.

In *Hadrian the Seventh* Dymoke advocates 'simplicity, going to the root of the matter' and is described as 'the only capable fighting man ever possessed by socialism, [who] had been spunged [sic] upon for fifteen years by socialistic cadgers, sucked dry, ruined, and cast out, a victim of socialistic jealousy and treachery'. Historian Henry Pelling was the first to identify Dymoke as modelled on Champion, named after the family who held the hereditary office as the King's champion and responsible for riding into Westminster Hall to challenge anyone who disputed the title at a coronation.[102] Jerry Sant is obviously Rolfe's caricature of Yorkshire-born Adolphe Smith. Attacked as a 'traitor' it is Jerry Sant who vilifies Dymoke for accepting 'Tory gold', prevents 'the traitor's letters' being read and orchestrates Dymoke's expulsion: 'If it hadna [sic] been for me he would have bought the bally show with his Tory gold. It was me as put my spoke in his wheel and got him expelled in time'. Sant's changeable persona is represented in geological terms as 'different strata', harking back to Champion's accusation of Adolphe Smith's 'Protean shapes'.

Some critics argued Jerry (Jeremiah) Sant is John Burns or Keir Hardie; in fact these two socialists are represented in the book as Burnson (Battersea) and Kerardy (Glasgow). However, Sant's first name has many clever allusions. Jeremiah is a biblical prophet prophesying destruction and the inspiration for the English word jeremiad, a text lamenting the state and morals of society. This also references 15 Jeremiah Street, Poplar, the Wade's Arms headquarters of the London Dock Strike Committee. Many of Sant's characteristics make Smith recognisable, including his affectations from Paris where he was part of the French ambulance corps during the Franco-Prussian war.[103] After his return to England early in June 1871 Smith wrote text for a photographic book, *Street Life in London*, published as a monthly serial from February 1873 to 1877, before joining the *Lancet* in 1878 as a freelance journalist. His surname is French for 'health', an allusion to his articles on sanitation and hygiene. For much of the novel he is called Jerry, a chamber pot, and described as 'a haberdasher's handbag', a reference to Smith's 1884 report on sweating of Jewish tailors in the East.

Explicitly 'a delegate from the north' who 'did not push forward, working in the background', he epitomized a plotter whose resting position was lies and schemes. Rolfe believed Sant was a backroom manipulator and his devious friendship with an influential woman, Mrs Crowe, is explicit and detailed. She has been identified as Mrs Gleeson White (née Annie Matilda Rose, daughter of Thomas Whittaker Rose and Matilda Clarke of Bath) and her husband Joseph Gleeson White was a friend of Rolfe's from Christchurch near Bournemouth. Multiple women in Adolphe Smith's life were named Rose, making Rolfe's assumption of his character's name, George Arthur Rose, seem more than coincidence. In July 1872 Smith married Alice, daughter of the editor of *Lloyd's Weekly*, and their daughter, Rose Hester, was born two years later; after his wife died in 1882, his second wife/boarder was Rose E.S. Wenham living in his Leeds house with her parents and two sisters in the census of 1891. When the Gleeson Whites moved to London late in 1890 Joseph became an artistic designer of book covers, illustrations and furniture while their house became a literary salon for artistic, literary and theatrical people in the afternoons and evenings.[104] After his appointment as editor of Covent Garden's *Studio* Gleeson White used Rolfe's Italian photography of young men for an article 'The Nude in Photography' in June 1893. His wife's advances were supposedly rejected by Rolfe with the novel's narrator pointing to her bitterness; his protagonist desires 'to squeeze all the acid out of her at one grip and toss her to the divinities who collect exhausted lemons'.

One of Champion's accusations against Smith was that he perpetrated 'slanderous lies'. According to Rolfe's novel, Sant knew 'secrets' and identified himself as 'the man and Mrs. Crowe is the woman that shall shame him'. She retains letters and albums suggesting Rolfe was a target for her enmity and tells her son, 'Yes indeed, he's just the sort of man your father would have liked, unfortunately. He liked that sonnet-man, too. A pretty kind of person'. Three articles were sent to the Aberdeen *Daily Free Press* throughout November 1898 detailing Rolfe's life as a fanciful exhibitionist clouded by debt. One of these anonymous attacks, '"Baron Corvo" His Further Adventures in Aberdeen: The Baron and Mr. H.H. Champion', was published on 12 November 1898 and Mrs Gleeson White was suggested to be the author. The timing is interesting because Joseph Gleeson White died from typhoid on 19 October leaving his family in dire financial straits and, with the demise of Major Beauchamp Colclough Urquhart, there was speculation Champion would inherit vast estates.

In the lead up to Champion's SDF expulsion, the diary entries of John Burns are revealing. Summing up the two men incisively in 8 September and 26 October 1888 entries, Burns wrote of Champion as 'a splendid friend but the most dangerous foe for any man to have, gentlemanly withal', while Hyndman 'never lost an opportunity of showing his jealousy, proving his cowardice and proclaiming himself a skunk'.[105] An argument with Hyndman around the London City Council elections in 1889 led to Burns resigning from the SDF in June. Champion's memory of 'a little knot of energetic and enthusiastic men' who became members of the Democratic Federation six years before, marked the date he resigned.[106] On the first day of February 1890 *Justice* lashed out, calling Burns 'a wholly untrustworthy "politician"' and 'a most treacherous man'.

Champion's failed attempt with Clementina Black to establish a branch of the National Electoral Labour Association at Southwark on Friday 7 February 1890 certainly demonstrated a concerted campaign by Hyndman's followers that ramped up after the successful Dock Strike. At the meeting interruptions, hisses and boos disrupted Champion's speeches with old allegations: he undermined both socialism and SDF's repudiation and received money from a 'gentleman'. *Justice's* headline the following day announced 'Justifiable Intolerance' and maintained workers 'positively refused to give the traitor a hearing' while beneath was an attack on Burns and his association with Champion under the title 'Beware of Traitors and Treachery'. The *Reynold's Newspaper* on 9 February picked up Hyndman's comments expressing no 'regret' for the 'boycotting' of Champion. Reports circulated on the various feuds and splits among socialists spotlighting Burns and Hyndman with 'daggers drawn'. Burns complained that Hyndman 'spends his time in rabid onslaughts on every able man and woman in the socialist and labor [sic] movement who dares to point out how his cowardly, egotistical and intolerant conduct of the social movement' and he bemoaned the fact that it had become 'a small clique of groundlings with Hyndman as the boss'.[107]

What first appeared to Morris to be an ambitious and significant socialist organisation was subsequently painted in historical record as an erratic combination of factions devoted to in-fighting and sullying each other's reputations. Hyndman's personality caused him to hate vehemently defectors from the SDF and within another four years, he recycled former hatreds and settled old scores, denouncing Burns for associating with Champion and the Fabians. Hyndman continued to write a river of grievances to the *Star* newspaper:

> Because he was hand and glove with Mr. H.H. Champion, both before and after Mr. Champion was expelled from the S.D.F.; was one of the editorial committee of the *Labour Elector*, and gave Mr. Champion the earnest letter of introduction to the workers of Australia, which enabled that gentleman to do so much mischief there ... Mr. John Burns has become, in short, an active and bitter enemy of the Social Democratic Party, and a chosen vessel of one of the great political factions ... Mr. Burns and his allies of the Fabian Society have done their utmost to upset and injure us for years past.[108]

Meanwhile, Burns retorted that Champion was 'a man of courage' while he accused Hyndman of 'cowardice and vanity' and explained: 'So anxious are they to reach the millennium that they sacrifice each other on the road'. In fact, Burns was dismissive of the whole organisation: 'the Labour movement has ceased to regard the S.D.F. as the mouthpiece of rational, sensible Social Democracy. Every movement must have its dustbin – the S.D.F. fulfils that position efficiently'.[109] Commentators in Australian newspapers took note of the tirades but seemed unsure about the nature of the argument.

Champion closed the *Labour Elector* after the final issue on 19 April 1890, having lost £10–12 a week following the Dock Strike. He later admitted the paper 'never paid for itself' and incurred 'a pecuniary loss per week'.[110] Mrs Humphry Ward in *A Writer's Recollections* (1919) wrote of Champion investigating a loan to keep the *Labour Elector* afloat, while in *Marcella* a bribe is offered to Harry to relinquish his newspaper to conservative forces. In 'Why did the *Labour Elector* die?' Maggie Harkness stressed the bid was conditional upon replacement of Champion as editor and attempted to justify his silence by 'pride' and restraint which fuelled more suspicion. With Champion's continuing and stoic public silence, gossip lingered and fanned the now-enduring accusations of 'Tory gold'.

His Place in History

Oh talk not to me of a name great in story.
The days of our youth are the days of our glory.
Lord Byron

Even though there was much ill feeling towards Champion from the founder of the Social Democratic Federation, Henry Hyndman's memoirs showed a firm belief in his abilities. Hyndman wrote that Champion 'completely wrecked one of the most promising careers a young man could have had before him' and that his selfless devotion drove him to socialism 'when assuredly nothing whatsoever was to be gained, personally, pecuniarily, or politically by doing so'. Hyndman's admission that he placed so much faith in him explained much about his bitterness and ferocity towards Champion when he abandoned the organisation.

> He worked hard in the movement, ran great risks, showed remarkable pluck and ability, and became the darling of the organisation ... I looked to Champion, with his initiative, trained intelligence and determination as the very man to carry on the work without faltering ...[111]

Champion was amused as he quoted Hyndman's interview for the *Windsor Magazine* in January 1896 where he was described as the man 'who wanted to make twelve o'clock at eleven'. Hyndman must have liked the phrase because he repeated it in his memoirs fifteen years later.

Interviewed by Walter Murdoch for over an hour on 18 December 1908 at his London home in Adelphi Terrace, Bernard Shaw also praised Champion:

> When there was need of instant action, when an unforeseen obstacle jumped up in front of the party, you were the man to go to; and you

were always ready with a solution of the problem. Your solution at 5.30 might be different altogether from the one you had suggested at 5; but you always had a solution. You also had a knowledge, which some of the more visionary members of your party sadly lacked, of the wires to be pulled when you wanted anything done; and you pulled them ...[112]

William Morris believed in his friend's sincerity and considered him forthright and without artifice while Mrs Humphrey Ward's fictional summation of Harry in *Marcella* depicted him as 'very good company, and very clever, but dreadfully sure of his own opinion'. In response to a biography of Keir Hardie in 1921 which described Champion as 'in appearance patrician to the finger tips; cool as an iceberg, yet emitting red-hot revolution in the placid accents of club-land', William Diack wrote that he had 'a caustic, saturnine humour, blended, however, with a ringing note of sincerity that even an occasional flash of cynicism could never wholly disguise'.[113]

Tom Mann thought Champion was 'cooler than a cucumber, would make statements of a revolutionary character, would deal with the weak points in the men's position, and would encourage them to rectify the same' and was a man 'genuinely devoted to the movement':

> Champion aroused considerable hostility amongst the members who were no less devoted than himself to the advancement of the cause. My own conclusion with regard to him was that he was profoundly convinced that his judgment was right, that situations arose which necessitated prompt and decisive action, and that he could not endure to wait several days before the committee met. Anyway, he was more sure of his own judgment than of theirs![114]

A picture emerges of a person who was very certain of his convictions, charismatic, confident, decisive, resolute, brimming with initiative and compelling in his arguments. In addition to being an inspiring speaker and writer, Champion possessed a rational, clear and analytical mind that gave him the agility required to formulate strong and practical opinions and plans.

Ernest Belfort Bax in 1918 remembered Champion wanted 'immediate results' for workers and showed 'a certain brightness and charm of manner combined with a ready mother-wit which made him good company in whatever society he found himself'. However, he also recorded his 'tendency for political intrigue with a view, as he in all probability sincerely thought, of obtaining immediate results in the improvement of the condition of the working classes and in general progress'. When the *Melbourne Punch* quoted from Bax's memoirs, Champion issued a letter to the editor titled, 'A Libellous Statement', pardoning his 'very good friend' Bax for his 'nervous alarms' about him in his youth but denying his parents were wealthy or he was ever gaoled, insisting the Dock Strike was a demonstration of 'how history is written'.[115]

Outside the recollections of various friends and enemies in England, Champion is associated in most people's minds with five key events: the riots in Trafalgar Square; the London Dock Strike; the Maritime Strike in Australia; and the creation of the Independent Labour Party in Britain. Still, Champion's role in a number of these important events is mostly ignored or relegated to minor historical notes.

Trafalgar Square Riots (1886)

On 'Black Monday' 8 February 1886 the Social Democratic Federation moved from their normal pattern of agitation in the East End and turned their attention to the affluent West End. They intended to capitalise on a planned mass meeting in the centre of London organised by the United Workmen's Committee on the issue of Fair Trade (protectionism). Champion and his colleagues in the SDF used the momentum generated around this event, keenly aware of the value of the press and publicity to escalate issues. Champion, Hyndman, Burns, Jack Williams and other members of the SDF arrived earlier than Kennedy's committee and from the base of Nelson's column spoke directly to a large crowd, with Champion's speech stipulating the provision of public works and an eight-hour day.[116] A small red flag was thrust into the hands of Burns and, when police removed the agitators, the men climbed the balustrade in front of the National

Gallery where they made four speeches. With the flag on a stick, Burns was carried on men's shoulders as the crowd proceeded to Hyde Park where the four speakers again addressed people from the statue of the Trojan War warrior, Achilles (positioned near the Queen Elizabeth gates).[117] Champion and Burns proceeded to Equestrian statue of the Duke of Wellington and again spoke to the crowd. 'There again I harangued them and induced them to disperse because the troops were coming', Champion claimed in an Adelaide interview some thirty years later.[118] Half the crowd dispersed, along with the four speakers who decided to find something to eat.

Calling their attempt to draw attention to the plight of the workers 'a great stroke of luck', the demonstration had unforeseen repercussions. The march quickly turned into a mob of people throwing stones from a cart in St James's Street; they broke windows (especially of gentlemen's clubs), destroyed carriages and looted shops. William Morris's shop escaped by a whisker, Joseph Chamberlain's and Hyndman's club at New University (for Oxford and Cambridge graduates) became another casualty of the mob's journey through the streets. According to Champion's interview for the *Trident*, he and Hyndman left the park with other speakers to dine at a Piccadilly restaurant, the *White Horse Cellars*, a well-known place just off St James's Street, on the corner of Dover Street. On the way, Champion had a surprise street meeting and relaxed conversation with his father who obviously knew nothing about the riots. Bernard Shaw was told late in the day and the riots came as a surprise to him. Mrs Humphry Ward wrote of being on her way from the House of Lords and surprised by broken windows in St James's Street and the large number of policemen waiting at Buckingham Palace. Two days after Black Monday William Morris believed Hyndman's credibility was now unfortunately renewed by the event although he heard the riots surprised SDF members.[119]

The day after the riots, an interview was conducted for the *Pall Mall Gazette* (Joseph Burgess later took credit) and this was circulated widely in Australia.[120] Champion admitted to knowledge of Dacre's shop looting because he saw some of the crowd in obviously stolen shirts and, although he personally witnessed damage to Raffini's wine shop in Piccadilly, he protested such events were 'entirely contrary to our wishes'. Using this interview Champion set out three questions for Joseph Chamberlain, president of the local Government Board, requesting a plan to alleviate the miserable conditions of the unemployed. He asked: 'First, whether he is personally in favour of relief works being undertaken? secondly, whether he will advise the Cabinet to start such works? and thirdly, if so, can he assure us that the Cabinet will take his demand into favourable consideration?' Champion's military background gave him a forcible style of argument and succinct language, as he pointed directly to the ongoing despair of the hungry and unemployed. He estimated 50,000 people lived in complete poverty in central London and this number, he envisaged, would grow.[121]

Four days after the riots Champion, Hyndman, Burns and Williams, were summoned and charged with using false seditious and inflammatory language against the government. Champion's surety came from Joseph Cowen, a Member of Parliament and proprietor of the *Newcastle Chronicle* who observed on the way out of the trial that Champion and Burns together could achieve 'great things', although he believed 'it was extremely unlikely' they could 'co-operate for many years'.[122] William Morris and Ernest Belfort Bax put up monetary security for the other men's bail with Morris believing the riots and trial could serve to draw the Socialist League and the SDF closer together. Percy Frost was unable to provide financial assistance as he faced a court case with Mrs Gordon Baillie, a charming charlatan he met while covering the Scottish crofters struggles on the Isle of Skye in November 1884. Mrs Gordon Baillie was described by police at her world-famous trial as 'an extraordinary woman – one of the greatest swindlers in the country';[123] Hyndman called her 'very dangerous', admitting his 'opposition' may have spurred Frost's obsession.

It was argued the four men arrested did not incite the crowd to violent acts and had actually departed Hyde Park in another direction when rioters caused substantial damage in Audley Street, Mayfair. However, they were accused of deploying words that caused violence. In the dock, guided in points of law by W.M. Thompson, a barrister for trade unions, John Burns argued: 'There must be some unusual agitation to prompt one of the idle classes like Mr. Champion, a skilled engineer like myself, an unskilled labourer like Mr. Williams and a middle-class man like Mr. Hyndman to stand in this box for one simple cause'. Hyndman later wrote in a foreword to Burgess's history on Burns, that the influence Burns had on the SDF was over-estimated, claiming his value was mostly as a 'stump-orator' and 'flag waver' and that he and Champion wrote his famous speech for the Old Bailey trial. Journalists covering the four-day April trial noted that Champion elegantly and successfully defended himself during cross-examinations of witnesses. In *Marcella*, Mrs Humphry Ward drew imaginatively on Champion's experience for a trial scene where Harry Wharton, the socialist aristocrat, a 'man of birth and power' and 'outcast from his class', expertly cross-examined:

> The crushing accumulation of hostile evidence – witness after witness coming forward to add to the damning weight of it; the awful weakness of the defence – Wharton's irritation under it – the sharpness, the useless, acrid ability of his cross-examinations; yet, contrasting with the legal failure, the personal success, the mixture of grace with energy, the technical accomplishment of the manner, as one wrestling before his equals – nothing left here of the garrulous vigour and brutality of the labourers' meeting![124]

A subpoena was served on Joseph Chamberlain by Champion to summon him as a witness, he reported at the ten-year anniversary of Black Monday in the *Champion*. He contended that, at the time, Chamberlain spoke in 'much stronger and more inflammatory language' as a Member of Parliament in Birmingham than those on trial.[125]

Champion attended only one more SDF Trafalgar Square demonstration on 25 August 1886 where, he boasted to Walter Murdoch, he was suddenly 'a very popular young man', picked up by the crowd on their shoulders and carried to Chelsea.[126] With many more constables, three speaker platforms, and people carrying red flags popularised after the Trafalgar Square Riot, this was a protest by Champion, Hyndman and Sam Mainwaring against the imprisonment of Jack Williams (originally arrested that February). However, at a dinner not long after the trial Champion gave a speech urging socialists to abandon 'random agitation' and to achieve their aims through a parliamentary route, which led towards divided paths.

London Dock Strike (1889)

During the summer of 1887 Ben Tillett was, according to Champion, 'the first' organiser of unskilled labour in the East End, mostly in tea warehouses around the docks.[127] With 12 years on the wharves, Tillett recruited 800 members from various Sunday morning meetings he held; after the strike, as secretary of the Dock Labourers' Union, his union counted 56,000 members. With its origins in a dispute over a bonus system paid for loading the *Lady Armstrong*, the London Dock Strike started on Wednesday 14 August 1889 with 3,000 dock workers forming a procession from South Dock to the other dock gates where momentum quickly gathered.

In 'my own story in my own way' for the *English Illustrated Magazine* in November 1889 Tillett told of his regular Sunday meeting with the dockers and their deputation the day after where he was asked to present their demands to officials and request a reply by Tuesday. When no answer was forthcoming, on Wednesday 14 August the strike began with Tillett addressing 12 meetings across the dockyards. In an interview with Walter Murdoch for the *Trident*, Champion told of Tillett coming to his office at the *Labour Elector* to tell 'a long story of a row' with employers, apparently just before the strike was called. Champion claimed he sent Mann to check the situation. (Tillett's wire was received at midday at their office asking to see Mann at the South West India Dock). When he didn't return that day or the next Champion admitted to being uneasy. An unemployed John Burns 'dropped in' to the *Labour Elector* and Champion asked him to look for Mann who hadn't returned. Finally, when Burns also failed to return, Champion went in search.[128] Tillett's first introduction to John Burns was on the third morning of the strike (Friday 16 August) when around 10,000 marched with brass bands through London streets.

For the next seven weeks all their lives were engulfed by the strike. A United Dock Labourers' Strike Committee was formed consisting of Ben Tillett, Tom Mann, John Burns, James Toomey and Champion with the *Times* reproducing one of their letters from Wade's Arms showing their five names appended to the bottom.[129] Champion's own book, *The Great Dock Strike in London, August, 1889*, recalled this period: 'I was the only man, not a member of the working classes by birth and education, who has been privileged to watch the whole movement at close quarters'. A sub-committee responsible for drafting the strike's manifesto calling on workers to join the strike on 2 September included Champion, Mann and 'Mr. Smith',[130] the latter possibly Hubert Llewellyn Smith, a social researcher for Charles Booth who later co-authored the first book released about the strike. Champion was there from the first few days until the final meeting of the Strike Committee addressed by Cardinal Manning where Champion himself moved the resolution which would end the strike.[131] The Strike Committee demanded the Dock Committee retain workers for a minimum of four hours and pay them six pence an hour (instead of five pence). They also demanded the abolition of the sub-contract system whereby the amalgamated association of privately-owned docks, controlled by the Dock Committee, sub-let to a third party and charged ship owners for the right to discharge ships. With London commerce and trade severely paralysed, this strike very quickly brought London to a standstill, much to the general population's alarm.

A street collection of £40 enabled the hiring of a headquarters as the Strike Committee moved their campaign business to the Wade's Arms in Jeremiah Street in Poplar. Champion admitted to seven weeks with 'never more than four consecutive hours' of sleep while Tillett's health collapsed many times and others suffered health issues in the aftermath. Members lived and breathed strike work, taking only short breaks to sleep at James Toomey's house five minutes away, before going to a meeting at Tower Hill every day.[132] Cunninghame Graham recognised the toll taken on Tillett when he called him 'thin, gaunt, hollow-jawed, fragile'[133] and Champion noted his struggles:

> Frequently Ben had to lie full length on his back on the ground to recover from a special effort at addressing the enormous crowds that had to be not only spoken to, but argued with, admonished, encouraged, advised, corrected, praised, disciplined.[134]

Nine days after the initial strike commenced, around 40,000 'orderly and quiet' men were in procession on 23 August through Aldgate and, on the first day of September, Maggie Harkness told a journalist that the march felt 'more threatening, more ominous' and a portent for future events.[135] A rash of other strikes erupted around the central strike as other workers showed sympathy with the dockers and sought their own wage increases and improved working conditions. Lady Charles Dilke's secretary and treasurer of the Women's Trade Union League (WTUL), May Abraham, was one who helped organise laundresses to support the Dock Strike[136] and Bryant and May's factory workers also joined.

Champion was a crucial part of the planning, organisation and publicity, laying claim to authorship of the Strike Committee's manifesto. This was published in one of the first contemporary histories of the Dock Strike, a book co-written by Hubert Llewellyn Smith and Vaughan Nash and released not long after the strike's conclusion.[137] From a room located behind the bar Champion was said to be involved in 'the arts and wiles of militant journalism', writing and issuing news about the strike for circulation to Fleet Street and overseas newspapers in Europe, America and Australia. With an articulate and clear explanation of the strike, the manifesto made its way by ship to Australia at the end of September, circulating quickly throughout the country. Champion's press release was intended to engage workers in faraway continents and dock owners were chastised as 'double handed sweaters, sweating ship owners on one hand and dock laborers [sic] on the other'. Readers were also informed that England's shipping fraternity and the general public wholeheartedly supported the strike. Success for the dockers would demonstrate a 'revolution in our social system, ordained by forces which no man can check, may be effected without the shedding of a drop of blood'.[138]

Between 120,000 and 130,000 were on strike by the end of August and it was a mammoth task to keep strikers and families from starvation. The distribution of relief moved from the Tea Operatives' committee located at Wroots' Coffee House to a local hall, subscriptions (including Australian cheques) were received and payments made to tradesmen by a cashless system of vouchers. Dock workers arrived in an orderly fashion to collect a relief ticket for one shillings' worth of 'solid provisions' for families each day and there was no panic or confusion, with police helping to control orderly admission into the hall. Three days later a person watching from the Trinity parsonage close to the Wade's Arms saw London on the edge of 'a social volcano' but watched in awe the staged movement of people through this hall.[139] Champion recalled that Mann, Burns and others controlled 'the volcanic eruption of the lowest strata of London labour' while Maggie Harkness provided a bird's-eye view of frenetic activity in her sketch of Mann:

> He willingly left the speeches to Mr. Burns, and the negotiations to Mr. Champion, while he flew about establishing law and order in the minds of the dockers. Sometimes he dashed through the committee-rooms with his eyes ablaze, throwing an amused glance at the hungry reporters, saying a few words to Mr. Burns; then he hurried off to superintend the distribution of relief-tickets, or to organize some new plan of campaign.[140]

Champion recollected having made speeches for years in the pre-dawn with John Burns and others at the dock gates, with *Justice* reporting Champion opening an SDF meeting at the entrance to the West India Dock as early as 1885.[141] With John Burns he walked at the head of processions and addressed meetings of the strikers while Burns made speeches to rally the men, 'preaching' at three dock gates and 'putting hope and courage' into strikers as he 'incited' them to 'revolt'. Champion fondly remembered Burns, 'a sturdy, swarthy, black-bearded man, clad in dark blue serge, a white straw hat on his head, a leathern satchel slung over his shoulder, his resonant voice reaching every ear in the square and arresting the attention of the passers-by in the streets'. Both his hat and his leather bag (used to carry strike money) were on display at his home, drawing admiring comments from journalists eager for interviews, his 'powerful voice, absolutely necessary for the control of large bodies of men in the open air and the physical strength to stand a tremendous strain without losing health, head and temper'.[142]

Cunninghame Graham saw Burns as 'burly, brawny, confident' in the *Labour Elector* on 7 September while Maggie Harkness thought he 'never had greater power with the workers than when he went black and untidy to meetings – hungry as a wolf and roaring like a lion' and wearing his trademark straw boater as showman.

> Probably the happiest moments he enjoyed during the dock strike were those he spent throwing packets of soap (it had been sent as an advertisement) to the ragged urchins outside the Wade's Arms. 'Mind, no one is to touch that soap but myself,' he used to tell the people in the room; and, whenever he had a few spare moments, he filled his straw hat with soap packets, and enjoyed the sight of boys and girls scrambling ...[143]

Free soap samples were provided by Robert Hudson whose advertisement for Hudson's Soap filled the whole front page of several editions. A drawing of a policeman holding a bull's eye lantern to a placard was underwritten by the words: 'ARREST all Dirt and cleanse Everything by using HUDSON'S SOAP REWARD'. Hudson was acknowledged in the *Labour Elector* on 31 August for his £50 donation to the Dock Strike, prominent subscribers included Augustus Harris, Lady Meux, the Countess of Carlisle and the latter's mother Lady Stanley of Alderley.

Neglected by many historians, women were also strike volunteers, with Eleanor Marx, Maggie Harkness, Annie Besant, Clementina Black and Martha Burns among those who played a constructive part and worked long hours. Maggie called Martha Burns 'charming' while Clementina Black's character depicted her as 'shrewd capable, and kindly'. Located in a room downstairs from the Strike Committee, these women assisted with administration including typing correspondence as well as visits to the homes of dock workers' families. Not only Cunninghame Graham and Champion, but Maggie Harkness (as John Law) contributed articles on the strike to the *Labour Elector* while Eleanor Marx and Annie Besant spoke on streets and at public meetings. On 7 September, the *Labour Elector* reported on a Hyde Park meeting attended by 100,000 people where Eleanor spoke:

> And so speaker succeeds speaker. To Mann and Burns succeed Mrs. Aveling [Eleanor Marx], Tillett and MacDonald. Curious to see Mrs. Aveling addressing the enormous crowd, curious to see the eyes of the women fixed upon her as she spoke of the miseries of the Dockers' homes, pleasant to see her point her black-gloved finger at the oppression, and pleasant to hear the hearty cheer with which her eloquent speech was greeted.[144]

A section of a letter in the *Labour Elector* was provided by Eleanor Marx: 'I envy you your work in the Dock Strike. It is the movement of the greatest promise we have had for years, and I am proud and glad to see it. If Marx had lived to see it'.[145] Engels also praised Eleanor in a letter on 17 October for developing into 'quite an East Ender' through her agitation and work for dock workers and had been privately thrilled to see no evidence of any followers of Hyndman involved in the strike organisation. He believed Champion was an unknown factor because of his Wolverhampton address to the Church Congress in 1887: 'If our lot here – I mean Champion especially – don't make mistakes, they will soon have it all their own way. But I confess I cannot get myself to have full confidence in that man – he is too dodgy'.[146]

The day after the manifesto of 2 September was issued, calling out all London workers, Maggie Harkness intervened by approaching Cardinal Manning and providing the names of dock directors so the Cardinal could speak with them. For three hours Manning gently listened to each individual's opposition to a 'nominal concession' before talking to the Strike Committee for ten minutes, after which assent was secured and a meeting at Stepney arranged, 'our last meeting of the strikers'.[147] The Cardinal spoke to a huge crowd of dockers assembled in a Poplar Catholic school in an almost theatrical and heavenly beam of sunshine where 'September sunshine blazed through an open window and struck the venerable old man with his quaint cap and long dress', his speech carrying the vote to end the strike. The scene was also depicted in the novel, *George Eastmont*:

> At 8 o'clock one night thousands of men streamed into a great hall filling it from floor to roof, leaning over the galleries to watch for Cardinal Loraine [sic], who came quietly to the platform. The pomp of the church was discarded; he stood before them a citizen like themselves; first an Englishman, and then a priest. The fragile old man straightened himself, and watched the men cheering him, his lips twitched, but his eyes pierced from gallery to floor, and when he began to speak every person in the hall heard him. Even the Strike leaders on the platform felt the spell that he cast over the audience ... Some of them told their wives afterwards that while he talked they saw a halo of light round his head, and his face seemed to shine like the face of an angel.[148]

Afterwards Maggie asked the Cardinal how he felt when the strikers cheered him, and he replied proudly: 'An Englishman'. Manning continued to read labour news till his death, keeping up with the Labour Commission evidence and trade union news and providing advice.[149] When he died, representatives of the London Dockers' Union attended his long funeral procession to the cemetery (and probably Maggie Harkness and Champion were among the street crowd). The strike ended on 14 September after weeks of struggle and a 'Dock Strike Supper' was held at the Central Democratic Club in early October 1889 for the leaders. A letter was read from Michael Davitt, co-founder with Charles Parnell of the Irish National Land League, who praised his 'old friends, Burns and Champion, and their able colleagues in the late glorious victory for the cause of Labour' and for achieving international recognition.[150]

Proudly Champion wrote his own account, *The Great Dock Strike in London, August, 1889*, just under 30 pages for the Social Science Series that published authors such as Edward Carpenter, Ernest Belfort Bax and Sidney Webb. At the same time as the London release, the book was published in Melbourne by E.A. Petherick. Bound in scarlet cloth, there were photos of John Burns and Ben Tillett and a youthful Champion with casually crossed arms, sitting backwards on a chair, a relaxed photographic style fashionable many years later. Champion's friend Walter Murdoch described this as 'a portrait of yourself, looking innocent to a degree quite impossible to our fallen nature'. When Murdoch later visited Bernard Shaw at his London home, he asked Shaw's opinion of Champion's recall of events surrounding the Dock Strike. Shaw expressed amazement at 'the exactness' of his friend's recall and judged it: 'Most interesting, and most accurate'.[151]

Following the Dock Strike, there was a meeting on 8 October at the Mile End Road Assembly Hall to promote female trade unions in the East End. Attended by 3,000 people including Clementina Black, Amie Hicks, Champion, Burns, Mann and Tillett, the meeting was pivotal for Clementina Black's establishment of the Women's Trade Union Association. Champion, Burns and Mrs Jane Tillett were on the committee as well as Amie Hicks, the first secretary of the East London Ropemakers' Union founded by Champion and promoted in the *Labour Elector*. Not long after, Engels showed displeasure that Eleanor had been excluded from the new committee of philanthropists, blaming Champion who 'used to go to Church Congresses and preach socialism'.[152] At this time Champion was also involved with Clementina Black in establishing the East London Confectioners' Union and she claimed the seeds sown at that meeting at Mile End were reaped a year later in the flowering of a variety of union organisations. Later she asked Champion to read proofs of her article 'Chocolate-makers' Strike' for the *Fortnightly Review* of October 1890, discussing a satisfactory mediation during a strike for Allen's factory (also highlighted by Champion for the *Age*).

Joseph Clayton's *The Rise and Decline of Socialism* (1926) judged that Champion's role was essentially neglected because he left England and lacked interest in 'fame'.[153] However, Champion would complain to a close Australian friend, Herbert Brookes, his quiet regret 'that his colleagues in London had ruthlessly pushed him aside' and 'had claimed to be responsible for the work he had done'. When speaking of John Burns nearly a decade later, Ben Tillett tried to re-position

Champion in labour history for his Australian audience: 'He [Burns], like so many others, owed his rise in public life to H.H. Champion' and 'probably it was largely due to the ingratitude of many who should have thanked him, that sent the iron into his soul and made him reactionary'.[154] Tillet's role in the Dock Strike was essentially lost because his health often took him out of the central action but was reclaimed when Champion assisted him to gather his thoughts for an article in the *English Illustrated Magazine* in November 1889. Other friends also suffered the lack of acknowledgement, with an 'informant' telling a South Australian newspaper of the largely unnoticed role played by Maggie Harkness in the Dockers' Strike:

> Merit does not, however, always enjoy its reward, for the honors [sic] went to others, and she who has given her time and energy and sacrificed her private fortune, was left with the sole satisfaction of a good conscience.[155]

Nash and Smith's book on the Dock Strike effectively glossed over the roles of both Champion and Maggie Harkness.

The success of the Dock Strike obviously rankled with Hyndman who went to Battersea on 6 January 1890 to denounce Burns and Mann as 'traitors to the Socialist cause', alleging they 'concocted' a balance sheet and disposed of strike funds dishonestly. As a result, the Melbourne Trades Hall Council wrote to Burns the following month openly worried about the dispersal of surplus funds sent from Australia and complaining their involvement was not sufficiently acknowledged. Burns replied on 28 February announcing the total sum of £38,000 from the colonies, although money continued to dribble into the strike fund over the following months.[156] The surplus received was finally handed over directly to the Dockers' Union and president Tom Mann for continued support for the dockers, now numbering 60,000 members. Using balance sheet figures from the Melbourne Trades Hall Council dated three months earlier, Champion wrote in *Nineteenth Century* of £20,887 sent from Australia (the general public provided £5,817 of the total) to assist striking workers and families.[157] Money continued to flow in for some time after the strike finished.

At the age of thirty, Champion had proved he was a successful leader and mediator. He was recorded as 'something of a social lion' in the aftermath, 'refusing hundreds of invitations' as socialism became fashionable in London society drawing-rooms. In fact, *Marcella* devoted a substantial section to his social appearances at political dinners and functions. Because of his notoriety after the Docker's Strike and a surge in membership for the New Unionism, he explained that he made a point of accepting many invitations, especially where there was opportunity to meet parliamentarians and push labour issues. Both he and Tom Mann turned up to by-election meetings, asserting they represented the Independent Labour Party and, with well-rehearsed questions, pointedly asked each speaker for their stance on the eight-hour day to get commitment and push public debate forward.[158] Even though the Dock Strike was exhausting, Champion pressed for 'An Eight-Hour Law' in a piece for *Nineteenth Century* in September 1889. In addition, he and Burns were asked to help found the General Railway Workers' Union, open to both skilled and unskilled workers and, six months later, the union had over 60,000 members.[159] This was part of a long drive by the *Labour Elector* for an eight-hour day, with train drivers and signal men expected to be on duty for up to 18 hours.

Maritime Strike in Melbourne (1890)

A year after the London Dock Strike Champion arrived in Melbourne, only days before the Maritime Strike. Before he sailed for Australia he wrote: 'I do not think that I am over-estimating the strength of the present revolt against the old order in the labour world when I state that there exist the will and the ability to send into the next Parliament men who shall be pledged to make the interests of labour, as judged from the trade union standpoint, their first consideration'.[160] Aged thirty-one, he was regarded as a two-edged sword by friends and enemies, laughingly revelling in the Melbourne *Age* that he was 'one of the most quarrelsome men in Europe' although his friends were 'much attached' to him. His enemies would increase many times over in Australia, as Tom Mann would remind him down the track in 1913:

'How I detest politicians – as much as you did those Labor [sic] and Irish politicians of a generation ago'.[161]

Champion's path was cleverly prepared over three Saturdays – from 28 June to 12 July 1890 – with carefully constructed articles sent to the *Age* as teasers for his lecture tour. The articles focused on the Labour Movement in England and the development of trade unions from a united group of skilled craftsmen who joined guilds and societies of artisans, to unskilled, casual and poorly paid workers. He explained to Australians the distinction between the old school of unionism suspicious of parliamentary power and a new unionism aimed at organising labour into a federation. By the end of 1889 there were 120,000 new union members in London and a battle had started between the new and old ideas in the London Trades Council. He praised John Burns as 'jovial and kindly' with 'courage and initiative', a man who fought his election campaign 'almost unaided'. He also paid tribute to Tom Mann, a strong orator and 'magnetic' personality; Clementina Black for her activities for female workers; and Ben Tillett for his ongoing extensive work outside of London in the ports of Bristol and Dundee.

En route to Sydney, he and Percy Frost docked at Melbourne on 12 August 'in absolute ignorance' of events.[162] Before departure Champion said farewell to Cardinal Manning and was given a commendation as a 'personal friend'. He imagined this as a document 'a man might tour this planet on'. Manning also gave him a copy of *The Garden of the Soul*, dated 8 July 1890, with initials written inside to facilitate the opening of friendly doors.[163] Three days before the Maritime Strike Champion visited the Victorian Legislative Assembly and presented his letter of introduction to Alfred Deakin, a former student at the Church of England Grammar School where Percy Frost's uncle, Dr John Bromby, had been headmaster. Champion was shown over the Assembly personally and given a distinguished visitor's free pass on the Victorian railways.[164]

It is well documented that the Maritime Strike had its origins in a dispute over wages and conditions when 50 Marine Officers of coastal steamships approached the Melbourne Trades Hall Council (THC) for affiliation on 24 May 1890. The Steamship Owners' Association tried to block the officers from joining, a THC Strike Committee of senior officials was formed and president John Hancock dismissively declared that a couple of days were adequate to restore 'a handful of pigheaded employers to their senses'.[165] Champion later equated this strike to the South Metropolitan Gas-Stokers' Strike of 1889 that collapsed in defeat in mid-December, only months after he, Mann, Burns and Thorne celebrated the success of their newly created union in Hyde Park speeches to a gathering of 12,000. J. Havelock Wilson, founder of the Sailors' and Firemen's Union, was later attacked by Champion for the loss of livelihood and homes of the 3,000 stokers as well as Wilson's lack of an effective union.[166]

Lauded for his role in the London Dock Strike, Champion was invited to speak to 150 delegates on 20 August, telling them he desired to study unionism in 'the workingman's paradise'. To lengthy applause he urged: 'Remember that by your moderation, your good sense, your good management and conduct of your affairs, you will be helping the labour movement from Siberia to San Francisco'.[167] His speech was widely reported and he was on the wharf a few days later to deliver another. As a prominent figure of the London Dock Strike, Champion was warmly invited by the Strike Committee to address 50,000 at Flinders Park on 31 August, the *Argus* reporting him as the president of the East London Ropemakers' Union. In the process of completing his civil engineering degree at Melbourne University, a young Herbert Brookes was in the crowd and heard Champion talk on the main platform with W.G. Spence (president of the Amalgamated Shearers' Union) and W.E. Murphy (secretary of the Trades Hall Council's Finance and Control Committee). Brookes was greatly impressed and in his unpublished manuscript told of becoming an ardent supporter of Champion's future candidature in elections, calling him 'gifted' with 'exceptional powers of appeal' and 'possessed of a daring and a dash' that would have ensured a wonderful career in senior army ranks.

Suddenly front and centre in the midst of workers and their grievances, and with a cherished public speaking role, Champion actively offered instruction and advice. Evidently, he ignored an ancient warning from Heraclitus that argued no man ever steps in the same river twice, for it's not the same river and he's not the same man, a cautionary warning about adjusting to conditions and circumstances. Champion inserted himself directly into the dispute, educating himself on the background, reading back-copies of newspapers from 1886 as well as four years of detailed reports on disputes, strikes and trade union meetings. Using the press as his favoured medium he urged workers to be moderate and restrained, arguing their reactions were driven by a 'fear that the power controlled by the other side is being used in a harsh, unfair, and arbitrary manner'. In response, David Bennet, THC secretary and later vice president, stressed that the 'tone' of the shipowners' letter of demand and past false promises forced the maritime officers to seek affiliation. He suggested conferences over two to three years, to work through issues to resolve 'recurring labour troubles'.[168] Three independent strike mediators agreed to lend their services and, after another interview with the Strike Committee, Champion was selected to deliver their proposal and discuss the prospect of negotiations for settlement.

Angry that the Melbourne THC asked for monetary help only for the relief of strikers' distress and not to win the dispute, the Sydney Labor Defence Committee gave their approval on 10 September for John (Jack) Fitzgerald to be their delegate to England to plead the case. Five days later Fitzgerald left Sydney on board the Orient steamer *Curzco* with a first-class ticket he had already booked for his six months' holiday in Europe. During his brief stopover in Melbourne Fitzgerald secured an agreement to be the Melbourne THC delegate to England, approaching the Finance and Control Committee's chair John Hancock and secretary William Murphy, before sailing on to Adelaide to give his pitch to journalists at his next port. Here a journalist recorded: 'England has its Mr. Champion; Australia is to have its Mr. Fitzgerald'.[169] Fitzgerald told reporters of his extensive agenda: he wanted to visit London to explain the facts of the strike, convene a conference of English trade unionists, the Dockers and the SDF, hold demonstrations in London, conduct extensive meetings throughout England, Scotland and Ireland, and bring John Burns back to Australia.

Champion sent him a letter extending 'any assistance in his

power' while hoping his 'mission would be productive of nothing but good'.[170] Champion failed to realise how determined Fitzgerald was to make his own name both locally and on an international stage and how quickly this opportunity would elevate his role in the dispute. He was the name on Australian lips, even if, in modern parlance, it was just fifteen minutes of fame. Originally a compositor from Bathurst and now a Sydney labour official, Fitzgerald was remarkably similar to Champion – youthful, enthusiastic, confident, well-educated and not a stereotypical agitator. Reporters too were amazed to find Champion did not represent their image of a labour advocate, seeing a personable, reasonable man, of youthful appearance, fashionable attire, patent leather boots, prince-nez reading glasses, military appearance and a black waxed moustache. One journalist described Champion as 'muscular', about six feet tall 'with a pleasant style of address and decided opinions, which he does not hesitate to express'.[171] Another journalist, Katharine Susannah Prichard, would later comment in her private notebook that his eyes 'gave him the gleam of iron'.

On the afternoon of 11 September and only days before Fitzgerald sailed, Champion travelled to Sydney on an express train accompanied by a former president of the THC, Fred Bromley, where he was met on arrival by William Trenwith, another former THC president, and F.J. Hall of the Wharf Labourers' Union. In his pocket Champion carried Andrew Lyell's proposal for settlement from the Melbourne THC Committee of Finance and Control, for delivery to Sydney members. As Champion arrived at a tram platform a journalist informed him that the Labour Council of New South Wales had already rejected any meeting with him, declining to accept him as mediator since he was not a trade union representative. The same day, Hancock talked in Melbourne of 'traitors in the camp', suggesting he and other unionists believed 'if the help from England can be cut off, then the struggle must be given up in Australia'.[172] The Labour Council's resolution on 12 September stated that 'his action since his arrival in Australia had been detrimental to the cause of labor [sic]'. When a reporter asked about chances of conciliation, Champion's reply was blunt and confident of a successful outcome, as he gave an outline:

> No Trades Unionist is to claim the right to dictate to an employer whom he should employ, or demand that an employer before taking on a man should ask him if he belongs to a Union or not. Nor is a Trades Unionist to claim the right to apply force, or the threat of force, or any form of persuasion other than that permitted and defined by law to men who are not unionists. During the last few days I have been conferring with Mr. Robert Reid, Mr. McLean, and Mr. Andrew Lyell, and they are willing to give their good offices at any time for the purpose of mediation ... I would rather not have discussed this matter at present, but I see Mr. Hancock has made a public statement very much to the same effect as what I am telling you, so there is no object to be served by my being silent.[173]

The other mediators were Matthew Robert Reid from Ayrshire in Scotland, an SDF member from Battersea in 1885, a delegate to the Melbourne THC in 1889, a foundation board member of the *Worker* and later a labour member for Brisbane;[174] Andrew Lyell, a well-known and successful negotiator in the 1880s, admired for his integrity, honesty, lack of bias and ability to find common agreement; and William McLean, a partner in McLean Bros. & Rigg, a large firm of ironmongers and general merchants. It was alleged the Committee of Finance and Control gave the proposal for settlement to Lyell without consultation with any other bodies and W.G. Spence, president of the Shearers' Union, saw the proposal for the first time when Champion arrived with this document during their meeting with the Sydney Lord Mayor.[175]

Advertised for the following weekend in Sydney was Alfred G. Yewen's lecture, 'H.H. Champion's Contentions and Pretensions Refuted', a recycling of old gossip and SDF recriminations from a member of the Socialist League who migrated from London four years before. The secretary of the Socialist League, William McNamara, dismissed Champion's role in the Dock Strike as 'clerical' and brandished a past copy of the *Reynold's Newspaper* from 2 February 1890 that focused on Champion's failed attempt with Clementina Black to form a branch of the National Electoral Labour Association at Southwark. According to the article, Champion had been subjected to noisy interruptions and charges of undermining socialism (mentioning SDF's repudiation, a Church Congress and money received from 'a gentleman').[176] The day before McNamara's interview, 'W.' (from the *Reynold's Newspaper*) referred to Champion as being 'hooted' from a London platform and 'posing' as an authority on labour in Australia. At a Sydney Socialist League meeting to this effect on 18 September, Yewen claimed Champion was 'playing the game of the capitalists', before a resolution was moved against Champion's interference in Melbourne's strike.

The THC secretary read two letters of recommendation to members, one from Cardinal Manning and one from John Burns (the latter dated 18 September 1890):

> Mr. Champion, late editor of the Labor [sic] Elector, the best labor paper we have ever had in England, has sailed for Australia. He has devoted a great deal of time and money to the labor question here, and has financially suffered very hardly indeed. He has done more for the eight hours question than any man in England; rendered us great service during the dock strike. I can only speak of him in the highest possible manner, and heartily recommend him to all Australians as being a man and a gentleman whom they can heartily trust in everything.[177]

However, the *Argus* reported murmurings from Melbourne Trades Hall members who denied knowledge of Champion's 'intentions' and 'darkly hinted at the presence of a capitalists' agent in disguise'.[178] Gossip had been stoked by a vicious fight between Hyndman and Burns in London papers at the time; in addition, there was a reference to Champion being 'an emissary from the Tory party' in the *Reynold's Newspaper*. The editor of this newspaper, William Marcus Thompson, was a former barrister for trade unions who defended Burns during the Trafalgar riots trial and after Bloody Sunday was the founder of the short-lived National Democratic League. Later, he slammed Burns for his 'swelled head' that like a fabled frog bulged 'with pride until he burst':

This diseased egotism carries him so far that, when men do not recognise that he is always in the right, he showers upon them a coarse and vulgar invective as if they were his personal enemies.

There is hardly a prominent man in the Labour movement whom he has not treated in this way. He must always be on the housetops shouting, 'I, John Burns, have done this or said that,' ... There are hundreds of men in the Labour movement of this country who have done infinitely more good than Mr. Burns, but they have not that gentleman's voracious appetite for flattery. Nor are they eaten up with jealousy of their co-workers. They allow others a due share of the credit for their performances, and they disdain to work the press oracle as Mr. Burns has done.[179]

Arriving initially as a labour star and celebrity, within six weeks Champion had incurred the enmity of THC members in Melbourne who, according to John Hancock, now threatened him with violence. The stage was set for an escalation of hate talk. Champion's early reference to a clash between the new and old ideas around new unionism in the London Trades Council, now seemed to describe his relationship with Melbourne's THC. The battle was transformed into cables across the ocean, all appearing publicly in the *Age* and repeated over the next two weeks in other Australian newspapers. G.A. Edwards (secretary of the Sydney Labor Defence Committee) believing English workers would reciprocate by sending money as Australians did in the London Dock Strike, telegraphed to England without authorisation in mid-October to appeal for £20,000, while Champion immediately sent his own telegram to John Burns who confirmed his wording: 'Strike grossly mismanaged; funds useless'. The money requested from Sydney could not stop the strike's 'absolute failure', Champion argued in the *Age* on 16 October. The next day the Labour Council of New South Wales and the THC declined to hear him, alleging that his interviews, opinions and journalism in Australia contributed to ill-feeling. While McNamara's *Australian Workman* talked of Champion's 'cloven hoof', the *Bulletin* weighed in to the debate using flamboyant, emotional rhetoric and hyperbole with a caricature of Champion as a capitalist embroidered with cartoon-like embellishments. Under a heading of 'A Prophet with an Eyeglass' the Sydney journalist wrote:

> That imported Labour advocate, Mr. H.H. CHAMPION, has been tried and found a failure ... The objection which Labour has to urge against this officious and self-appointed prophet is simply that from first to last he had urged unconditional surrender, and the acceptance of terms which would make Labour the hopeless slave of Capital; and the Employers' League, in its rampant mood, could do no more ... his eye-glass, and his dress-suit, and his bank-account, and the exotic plant in his button-hole, will all survive the general carnage ... the capitalists, and the prophet with the eye-glass and the dress-suit, have managed between them to discover the most hopeful means for the achievement of that object. As a rampant Conservative and a man who howls in defence of Property Mr. CHAMPION has many good points, but as a social reformer he has some conspicuous disadvantages. The eye-glass and the dress-suit have eaten into his soul, and cannot be eradicated.[180]

Subsequently, Champion discovered a telegram to England signed 'Murphy' sent on 1 October stating Champion was an 'enemy of the labor [sic] party'. Champion's letter to the editor of the *Age* requested formal permission to address THC members for 30 minutes. As hostility increased, the request was denied, with John Hancock weighing in with an angry tirade that presented the THC as a violent and unruly mob threatening Champion's personal safety and this was used as a reason not to grant him a hearing. This caused *Melbourne Punch* to question: 'If the Trades Hall quarrel with Mr. Champion is just, why are they afraid to meet him?'[181] However, within the THC the rank and file were unhappy and not unified, with one member arguing that the trades needed to be consulted on important executive decisions and another accusing strike leaders of stifling free debate and resigning.

Armed with a barrage of union complaints against Champion, Fitzgerald arrived in Naples to visit tourist sites and made his way to Paris and then London. John Burns accompanied him to the *Pall Mall*

Gazette office for Fitzgerald's first interview. His interview was only days before Hancock sent telegraphic advice to W.G. Spence advising that the strike was ended in Victoria, and Spence sent circulars to members to that effect. Fitzgerald addressed a meeting at the Mile End Assembly Hall in Stepney on 4 November 1890, hotly denouncing Champion and requesting repudiation by the Dock Labourers' Union leaders. Stirred up by Fitzgerald, the assembled crowd turned on an absent Champion with emotional cries of 'kill him', 'Shoot him' and 'He dare not return', comments recorded by bemused London correspondents and reproduced across various Australian newspapers. Burns told the crowd that £16,000 had been sent to Melbourne and read a letter aloud to the crowd from 'Mr. Laws' [sic], obviously Maggie Harkness. Fitzgerald countered this with a blatant lie, saying the Marine Officers' affiliation was raised after the commencement of the strike and was not 'the cause'. Instead, he insisted, the strike was to help a 'weak' union and a battle for 'trade unionism, whether it should live or whether it should die'.[182]

Reynold's Newspaper also stirred the pot by quoting Sydney's *Truth* scandal sheet, written to demonstrate the whole nation's opinion of 'chameleon' Champion. Added to his sins was 'reading namby-pamby papers at Church Congresses, where he has been petted and caressed by port-wine bishops and truly rural deans, who serve the Lord for the most part on horseback hunting foxes to death and trampling down poor farmer's crops'. The accusation was that, like the Bible's dog and sow, Champion 'has gone back to his vomit and to wallowing in the mire of class prejudice and monopoly'.

On Champion's return from a trip to a gold-mining town of Walhalla in the Gippsland region to speak to workers in October, he angrily responded to the *Age* about reports of the Mile End meeting and inflammatory rhetoric. He labelled Fitzgerald's speech as a 'mean piece of dishonesty', an attempt to secure money for a strike that would fail, declaring 'poverty-ridden laborers of the old country' should never be asked to support a falsehood; the strike's failure was a direct result of 'the arrogant imbecility of the strike leaders'.[183] His disappointment with people believing Fitzgerald's 'wild mis-statements' carried over to Burns and Mann who left him unsupported at the meeting.

Indeed, Mann's statement, 'Mr. Champion represents nobody but himself', caused newspaper headlines to howl: 'Tom Mann Disavows Champion'. He admitted to understanding his friends' worries about northern strikes, as well as clashes with the Trade Union Congress and Dockers' Union with their 'endless bickerings and jealousies amongst those who envy them their temporary popularity'. This was certainly true with Ben Tillett complaining to a crowd at the gates of the East India Docks that as a leader 'rose to eminence, many of his own class seemed to be jealous'.[184] As the Maritime Strike concluded, Champion announced his intention to write a full account and to take up an appeal for any Marine Officers now permanently unemployed. After checking with subscribers, if any surplus remained, a public monument also would be erected to Hancock, Murphy and Trenwith inscribed with their current triumphs, a statement of ridicule probably enjoyed by many.

Reports continued to filter back to Champion, including some from Maggie Harkness who was still in London. Now the face of the Maritime Strike, Fitzgerald continued to demonise Champion and incite antagonism amongst friends and colleagues in the Dock Strike's iconic pub. He generated a 'storm of abuse' at Wade's Arms and also the Central Democratic Club, angrily denouncing Champion's telegram to Burns. The radical barrister and member of Giuseppe Garibaldi's armed volunteers in Southern Italy in 1860s, John Morrison Davidson, strongly believed Fitzgerald was incorrect and felt Burns believed Champion to be sincere.[185] In Scotland, the Aberdeen Trades Council were very unhappy about him being condemned without a hearing and mounted a defence in the *Aberdeen Free Press* that was reprinted in Australia. Their members tackled Fitzgerald's accusations, distilled into three charges: Champion altered the strike situation by providing advice; dined at 'swell' clubs; and met with employers. The second and third charges they called 'flippant', 'ridiculous' and 'beneath notice', his contributions to the *Age* articles considered correct. The Aberdeen Trades Council's resolution was that they were 'convinced that the course he pursued in the Australian strike was a true, just and proper one entirely in the interests of true trades unionism' and proclaimed support for Champion as a labour leader.[186]

Meanwhile, Fitzgerald wrote excitedly from Hull, detailing an extensive list of Champion's friends and colleagues he had met in November and December. Consciously or unconsciously Fitzgerald immersed himself in the life of the docks, places central to the Dock Strike and Champion's circle. In a letter dated 2 January 1891 and released to the *Australian Workman*, Fitzgerald wrote that Cunninghame Graham was 'mad with me for denouncing Champion'. Suggesting enticingly that there was some 'conspiracy' by Champion who was paid by shipowners to 'break' the Seamen's Union, Fitzgerald claimed he would expose Champion in a pamphlet.[187] This never appeared and talk about conspiracy quietly dissipated. Travelling widely through Britain he spoke at Cardiff, Liverpool, Leeds, Hull, the Tyne (Newcastle-on-Tyne, Gateshead, North and South Shields) and in Edinburgh and Glasgow. He organised interviews and claimed friendships, providing an extensive laundry list of people Champion knew.[188] It is probable that a star-struck Fitzgerald had simply met many of these individuals at large events. Before he returned to Australia he went for a few days to Berlin and Hamburg where, though 'prepared to face the burden of a demonstrative reception', he was 'disappointed' at a lack of meetings with the labour movement leaders though he started correspondence with Liebknecht sailing back to Adelaide.[189]

Apart from his speech at Mile End, Fitzgerald held no mass demonstrations in England to support the Maritime Strike, which by now had collapsed; there was no great case to lay before the SDF, an organisation who weren't involved in the London Dock Strike; and John Burns never came to Australia. Fitzgerald did attend one SDF meeting with Hyndman in the chair and received an indifferent reception. He was also given some pamphlets by the Fabians. Fitzgerald arrived back in Australia in February 1891 on the *Ormuz* for a victory procession of ports, stopping firstly in Adelaide and then Melbourne. In mid-March a band led him through the streets from Circular Quay to Trades Hall for his welcome home banquet, attended by E.J. Brady who represented the Socialist League. Fitzgerald returned to his favourite topic, presented only a few days before to an enthusiastic audience of Melbourne THC members: 'Mr. Champion, a middle-class man, had dropped from his middle-class heaven in order to champion the cause of labor [sic], but he had not done so. They knew all about him'.[190] Returning to the Sydney Trades and Labour Council as a decorated warrior, complete with a scarf and medal from English labour bodies, Fitzgerald was soon elected a member for West Sydney.

Informing an Adelaide journalist that Fitzgerald 'much misrepresented' him, Champion returned to England, announcing that Aberdeen trade unions enthusiastically desired him to stand for parliament. His article 'The Crushing Defeat of Trade Unionism in Australia' explained the strike's failure and, not one to take a backward step, he blamed 'the wanton mismanagement of the strike' for the failure of the Maritime Strike which ended after 10 weeks. The THC leaders were 'unmistakably and avowedly beaten on every point at issue', Champion informed his English audience, and

> ... have had to surrender unconditionally, have caused enormous loss, principally to the working class, have wasted all the money sent from England, have lost their prestige, have welded the employers into a solid and irresistible force, and have destroyed the possibility of even intercolonial federation of labour for ten years.[191]

He argued that the responsibility lay firmly on the 'blunders' Hancock and his Strike Committee perpetrated in their handling of strikers' grievances. In a now infamous phrase, 'an army of lions led by asses', he alleged that they blamed him to deflect interest away from the THC failure. The phrase evoked antipathy and anger towards Champion and would continue to do so throughout his life and well into modern times. The words harked back to Thomas Paine's pamphlet *Common Sense* (1776) during the American War of Independence where he questioned monarchy and 'the folly' of hereditary succession: 'nature disapproves it, otherwise she would not so frequently turn it into ridicule by giving mankind an *ass for a lion*'. The phrase is also attributed to Napoleon as well as soldiers in the Crimean War. The THC was deeply offended by Champion's reference to workers as courageous and strong lions, while leaders were allocated the role of braying asses. Also quoting Defoe to support his fearless position, Champion noted he stood 'on the dangerous precipice of telling unbiassed truth'.

Fitzgerald's reply to Champion's allegations pointed to his repudiation by Sydney and Melbourne trade unionists and so, he wrote, the 'naturally embittered and rendered vindictive' Champion took his vengeance out on their movement.[192] Champion did not reply and, when asked why in Aberdeen, explained that the editor (Knowles) did not think it warranted a reply and interest was not there to justify further space; indeed, without oxygen to feed the issue, interest dissipated. The Maritime Strike guaranteed a number of enduring enemies who formed Champion's most vocal and strident detractors. He was annoyed that the workers were 'blindly following incapable and unscrupulous leaders' and knew that he was regarded as being without knowledge of local conditions by men who didn't appreciate his frank and fearless advice.[193] Joseph Burgess, friend of Henry Broadhurst, denounced him on the front page of the *Workman's Times* as a meddling outsider: 'The working man can choose his own leaders without recruiting them from the class from which Mr. H.H. Champion sprang'.[194]

A year later Fitzgerald would face 'an indifferent reception' and laughter from constituents when he informed them that he had business that required his departure for London within two weeks.[195] The following month he returned overseas for another six months to marry to a French woman and enjoy a honeymoon while courting Keir Hardie, Cunninghame Graham, Tom Mann and John Burns (the latter asked to witness his Chelsea marriage). During this period, Fitzgerald also strongly opposed Champion in his 1892 quest for the seat of South Aberdeen, sending letters that turned into election handbills to support a Liberal candidate, Professor James Bryce.

Apart from Fitzgerald, whose career flared briefly and then gradually faded, there were a number of the Melbourne THC Strike Committee who were ambitious. Many had, or were to have, high office within the THC and also political seats, especially in the Legislative Assembly. Champion's vocal critics included six men: Fred Bromley, born in England, President of the THC (1885) who was the parliamentary leader of the party in Victoria; William Trenwith, born in Tasmania, President of THC (1886), who was a member for Richmond (1889–1903); William E. Murphy, Irish-born Secretary of the THC (1888), who contested the seat of North Melbourne; John Hancock, born in Clerkenwell, President of THC (1889–90), who was a Legislative Assembly member for Collingwood (1891–92) and Footscray (1894–97); Edward Findley, born in Bendigo, President of the THC (1896–1897), who was a member of the Legislative Assembly for Melbourne (1900) before being expelled; and George Prendergast, born in Adelaide to Irish parents, President of the THC (1893), who was a member for North Melbourne (1894–1897, 1900–1927), succeeded Bromley as leader of the Labor Party and was later Premier of Victoria.

Although Champion would continue to be regarded as an Englishman even after nearly 35 years of life in Australia, all of his opponents were either born in Great Britain or Ireland, or first-generation sons of British parents. These senior THC leaders not only solidly opposed Champion but obsessively opposed any ambitious moves by this interloper within the closed shop of labour politics in Victoria. He was not only a thorn in the side of their ambition, he became a sharpened stake and THC leaders had long memories and deep-seated animosity. When trying to tease out the cause of the overwhelming hostility and resentment of THC senior members towards Champion, one newspaper argued that a fear existed of the 'imported' competitor, one who now stood between the local labour leaders and executive THC positions. 'Champion is in fact a cleverer man than any in the crowd, and what is most dreaded is that he may prove a dangerous rival, and by stepping to the front spoil the cherished aspirations of the Trades Hall bigwigs'. Specifically named were Hancock and Prendergast who 'do not trouble to consider whether Champion can serve the labour cause, but they are certain that he can only spoil their little cause, and they feel that they are all the champions labour is in need of'.[196]

Champion greatly surprised many senior THC members by returning to Australia a second time and when his political ambitions became known, a letter was sent in late 1894 by Frank G. Anstey, assistant secretary of the United Labor and Liberal Party of Victoria, requesting information about Champion's expulsion from the SDF. Keir Hardie's response on 17 December 1894 to Anstey tried to defuse antagonists; he explained that he had no knowledge of any issue that made Champion 'a friend to the capitalists'. H.W. Lee's reply from the SDF's central office, dated the day after Hardie's, summarised the organisation's considerations that Champion's actions over the years 1887–88 showed he was not 'a fit and proper person' (as previously discussed). A week later, at a committee meeting at the Democratic Club for May Day 1895 the THC representative, Edward Findley, read both letters. Champion's defence was to point to 'men of ability and stability' in the SDF such as Morris, Aveling, Bax, and Burns who were expelled or 'compelled to sever themselves' because of their criticism of senior leaders and who afterwards were 'maligned and stigmatised' as traitors; he deemed that 'the present object of its spite was no less a person than Keir Hardie himself'. Champion also wrote a letter to the editor, placed underneath this article, announcing: 'I have made plenty of such enemies. I shall make more' and quoted George Higinbotham's 1858 statement on 'the political quack, the trader in sedition' who 'scare from public life all men of cleaner hands and nobler aspirations'.[197]

The publicity over the Maritime Strike ensured SDF labels such as traitor, conspirator, agent of capitalists and of employers, were attributed to Champion. He was constantly viewed with suspicion by senior figures in Trades Hall, the union movement and often the public. Years later, still nursing a grudge, William Trenwith would go over Champion's mistakes with Herbert Brookes, pointing to Champion's actions during the Maritime Strike as demonstrating that he was untrustworthy. Throughout all the events, the focus was on personalities, scandals and opportunities, and power plays by those holding collective power at Trades Hall. This would erode Champion's credibility for decades, as well as setting the tone for future histories of the Australian labour movement.

Independent Labour Party (1893)

The old adage 'success has many fathers, failure is an orphan', could well describe the formation of the Independent Labour Party (ILP). Very few of Champion's contemporaries gave him credit for his role in the creation of a new party, which was something of a forerunner to the modern Labour Party in Britain. While reviewing A.W. Humphrey's *A History of Labour Representation* (1912), the *Athenaeum* recognised Champion as 'that singularly able and undaunted man' who founded the ILP, with Keir Hardie its 'most conspicuous figure'. It recognised that both had been 'abused, denounced, and calumniated' for years. Another contemporary, Joseph Clayton, wrote in *The Rise and Decline of Socialism in Great Britain 1884–1924* that an unbiased 'student of history' would recognise in the future that Champion was 'the real creator of the I.L.P.'[198] One of the strangest explanations for the ILP's foundation was Keir Hardie's small pamphlet which skirted the issue about where the name originated, blaming 'influences of nature'.[199]

As early as 1885 Robert Hudson recalled Champion visiting him with ideas of founding a new political party. Although the official date for the founding of the ILP is recognised as 1893, it is 1888 that really marks the initial moves for the formation. As secretary of the Labour Electoral Association's Metropolitan Section, Champion gained momentum to run Keir Hardie as a candidate for the by-election on 27 April 1888 of Mid-Lanark in a Scottish community of miners where there was a strong Irish vote. The election showed 'a straight-out Labour Party was in existence'.[200] Their small team was therefore the driving force behind Keir Hardie's claim to the title of first independent labour party candidate. Champion was a man with an ambitious plan.

Only days before the by-election, Champion spent two hours alone with Charles Parnell discussing a party for labour and the possibility of an 'alliance'. He received a letter in red ink requesting he meet with Parnell the following day in the lobby of the House of Commons and, upon leaving their discussion, felt that this politician 'had no equal'.[201] Champion immediately sent details of this meeting to the *Times* to outline the proposed tactics for labour candidates before an election:

> If it was agreed that the majority of the electors in the constituency were workmen, the support of the Parnellite party should be given to a labour candidate. If it was agreed that working class electors were in

a minority, no labour candidate should be run to divide the Liberal vote. In case of disagreement as to the composition of the electorate, the point should be referred to the final decision of an arbitrator.[202]

This invitation was politely rejected by Parnell. While Hardie received less than 10% of the vote, Champion went on to establish the *Labour Elector* in June 1888, the title a direct statement of his intention to create a new independent labour party. A month later he argued for 'The New Labour Party', styled upon Parnell's leadership of Irish Nationalists, to put pressure on other political parties. He stressed 'the times are ripe, and a field is open, for the action of a Party which places the rights of labour before everything else'.[203] After the Independent Labour Party proved successful, Hyndman admitted that 'time was ripe' for a new party although he relegated Champion to one of the 'short-cut intriguers', linking old SDF accusations suggesting personal gain. His partisan views became received knowledge for Champion's activities.

Not long after Champion promulgated the idea for a new party of labour, a Trade Union Congress was held in September 1888 at Bradford. A private meeting to discuss a new party was quietly arranged just a few minutes' walk from the Congress in the Bradford Coffee Tavern, a venue able to seat 90 customers, located at the old Mechanic's Institute in Well Street. At this venue Champion, Keir Hardie, Tom Mann, Clementina Black, George Bateman, William Matkin and a few unnamed local politicians met. Bateman was a former SDF member from Trafalgar Square days, a candidate for Holborn and a retired Royal Welsh Fusilier whose pamphlet *Socialism and Soldiering* (1887) contained a preface by Champion. Together the two argued forcibly for the foundation of an independent party devoted to the cause of labour.[204]

Champion continued his theme of the Federation of Labour in the *New Review* for June 1890, warning of a 'revolt' against previous attitudes in the labour movement and stressing a growing desire to place candidates in parliament to work for labour. He stood out as a persuasive and energised leader and even Lord Randolph Churchill, who was 'on the stump' at Walsall on 29 July 1889, arranged for

Champion to visit him and outline issues of concern to workers. Champion wrote:

> He was going to speak at a meeting at Wolverhampton, and had not the remotest idea of what political points were likely to please the men of the Midlands. To my surprise, he sent for me and asked me to recite the chief social points which burdened the working man. I did so, with a shorthand writer rapidly taking it down. Lord Randolph went and incorporated the whole of my socialist doctrine in his Wolverhampton speech.[205]

Champion had been asked to run for the seat of South Aberdeen and while his candidacy as an independent for labour was being considered by the Aberdeen Trades Council, he visited his relatives and Cunninghame Graham. Recognising a mood resistant to those who were not part of a union, Keir Hardie wrote a public letter advising the Aberdeen Trades Council not to turn their backs on people like Champion and Cunninghame Graham who, as social reformers, were germane to the movement even if outside the trade. Before the Dock Strike there had been a belief that trade unionists, who formed only 10% of workers, were the only ones able to represent labour, forcing Cunninghame Graham to write that he represented the other 90% left without representation.[206]

Champion and his friends were shaping up, not only as a threat to many trade unionists but also to SDF members who believed that only they were the hope for the working man. Champion's speech on 'The Future of British Democracy', due to be given on 19 June 1891 at St Katharine's Hall in Aberdeen, attracted a visit by an SDF member and a storm of controversy erupted in the press. In a strategic move to undercut Champion's ambitions, the SDF sent Herbert Burrows to Union Street that week. Here Burrows talked freely and at length with journalists and members of the Aberdeen Trades Council, the latter a group who supported Champion for parliament and rejected Fitzgerald's charges. Employing the same old gripes, Burrows complained of Champion's betrayal of their movement for personal profit, reminded them of Fitzgerald's charges against him from the

Maritime Strike in Australia and attacked Maltman Barry (now editor of *Labour Elector*). This incited George Gerrie, a founder of the Scottish Labour Party, to criticise Burrows for his 'intense bitterness and hatred'.[207] One paper complained about the personal rivalry and suspiciousness plaguing socialists:

> How these Socialists love each other! It seems that a Mr Burrows has come all the way from London to enlighten the people of Aberdeen on the subject of Social Democracy; and one of the first things he did was to warn them against the teaching of Mr H.H. Champion, who is also believed to be a Socialist.[208]

Comments, accusations and charges took up many columns in Aberdeen's newspapers and, while ensuring a large crowd for Champion's speech a few days later, the audience was divided between those applauding and those hissing. 'He belongs to Aberdeenshire', Burrows was bluntly told by locals. Aberdeen was the birthplace of Champion's father, who was baptised in Union Street, and the area home to generations of Urquharts and Duffs. Champion had just visited Hatton Castle to see Champion's cousins Annie and Beauchamp Duff who was now ADC to the Earl of Aberdeen. One supporter of Champion for the seat of South Aberdeen was John Morrison Davidson, born in Hatton and founder of Greenock's *Fiery Cross* newspaper in 1885; he was the brother of philosopher Thomas Davidson from The Fellowship of New Life.

George Gerrie (a founder of the Scottish Labour Party) had recognised a kindred spirit in Champion during his campaigning for Mid-Lanark and his May Day 1890 speech at Aberdeen to a crowd of 20,000. His examination of the origins of the eight-hour movement in the Antipodes, published in the *Economic Journal* (March 1892), attributed the first May Day to New Zealand's Otago settlement in 1845 followed by Victoria's 'small knot of workmen' (stonemasons) who laid the foundation on 21 April 1856 for an international May Day in 1890 for working-class solidarity. Champion's early research led him to an interest in the colonies and, as early as 5 June 1888, he expressed an early desire to visit Australia.[209]

George Gerrie collected friends such as George Bisset (a past president of Aberdeen Trades Council) and formed the Aberdeen Labour Committee to support Champion's candidature. In April 1892, in preparation for the election, Gerrie

> ... drafted a constitution of an 'Independent Labour Party of Great Britain and Ireland.' Membership was to be open to all who would sign a declaration to the effect that the 'interests of labour are paramount to, and must take precedence of, all other interests, and that the advancement of these interests must be sought by political and constitutional action.' The party was to be formed for 'the sole purpose accomplishing the emancipation of the workers from their present economic slavery'.[210]

Champion obviously played a large part in the preparation of this document, which was similar to one written in 1891, 'The Labour Platform at the Next Election'. In that article he envisaged a labour party united around strong rallying points of social reform for workers, including one man one vote, an eight-hour day, a graduated tax system, health and safety legislation and national pensions. The draft constitution of the Independent Labour Party was printed by the editor of the *Workman's Times*, Joseph Burgess, on 30 April. Burgess later claimed he saw the need for an Independent Labour Party prior to the July general election and his own role was an 'essential factor in the evolution of the Labour Party', patently a self-important overstatement.[211]

In this election, William Diack recorded Champion was 'in fine fighting fettle, and made the campaign a memorable one in the annals of political electioneering in Aberdeen' and that his radical days seemed tempered.[212] Champion's alleged traitorous actions in Melbourne, contained in the *Aberdeen Evening Gazette's* article, 'Down with the Infidel', was settled in a libel action in Champion's favour for £250.[213] Champion's old nemesis Fitzgerald arrived on his honeymoon and claimed he assisted the election of five labour candidates (including John Burns and Keir Hardie) while opposing Champion and supporting a Liberal candidate, Professor James Bryce for South

Aberdeen. Calling Champion, one of 'our opponents', Fitzgerald remained vigilant in his crusade and sent a letter to Bryce attacking Champion's 'treachery' during the Maritime Strike in Australia.[214] The cycle of escalation began again with Bryce's supporters copying and handing out Fitzgerald's letter to Aberdeen electors and by 4 July the accusation of Champion being an agent of the Tories in Scotland was taken up by Bryce. Even though he suffered defeat, Champion gained the largest Independent labour vote polled in Great Britain to that period with 15.8% of the vote.

Mischief was being propagated by the *Workman's Times* and suspicion was directed at Champion's intentions even after the election. John Burns was informed around August that money for his election expenses (totalling £453 1s 11d)[215] that the *Workman's Times* provided, came from Champion, with Joseph Burgess and James Shaw Maxwell described as unwitting puppets of Champion. Burns complained that Shaw Maxwell (candidate for the Scottish Land Restoration for the 1885 Glasgow election and editor of *People's Press*) was about to publish internal discussions presented as an interview between the men. It was also alleged that Champion's aim was to use 'a secret' as leverage over Burns and a source had told of Champion's nefarious plan.[216] Recognising another 'Tory gold' scandal in the making, Burns felt compelled to write to the *Daily Chronicle* the next day to explain the source of election money. In September 1892 Engels wrote to Eduard Bernstein that Burgess now wanted to be leader of a party and the election money was either derived from Champion or channelled through him from Hudson's Soap. With another round of accusations and suspicions, it seemed no-one had learned any lessons from the last time, the reappearance of 'Tory gold' helping fuel more distrust.

In hindsight, it appeared that Champion made a serious error in not attending the Bradford Conference in Yorkshire on 13–14 January 1893. This conference drew up the blueprint for the fledging Independent Labour Party. However, it was not a mistake or miscalculation but an accident that resulted in his fractured kneecap. The *Labour Elector* in December reported Champion 'knocked his knee against a bedpost, or table, or something, and had to get it cut' before Christmas. This was true and a year later, an interview with Morley Roberts published in

To-Day (using Champion's pseudonym 'Leslie Orde'), told a humorous story about Morley spending an evening at 'the bedside of a friend who was laid up with a cracked knee-pan'.[217] He was incapacitated and could not walk or straighten a knee: frequently these injuries required surgery to remove pieces of bone and immobility for a couple of months. Since Champion was confined to bed with a nurse in attendance he could not travel to Bradford.

Because Champion wasn't at the conference, he had no place in the historical formation of a national party for labour, something he had been arguing for and working towards for many years. He therefore had no input to the crucial planning or decision-making of an organisation that gradually morphed into a future Labour Party. As a representative of the Aberdeen United Trades Council Labour Party, Champion was notable for his absence and two weeks after the conference Maltman Barry, as new editor of the *Labour Elector*, took a swipe at the *Workman's Times* over the handling of election money (described as an error) although he approved the decision to set up a central election fund. Burgess previously had advised Champion to disassociate himself from Barry although Champion stood his ground: 'I have lost pretty well everything a man can lose over this Labour business – except my self-respect. Before I abandon my tried and true friends at the dictation of my enemies, I trust I have the decency to cut my throat'.[218]

The National Administrative Council (NAC) of the new Independent Labour Party, chaired by Keir Hardie, appointed Shaw Maxwell as secretary. As an elected member, Burgess confessed he 'had to bell the cat' (issue a warning) about Champion's 'irresponsible activities' and was one of 11 members to sign a condemnation of Champion. Burgess also tried to persuade the Council from accepting 'no money whatever, under any circumstances' from Champion.[219] One anonymous letter to the editor effectively summed up the in-fighting, pointing to the ILP as now 'split up into two rival camps, with the *Clarion* [Robert Blatchford or 'Nunquam'] and the *Workman's Times* [Joseph Burgess] as opposing leaders'.[220]

On behalf of the National Administrative Council, Shaw Maxwell identified and exposed Robert Hudson's role, layering this with snide criticism of Champion: 'The Tories twist him round their fingers, and reap all the benefits of the few hundred pounds which he gets now and then for Labour purposes from his friend Mr Hudson'.[221] The identity of the radical who contributed to campaigns was divulged and out in the public arena, with helpful input from Burgess. Champion's response was swift as he argued the funds were:

> ... the money of a gentleman who is known personally to almost every one of the Labour leaders of the Independent Labour Party, who has helped the cause for many years with voice, purse, and pen, and whose bona fides and independence of political parties are questioned by no man.[222]

In his memoirs of the Scottish Labour Party, David Lowe recalled that he spurned Champion's offer of help at that time because 'by private letter and otherwise' people undermined his opinion of him. Champion was 'a born general' and Lowe regretted he 'may have effectively assisted to put an end to the activities in Scotland of a man who, by education, sincerity, and courage might have been a valuable asset to our cause'.[223]

Champion was made honorary president of the ILP in Aberdeen in June 1893 and again in March 1896 when a letter was sent to him stating: 'Williamson Innes, Secretary of the I.L.P. in Aberdeen, will be writing to inform you of your re-election as Hon. President of that body. That was all we could do in return for your great services to us'.[224] Champion attended the International Socialist Workers' Congress held in Switzerland in August 1893 as one of four members of the Independent Labour Party, with Shaw Maxwell (general secretary), Arthur Fields (Leicester) and L.A. Glynn (Leeds). This conference was followed by a Trade Union Congress held on 4 September in Belfast, the first city in Ireland to establish an ILP branch, and attended by Champion, Edward Aveling, Keir Hardie, Ben Tillett, and Maltman Barry. In an address to the Aberdeen Trades Union Congress eight days later, Champion talked of issues raised and explained that the labour movement was now at a crucial fork in the road; one way led straight, the other one was a destructive 'broad and easy' path.

He was going to act once more as the candid friend to some of the leaders of the working classes, and as the candid enemy to a good many more of them. He had done that once or twice in the past, both in this country and on the other side of the globe, and the result had been that he had been subjected to a good deal of misrepresentation, a great deal of opposition, and a great deal of hostility of a bitter and prolonged kind.[225]

Believing that people would see envy or 'personal hatred' behind his criticism of labour leaders, Champion took aim at two suggestions proposed: Keir Hardie's impractical Utopian suggestion of placing the unemployed under the care of the Board of Guardians to cultivate small land settlements and Aveling's suggestion for wholesale radical political reform measures. The actions of John Burns, Henry Broadhurst and Havelock Wilson were also heavily criticised. Knowing the animosity of both friends and enemies would be guaranteed by his forthright speech, it appeared Champion didn't care. Hardie was hostile enough to complain that Champion and Maltman Barry tried 'to poison' people against him.[226]

Champion's return from Ireland to address the ILP's Dundee Branch saw 'Tory gold' take centre stage once again, precipitating another replay of earlier rumours and innuendoes. At the end of one meeting Champion responded to a question about whether Hudson gave him an imaginary sum of £30,000:

> He denied that he had charge of this or any other sum, but explained that certain moneyed men of Socialistic views had offered to defray the official expenses of labour candidates, and simply asked him to give the benefit of his experience.[227]

These were expenses paid for a candidate fee of £100, as required by the system, to enter a political election. As Burgess increasingly manoeuvred for prominence in the Independent Labour Party, the *Workman's Times* promoted a Burns/Hardie discord, with articles such as 'John Burns *v.* Keir Hardie: Which Is Right?'[228] Beatrice Webb

[Potter], like many others, now believed the two men were completely at odds with each other. She wrote in a diary entry on 12 October 1893 that John Burns carried the 'burning sin' of 'jealousy and suspicion' of others in the labour movement and believed 'his hatred' of rival Keir Hardie extended to 'dimensions of mania'.

With one last attendance on 2 February 1894 at the second annual conference of the ILP in Manchester, Champion again headed back north. Although Burgess had nominated again for the NAC, he resigned in order to position himself as an ILP candidate for the Leicester election, after Arthur Fields, who supported Champion on the NAC Council, was ousted in his favour. The Manchester conference opened with a meeting at Harpurhey, with Aveling on the platform, Barry in the press section and Champion in the gallery. Champion had not expected to be there as he was to journey to America on 'an enterprise of considerable magnitude' [to accompany Morley Roberts].[229] An orchestrated attack was made on Champion who sat through a stage-managed reading of the NAC's minutes. These contained the NAC's official repudiation of Champion and Barry, accompanied by much applause; it was claimed that the latter two men were pointedly disregarded by every delegate in the room.

From the Grand Hotel in Aytoun Street Champion wrote a letter to the editor of the *Manchester Guardian* addressing three points of the ILP program: firstly he directly opposed a proposed name change to the Socialist Party, insisting that the words Labour and Independent were understood at this time by workers who would rally to this title; he agreed to the ILP's plan to 'abstain from voting at all parliamentary elections at which it does not run a candidate of its own'; and urged members not to squabble or demonstrate division.[230] Champion 'left in disgust' the next day without attending the rest of the conference. Three weeks later he sailed for Australia.

As sales of the *Workman's Times* declined, the newspaper was moved back north to Manchester and, after a failed attempt to convince the ILP to adopt it as their official journal, the paper soon ceased publication. Burgess was unsuccessful as an ILP parliamentary candidate for a by-election in Leicester, although persisted in Scottish elections in 1895, 1906, 1908 and 1910. Burns moved away from the ILP towards the Lib-Lab Party for Battersea and lost votes to the ILP in 1895; by July Champion saw Burns 'at the tail of a dwindling party, instead of at the head of a growing one'. Mann was national secretary of the ILP from 1894–96 and pointed to this involvement as causing a break in his friendship with Burns. In 1897 Champion was able to forecast with great accuracy: 'In the long run – it may not be a very long one – the I.L.P. is going to swallow the Radical rump by the process of converting its more advanced and earnest members'.[231]

Mrs Humphry Ward's *Sir George Tressady* was subsequently praised by Champion as 'prophetic' for her insight into 'the trend of British politics':

> The old Liberal party had been almost swept away, only a few waifs and strays remained, the exponents of a programme that nobody wanted, and of cries that stirred nobody's blood. A large Independent Labor [sic] and Socialist party filled the empty benches of the Liberals – a revolutionary, enthusiastic crew, of whom the country was a little frightened, and who were, if the truth were known, a little frightened at themselves. They had a coherent programme, and represented a formidable 'domination' in English life.[232]

The Labour Party in England was 'muddling along very well on the lines every man Jack of them vilified me for laying down in 1888', Champion complained to Morley Roberts on 23 April 1897, accurately predicting the party would 'get there' without his help after one or two generations. Ramsay MacDonald became Prime Minister of Britain for the Labour Party, one Champion envisaged as early as 1891. Ramsay visited Tom Mann in prison where he was serving a five-week sentence for street obstruction in Prahran. Champion reported on Ramsay's visit to see Mann and had breakfast with his old friend from the early days of the SDF.[233]

In Melbourne to speak as a member of the House of Commons, Ramsay was welcomed by the Trades Hall Council and members of the parliament and his speech was generous and self-effacing in the face of Australian tributes: 'He was one of those who reaped, to some extent, the harvest where others had sown, but he felt that in honouring him, Australian Labor [sic] honoured those who had gone before him, as well as the other reapers in Britain today'.[234]

Certainly, Champion can be credited with proposing an independent Labour Party and a united labour platform for a new party. In 1894 Champion claimed he 'commenced single-handed the movement in practical politics' reworking a political narrative of a 'normal' eight-hour working day to give prominence to the need for an independent party.[235] He would continue this political push when he moved permanently to Melbourne, eventually becoming one of the founders and vice president of the Socialist Party in 1906.

The career of John Burns as written by Joseph Burgess was a cautionary tale for anyone interested in a role in politics, Champion quietly stated in a review of the biography of Burns. Achievement was assessed by outcome in the service for a cause, he advised, not in 'the horrible murk of slander and misrepresentation in the places where it is grown'.[236] It was a subtle dig at Burgess and probably too discreet for many to understand. Meanwhile, Champion saw his own transformation from fictional hero to a minor role in the memoirs of Burgess and Hyndman, both published that same year. Indeed, both memoirs have guided historical attitudes until recent times. A 'most unorthodox biography', according to the London *Evening News*, this book certainly sold well with four editions within six weeks. Hyndman's own book was also well received and he rapidly followed it with *Further Reminiscences* (1912) filled with distrust, intrigue, jealousy and malice. Keir Hardie was called an 'inveterate intriguer', Burns 'a self-seeker' and Shaw 'the poser-in-chief of our period'. Champion wrote sympathetically to Hyndman when his wife Matilda died and, upon Hyndman's next marriage to Rosalind Travers the following year, asked him to give his 'respects to Mrs. Hyndman, who may have heard of me as "the bad boy in the nursery"'.[237]

There is no doubt that socialism defined Champion's life and that his political life was shaped by four momentous events: the Trafalgar Square Riots or 'Black Monday', two large-scale strikes and the desire to create a new party to represent the labour movement. There is no doubt that there were two issues which overwhelmingly helped to blacken Champion's name: his actions in the Maritime Strike in Melbourne; and a campaign against him for control of the Independent Labour Party in Britain. In fact, political knives were sharpened not only for Champion but also some of his friends.

In many ways, Champion's compelling belief in emotional self-restraint, dignity and discretion was a result of his upbringing, identity and values. This gave him a sense of control over both his emotions and environment. Champion remained mostly reticent about the inner workings and his own role in political struggles and history-making events. No wonder many have experienced a confusion about his persona. Champion could be considered partly responsible for his own enigmatic reputation and may have unwittingly colluded in his own historical neglect.

One of the People
Juliet Bennett (1855–1886)

'I'm so unhappy. Oh! I'm so unhappy.
Why did you marry me, if I'm not good enough to be your wife,'
(*George Eastmont: Wanderer*, p. 62)

Champion freely discussed intimate details of his early life in an interview with his friend, Havelock Ellis, who used him as a case study for his research, appearing in Appendix B as History VI.[238] At the time, Champion was in his mid-twenties and married. He recalled his own lack of sexual curiosity and knowledge when a schoolboy and the fact he was 'never taken into the counsels of prurient schoolmates'. Still, he was a 'great reader' and at the age of fourteen obtained *The Fruits of Philosophy, or the Private Companion of Young Married People* (1832) by Charles Knowlton, a pamphlet on the human reproductive system and contraception as a means of preventing unwanted pregnancy and sexually transmitted diseases. He read this guide with great interest, as well as an amended work republished by Charles Bradlaugh and Annie Besant.

Consulting his diary during the interview, he claimed inexperience, being 'still ignorant' about the nature of sex at twenty-one when 'a clever friend' educated him. With a 'preponderating interest in the romantic side of things' rather than the physical, he admitted 'feeling that the knowledge lay always within my grasp kept me from that curiosity which so oft consumes those who think it is hidden away from them'. A 'conspiracy of silence', he believed, tended to emphasize physical detail, though the idea of 'close physical intimacy appealed' to him as 'quite poetic and beautiful between two loves'. A female playmate from his early youth came to London after he married and he recalled an intense 'flutter of heart' even though their families had lost contact for sixteen years. This girl was close in age and was probably his

Aberdeenshire cousin, Annie Isabel Urquhart, who married at the age of twenty-one another cousin, Garden Alexander Duff, five years prior to Champion's own marriage to Juliet Bennett. Without guile he explained to Ellis:

> The physical in sex has never been any bother to me, neither have I bothered about it. I have recognized it, frankly, and don't see why I shouldn't, but my unashamed recognition has probably been because the merely physical is less absorbing to me than to most. Mental and emotional interest in passion has absorbed me greatly, but the merely physical has sunk into what I call its natural place of subordination.

The case study makes an interesting psychological background to Champion's assumed plan to marry his first wife in order to integrate him into working-class life.

At the age of 24, three years after receiving orders for Kandahar, less than a year after resigning from the army, and with the traditional trappings of a religious ceremony Champion married Juliet Bennett on 9 August 1883 at the Anglican St George's church in Bloomsbury. With a soup kitchen for the poor, the church was close to the Rookery and Hogarth's Gin Lane, a notorious area filled with 'Mother's ruin', stretching from the St Giles High Street to Great Russell Street. At the time Juliet resided in Bloomsbury at 4 Torrington Square, an attractive location close to the British Museum, Gray's Inn Court, Westminster Hospital and Covent Garden, and popular with the medical, university, law and theatrical fraternity. A few decades earlier, next door 3 Torrington Square was the residence of Charles Kean, actor and stage manager, as well as Miss Taylor's establishment dedicated to Christian education for young ladies.

Juliet was 28 years of age and her father, Samuel Bennett esquire, was listed as deceased. Her father may have worked in London either with the theatre or around actors, given his daughter was named after a Shakespearean character. During Queen Victoria's time there was a revival of interest in the Italian-set plays *Romeo and Juliet* and the *Merchant of Venice* and one journalist, J.S. Fletcher, wrote his novel about two sisters with Shakespearean names, Miranda and Juliet, the latter even referred to as 'Jewleit' or 'Jew-liet', a young Jew. Juliet Bennett was probably employed as a live-in domestic for the family of a stockbroker who lived in the house at Torrington Square.[239] Activist and author, Clementina Black, whose friendship with Champion lasted many years, wrote in her novel, *An Agitator*, about a socialist married at 24 to a girl who 'was working twelve to sixteen hours a day for a wealthy employer in this town, and earning three-farthings to a penny-halfpenny an hour. She had nobody belonging to her, and her health had begun to break down'. Her husband, a socialist and street speaker, was 'a ringleader' in the unemployed demonstrations and sacrificed everything to help workers.[240]

The witnesses to their marriage ceremony were Champion's friend, Percy Frost, and Sarah Taylor, possibly a relative of George Warrington Taylor, business manager for socialist, poet, and artist, William Morris. Eton-educated from 1850 and in the army for a short period, Taylor was a bankrupt from Liverpool and 'check-taker' at the opera theatre in Covent Garden until Dante Rossetti introduced him to Morris. Having just met Morris at the Democratic Federation on 14 May 1883 and struggling for acceptance among the working poor, Champion admired his marriage as one worth emulating, his seemingly happy relationship with a groom's daughter he encountered at a theatre production in 1857.[241] Champion called Janey 'one of the most beautiful women in England' pointing to Rossetti's famous paintings as proof.[242] However, he could not have been aware of the lengthy liaison Janey Morris and Rossetti conducted after Rossetti's wife died of an overdose of laudanum in 1862, their affair lasting twenty years.

During their brief life together as husband and wife, the Champions resided at 10 Gray's Inn Place in a drab, confined flat where they 'lived inexpensively'. Gray's Inn's Workhouse, passed on the way home, was notable for its severe overcrowding and Champion argued with conviction and eloquence that the Board of Guardians, looking after such places, was unable to move 'their paupers' to other places because 'every workhouse in London was overfull'.[243] After long days at the office of Modern Press it must have seemed appropriate to return to a squalid building, but it was depressing for Juliet who was forced to live within the confines of tiny walls on a daily basis and to see her husband devote much of his free time to work. Champion took to public speaking with increased enthusiasm, his political passion keeping him away from home quite often during his marriage. In a fashion reminiscent of Bernard Shaw, his devotion to street corner speaking and lecturing was recalled in an interview: 'between 1883 and 1886 he worked unceasingly, speaking from six to ten times a week all over England'; Shaw thought he was 'the most industrious' of the whole group of activists.[244]

Apart from Percy Frost, Champion's closest friend and witness at their wedding, a number of people had contact with Mrs Juliet Champion either at the Modern Press or the couple's home. Shaw records simple notations of dates when he visited their tenement from March to September 1885. He even chatted to Mrs Champion alone and saw her at the office with her husband. A number of *Justice* and the SDF members probably met her, as did various colleagues, including Jack Williams, James MacDonald, John Hunter Watts, Henry Hyndman, William Morris, John Burns, Edward Carpenter, James Joynes, H.S. Salt, and William and Frances Archer.

Less than three years after her marriage, at age 31, Juliet died suddenly and catastrophically on 17 March 1886, two weeks after Champion was committed for trial and nearly three weeks before his court appearance. Eight days after Juliet's death Shaw wrote a letter about her to Joynes, Frances Archer and others, although nothing is known about the contents and it is not known if he attended her funeral. Her death notice was one line in the London *Standard* on 23 March, the same newspaper in which Champion's mother received a small notice on her death on 12 September 1895. Juliet's death certificate, obtained by writers such as Whitehead and Barnes, showed she was an alcoholic for 'a few years', a condition impossible to hide in their marriage and also observed 'menorrhagia', an umbrella term meaning abnormal, excessive uterine bleeding suffered for 'a few months', accompanied by syncope or insufficient blood flow to the brain, and heart failure. One cause for this prolonged blood loss may have been an incomplete, spontaneous miscarriage suffered months earlier and not detailed on the death certificate. Champion had stepped down as secretary of the SDF in August the previous year (replaced by H.W. Lee) to run for the October School Board elections but was unable 'to devote that personal attention to his [Finsbury] candidature'. Champion's letter to the editor pointed to 'private affairs' precluding him from activism for a period.[245] It appears there were many months prior to Trafalgar Square when Champion's personal life was overwhelming his political activities.

After their first nine weeks of marriage, in a letter to Thomas Davidson about The Fellowship of New Life, Champion suggested he was anticipating parenthood.[246] Juliet may have lost a baby very early in their marriage and Clementina Black's novel does refer to the parish churchyard holding the graves of both his wife and baby. Later, Juliet must have been increasingly worried and isolated during the September 1885 agitation and free speech arrests in Dod Street, and then after the arrests at Trafalgar Square, his formal arraignment and preparation for trial. She may have experienced another miscarriage months prior to his trial and the persistent bleeding recorded on her death certificate suggests two possibilities: it was hidden either through a Victorian embarrassment or ignorance, or she may not have wanted to add her angst to her husband's worry during the trial. Maggie Harkness also suggested in her writings that Victorian coronial inquests often used heart failure as a euphemism for suicide and in her novel on a labour leader, *George Eastmont: Wanderer* (1905), she writes that 'she killed herself' and suggests 'an overdose' (pp. 93–99).

Whatever caused her heart failure, an unusual steadfast silence was maintained by friends and colleagues about Mrs Juliet Champion even in their numerous histories, reminiscences, memoirs and reflections. In essence, it was as if Juliet never existed. In an unsentimental age when death was commonplace, Champion kept his own counsel and never placed his grief on display except perhaps in private conversations. However, two female friends recorded Juliet's existence in fiction and a Fleet Street journalist seemingly knew of her circumstances. Clementina Black was involved in campaigns on female labour in the East End and modelled her main character on Champion. She described his wife briefly at the start of her novel through Dick Harris who she based on John Burns. Harris saw her as 'a sweet-looking creature' who was 'fair wrapped up' in her husband until her lack of health and 'the worry and the trouble wore her out'. Harris believed her husband was 'careful and considerate' but quite 'wearing' because no-one was able to predict 'what he'll do next'. After her death her husband's memory was of his wife's 'delicate, anxious face' as he arrived home in the evenings.[247] Journalist J.S. Fletcher also wrote *The Quarry Farm* (1893) about two sisters managing a farm after their father's death, with one sister, Juliet Bennett, running away to the city to be with a soldier and 'rover' who served in India. Meanwhile, Fletcher's *Daniel Quayne: A Morality* (1907) features a 'Mr Campion' whose family dates back to 1689 living at Middlethorpe Grange, Yorkshire; he forms a relationship with a young working woman.

Two years after Juliet's death, Maggie Harkness's story 'The Gospel of Getting On' focused on a schoolboy who 'got on' (climbing the ladder of success) according to his mother's ambitious desire. He becomes a friend of Lord Tom Noddy, a character of Richard Brough's satiric poem. Subsequently he is seen rowing a girl, 'a little thing, weighted by ignorance, tethered by poverty, with just enough sense to love and worship' who, with 'a sickening sound of pain', is singing a song containing two powerful lines drawn from Lord Byron's poem, 'All for Love': 'Oh talk not to me of a name great in story. / The days of our youth are the days of our glory.' Later at his wife's grave he is said to be responsible for her death because of his obligation 'to get on'. The story concludes with a few socialist martyr figures intent on saving humanity.

More substance is given to Juliet in a novel, *George Eastmont: Wanderer* (1905), and the author seemed sympathetic to Juliet's deep loneliness. Nearly two decades after the trial for Trafalgar Square Riots, Margaret Harkness, under her pseudonym 'John Law', finally published her novel about Champion and the events of the London Dock Strike. Close examination of the novel shows a number of elements in character development and plot that revealed Champion and his wife's identity. The book also contained specific details and traits evident in Champion's other relationships.

In the novel, George Eastmont has a black trimmed moustache and is an ex-British Army Officer, 'a soldier's son', recuperating from illness. His adherence to socialism develops after meeting Charleston (who is modelled on John Burns) and the couple meet at his home. Eastmont 'did not take long over his courtship, but proposed and was accepted' (p. 24) and they marry six weeks later. Like Juliet Bennett, Julia Hay is five years older than her new husband. Julia's father is a small farmer near Leigh in Essex similar to Juliet's father who was listed as esquire on her marriage certificate. She is described as 'a simple guileless woman, clever about a house, and domestic'. Reverend Podmore is responsible for delivering an incisive declaration of Julia's state of mind: 'I fancy she was flattered by Eastmont's offer, and pleased to marry a gentleman' (p. 48). Podmore may have been a composite of many people, including Frank Podmore, a Progressive Association member and Fabian; Stewart Headlam, ex-clergyman, student of Frederick D. Maurice and a Fabian; and Edward Carpenter, ex-clergyman and curate to Maurice. Many sons and daughters of clergymen in London were part of the author's circle of SDF, Fabian and Socialist League friends, although Maggie's association with Edward Carpenter and Olive Schreiner provides the major clue to Podmore's identity.

From an aristocratic family, George's grandfather is Lord Cashel, a name from County Tipperary that Bernard Shaw used for the hero of an early novel Champion published. His grandfather is Laird of 'Castle Crag', an allusion to the Urquhart family's Craigston Castle near Turriff and the Cromarty seat of Castle Craig on the Black Isle. The estate provides a youthful George with his vision of a 'savour of the masses'. George's aspirations provide the impetus for a gentleman's marriage to a working-class girl:

> Because I am so far off from the People. The men I am working with are of them, but I am not. I have tried to be of them, and I have felt all the time so different. They look on me as an outsider. I want to be one of them, that is why I have done it. (p. 5).

Presented as his desire to become one of 'the People', his union with a working girl is designed to change the direction of his George's life: 'I have thrown in my lot with them; and by this marriage I hope to become one of them; living as they live, suffering as they suffer' (p. 5).

His marriage is 'a matter of forethought, hastened by meeting the woman he thought the right person for the experiment', a working-class girl. His friend the Cardinal was said to have 'watched him from childhood' (p. 10) and directly challenges 'the wisdom' of their marriage; he was based on Cardinal Manning (to whom the book was dedicated). Lord Cashel sees him, in time, as prone to 'atavism' where he would eventually revert to ideas of his ancestors (pp. 23–25) while his 'proud, autocratic' father Colonel Eastmont views him as 'a rebel' (p. 171).

Julia is uneducated, the extra glottal 'h' (termed 'aitch dropping') inserted at the start of her words, to emphasise her underprivileged background when she discusses her husband's work: 'The working-class is hungrateful [sic] and hidle [sic], Miss, and he'll find it hout [sic] before he's finished' (pp. 51–53). In contrast, George is depicted as a refined gentleman who wants his wife's transformation and so 'hoped that Julia would drop the peculiarities she shared with the People, and copy him when they were married'. Since he is always at the office, doesn't speak to her about his work and retains membership of his club, Julia sees little of her husband. He leaves early and comes home to the tenement late at night, although she admits she is 'better hoff than some' (p. 25). This especially has a truthful ring since Champion admitted that he worked incessantly around London during the three years of his marriage and frequented his gentleman's club. With no friends, Julia remains desperately isolated. Her father visited the pub every night and is an obvious role model for her addiction to laudanum (a point of similarity to Rossetti's wife).

Like Champion's real wife, George's fictional wife dies suddenly when he is gaoled for riots at Trafalgar Square. Following an inquest and post-mortem, Podmore explains that Julia died from a 'disease of the heart'. Although a poignant suggestion of her physical and romantic affliction, the author suggests elsewhere that this was a 'time-worn verdict' of an inquest suggesting suicide.[248] George is shown returning to their drab tenement in 'the great beehive' where the scene focuses on a bunch of violets on the floor and a small American clock on the shelf of the fireplace – domestic signs of his past life. Later, Shaw would also use these details in *Pygmalion*.

While violets are associated with George's wife, red roses are a symbol of desire for a county rector's daughter in the story, her expectation of something more than friendship hangs in the atmosphere. Six months after his wife's death, while working at George's office, Miss Mary Cameron, who 'no man had ever kissed' or 'whispered words of love', attempts to turn a platonic friendship into a romantic relationship and races into the street to buy crimson roses from a flower girl to brighten her tiny room for his visit.

Julia's funeral procession leaves from the Socialist Club so George catches a train from Blackfriar's Bridge to Mile End station. It is a public funeral in which her coffin is on a horse-drawn hearse with policemen either side, George following behind as the stoic chief-mourner 'determined not to show what he was suffering' with a band playing a funeral march. The reader gains a glimpse of a Victorian funeral procession not associated with royalty or high public office as the hearse proceeds to a cemetery opened for London's poor. Depicted as isolated, grieving and unable to understand the death of his wife, George attends her burial in the 'People's Cemetery' while the author cynically records: 'propaganda was being made out of the tragedy in which he [George] took a leading part' with socialists turning 'his sorrow turned into an advertisement' (pp. 108–9). Whether Juliet was buried in the Tower Hamlets Cemetery ('Bow Cemetery') near Mile End or a small Anglican parish cemetery is unknown. The fictional Julia, whose husband doesn't understand her desire for their wedding announcement to be advertised in newspapers, is transformed in death into a socialist celebrity, while the real Juliet received only a short obituary notice. Julia's funeral is represented as a grand display that serves the socialist cause, reflecting the personal disappointment of the author's later opinion of socialists in *Imperial Credit* (1899).

Whether Maggie Harkness actually attended Juliet's funeral in March 1886 or merely recorded newspaper accounts of other funerals is uncertain. Alfred Linnell, a law clerk of no political persuasion wandered towards Trafalgar Square to watch the spectacle and, as the crowd surged forward, he fell and was trampled. Alfred Linnell's thigh bone was fractured by a constable's charging horse and he died of medical complications on 2 December 1887. Subsequently, the Chief

Commissioner of Police Sir Charles Warren issued an inflammatory edict banning public meetings in the Square and included Linnell's funeral procession in the decree. Many newspapers reported the event, with his black coffin draped in a red flag and carried in an open hearse drawn by four horses. After leaving the undertaker, the hearse travelled through Coventry Street into the Strand where the funeral gathered a massive crowd in the journey through the area of Fleet Street, Aldgate, Whitechapel and Mile End to the Tower Hamlets Cemetery. William Morris, together with a Salvation Army Officer and a member of the Irish Land League, were on one side of the hearse, with Annie Besant, Herbert Burrows, William Stead and Cunninghame Graham on the other, while the Linnell family were accompanied by Dr Richard Pankhurst, his wife Emmeline and John Burns. Eleanor Marx was in a horse-drawn dray as part of the cortège while Hyndman watched from a tram's front seat. Behind the procession marched clubs, with bands and banners, while above fluttered red, yellow and green flags signifying socialism, radicalism and Irish nationalism. Graveside speakers included William Morris for the Socialist League, Harry Quelch (editor of *Justice* for the SDF), and a couple of other radical group members, while a choir sang 'A Death Song' composed by Morris for the unknown man in memoriam. Some people argued Linnell was merely a spectator and not 'the ideal type of a Trafalgar-square martyr' while others believed he represented those who died of injuries in the cause. Meanwhile, Maggie was at Wolverhampton listening to Champion's speech and working on Keir Hardie's spring election in Scotland with Champion, Mann and Mahon.

Another funeral was the subject of one of Maggie's articles on 25 April 1892 titled 'An Anarchist's Funeral'. The article was about Charles Mowbray's arrest for charges against *Commonweal* only four hours after his wife Mary died of tuberculosis. With her body still in their flat, he was released for his wife's funeral which left from the Anarchist Club in Berners Street, not far from the British Museum. John Hunter Watts, the SDF executive who sparked the 'Tory gold' saga, addressed a crowd from the window while a Paris Commune personality, Louise Michel, whose writings were translated into English by Maggie's friend, Louisa Sarah Bevington, attended. A band played the 'Marseillaise' with a procession of thousands accompanied by anarchist banners, flags and police. Noticing a familiar pattern, Maggie concluded that an individual's grief was used for political defiance, citing one flagbearer as excitedly proclaiming: "'It's just like the old days ... just like the S.D.F." So history repeats itself!'.[249]

Such funeral processions provided a wealth of material and highlighted Maggie's vision of the SDF as an event-driven agent of propaganda. Though these funerals were sometimes turned into an advertisement for radical groups, Juliet's funeral was probably on a small scale. Her death in the lead-up to the trial had the potential to generate much emotion among socialists and so policemen would have been rostered because of a surge in public support for Champion and the other arrested men. Though Juliet Champion's funeral was never destined to be as dramatic as Linnell's procession of 100,000 people, many of Champion's friends, colleagues and sympathisers would have attended.

Facets of the Champion's marriage also were germane to Shaw's *Pygmalion*. Although Juliet Champion was not a flower girl and it was Eliza's father who married at St George's church, Champion and his wife certainly enriched Shaw's play. No doubt Shaw read *George Eastmont* with interest when it was published and it is also within the realms of possibility that the work was discussed in depth amongst mutual friends in London. The year 1886 was seminal to Shaw, with a number of intersecting events serving as important material for his creative output. Occurring primarily between March and June, these events occurred after the arrest of Champion, Hyndman, Burns, and Williams for the Trafalgar Square Riots and around Juliet's death on 17 March. They include the Shelley Society's first meeting at the Botany Theatre in University College on 10 March; Professor Henry Sweet's scheduled paper for the Shelley Society on 4 May; the Shelley Society's private presentation of Shelley's play *The Cenci* on 7 May; Champion, Carpenter and Shaw in discussion in the garden of St Paul's Church, Covent Garden on 4 June; and Shaw's 'slumming' with Annie Besant as they walked together from Leman Street along Ratcliffe Highway to Stepney and the East India dock area in the middle of June.

Shaw frequently used his acquaintances for dramatic purpose, exploiting life around him as a framework for writing scenes. In a letter to actress Ellen Terry on 8 September 1897, written a decade after Juliet Champion's death, he stated: 'Oh, I do not neglect "the material at hand." At my side people do not suffer from cold neglect: life is one long scene sometimes'. Rather than portraits he admitted that 'certain people inspire one to invent fictitious characters for them'. One new concept was a play for actors Forbes-Robertson and Mrs Patrick Campbell: 'he shall be a west end gentleman and she an east end dona in an apron and three orange and red ostrich feathers'.[250] Only weeks after the death of Juliet, Shaw was in charge of promoting the Society's private presentation of *The Cenci* in Islington in May 1886. At this time the British Museum had on display a humorous print by Charles Williams, 'The Rival Queens', showing two Covent Garden actresses, Eliza O'Neill and Sarah Siddons, both wearing Regency head-dresses with three tall ostrich feathers. It seems only natural Shaw named the flower girl in *Pygmalion* after Eliza O'Neill, the actress for whom Shelley composed *The Cenci*.

Shaw's central characters, a 'west end gentleman' and 'east end dona', pointed explicitly to London as a city of two halves, graphically underscored by Champion's drawing in his newspaper, *Common Sense*, with an image of an east and west divide to represent London's destitution and prosperity. Champion's Australian newspaper argued in 1896 that,

> ... good manners, courtesy, and the rest of the small change of the currency of civilized life, ought to become public possessions, ought to be democratized until they are national attributes. It can't see any sufficient reason why the qualities which made up 'the very perfect gentle knight of Chaucer' and the gentilissima donna of Dante should not appear, slightly adapted to modern requirements, in the larrikins of Collingwood and Toorak.[251]

Similarly, in Champion's *The Root of the Matter* (1895), George Blake argued the need to turn the social system on its head:

> I told you that my object was to make the working classes ladies and

gentlemen ... I have said that we make our brewers and bankers peers, and we also make our peers into tradesmen. With our premier earl as a cab-proprietor, a marquis as a coal-dealer, a future duchess behind the counter of a flower shop, the landed gentry turned dairymen and game dealers, and the names of all our old nobility on the boards of hundreds of commercial companies, you must see that commerce has absorbed feudal aristocracy (p. 118).

Shaw also employed the flower girl motif as a social distinguisher in *Man and Superman* (1901). His stage directions for the character, Ann Whitefield, in the first act were: 'Turn up her nose, give a cast to her eye, replace her black and violet confection by the apron and feathers of a flower girl, strike all the aitches out of her speech, and Ann would still make men dream'. In the third act of *Major Barbara* (1905) a young Professor of Greek, reminiscent of an Australian, Gilbert Murray, announces that a young Salvation Army officer and 'an east ender',

... bought my soul like a flower at a street corner ... But I was romantic about her too. I thought she was a woman of the people, and that a marriage with a professor of Greek would be far beyond the wildest social ambitions of her rank.

Premiered at the Court theatre, just after the release of *George Eastmont*, it finds an echo in Podmore's analysis of the marriage of Julia and George.

Around the time of the performance of *The Cenci*, Henry Sweet, an expert in phonetics and grammar, and credited with describing scientifically educated speech in London, was scheduled to deliver a paper to the Shelley Society in May 1886.[252] It is widely recognised he was a model for Professor Henry Higgins. Around Federation, Champion strongly supported the political aspirations of an Australian lawyer and politician, Henry (Bournes) Higgins, who took elocution lessons when young and chose law to help correct his stutter. Henry Higgins is the play's agent for social change, believing a flower girl could be passed off as a duchess if he taught her to speak correctly. Eliza becomes his 'experiment' with her speech corrected and her social transformation realised by a 'book-learned gentleman' or, as Havelock Ellis called Champion 'a man of letters'.[253] A bright future is predicted for Eliza when Higgins announces the potential for her marriage to 'an officer in the Guards, with a beautiful moustache: the son of a marquis, who will disinherit him for marrying you' (p. 45). In fact, Champion claimed in a speech at Albert Park that he was 'disinherited' and had 'sacrificed' between £7,000 to £8,000 a year for 'espousing the cause of the working classes' in his commitment to socialism. [254]

Drury Lane was chosen by Shaw as the location for Eliza's little room, its desolation serving to highlight the difference between east and west London. Mrs Humphry Ward, in book three of *Marcella*, provided a contemporary description of the street:

> With its condemned houses, many of them shored up and windowless, its narrow roadway strewn with costers' refuse – it was largely inhabited by costers frequenting Covent Garden Market – its filthy gutters and broken pavements, it touched, indeed, a depth of sinister squalor beyond most of its fellows.

Pygmalion's opening scene in the portico of St Paul's Church, Covent Garden, was also the scene of Champion's discussion with Carpenter and Shaw in the aftermath of Juliet's death; it was in this garden that Champion unburdened himself to his friends during a period of 'deepest dejection'.[255] In this same setting, Eliza's bunches of violets are crushed into the mud and the first scene concludes with her return to a small room in Drury Lane, rented for four shillings a week, furnished bleakly with an empty birdcage and the fireplace shelf holding an American alarm clock.

While it is tempting to be dismissive of such exact detail, Shaw was very particular about stage directions, devoting specific attention to each setting. The scene becomes a framing device recalling George Eastmont's tenement with his American clock on the fireplace, and a birdcage brought on a visit. The clock is a striking and strange detail for Shaw to place in an essentially empty room of an East End flower girl who had no money, though we might infer that this object was purchased by Champion in Boston. Perhaps because it was so out of place in the Champions' flat at Gray's Inn Place, it formed a touchstone for the creative imaginations of both Maggie Harkness and Bernard Shaw. In the same way William Morris's furniture and decorations for the drawing room of Mrs Higgins stand out prominently as stage directions and highlight Champion's own memories:

> Twenty years before, the decorative horrors of the British home of all classes were appalling. Morris altered all that. In the teeth of the tendencies of his time, he forced his countrymen to appreciate and demand beauty in their domestic surroundings ... He brought it into the furniture, the wall-paper, the carpet, the lamp, and all the common things of life.[256]

Eliza Doolittle, her name suggesting an inherent lack of purpose, receives food, clothes and a home, not wages, because Henry believes, if given money, she would buy drink. She is represented as socially isolated, with no friends, no past, and so driven to alcohol through loneliness. Eliza's attempt to shake Higgins into reality, by questioning whether he would care if she died only elicits a stunted emotional response. If the Champions were the genesis for Shaw's ideas, then Eliza's plea and heartfelt cry, 'I only want to be natural' (p. 136), is all the more poignant when placed alongside Julia's statement to her husband in *George Eastmont*, 'Why did you marry me, if I'm not good enough to be your wife'. Indeed, Eliza and Julia effectively damn the experiment of both the play and novel. The real Mrs Juliet Champion's tragic end as a youthful, unhappy and alcoholic wife, retains a poignancy dominated by the silence of Champion and friends.

Throughout the stage history of *Pygmalion* Shaw was against romantic convention, fighting doggedly against the idea that Eliza and Henry were to have a happy ending, one that transcended her dependence on a gentleman who believed himself responsible for her social transformation. Eliza was Shaw's spokesperson for a generation of frustrated women: 'I sold flowers. I didn't sell myself' (p. 107). The surrender of her independence to a gentleman also echoes Podmore's summation of Julia position in *George Eastmont*: 'I shall be surprised if the marriage does not end in trouble for her ... she had been her own mistress for many years' (p. 48). The ideas touch on the concept of the 'New Woman', which represented her move to independence in the political and social spheres, often with a life outside of marriage. Encapsulating a social and political conversion from a stereotypical domestic role, it was an adventurous imagining of what it meant for a female to be an agent of change. While Champion disliked the title, 'New Woman', he promoted the concept in his Australian newspaper, arguing for the education of women, quoting research by Havelock Ellis, and becoming incensed when people diminished the cause as a 'fashionable doctrine'.[257]

Pygmalion was still in shorthand manuscript when Shaw read it to George Alexander, theatrical manager of St James's Theatre, a few days prior to Shaw's reading on 20 June 1912 for the performer, Mrs Patrick Campbell, and only a couple of months after Henry Sweet's death.[258] Champion was in England at this stage but continued to correspond as his newly appointed Australian theatrical agent during Shaw's six weeks holiday in Europe late August. As early as January 1912 Champion had told the *Pall Mall Gazette* of the role in repertory theatre in Melbourne, and of theatre audiences who longed to see recent dramas. Again, Champion wrote that August about 'a good company, armed with half a dozen plays of Shaw's, to take the field' in Australia, citing Gregan McMahon as a key director. He provided an analysis of Shaw's box office, calculating a significant amount gained in royalties from the five companies touring England with Shaw's plays, with one play having 600 performances.[259] Champion also disclosed that Shaw's uncle, Edward Carr Shaw, was a well-regarded Tasmanian colonist since 1831; Shaw admitted that he was a first cousin and complained about his snobbish 'family of Pooh-Bahs'.

Shaw apparently was aware his new play about a gentleman and a working-class girl may cause difficulties. As part of Shaw's arrangement with Champion in September 1911 to become his theatrical agent in Australia, he insisted Champion's 'appointment' was 'personal' and 'revocable when we please or when we quarrel or when you are tired of it'. By January 1913 – only eight months prior to *Pygmalion's* opening night in Berlin – Shaw again wrote to Champion stating: 'I have had to introduce a limiting clause lest you should take extensive libel action ... and ruin me'. Shaw's legal proposal was coupled with a reference to Tichborne, the aforementioned case about a claim of identity to a baronetcy. Shaw cited the case in his preface to *Androcles and the Lion: A Fable Play* in 1912 and was now using this humorously to undercut the seriousness of his suggestion to Champion.[260] A subject of great interest in England, the Tichborne trial was covered in 'Famous Trials' by J.B. Atlay, reviewed by Champion as suitable for late night reading 'when suicidal moths make the flames turn blue'. As discussed earlier, Champion heard the case discussed as a schoolboy while lunching with patients as 'a visitor only' at a private asylum, with many inmates believing Arthur Orton's claims and some buying bonds issued by supporters.[261]

Just prior to *Pygmalion's* first performance in London on 11 April 1914, Shaw admitted in a letter to Champion that *Major Barbara* (1905) was based on people he knew very well: 'The original of Cusins is Gilbert Murray, the most famous living Australian. Lady Britomart is Lady Carlisle, his mother-in-law. Both are lifelike portraits'. Having used real people as characters in that play, Shaw already found himself in trouble with his friend, Murray, son of Sir Terence Murray, a member of the Legislative Council of NSW. Murray was very involved in reading Shaw's manuscript for *Major Barbara*, actively suggesting revisions, even attempting to change character development, the ending and some dialogue. Murray also expressed his disappointment that Shaw was 'imitating' Mrs Humphry Ward by using real people.[262] This was something Champion knew about from personal experience as a character in *Marcella* and now *Pygmalion*, which had 'touches' of Champion and Juliet. It was well-known that Champion, Margaret Harkness and Lady Carlisle appeared in Ward's 1894 novel as inspirations for the characters of Hallly, Marcella and her mother. *The Woman's Signal* had noted a stir in fashionable circles as people recognised the 'very thin disguises' of real characters in London in *Marcella*. Champion could also identify the economic historian, Arnold J. Toynbee, as Hallin in *Marcella's* sequel *Sir George Tressady*.[263]

Nearly ten years later, on 13 November 1923, *Pygmalion* had its first performance at Melbourne's Her Majesty's Theatre and the *Herald* reported that in the audience were Champion and his second wife, Elsie Belle, along with Norman Brookes and his wife. Playing Eliza's role was the Honourable Mrs Emily Pitt-Rivers, daughter of the Governor-General of Australia, Sir Henry William Forster. Forster was a former Dragoon Guards officer and president of the London Marylebone Cricket Club, and his wife was interested in social questions and the women's movement, credentials greatly favoured by Champion. An original sketch by Cyril Dillon of the play's flower girl, autographed by the company and used for the program cover, was bought by Forster. Directed by Gregan McMahon, a close friend of Champion and Elsie Belle, the performances aided the Queen Victoria Hospital Appeal, the Actors' Benevolent Fun and the J.C. Williamson Sick Fund. An outstanding success as a play, the Wednesday afternoon session netted an amazing sum of £1500. A section of Shaw's reply in January 1924 to Champion's letter about that first Melbourne performance stated: 'It does not seem to matter who plays it or where it is played', *Pygmalion* always 'boils the pot' with audiences.[264] Unique features linking Champion to the play were not evident as were the details embedded in stage directions.

Salvation and Socialism
Margaret Elise Harkness (1854–1923)

> *He has many faults, but his invariably sweet temper,*
> *& his affection have helped me. I have helped him, too, I think ...*
> *I shall never see him again, of course.*
> (Maggie Harkness letter to Beatrice Potter, 1889)

How did a country rector's daughter become an author and social reformist in London? The key to unravelling Maggie's journey from finishing school to radical politics, lies in records kept by her cousin Beatrice Potter, her fiction and her relationship with Champion. Well before Champion became one of the luminaries of the Social Democratic Federation, he was part of a growing number of people seeking change and reform. A number of weeks before the SDF was formed from the bones of the Democratic Federation, thirty-year-old Maggie Harkness ventured out to one of Foulger's Progressive Association meeting, attended and often chaired by his publishing partner, Champion. It was July 1884. While she may have attended a few months prior, this date confirmed Maggie's involvement with a new radical circle that led her to a relationship with a young firebrand on the SDF Executive. Gossip would eventually circulate amongst friends and also in newspapers about Maggie's visit to Champion's rooms at Gray's Inn Place and her discussions with Cardinal Manning 'about her feelings' for him. She would join him in working for Keir Hardie's election campaign, the fight for dock workers in the Great London Dock Strike, travel to Australia and eventually write a book about him as a labour leader.

Known as Maggie by friends and family, she was yet another clergyman's child drawn to London where, after a brief and unhappy stint in nursing, she turned to journalism to earn her living. Born at Upton-on-Severn in Worcestershire on 28 February 1854, Maggie was one of five children of Robert Harkness, the Rector of Wimborne St Giles in Dorset, and his wife Elizabeth Bolton (née Seddon). Burke's Peerage is comprehensive about her ancestors as landed gentry from Garryfine in Limerick and Temple Athea in Dublin. Her immediate family were ministers: her grandfather, Robert Harkness was married to Jane Waugh Law (daughter of the Bishop of Bath and Wells), and was Vicar of East Brent in Somerset; many of Robert's brothers were ministers. Maggie was related to Captain William Harkness, an officer in the Dragoon Guards in Dublin, and to Mr Robert Law Harkness, Salisbury, Major J. D'Alton Harkness, and Captain William Bathurst Harkness.[265] Through her maternal grandmother Maggie was also related to the first Earl of Ellenborough, a past Governor-General of India. Her maternal aunt Mary Seddon married Richard Potter and so her kinship with Beatrice Potter was established.

Maggie's decision to use the pseudonym 'John Law' was a direct response to her father's written request before his death that her name should not be printed, a fact she revealed after her identity had been exposed.[266] Since her father displayed no apparent concern about the use of her name in the early 1880s, this obviously related to his daughter's increasing political activity. While Maggie's masculine pseudonym gave her the ability to enter the public arena without engaging with public hostility towards her or her family, this benefit was short-lived. Inevitably there was a lifting of the veil when it became public knowledge that she was John Law, a name many Harkness relatives traditionally were given as a middle name. Maggie experienced both the pleasure and pain of public recognition but continued to use the pseudonym. She admitted to inheriting her father's 'prejudices' and revealed it was never her wish to be a platform woman or have her photograph displayed in society magazines, wanting instead a reclusive life. Her work for the unemployed and poor was performed with her pen, her writing a solitary act suiting her disposition and setting her apart from others. In 1899, twenty years after her arrival in London she explained in *Imperial Credit* that her 'birth, sex and temperament' prevented her from seeking a more forthright public role within the labour struggle. The tension between these three factors – family, gender and personality – served to shadow her obvious political involvement and writing.

Most of what we know about Maggie's early life is seen through her relationship with younger cousin Beatrice Potter and recorded in the latter's personal diary, now preserved in the London School of Economics.[267] From their early life both women suffered the agony of insignificance, the desire to achieve something they couldn't identify and which was just beyond their reach. Behind the confining walls of St Giles Rectory, Maggie was seen by Beatrice as 'an hysterical egotistical girl' who was in 'wretched health and still worse spirits', with her religious family seeking 'to repress her extra-ordinary activity of mind'. Writing on 24 March 1883, Beatrice saw her parental restraint as 'causing a state or morbid sensibility and fermentation which gave almost a permanent twist to her nature'. Beatrice felt no real 'liking' for her relative when young, only a sense of pity and, after the Dock Strike on 13 November 1889, noted Maggie's emancipation was a battle to escape from 'the prejudice and oppression of bigoted and conventional relations'.

In *Imperial Credit* Maggie admitted to frequent ill health as a child, often spending winters with her governess in the fresh sea air of Bournemouth, while her cousin's childhood was marked by continuous illness until her health broke down in the year before finishing school. Both girls continued to have difficulty with their physical strength while living in a polluted London and would suffer depression later as adults.

Family decisions were made to send both cousins for a year to Stirling House, a finishing school in Bournemouth. Maggie read Latin, French, studied Peter Roget's Bridgewater Treatise on health and physiology, loved astronomy, played the piano well, and knew her Bible, a priority for admission. The cousins gravitated to each other as companions and confidants and, observing the sunset over trees on the moorland near to the school, talked endlessly on religion and their frustration about 'world-sorrow'. Parental expectations saw their future as one of marriage and household duties so they speculated about life as wives and mothers, 'of cooks and baby-linen – boys going to their first school – and other matronly subjects'.[268] In 1874 Maggie consulted a dictionary and (of course) her Bible to define the nature of love and questioned whether a woman lost her identity when she fell in love. Home education for a young girl, she later believed, was intended to repress their unique character and 'to teach her to sink her personality in the other sex'.[269]

After leaving school, Maggie was twenty-one years of age and Beatrice eighteen. Novelist and journalist, Mrs Humphry Ward, was a frequent researcher at the British Museum Reading Room and in the first chapter of *Marcella* (1895) described her character as 'a "finished" and grown-up young woman of twenty-one',

> ... no longer the self-conscious schoolgirl, paid for at a lower rate than her companions, stinted in dress, pocket-money, and education, and fiercely resentful at every turn of some real or fancied slur; she was no longer even the half-Bohemian student of these past two years, enjoying herself in London so far as the iron necessity of keeping her boarding-house expenses down to the lowest possible figure would allow. She was something altogether different.

Robert Harkness had undoubtedly kept his daughter 'stinted' and Maggie's letters to Beatrice complained of her family's poverty, even though her father's estate was worth nearly £10,000 when he died in 1886. She later regarded Cardinal Manning as 'more than a father'. On returning to the family home, Maggie couldn't envisage a career or a fulfilling life and complained to her cousin on 13 August 1876 that she was 'all alone', ignored and, 'if I speak, I am simply thought wrong or idiotic'.[270] She thought Beatrice was lucky to have an environment in which to nurture self-expression; even more horrible to Maggie's sense of intellectual worth was a fear she may become 'a nobody, or still worse a general nuisance'.[271]

After surviving another year of family constraint, Maggie departed Dorset in 1877 for nursing training at Westminster Hospital. After ten-hour days, lectures after work and study of clinical cases, she returned to a room rented at a boarding house in Broad Sanctuary close to Westminster Abbey. Her parents regarded this residence as unsuitable for a lady, their concerns forcing her departure even though living there gave her a sense of liberation. *Macmillan's Magazine* later wrote that a 'Glorified Spinster' who sampled a less restricted and more independent life was reluctant to give this away and a glimpse was provided into the bohemian life of a working female renting a small boarding room, including details of daily routine and habits.[272] In January 1878 Maggie made a side-ways move into training as a nurse-dispenser at Westminster for a Miss Granville, where the long hours were exhausting, the work strenuous and her choice to be an unmarried, working woman questioned as self-centred.

Her streak of independence was briefly crushed when she was called home to nurse her sick mother for a few months and she experienced despair and depression, feeling it was 'hard work to go on living'.[273] Returning to Kensington, she trained at Guy's Hospital in Southwark and *Marcella* described her nurse's attire as 'plain brown holland, with collar and armlets of white linen' with a bonnet. A nursing career provided no great fulfillment or intellectual stimulation only perpetuating her sense of isolation. Her 1884 article 'Hospital Nurses' for the Religious Tract Society's magazine, *Leisure Hour*, detailed the unpleasant and exhausting tasks undertaken in hospitals and exposure to 'moral and physical strain'. In her later serialised story, 'Called to the Bar', Maggie's main character complained:

> 'Well, it has always seemed to me an absurd fallacy to represent nursing as a suitable occupation for females in distress, to gild the nastiness of the work by sentiment. Florence Nightingale made nursing the fashion, the Royal Family patronise nurses, so nursing has become the vogue for women whose lives are out of joint, in fact a sort of Protestant make-shift for a Convent.'[274]

The Nightingale figure of a ministering angel of self-sacrifice held no appeal. Aware of the tedious work and long hours, even Champion was scathing about a 'diatribe' written for January's *Nineteenth Century* on 'rewards in the shape of husbands' for nurses.[275]

With the dawn of a new decade, Maggie lived independently and was developing intellectual pursuits. She felt the first stirrings of a political nature, reading newspapers and conducting research. In her first published article under her own name for a well-known journal, *Nineteenth Century*, she argued there was demand for 'remunerative employment of women', especially female civil servants, arising from a new practice of employers of engaging 'ladies in reduced circumstances'. However, she defiantly questioned why women received less than half the pay of men, pointing to significant savings afforded by using women as 'cheap labour'.[276]

On 13 February 1882, Beatrice's diary captured Maggie's entrance into a new world of research at the British Museum.

> The little glimpse into the British Museum life through Maggie Harkness and the Pooles interested me – There you get real intellectual drudgery, and though the various curators with their various hobbies, sometimes verge on boring you, there is a strong and refreshing flavour of earnestness and thoroughness in their conversation.

At the time, Maggie was lodging in Gower Street with Stanley Lane Poole, a noted Egyptian archaeologist at the British Museum, and his wife Charlotte. Under the influence of her adopted mentor, Maggie was lecturing and researching ancient civilisations and delivering lectures, advertised as far afield as Boston.[277] She also funnelled a range of historical interests into small books for the Religious Tract Society, admitting she sold her copyright 'to an inferior publisher' for both *Assyrian Life and History* (1883) and *Egyptian Life and History According to the Monuments* (1884). In addition, she was also writing for the Society's *Leisure Hour*. The good income she secured through freelance journalism made her self-supportive even though her health suffered from the lengthy days and nights. Over three years from 1881 till her letter to Beatrice on 29 February 1884, her earnings totalled a surprising £150.[278]

When Beatrice returned to her family home, Standish House in Stonehouse, Laurencina Potter was suddenly struck down with a terminal sickness and the reliable Maggie was sent for and stayed to assist until she died in April 1882. Christmas was spent by Maggie consoling her cousin rather than with her own family and after leaving Standish House Maggie severed ties with nursing. Beatrice wrote in her diary on 24 March 1883 that Maggie's whole attitude and manner altered.

> It's extraordinary the improvement in M.H. since she has given herself up to work ... Now that she has broken loose from all ties, supporting herself by literary piecework, living in a queer unconventional family with whom she is by no means one, she is blossoming out into a clever, interested and amusing young woman with much charm of looks and manner.

Beatrice still saw Maggie inclined towards moodiness and recognised in her an 'absurd distrust of the faithfulness of others'. Firmly entrenched amongst London's medical students, artists and female journalists, as sketched in *George Eastmont*, Maggie was earning a steady living, networking with writers and people in the publishing world and attending various political meetings that would eventually lead to friendship with Champion whose political agitation was already generating waves in London.

A frequent visitor since 1881 to the British Museum's Reading Room, Maggie joined a number of female writers such as Mrs Humphry Ward, Olive Schreiner, Annie Besant, Eleanor Marx, Clementina Black, Amy Levy and Dollie Radford (Caroline Maitland), who all lived within walking distance and knew each other through their writing and activism. The Reading Room was one of the most important institutions for writers at that time, a vast, airy, warm and comfortable space with a large desk, two ink wells, quills, blotters, book weights and an adjustable bookstand, with a choice of three types of chairs.[279] A warm position in cold London was sought after and, if the walls of the Rectory at St Giles confined Maggie's spirit, these academic walls set her free. Dr Richard Garnett was Superintendent of the Reading Room from 1875 and later Keeper of the Printed Book and an essential guide and mentor to many researchers, his son Edward marrying Constance Black, sister of Clementina.

Olive Schreiner arrived in London to pursue dreams of a medical career and in June 1883 applied for a reader's ticket for the Reading Room where she met Maggie and Eleanor Marx, the latter helping

Olive find rooms at Fitzroy Street. Olive was born in South Africa, daughter of a German missionary, while her maternal grandfather had been an East End Presbyterian minister. Recognised by George Meredith, reader for Chapman and Hall, she was now the newly acclaimed author of *The Story of an African Farm* (1883). In a letter to Beatrice on 29 February 1884, Maggie referred to George Bentley having rejected the work and to a novelist (obviously Olive) who believed her first novel, which opposed to capital punishment, showed promise. A current topic in England, this was fuelled by a gruesome interview with a hangman in Sheffield's *Daily Telegraph*,[280] Gericault's evocative drawing of a public hanging in England and the popularity of Victor Hugo's *The Last Day of a Condemned Man*. Over a decade later Champion revealed insider knowledge when writing about a charity dance where young ladies knew nothing of Olive Schreiner or that, like Jane Austin's first attempt (*The Professor*), Olive's first novel had been declined by publishers.[281] Since Olive's *Undine: A Queer Little Girl* was only published posthumously in 1929, its early rejection was not common knowledge and suggests Olive's sympathetic admission to Maggie who, in turn, told Champion.

Olive recorded in June her particular liking for Maggie who was 'making a path for herself in the world' through journalism.[282] At this time, Olive was growing closer to Champion's friend, Havelock Ellis, who noted on 20 July that Maggie attended a Progressive Association meeting at Islington with poet and anarchist, Louisa Sarah Bevington.[283] Ellis had invited several of his colleagues to be case studies for his *Studies in the Psychology of Sex*, including Olive who imagined herself as a 'heroine' in 'erotic' dreams. Her friend, Eleanor Marx, was another study and was German 'on both sides', dreamt of being a 'knight rescuing damsels in distress' and Eleanor's lover, Edward Aveling, was also interviewed. Aveling studied medicine and science in London from 1867 and lost his religious faith after the sudden death of his mother, the daughter of a Cambridgeshire farmer and innkeeper in Wisbeck. Aveling discussed his maternal grandfather, a small farmer married to a farmer/innkeeper's daughter, and subsequently their daughter's pregnancy to a local doctor that caused her to flee her family home. The case study of Aveling, discussing a man of 38 with an 'abnormally strong' amount of 'sexual feelings' who came to London at 20, quoted his use of medical terms such as 'dolicocephalic' and 'occipital' and believed he was 'violent and tenacious in temper, high strung, and rapid in thought and action'. He also had sexual dreams centred on 'a dead woman'.

Eleanor Marx first met Edward Aveling at the British Museum's Reading Room[284] and from 1884 for 14 years she lived openly with him, aware he had left his wife (Isabel Frank) two years before and waited for a divorce. Her contributions in *Justice* were signed as Eleanor Aveling and sometimes Eleanor Marx Aveling, although many referred to her as Mrs Aveling, his common law wife. As early as 2 August 1884, Olive expressed her intense and distressing emotional hatred of Aveling and her serious concerns about his infidelities as rumours circulated about his philandering. After Maggie read Balzac's analytical sketches on infidelities and advice on unhappy marriages in *Physiologie du Marriage*, she loaned the book to Olive so both women held concerns for Eleanor.[285] Two women involved in sexual health campaigns, Annie Besant and Gertrude Guillaume-Schack, called 'Mother Besant' and 'Mother Schack' by Engels, were openly antagonist to Aveling and in June 1887 Eleanor insisted on knowing what prohibited Mother Schack remaining in the same room with her partner;[286] two years later Engels would also call Maggie 'another Mother Schack'. Aveling's reputation grew 'as a borrower of money and a swindler and seducer of women' and he became Shaw's model for Louis Dubedat, the gifted, amoral womaniser and bigamist in his play, *The Doctor's Dilemma* (1906). A rift finally opened between Maggie and Eleanor, noted in Shaw's diary entry on 3 August 1888: 'Asked Miss Harkness a question about the Avelings and received such a disagreeable, brusque reply as to suggest that she has either quarrelled with the Avelings or with him'.[287]

On the death of his estranged wife in 1892 Aveling was appointed administrator and in July 1897 secretly married an actress under his playwright's name Alec Nelson. The following year Eleanor discovered the marriage and her suicide note was reproduced in *Reynold's Newspaper*: 'It will soon be all over now. My last word to you is the same that I have said during all these long, sad years – love.' *Justice* pointed the finger directly at Aveling by publishing Eduard Bernstein's 'What Drove Eleanor Marx to Suicide'[288] and in *Further Reminiscences* (1912) Hyndman dismissed Aveling's theatrical suffering at Eleanor's funeral as heartless and labelled him a 'scoundrel'. Only weeks after her suicide, Olive wrote to Dollie Radford, detailing Eleanor's distress about one of Aveling's sexual encounters when she caught him in her bed with two prostitutes. Champion knew Aveling 'exceedingly well', describing him as 'a man of more ability than character' and knew of rumours the SDF had invited him to resign.[289] Aveling did, claiming probate of Eleanor's will and taking a holiday although he did not claim her ashes which were placed on a shelf in the SDF premises at Maiden Lane until they were buried in 1956 at Karl Marx's tomb.

After Maggie and Beatrice returned from their August 1884 trip to the Bavarian Alps, Beatrice became a voluntary rent-collector for philanthropist Octavia Hill. A new venture in the Katharine Buildings in Cartwright Street, Aldgate opened in January 1885. This was intended to accommodate dock workers employed on a casual basis and unskilled labourers. Beatrice and her co-manager Ella Pycroft were assisted by a medical student, Maurice Kegan Paul, manager of the residence's Boys' Clubs and son of the publisher in whose business Champion originally invested. Maggie joined Beatrice and resided with the unemployed occupants 'a whole winter, in a block, sharing their mode of life and becoming intimately acquainted with their feelings'.[290]

> The outward and visible signs of government were manifest to the tenants in the form of lady-collectors. Several times in the week ladies arrived on the Buildings armed with master-keys, ink-pots and rent-books. A tap at the door was followed by the intrusion into a room of a neatly-clad female of masculine appearance ... 'Females like 'er don't marry,' mumbled a misanthropic old lady ... Some tenants grumbled against petticoat government, but others liked it; and all agreed that 'an eddicated [sic] female' was a phenomenon to be much watched, criticised and talked about (pp. 10–11).

From January to around the end of March Maggie wrote half of

A City Girl at this location in the Katharine Buildings. On 12 April 1885, Beatrice noted running into Maggie who had just returned from Berlin.[291]

Despite individual differences, the cousin's lengthy ties remained intact and they moved together in September to a flat owned by Beatrice's sister Kate and her husband on Chelsea's Cheyne Walk, allowing Maggie the solitude to finish her novel. When Beatrice returned home at the end of the day, Maggie would play the piano, a wedding day gift from Leonard Courtney's parliamentary colleagues when he married Kate Potter. Both cousins were now engaged in work concentrating on the East End, one translating her experiences into a novel of social realism and the other analytical writing. In a diary entry on 15 September 1885, Beatrice rejoiced that they were independent women who 'passed through the misery of strong and useless feeling' and now worked outside the domestic environment.

Beginning with the momentous Trafalgar Square Riots, the year 1886 was a perfect storm of events. The period also signalled changes in political and personal contacts as Maggie became friendlier with Champion whose personal crisis after his trial and death of Juliet was evident to many friends. Two weeks after Champion's discussion in St Paul's Church, Covent Garden following Juliet's death, Edward Carpenter invited Olive Schreiner, now staying at St Dominic's Catholic Convent for a six-month retreat, to visit his home in Sheffield. Visiting Millthorpe seemed to be a healing process for emotionally distraught friends who found events overwhelming. Champion also took up his invitation to Millthorpe and stayed three days, a period that 'materially altered' his life.[292] One devotee who listened to Carpenter's Sunday evening Sheffield lecture, 'The Simplification of Life', recalled the effect of his words, envisioning 'a reconquest of the green and beautiful England by a happy and healthy people.'[293]

On 7 August, Olive wrote about her Bournemouth friend, Maggie, supporting herself by journalism and apparently contemplating motherhood outside of marriage.

> She was talking about the impossibility of finding a man whom one could marry, and I asked her whether she never wished to have a child.

The impassioned way in which she turned to me quite astonished me. 'Ah, that is the bitterness,' she said, and she described all the feelings of longing – the main thing seemed to be that she would never have a little child to clasp its fingers round hers! ... She said she had often thought whether it would be very wrong to have a child and send it away to the South of France and go away secretly to see it every year.[294]

It is apparent Maggie suggested Olive's retreat to St Dominic's Convent because the prioress (Catherine) once cared for her orphaned aunt, Jane Harkness. Mothers who leave their children in a convent appear in two of Maggie's stories, 'Roses and Crucifix' and 'Called to the Bar'.

In Maggie's novel, *George Eastmont*, a country rector's daughter had a visit to her home from a labour leader only six months after the death of his wife. The novel also described a demonstration where the crowd carried Eastmont on their shoulders to Chelsea, mirroring Champion who was carried by the crowd at Trafalgar Square on 25 August 1886. It is probable that Champion at this time further opened Maggie's eyes to the world of poverty and despair not seen in the structured activities at the Katherine Buildings, for she recalled being 'introduced to the inhabitants of the London slums shortly before [her] father's death' in late November 1886. In her trip to Berlin, Maggie had seen the widespread use of porters and messengers (or Dienstmänner) and considered this a possibility for the London unemployed, so she took the idea to a committee, prepared for significant personal expenditure. 'It was a very influential committee, but they did nothing but talk – and quarrel. I had three committees in all, one after another; but they could not agree upon anything, and had to be broken up.' In an interview, Maggie 'confessed that there was one man, and one only, on her committees who had got any work or energy in him, and that was Mr. Champion'.[295] After her return from Germany, Maggie entered the political sphere by joining the Social Democratic Federation for 'a few months'.[296]

Following Olive's lengthy stay at St Dominic's, Maggie travelled to Mendrisio in Switzerland to see her and recalled for the *Novel Review* Olive's statement in the mountains, 'Nothing will satisfy me but God Almighty'. On 22 March 1887 Olive complained to Ellis that Maggie arrived without money 'and came thinking I would support her'. However, Maggie's situation changed dramatically when Henry Vizetelly published *A City Girl: A Realistic Story* (1887) based on her first-hand experience observing rent-collectors and tenants. Evidence indicates that on 2 May 1887, when Bernard Shaw called on Champion, the lady in the adjoining room was Maggie. Champion's tenement rooms at Gray's Inn Place were neither numerous nor spacious; a sitting room, bedroom and perhaps a small kitchen. With the discretion of a Victorian gentleman, Champion did not name his female companion. Only one day before the visit, *A City Girl* had been favourably reviewed by *Lloyd's Weekly*. It is interesting to speculate whether Maggie shared her excitement about her first review with a close colleague and that this visit was one of many. Certainly, she had been working closely with him on committees. The death of Champion's younger sister Mary Leslie, married to barrister William Hacon for less than a year, occurred only two weeks earlier so perhaps they consoled each other, for Maggie had also lost two siblings and her father the year before.

At Maggie's request a copy of her novel was forwarded to Friedrich Engels and he 'read it with the greatest pleasure and avidity', praising the novel for 'its realistic truth' and commending the work as 'the courage of the true artist'. However, he complained about her depiction of workers 'as a passive mass, unable to help itself and not even showing (making) any attempt at striving to help itself'. Engels placed a caveat on his appraisal, acknowledging East End workers were 'less actively resistant, more passively submitting to fate, more hébétés [stupefied]' than any workers in the 'civilised world', perhaps anticipating or encouraging her towards a future more 'active' novel.[297] Maggie responded to Engels in April 1888, pointing to her lack of confidence in her writing skills and to her gender, a continuing chronicle throughout Maggie's life.

Maggie joined Champion in travelling north, hearing his address to the Church Congress at Wolverhampton in October 1887 where she admired his 'ability' amidst 'uproar and hisses', and later writing of this event during his election campaign for the *Aberdeen Journal*.[298]

The period spent in Scotland enabled more intimate contact, with trips to Aberdeen and south to Brechin, Arbroath and Dundee as she worked with Champion, Tom Mann, John Mahon, Robert Smillie, T.R. Threlfall and Cunninghame Graham for the spring election of Keir Hardie. From Hardie's Scottish home in Old Cumnock, Ayrshire, on the borders of the Mid-Lanark constituency, Maggie gave her return address to her cousin as care of Keir Hardie at the Miners Union in Ayrshire where the small election team were no doubt invited to join family Christmas festivities. A month of ten-hour days and many nights were spent electioneering in Glasgow, from the Steel Works at Newtown along the collieries and 'through a dozen townships strung in a line by the mouth of the mineshafts' dotting the moors. Although Hardie received under a thousand votes Champion believed it demonstrated 'a straight-out Labour Party was in existence'.[299] Maggie had worked for a year, 'hand in glove with the underground labour party – with Champion, Burns, Mann etc', Beatrice later confirmed on 13 November 1889.

Activities in Scotland also led to Maggie's affection for Champion's friends, including Cunninghame Graham, elected to parliament for North West Lanarkshire. Champion had drafted 'an amendment to the Address in Reply' to parliament for Cunninghame Graham 'to recite' during the Coal Mines Regulation Bill in September 1887 and, as a result, this protest speech against the House of Lords unelected nature earned Graham a brief suspension but established a platform for labour.[300] Maggie subsequently advised Graham's critics to listen to his constituents, Scottish miners who loved their 'toozled-headed darling'[301] and wrote a telling appraisal for an Adelaide newspaper.[302] She also dedicated *A Manchester Shirtmaker: A Realistic Story of To-day* (1890) to Champion's aristocratic friend, the Laird of Gartmore, a descendent of Robert Bruce and immortalised in William Strang's quintessential etchings of *Don Quixote*. Champion wrote later of Graham's inheritance of Scottish estates of Ardoch in Dunbartonshire and two 'dormant earldoms' of Strathern and Menteith and recalled he had the 'keenest wit and the worst handwriting of any one I ever met', and that he believed his friend was 'the handsomest man in London' until he met his brother [Charles, a naval officer].[303]

Just prior to Keir Hardie's Mid-Lanark election attempt in April 1888, rumours circulated in London suggesting a siren-like woman whose powers of allurement had coaxed Champion away from the SDF into alternate political paths. A London correspondent, writing as J.M.D. for the *Argus* and claiming a 'Social Democrat friend' as the source, was spreading misinformation.

> H.H. Champion, the ex-artillery officer, has also broken away from the Hyndman combination, and stands by himself. He was demoralised some time ago by the blandishments of a fair Primrose League canvasser, who visited him in his chambers at Grey's [sic] Inn, to ask for his vote at a Parliamentary election. After many visits and much tender talk, he half converted her, and she half converted him, and he left the Social Democratic Federation, joining, by way of compromise, a Gladstonian Caucus. (10 March 1888)

Later, during the London Dock Strike a similar reference was made to Maggie Harkness, identified by her relationship with Beatrice:

> Mr. Champion is a handsome, 'interesting' gentleman, of most persuasive manner and fascinating address. He can get money out of almost anybody, especially out of women of intellect. Certain people give him money freely for his objects, some of these persons being Tory men, and one being a Liberal-Unionist lady, a close friend or a relation of Mr. Leonard Courtney. (19 October 1889)

After Champion was made honorary president of the ILP in Aberdeen in 1893, the journalist again reported rumours of Maggie's visit to Champion's rooms.

> Mr. Champion is a good-looking man, as you know, and rumoured to be very fascinating and magnetic. One day a woman who writes under the name of 'John Law' – I believe her real name is Harkness – called on Mr. Champion at his chambers in Gray's Inn. When she entered the room 'John Law' was a violent Primrose Leaguer. He talked to her for an hour or so without looking at her, and she left the room a violent

Socialist. Then she took to worrying poor old Cardinal Manning about her feelings. (30 December 1893)

Maggie's significant writing activity ran parallel to Champion's frenetic pace of activism at this time. The editor of the *British Weekly: A Journal of Social and Christian Progress* (an associated publication of Hodder and Stoughton) wrote to Maggie in the belief that John Law was male and they shared a laugh over his mistake at his office.[304] From October 1887 a pattern developed in Maggie's writing where her serialised articles tested the market before publication as books. 'Tempted London: young men' (October 1887–April 1888), its companion piece on women workers 'Toilers in London' and 'Captain Lobe: a story of the East End' (April-December 1888), were subsequently published as books over a two-year period. The latter novel achieved substantial overseas success when Eduard Bernstein's wife, Regina, translated the novel into German; Russia and Sweden also requested the rights.[305]

The Salvation Army and their practical assistance were a feature in Maggie's writing even though she had no sympathy with their religious evangelizing. She argued that the SDF and Salvationists had mutual interests and should work together more.[306] However, Champion argued for the treatment of the root cause:

> I have no wish to belittle the great efforts made by charitable and philanthropic persons to sweep back the rising tide of misery. They themselves admit that it is gaining upon them. And this is natural, for their efforts are condemned to impotence by the fact that they are directed, not at the causes, but at the effects of poverty ...[307]

Champion later praised General William Booth as 'one of the remarkable men of the time' whose success was attributed in large part to women in his organisation engaged in philanthropy and proselytizing, with their 'mission of soul-stirring dimensions'.[308]

Drawing on Harry Quelch's article with the same title in *Justice* a week before Christmas 1885, Maggie's new novel *Out of Work* (1888) featured the November 1887 Trafalgar Square skirmish involving Burns and Cunninghame Graham who were arrested on 'Bloody Sunday'.

This novel could not have come out at a better time, published not long before the London Dock Strike and translated into several languages. Maggie's new novel countered the criticism of a 'passive mass' of working class and centred on Joseph Coney, a man seeking work as a temporary, casual dockworker. It included a section of 'Girl Labour in the City' (originally written for *Justice* while she was in Scotland) and described thousands of starving unemployed in queues on the docks 'pressed so hard on starving men in front, that the latter were nearly cut in two by the iron railings which kept them from work'.[309]

The lady in Champion's room again became the subject of gossip among his friends and on 15 February 1889 Shaw recorded a discussion about the pair at William Archer's home with Ernest Radford and Clementina Black.[310] As their relationship became public knowledge Maggie fled north to Manchester. Her political activities with Champion in Scotland and dissatisfaction with socialists, especially the SDF, couldn't help but play out in her story about the Salvation Army. While the SDF was frequently prone to extensive criticism of others, members became angry about their portrayal in *Captain Lobe: A Story of the Salvation Army* (1889). The novel focused on assistance by 'slum saviours' to the poor and featured a female factory labour manager and socialist, Jane Hardy. One chapter, 'Among the Socialists', named Hyndman and the SDF, as well as Morris and the Socialist League. In a discussion with a Salvation Army Captain, Jane discusses the inherent fragmentation and distrust of socialists:

> These men see the misery of our present social conditions, and throw themselves into Socialism as a forlorn hope, expecting to be worsted. The amusing thing is that these men, who are all well-meaning, are so suspicious of one another ... So why they do not swallow their petty jealousies and pull together I cannot think. But I suppose they cannot help it ... But why indulge in personalities? That is a common fault among Socialists, and one that ought to be avoided (pp. 115–16).

Political and personal advantage were now gained by those who released information about the identity of John Law and old scores were settled with Champion. Shaw and Bax called at Champion's place on 23 March 1889 to find him in discussions with Hudson, believed to be Frederic Hudson, [311] a Fabian solicitor and partner of C.J. Smith and Hudson of Fenchurch Street. With experience gained from his dealings with Lewis Lyons and Adolphe Smith, Champion evidently assisted in the crafting of strategy. When Maggie wrote her simple letter from the Manchester Cotton Exchange in St Anne's Square on 29 March to the *Pall Mall Gazette*, it was intended to free her from any sensational legal case. The steps devised were cleverly structured to this purpose: (a) reveal the practice of selling a paragraph of gossip (true or false) shaped as an interview to a society newspaper (b) highlight harassment over unsought attention using words like 'victim', 'nuisance', 'degrading' and 'molested' (c) assert an individual's rights to privacy and (d) represent the attempt 'to drag forward a woman writing under a pseudonym' as a restriction of a British subject's 'rights'. As rumours continued to spread, Maggie freely admitted she could not live like a recluse anymore because of the exposure that increased public interest. Her final question pleaded, 'why should I be molested like this? There are plenty of women who like to be written and talked about. I do not'.

Lawyers threatened Maggie with a substantial £200 claim for libel over her portrayal of socialists and she admitted the novel brought a large amount of trouble. A month after her exposure, after attending Annie Besant's lecture in Manchester, Maggie wrote an urgent letter of apology and a plea to *Justice* on 20 April. On the defensive over the SDF's outrage she wrote contritely: 'I am sorry to think it gives an untrue account of London Socialists'. Written week by week the previous year with little thought to the ending, the offending section of her work was written after Maggie 'suffered a good deal from Socialists' (around the time of Champion's SDF expulsion). She admitted to being unsuccessful in retrieving the book before it was printed. 'It is not true, and I am sorry for it', she apologised unreservedly and passionately told *Justice* she was 'without a relation or a friend' because of her beliefs while socialists emptied 'vials of wrath' upon her.[312] She later recalled the harassment by lawyers as well as blackmail from 'religious adventurers' that she suffered at that time, 18 months prior to her Salvation and Socialism article in the *Pall Mall Gazette*. Anger towards her and accusations about her allegiances, mainly from SDF members, appear to be the result of a relationship with Champion. When he lashed out at Adolphe Smith to accuse him of using an alias to reflect changed beliefs, Champion opened an opportunity for an assault on Maggie, now vulnerable after the exposure of her own alias.

Maggie turned to Cardinal Manning during this time and received a letter back addressed to 'My dear Child' from his office in Westminster dated 17 May. His advice was still treasured ten years later in Adelaide when she printed his letter to her:

> 'Write and work for OUR PEOPLE as before. Do not be weary or fastidious or disappointed. If they quarrel, or are rash, or FOOLISH, or violent, they need YOUR HELP ALL THE MORE. Our Lord said, "They that are whole have no need of a physician but they that are sick," and the more SICK THE GREATER THE NEED'.[313]

Upon Cardinal Manning's death, Maggie wrote that she 'forgot the priest and loved the man', remembering her 'best friend'; she knew his personal staff and frequently visited him at his rooms where he read her proofs and gave advice on the *City Girl* and *Out of Work*. '"Pride has kept you from religion", he once said to me; "and from sin"', his words accompanied by tears.[314]

Beatrice found money to assist with Maggie's law suit although increasingly doubts were expressed about Maggie's reliability. With personal experience from Maggie's publication of sensitive information (three months before) Beatrice was wary and not too sympathetic about her difficulties. Using a patronising tone, she wrote on 19 May 1889:

> Poor Maggie Harkness! Her bitterness has cost her £200 as compensation for the libel on her former lover! Poor child! With her, life has embittered relations instead of repairing affections. Lent her £50. But one feels it is as likely as not the next libel will be against oneself!

On holiday with her father at Argoed in the summer of 1889, Beatrice advised Dr Garnett at the British Museum Reading Room that very soon her cousin would return from Manchester to London with her 'bottomless pit' now full. Maggie had written to Beatrice at Argoed about departing England after Christmas, the only anchor holding her was 'one more slum story' about Manchester. She wrote of her strong emotional ties to Champion who had sustained her through difficult times but claimed that she would not see him in future. Her wistful announcement about ending their liaison pointed to a decision to abandon any hope of further involvement:

> I feel I shall always be grateful to Mr --, for he came into my life when I might have become very bitterly sceptical. He has many faults, but his invariably sweet temper, & his affection have helped me. I have helped him, too, I think. I never hear of that man, but I do so wonder if he has a child. He wanted children so much. If you hear, do tell me. I shall never see him again, of course. We women, with strong individualities are not meant for marriage. [315]

However, the pledge to break contact was thrown out because of political upheaval during the London Dock Strike, with Maggie and Champion renewing their close friendship (but not romance). Maggie recommenced work during the Strike, spending long hours in the basement and back room of Wade's Arms, a pub in Poplar run by Mrs Hickey. Watching the peaceful protest on 23 August 1889, Maggie worried about the mass of 40,000 people that seemed 'more threatening, more ominous' as a portent for conflict and the same day she wrote a letter on the human face of the strike, noting that people didn't want charity only work and a fair wage. Maggie turned to the *British Weekly* for 'The Dockers' "Tanner"' to appeal to a concerned readership worried about starving families after she discovered one wife at Aldgate trying to feed her eight children on a handful of peas; she also reported on Ben Tillett's Tea Operatives and General Labourers' Association members.[316] She cited Champion as an inspiration with his written arguments supporting the strike and celebrated the hands-on approach to workers by Burns and Mann, writing about labour leaders avoiding 'a revolution' and maintaining peaceful order.[317]

Maggie's role in the strike became public knowledge in late August when she requested that Cardinal Manning act as a mediator. Later she expanded on a proposal for an extension of the strike with London's shutdown a real possibility, of a sleepless night as she feared bloodshed, and how she obtained a list of dock directors for Cardinal Manning.[318] Before the Strike Committee was dissolved, a manifesto was crafted thanking her as 'the first to ask for the help' from the Cardinal. Champion later recalled, 'A lady told me that I had better go and see Cardinal Manning who would listen to me' and this led to Manning's final address to end the strike.[319] The Port of London reopened on 16 September 1889, although an underclass of temporary, unskilled and despised workmen remained, Maggie's letter explained; she pointed to a parliamentary avenue and stressed concepts Champion espoused in the *Nineteenth Century* the preceding year including the importance of an Eight Hours Bill.[320]

In the aftermath of the successful London Dock Strike, jealousies erupted and Maggie sent a letter on 'Labour Politics' trying to dispel old rumours again plaguing Champion.

> I think it is pretty well known that I paid my friend Mr Keir Hardie's election expenses at Mid-Lanark; also that I am not a Conservative but a Socialist ... Tory gold is a myth. John Burns knew this when he became treasurer of the Labour Elector some months ago; he was satisfied that the money of the Labour party had come from Socialists.[321]

Fresh from personal experience of SDF outrage and five days after her first letter the *Star*, Maggie continued to take aim at old adversaries. She argued that Champion's departure from the SDF ensured their continuing attacks against him and provocatively denounced the SDF as defunct. Her admission about payment of the Returning Officer's charges demonstrated Maggie was 'mad with vanity', according to Beatrice, who asked her to explain why, with substantial money to spend on a Scottish election, she was forced to borrow £50 to settle her libel suit. On 13 November 1889 Beatrice noted: 'to account for borrowing money she tells me that the money was hers "for that purpose and that purpose alone" which simply means that she served as go-between', her interpretation coloured by 'Tory gold'.

At this time, Maggie was writing a new novel on Champion as a labour leader and told Beatrice, "'I can tell you nothing now, but I shall get out of the whole thing someday – then I can tell you all.'" This news was greeted with hostility by her cousin who wondered at Maggie's 'utter deficiency of sense of honour'. The use of insider knowledge in the form of fiction, Beatrice regarded as one that allowed her cousin to take 'a crooked path' to fact and observation, as opposed to her own preferred method of analytical and research-based reasoning. As their long friendship dissolved, passionate words spoke of treachery:

> Poor Maggie! a strange weariness and chronic depression add pathos to her curious contortions: there is still pity for her suffering, admiration for her pluck, and appreciation of her kind-heartedness towards others' suffering – but can there be real friendship where there is no respect – no confidence? At times I feel that the pretence of the old feeling is a hollow sham: that a relationship in which one is perpetually trying to guard oneself against betrayal cannot be healthy or lasting and must end in Death. But pity will keep me her friend, until I cease to interest her and she slips from me – not I from her.

Months later a Lancashire journalist announced Maggie's two-year study of the labour movement formed the basis for her new novel about a labour figure. Tentatively titled, *The Labour Leader*, the novel was slated for publication at Christmas and was regarded as a truthful historical record.[322] This marked the genesis of *George Eastmont: Wanderer*, the new title drawing on her school text, *Pilgrim's Progress*, to highlight moral difficulties. George's assent, implicit in his surname, suggested his 'wilderness wanderings', a moral choice of a hard 'right way' compared to an easy 'wrong' path that Champion's speech to the Aberdeen Trades Union Congress in 1893 had warned about. To Maggie the Bunyan classic was now 'little read because most people fail to see that the author brought his experience of this life to assist him with descriptions of another world'.[323] Although there would be a hiatus of fifteen years to publication, her dedication of the book to Cardinal Manning, her firsthand experience of the Dock Strike as well as controversies surrounding Champion, guaranteed a wide reader appeal.

On 14 February 1890, at the Devonshire House Hotel where Beatrice was staying for two weeks, she recorded Maggie's dramatic tales of Champion and his friends:

> She is in a much more satisfactory state. Her position with the New Trade Unionists and the genuine affection the leaders have for her, has softened and enlarged her life – and her faith in their aims has transformed her from a cold blooded journalist in search of 'copy' to an honourable colleague. From her I catch a glimpse into the inner workings of the movement. Champion with his Tory sympathies, his money troubles and his somewhat crooked ways is loosing [sic] his hold on Burns and Mann ... As usual she represents the society she lives in as a huge whirlpool and her friends seem like monsters (of virtue or wickedness) in a nightmare: but this time they are loveable monsters with fine manly instincts.

Beatrice joined Maggie a couple of days later at St Dominic's Convent where Maggie had a retreat after the exhaustion of the Dock Strike and where Olive Schreiner had found peace years earlier. After Sunday lunch the pair went down to Peter Kropotkin's cottage for afternoon coffee and cigarettes. Maggie remembered Kropotkin fondly as inspiring whereas Beatrice had no such rosy glasses, viewing him as a chamberlain in Tsarist Russia but now a 'poverty-stricken nihilist' and journalist.

Through critical eyes, Beatrice saw the convent as 'a bare unlovely place, with a perpetually-smiling buxom old prioress' who was Mother Catherine Bathurst of the Sisters of the Third Order of St Dominic. Catherine was the daughter of General Sir James Bathurst and Lady Caroline Stewart, daughter of the first Earl of Castle Stewart in Ireland. Catherine's brother, Robert Andrew Bathurst, was Rector of Birchanger in Essex who in April 1852 married Maggie's orphaned aunt, Jane Harkness. Catherine's conversion to Catholicism after hearing Cardinal Manning preach on the top of a tub in London slums, took her to Birmingham where Cardinal Newman found her in the slums. Newman arranged for Catherine to join the Dominican order in Ghent and in 1878 asked her to establish a Catholic 'motherhouse' at Harrow-on-the-Hill. The two Cardinals and Mother Catherine met annually at St Dominic's[324] and the convent was the background for Lilian, an orphaned daughter of an Anglican curate who featured in Maggie's story, 'Roses and Crucifix'. Catherine also attended Tillett and Mann's Christmas dinner, featured in her article, 'The Children of the Unemployed'.[325]

Maggie's new novel, *A Manchester Shirtmaker*, was to be printed by the newly formed Authors' Co-operative Publishing Company and centred on one of the worst slums in Angel Meadows. Inspired by the *Labour Elector's* January 1889 issue about a man's suicide that left seven family members to support themselves on starvation wages as shirt-makers, it was one of the first success stories for the Authors' Co-operative. Maggie felt deeply and emotionally about slum dwellers: 'The filth and moral degradation of the English slums fill one with despair. Ink turns to blood when one writes about them, tears make words fall like lead from one's pen'.[326] As she flagged to her cousin, Maggie had decided to leave London and in a farewell letter to the *Labour Elector*[327] acknowledged Champion's foundation role.

The following month Champion closed his newspaper after the final issue in April 1890. Together they went to Aberdeen for May Day where, invited by the Aberdeen Trades Council – Burns, Mann and Tillett didn't attend – Champion addressed a crowd of 20,000 at one of the largest rallies outside of London. He spoke at the Links on 17 May on the eight-hour day and Maggie mentioned specifically this May Day as a turning point for her belief that parliamentary seats could be won for a Labour party.[328] Later, she reported that Champion's constant companion in Scotland at that time was a copy of Thomas Carlyle's book.

Both Maggie and Champion appeared on the Continent, apparently travelling some part of the journey together. Champion's three-week journey in June took him to Berlin, Belgium and Holland (Netherlands)[329] while Maggie wrote articles for the *Pall Mall Gazette*, travelling to Berlin where she saw Eleanor Marx's godfather Wilhelm Liebknecht in the lobby of the Reichstag, interviewed August Bebel and chatted about quarrels among London socialists. Maggie also visited the strike district of Felshammer to write on 'The Loafer in Germany' and travelled to Vienna comparing conditions there with the English workhouse 'Viennese Pauper' and interviewing Austrian socialist Dr Victor Adler.[330] Champion returned to England to collect Percy Frost and wrap up loose ends with his newspaper before he sailed for Australia in July 1890. Meanwhile, Maggie, having contracted a severe illness, was forced to return to England just prior to the release of General William Booth's *In Darkest England and the Way Out*.

Beatrice's quiet dinner with Bernard Shaw, a seemingly casual event at the Devonshire House Hotel on the first day of September 1890, was transformational for both cousins. Eight days later there was an estrangement, with Maggie dispatching 'a curt letter' advising she was leaving England forever and rejecting her cousin's offer of a visit. Beatrice understood the predicted schism was happening:

> It could hardly end otherwise – she had lost my respect and my confidence – and her feeling for me was undermined by jealousy of my small success and possibly by a consciousness of the change in my attitude. It is sad. One always feels the worse for a broken tie – feels to some extent a traitor. And she was as tender to one in one's trouble as she has been traitorous to me in success. A strange nature – the two dominant impulses – Pity and Envy – Helpfulness and Treachery.

Whatever was discussed at dinner altered the dynamics of their close familial affinity and dramatically spotlighted their disunity. They may have discussed Champion's role in the Maritime Strike in Australia but whatever words were spoken, Maggie was furious enough to signal the end of their friendship.

Only eight months after Maggie introduced Beatrice to her future husband and four months after Beatrice claimed Sidney Webb transformed her into a socialist, the trusted fifteen-year friendship between the two women suddenly ended. The break was catastrophic and their closeness never re-established. Beatrice couldn't bring herself to name her cousin in her future memoirs and talked of 'an intimate friend' with whom she travelled in Bavaria and 'a friendly woman journalist' responsible for her introduction to Sidney.[331] Her cousin's name effectively disappeared from Beatrice's recorded history with an intent calculated to erase both memory and influence and Maggie became inconsequential to Beatrice's new life.

After the fracture of their relationship, Maggie launched a stinging attack on the failure of socialists to unite, pointing with regret to quarrelsome men. She argued the combination of 'John Burns's strong lungs and cheery presence, H.H. Champion's diplomatic skill, and Tom Mann's organizing genius' and their ability to unite had ensured success. At the same time, she condemned individualism and disunity of others, just as in *Captain Lobe* she had pointed to their 'petty jealousies'. Praising practical actions, she highlighted the Salvation Army's more immediate and everyday methods believing history would record them as the 'Slum Saviour'.[332] General Booth, who she saw prior to departure, was especially praised. Beatrice denounced her 'sensational article' and dismissed her condemnation of socialists as 'another treachery added to the long roll', a betrayal of old friends.

Over the years of her close association with Champion, Maggie received anonymous letters, many a vicious replay of the unrestrained fury to which Champion was subjected. The vitriol affected her deeply and wore her down. She complained she 'was accused of every imaginable sin'; the less vehement claims asserted 'she ought to be shot as a Tory spy and hung for taking money from Tories', with others speaking of 'vulgar intrigues' and 'disappointed ambition'.[333] Maggie laid out less obvious reasons for ongoing socialist censure in her pamphlet, *Imperial Credit*, claiming that because she was a middle-class female who preferred a writer's solitude, research and study to a battleground of public speeches and agitation, she attracted open hostility, suspicion and a questioning of her motives.

While platform women such as Eleanor Marx and Annie Besant were at the forefront of debate and regular speakers at street corners, demonstrations and halls, women like Maggie eschewed public speaking instead using either creative fiction or journalism as mediums for political impact. Tom Mann's memoirs mention 'opponents' in crowds frequently being 'disguised as friends' while any unknown voice in the crowd was able express an opinion, denigrate or provoke fights so that speakers were expected to deal with hecklers or offensive remarks. A form of street entertainment, often it was a difficult arena for all speakers but women speakers were subjected to particular criticism because of gender. As early as 1884 an article appeared in the *Nineteenth Century* on women who spoke in public on social and political reform and on philanthropic concerns, who wanted to be 'seen as well as heard'. According to this discourse, these modern women exhibited negative traits, a suppression of womanhood and an 'unnaturalness'.[334]

Vaughan Nash, assistant editor for the *Workman's Times*, former editor of a short-lived weekly newspaper the *Trade Unionist* and co-author of a Dock Strike account, helpfully fuelled Beatrice's distrust of Maggie. A couple of years earlier, on 19 November 1889, Beatrice had seen Tom Mann at Toynbee Hall speak about an eight-hour day and took an instant liking to him as 'absolutely straight, and a warm enthusiast'. Sensing Mann's reserve towards her early in 1891, Beatrice pointed this out to Nash who directed blame towards two culprits: 'He looks upon you as a schemer – a person with tin-pot schemes as he calls them – possibly it is your cousin Miss Harkness who has given him that idea'. Adding Champion to the mix, Nash insisted Burns and Mann had 'to live down the calumny and the treachery' and perfidy of Maggie and Champion, an opinion with which Beatrice agreed. In the aftermath of the Maritime Strike in Australia and with Fitzgerald's various London speeches sowing hatred of Champion, Beatrice tried to look objectively at Nash's statements that fuelled innuendo and suspicion. On 13 January 1891 Beatrice noted other people, such as Octavia Hill, Florence Nightingale and Annie Besant, had misgivings about her, and now it appeared Mann and Burns saw her as a manipulator.

She argued with surprising self-appraisal while still apportioning blame: '*There is always some foundation for a deeply graven impression* – despite traitors like Margaret Harkness'. Perhaps Octavia and Florence's qualms also flowed from Nash, for Florence Nightingale was his wife's aunt and a benefactor of Octavia's projects. In the blame-game John Burns also coupled Maggie and Beatrice with Nash in his diary on 26 April 1892: 'Mann is disenthused to a great extent.

The Laws, Nashs, Hollands and others have damaged the Tom Mann in him'.[335]

A series of articles on labour leaders throughout February 1891 had personal repercussions when Maggie wrote about Henry Broadhurst MP, a former stonemason, colleague of Sir John Brunner and secretary of the Parliamentary Committee on the Trade Union Council, who represented the old school of unionists. Despite Beatrice's appeal not to repeat the story, Maggie re-retold Beatrice's tale of Henry Broadhurst and Cunninghame Graham at breakfast during the Trade Union Congress in Dundee at the time of the Dock Strike.[336] Broadhurst endorsed the blatant use and disposal of socialist 'gentlemen' such as Champion and Graham, saying 'but directly we can do without gentlemen we shall chuck them up. We want no gentlemen amongst us'.[337] Mrs Humphry Ward's scene in *Marcella* depicted a Union official and Labour candidate Wilkins who views Harry's captivating 'youth, good looks, and easy breeding' while addressing a crowd and thinks: 'A day would soon come when the labour movement would be able to show these young aristocrats the door'. It was not the first time Maggie used personal information, with Beatrice affronted on 21 February 1889 over 'an unpardonable act' when Maggie divulged 'a silly story' about Herbert Spencer in the *British Weekly*.

> Probably we shall be firm friends again; for though I do not trust her, I love her and she loves me – we have the same troubles and the same difficulties, the same eternal struggle without result ... But in the nature of things it cannot be secure; and when the breach comes, it is all the more painful.

Using her knowledge of her friends – Champion, Burns, Mann and Cunninghame Graham – Maggie's series of intimate portraits on labour leaders for the *Pall Mall Gazette* were reprinted in many Australian newspapers and guaranteed much-needed income. Called 'a patrician' by John Burns, she emphasised Champion's bravery as shaped by military service, his reserve and efforts to 'declass' himself. Forcefully tackling the mantra 'no gentlemen' in the union movement, she pointed to speculation surrounding the demise of the *Labour*

Elector, 'a house divided against itself'. Maggie's character appraisal of Champion also quoted one of his favourite authors, Charles Kingsley. Frequently Champion used his words from *Letter to Ladies* in 'The World of Women' column. 'Here is a wrong. Right it!' was a concept that to Champion embodied honour, sacrifice and integrity. Maggie asserted:

> He has done his best to declass himself, but he remains what his forefathers made him – a soldier, brave and tender-hearted, a proud and very reticent man. When he was a boy he used to say, 'There is something wrong somewhere,' and after he became a man he tried to right that wrong by joining the Socialists ... gave up his position in the army, his relations and friends; in fact, he declassed himself. But it is one thing to become a Socialist because your class is oppressed, and another to throw in your lot with the oppressed because your class is the oppressor.[338]

As further evidence of Champion's integrity, she quoted Burns, 'the strongest man is he who stands alone' and repeated this again in *George Eastmont*. Maggie also portrayed Tom Mann's reaction after both he and Burns were strongly criticised by Champion following Fitzgerald's attack at Mile End: 'woe betide the man, or woman, who injures Mr. Mann's pride; for he will never forget the injury or forgive the culprit'. Champion's letter to the *Age* on 8 November 1890 pointed to lack of 'pluck' for taking an easy way out because Burns thought his telegram 'a hoax' and Mann said he was not authorised by the Dockers' Union. A successful movement was conducted by those 'who never sold the truth to serve the hour' was Champion's reply.[339] Maggie was the only person to defend Champion at Mile End when she sent a letter for Burns to read on the strike's origins.

Maggie finally arrived in Sydney in 1891, so plans had been made to rendezvous although she missed Champion by months. From Australia, she able to contribute a background piece to the *Aberdeen Journal* to help his election attempt, presenting him again as a 'patrician' who tried to 'declass' himself and including Broadhurst's claim, 'directly we can do without gentlemen we shall chuck them up'.[340]

While in Sydney Maggie stayed on the harbour foreshore at Watson's Bay at 'The Bungalow' with English-born mariner, Captain Andrew William Jack, a Port Jackson pilot. His son, Leslie Jack, worked for the Sydney *Evening News* and his youngest daughter Vera later married Edward Burns Harkness, first private secretary to Sir John See and later Premier Carruther. Maggie gained plenty of source material for her novel, *George Eastmont*, visiting the Premier, Sir Henry Parkes, at his Hampden Villa residence in Balmain which overlooked the bay, his magnificent garden populated with pet wallabies and kangaroos. Her scenes were quite remarkable for capturing the mood in Sydney in the middle of an election, the Shearers' Strike and with the New Australia Movement gathering momentum.

William Lane, who was editor of the *Worker*, drew his journalistic pseudonym from 'John Miller' in William Morris's novel *A Dream of John Ball* (1887) and was working on his novel *The Workingman's Paradise* (1892). Champion had gone to Australia 'to study Labour Questions in the Workman's Paradise', so Maggie was well aware of Lane's novel that sought to explain socialism and unionism. According to Herbert Brookes who heard Lane speak in country Queensland, he was 'a sincere enthusiast and idealist who was consumed with the desire to assist in the uplift of his fellow men and women'. Lane's planning process for a socialist settlement in South America commenced with the appointment of Alfred Walker for discussions with governments while he purchased the ship, *Royal Tar*, to transport colonists to a new settlement.

Based on Champion, Maggie's novel about a labour leader included one of earliest attempts to draw attention to the newly emerging Utopia of the New Australia Movement and used Sydney's Domain for George's meeting with a shearer bound for the 'experiment' (pp. 193–95). Maggie's alter ego's name, Miss Mary Cameron, was derived from writer Mary Gilmore (née Cameron) who joined Lane's colony in Paraguay, married another settler and later became a journalist for the *Worker*. At one stage, Maggie even talked in an interview about travelling to New Australia in South America.[341] Champion's previous experience with the Fellowship of New Life in England left him with little faith in Utopian movements and he refused to applaud Lane's experiment. In typical straightforward argument, he noted that the New Australia attempt was an 'ill-advised, ill-placed, and ill-managed attempt to found a Communist Colony in Paraguay', calling it 'doomed to failure from the first', although not because of socialist or communist reasons.[342]

On a world tour to discuss colonisation movements, Maggie's much admired General Booth had attended a large reception in Sydney at which Henry Parkes presided. The occasion was the Salvation Army's celebration of seven years in Australia. Rumours now abounded in London that John Law was a member of the Salvation Army and in a letter addressed from the Fleet Street *Daily News*, Maggie clearly dismissed this religious conversion.[343] However, the idea was still a source of gossip, with one London columnist telling Australians: 'I fancy she had finally joined the Salvation Army'.[344] Interviewed on board ship before his departure to New Zealand, Booth complained that NSW labour and especially J.D. Fitzgerald, misrepresented his labour settlements proposal to tackle East End misery.[345] Champion had praised Booth's practical efforts but believed that 'until the causes which create that widespread destitution are removed, the reserve army of labor will find recruits to fill every place vacated by the people rescued from degrading conditions'.[346]

Maggie's one-year review presented her sea journey to Australia as one of calm optimism rather than despair and told readers that she learned from 'the sea and the stars', nature's animating force. Her trip allowed time for reflection on the aftermath of the Dock Strike, the rise of new trades unionists and hopes for a labour party although there still remained the unemployed and unskilled in the East End now approaching a crisis level of 30,000. She also continued to express disappointment with personal attacks, denunciation and in-fighting of socialists.[347]

Meanwhile, hearing nothing from her cousin, Beatrice claimed on 27 December 1891, almost with a sense of relief, her family connection was severed:

> Margaret Harkness has finally disappeared: her strange ways, deliberate lying, mysterious financial positions have killed all respect

on my side. Gradually I began to doubt the truth of her accusations, presently I became aware of a certain sordid side to her manoeuvrings which cut at the root of affection, and confidence – so I allowed her in a fit of pique and envy to cut the tie that bound us together. It is a sad ending to an old friendship.

In fact, Maggie had returned to London before Christmas. Sidney Webb informed Beatrice of Maggie's serial 'Roses and Crucifix'[348] in the very paper where Champion wrote under his old *Justice* newspaper pseudonym of 'Diogenes', a 'crusty old bachelor' living alone and visiting relatives for Christmas chaos. Maggie was also visible in January as she reported on Cardinal Manning's death and his final request to arrange a meeting with Charles Booth.

Shortly after the death of her father, Beatrice and Sidney were engaged. In what seemed to be a replay of Champion's own desire for credibility as one of 'the People', Beatrice recorded her conversion to a working woman through marriage. The man who wore a shabby 'bourgeois black coat shiny with wear' to dinner with her and the Booths, her 'retail tradesman with the aims of a Napoleon!', as she called him on 26 April 1890, was now Beatrice's catalyst for social transformation. Using a school-text phrase from Dr Peter Roget's Bridgewater Treatise, she noted on 21 January 1892: 'And now the old life is over – or rather the old *shell* is cast off and a new one adopted'. By throwing off her trappings of wealth she assumed her 'place as a worker and a help-mate of a worker – one of a very modest couple living in a small way'. She would initially 'suffer', she thought, because of her 'step downwards in the social scale' and because she defied social and family expectations. Herbert Spencer's literary executorship was lost to her although she gained entrée to an exciting political life of the Fabians, which included a fascinating friendship with Bernard Shaw. The London columnist who reported gossip on Champion and Maggie for the *Argus* had also obtained from an SDF friend news of Beatrice's engagement and of her inheritance of £40–50,000.[349]

Although Maggie returned to London prior to Christmas, she was not invited to their wedding ceremony at St Pancras Vestry Hall registry on 23 July. The strong-willed and intelligent cousin who originally chose an unmarried life had backflipped. As an olive branch, Maggie posted one issue of her *Novel Review* to Sidney Webb which failed to re-establish connections. Sidney didn't think much of the magazine and believed it lacked anything of importance to either of them, was of low quality and destined to have a short lifespan.[350] Maggie was a 'Lady correspondent' writing to the *Pall Mall Gazette* the day after their marriage who was intimately acquainted with Beatrice's career, her new husband's background and three visionary socialists, Edward Carpenter, Olive Schreiner and John Barlas. There were obvious tensions in her letter as she vacillated between praise for Beatrice's work, overt criticism of her detailed economic philosophising on labour issues, and the fact she held the same opinions as her future husband.[351] Beatrice's union brought no great romantic passion. Her life was a dedicated, analytical one that saw Sidney Webb's political rise and, like her two sisters, her husband would be made a peer of the realm. Together she and Sidney founded the London School of Economics in 1895 with a bequest from Henry Hutchinson, a Fabian lawyer, and the couple achieved a full and successful public life with honours bestowed on Sidney as Baron Passfield.

When Sidney and Beatrice came to Adelaide in November 1898, she and Maggie didn't meet and, after Sidney delivered 'Some Impressions on Australasia' back in England, Maggie found 'inexcusable' his '*reductio ad absurdum* of Australasian politics in general, and South Australian politics in particular'. Champion's friend and benefactor, Herbert Brookes, invited them to visit his alluvial mines at Allendale near Creswick and found Sidney 'a quiet, meek little man' and his wife a dominant partner who lawyer-like cross-examined Brookes about the operations and informed him she was private secretary to Herbert Spencer for several years before 'he dispensed with her services' because of her socialism.[352]

On return to London, both Maggie and Champion were engaged in editorial work. Champion was snapped up early by James Knowles for a position as his assistant editor on the prestigious journal *Nineteenth Century*. New editions of Maggie's two books (*A City Girl* and *Captain Lobe*) were re-released by the Authors' Co-operative Publishing Company who had also published *A Manchester Shirtmaker*.

They were new proprietors of *Tinsley's* Magazine which they renamed the *Novel Review* and appointed Maggie editor in February 1892. The journal had a short life and ceased publication at the end of the year. Maggie was forced to source additional money from contributions to other papers and so, as John Law, she enthused on old Egyptian and Assyrian research interests, writing on Egyptian clay tablets from Tel-el-Amarna held in the British Museum, while a more political tone was added by 'An Anarchist's Funeral'.[353] The latter article focused on Charles Mowbray's arrest in front of his distraught children, only four hours after his wife's death, with mourners calling for Annie Besant, Mrs Schack and Louise Michel to be contacted for assistance, and bail provided by William Morris.

As Maggie sought writers for the *Novel Review*, Champion warmly encouraged friends to help in creative ways and they rallied behind Maggie in a generous and supportive effort. Shaw was one of the first, writing a quirky and frank recollection about his early writing and returning Maggie's cheque for the article because he didn't think the review was making money at this stage. Champion commissioned Morley Roberts to write on his friend, George Gissing, while the actor Raymond Blathwayt interviewed Morley at his rooms in Bloomsbury. John Barlas wrote a beautiful sonnet 'The Flute' and an article in praise of his close friend Oscar Wilde while Maggie (as John Law) wrote of Olive Schreiner who felt England was a birdcage and Europe 'a bandbox'. The *Novel Review* folded in December 1892 at the time Champion smashed his knee-cap and not much is known of how Maggie spent 1893 while he and Frost travelled on the continent. She turned to other avenues for income and wrote a serial story about a pregnant woman ('Connie') using the name of her younger sister, with her last chapter for Maltman Barry's *Labour Elector* in December 1893 published alongside Champion's 'An Aberdeenshire Poet'.

Champion had again sailed to Australia to meet Morley and his lover in Melbourne, leaving London on the *Orient* on 23 February 1894, while Maggie departed for Sydney. In their absence Mrs Humphry Ward's *Marcella* (1894) and Clementina Black's *An Agitator* (1894) were released documenting recent historical events involving the pair. Socialism had become 'a vogue in the drawing-rooms' after the London Dock Strike and Champion was one of the faces of this now 'fashionable fad'.[354] *Marcella* was reviewed early in April 1894 and quickly went to a third edition within weeks when discussion raged throughout England, America and Australia about the thinly masked personalities. Readers were quick to recognise Champion, 'the once petted demagogue', as 'the Radical candidate' Harry Wharton who 'was far too well dressed and too well educated', Henry Broadhurst as Wilkins and Thomas Burt MP as Bennett.

The heroine was loosely based on Maggie and one reviewer recognised her in the character and labelled Maggie a 'patron saint of the dockers and guardian angel of the Labour elector'.[355] Marcella Boyce attends a 'school for young ladies' until she is 21, lives in a boarding-house, is a member of the Venturist Society (clearly the Fabians) which examined philanthropic and social problems, and works as a rent-collector in the East End, finding purpose by reading articles in addition to 'blue-books on Sweating and Overcrowding'. She leads a Bohemian life for two and a half years, trains in a hospital, finds work as a nurse amongst the sick and poor of London's slums and helps to organise a union for female shirt seamstresses. In details, Marcella was obviously an amalgamation of Maggie and Beatrice.

Harry is rendered as a gentleman 'of birth and power', a 'Socialist aristocrat' of the 'People' and 'Chevalier des Grieux', the latter referring to a French novel about a nobleman who gives up hereditary wealth. Ward provides a picture of a 'very brilliant and gifted' man with 'great eloquence and ability' whose 'manners [are] perfect'. With family ties to Scottish nobles, the first book mentions he is 'a connection of the Levens, and used to be always there in old days'. The Urquharts were related to the Scottish Leslies of Wardis and Leven, ancestors of the Earl of Aberdeen, Leslie was the middle name of one of Champion's sisters and he used 'Leslie Orde' as a pseudonym; the Earl's Glenferness House near Nairn was purchased in 1869.

Harry is proprietor of the *Labour Clarion* purchased with 'a small legacy' from a relative, a reference to the *Labour Elector*. Friends, relations and class have repudiated Harry because of his advocacy for workers and for an eight-hour day. As 'an outcast' he explains: 'I have not a relation or an old friend in the world that has not turned his back on me ... My class has renounced me already'. At the conclusion of Book III rumours circulate of a 'bribe' paid to Harry by employers for his newspaper to end its support for the strike. Champion's contemporaries also saw Harry's mother as inspired by women's suffrage activist, Countess of Carlisle (Rosalind Howard). She and her husband were close friends of William Morris, their residences at Castle Howard in Yorkshire, Castle Naworth in Cumberland and Kensington decorated with Morris's wallpaper designs; Bernard Shaw later used the Countess as an inspiration for Lady Britomart and Maggie for his Salvation Army character in *Major Barbara.*

Marcella reappeared in Ward's next book, *Sir George Tressady* (1896) also serialised in *Century Magazine*. Under the pseudonym, F.F. Juvat (Fortes Fortuna Juvat or 'Fortune favours the brave'), Champion pointed to Ward's earnings of £10,000 per book and believed the author's focus on contemporary issues in politics assisted the novel to maintain currency when 'interest and the excitement faded about finding points of resemblance between the characters and real personages'. Even so, he identified several, Randolph Churchill, George Curzon, the Countess of Aberdeen, Margot Asquith and Arnold Toynbee. He drew specific attention to Ward's bloodline through her famous uncle Matthew Arnold and the inevitable intellectual constraint behind her presentation of political difference or 'the great questions'. Arguing that Ward held herself back from sufficient emotional engagement with socialism in an English setting, he nonetheless added: 'Mrs. Ward has been to some extent converted by her own creation and by the patient researches she has had to make, in the collection of her material'. According to Champion, her inquiry generated an inherent, noticeable and laudable compassion for the disadvantaged in England, both in the reader and author.[356]

Clementina Black's *An Agitator* was set a few years after the Trafalgar Square Riots and the death of Champion's wife. Champion was close to Clementina, and one of her 'old friends' specifically thanked for his input to her book on anti-sweating. Her novel had characters who were 'professional agitators', Kit Brand ('a firebrand') and engineer, Dick Harris, clear representations of Champion and Burns respectively.

The name Brand was also Clementina's nod to Ibsen's play

Brand, playing at the Opera Comique in Westminster in 1893 after the Bradford ILP Conference. Clementina's disclaimer, preceding the title page, tried to direct attention away from the identification of individuals: 'It may perhaps save a little time and ink, both to my reviewers and myself, if I say plainly beforehand that these pages contain no portrait of any person whatever'.

In one interview, she spoke of her novel as an imaginative rendering and insisted she had battled any urge to use real characters.[357] These comments were obviously made to eliminate gossip surrounding the characters' identities although it did not stop recognition by reviewers and readers.

Indeed, Clementina's reviewers saw 'a startling resemblance' between her central character and a labour figure who intrigued many in London.[358] Certainly, Kit Brand separates from an older group of 'unpractical' socialists based at Cinderbridge (SDF meetings were at Bridge Street). He shows traits of an 'aristocrat' and 'a born leader' and is 'different' from the workers he wants to help. To his dismay, his 'aloofness' makes him an outsider, not one of the 'masses'. Distanced even from 'comrades', he sees Harris gaining 'affection and confidence from whole groups of men who doubted and mistrusted himself'. Kit is 'a very able and scrupulously honourable man' who subsequently decides 'to stand alone' as an independent candidate for labour issues. Threatened with prison over defending 'the right of free assembly' his defence without legal training gains an acquittal.

In *An Agitator*, attendees at a Russell Square Socialist Society (Fabian) meeting include a devotee of Dr Jaeger's ideas of woollen clothing (Shaw) and a woman of 'the most revolutionary views on all social subject, especially marriage' (Annie Besant). The society's motto, *Festina lente* (make haste slowly), is a nod to the Fabian belief in incremental change, although Kit complains they are 'mere parlour socialists' who, in military terms, 'want to take the citadel without fighting for it'. One intriguing cameo not pursued in any detail is Miss Mayne, with her auburn hair and 'starry eyes' that are 'beautiful blue-grey', who chooses to sit 'in the remotest corner of the tea-room'. She makes a brief appearance at a socialist meeting and there is speculation she very much desires an introduction to Kit. Later Miss Mayne is seen as an enthusiastic election worker but remains a peripheral character who is never fleshed out and fades into the background. Perhaps Clementina deleted sections after gossip about Maggie's visit to the rooms of a 'very fascinating and magnetic' Champion began circulating in London.

Having escaped London chatter associated with their fictional appearance, Champion and Maggie were now in different cities of Australia. Maggie arrived well before the *Royal Tar* departed for Paraguay with its second Australian contingent. She visited a cooperative village outside of Sydney at Pitt Town where she spent a few weeks in late February and March 1894. While working as a correspondent for the London *Daily News, Fortnightly Review* and *Westminster Gazette*, she wrote an article on Pitt Town's labour settlement in August for the *Fortnightly Review* which showed a desire for collective social harmony, obviously at odds with a reality experienced by some participants. The visit to the settlement was also given an imaginative interpretation at the conclusion of *George Eastmont* where she appropriated her own experiences.

An English woman working in a Sydney newspaper office committed suicide on 21 April 1894 and Maggie had recently met her. In her early thirties, Alice Caroline Moon, daughter of a Brighton doctor, wrote weekly literary columns for the *Daily Telegraph*. After an autopsy Alice was buried in a gravesite she had located before her death. The site overlooked the ocean at South Head Cemetery in Vaucluse where she often walked. Her salary had recently been cut because of belt tightening at the paper so she was unable to save enough to return to England after the death of her invalid brother. This memory stayed with Maggie and she later recalled the tragedy in the *West Australian*:

> "'Don't leave me today,' she pleaded. 'Don't leave me by myself.' But I did not understand, and I left her alone in the office. The next morning, her sudden death was announced in the newspapers. I hurried to her boarding-house. At the door I met the doctor, and I asked, 'How did she do it?' 'How came you to guess?' he demanded. There was an inquest, and snake-poisoning (she had been experimenting with

the poison of snakes) was brought in "disease of the heart." I went to her funeral, and saw her laid to rest in a little graveyard beside the Pacific. The proprietors of the paper were there; also some men who had loved her, but whom she had not cared about. I blame myself yet for having left her alone that day; but she was almost a stranger to me, and I had been in Australia then only a few weeks'.[359]

After Alice's death and for a brief time, Maggie appears to have written Alice's column 'Literature: Books up to Date', following her own reading interests, particularly 'Pictures of the Socialistic Future', the Webb's history of trade unionism, and Olive Schreiner's work. When Annie Besant arrived in September at the Opera House to lecture on theosophy as a religion, philosophy and science, she was in conversation on arrival and departure with a *Daily Telegraph* representative who was probably Maggie.

Not long after, Maggie made a decision to leave Sydney, travel to Melbourne and see Champion. From there she visited the Victorian Mallee district where she was taken to see the body of another Anglo-Australian suicide, a boy in farm service who swallowed rabbit poison. Towards Christmas she was hosted in Ballarat by the 'handsome' Theodore Stretch, Archdeacon of Melbourne, Geelong and the Ballarat goldfields whose daughter Mrs William Rowe ran the Glenfine sheep station. Her trip to the gold-mines was probably inspired both by Champion's talk of Walhalla miners and by Stretch's experience in the region because by December she was speaking with miners at Creswick. This rural town was the birthplace of five Lindsay children (Percy, Lionel, Norman, Ruby and Daryl) and close to where Herbert Brookes managed mines.

In search of characters, setting and motivation, it is possible that Maggie's interest in Western Australia was piqued by Henry Parkes noting several 'titled members of the English aristocracy' living on the goldfields.[360] Aristocratic outcasts and black sheep finding refuge in anonymity featured in many Western Australian articles, one pointing to a camp exploring for gold with a Viscount working as cook, along with younger sons of dukes.[361] By mid-1895 Maggie was ensconced in the west and sufficiently attuned to Coolgardie to write about the town for *Cosmos*. Typhoid was rampant and a constant presence in the fiction she wrote about the goldfields. Caused by contaminated water and unsanitary conditions, medical treatment was administered in hospital tents and fever could last up to three months, 'followed in many cases by severe rheumatism in hands and feet' or burial in the 'red earth' in 'a lonely spot' out of town.[362] Maggie's free time in the west was spent writing a newspaper serial dealing with death and murder on the goldfields, 'Called to the Bar'. This title cleverly used a metaphor for the crossing between life and death from Tennyson's poem and was an allusion to barmaids, drinkers as well as the divide between western and eastern Australia.

A nine-day visit to these goldfields in October 1895 by Champion's old friend, Michael Davitt, leader of the Irish Land League and now a member of parliament, provided a glimpse into the arduous journey Maggie faced getting to an outback mining area. Davitt reported in his *Life and Progress in Australasia* (1898) that the journey from Perth to Coolgardie took three days and was 360 miles by rail and then coach, with blazing sun and bush flies in abundance. Maggie compared these offensive clouds of flies, drowning in miners' tea or attaching themselves to bread and jam, to an Egyptian plague. Describing January in summer, she provided a raw but breathtaking picture of the outback town that

> palpitates under the hot sun at eight o'clock in the morning; by twelve it will swelter beneath vertical rays of molten sunshine, between five and six – when the sun sinks in a glory of gold and purple behind the banks of eucalyptus – a quiver of relief will be felt … The wind has risen, and is sweeping clouds of dust before it. In the distance willy-willies, like the ghosts of snakes and serpents, writhe on the ground or wriggle upwards – spiteful, destructive, mischievous. The sky is streaked with soft, white cloudlets that in any other place but Western Australia would presage rain; here they only tell of coming dust-storms and dangerous willy-willies.[363]

Her images are of a multi-racial population drawn from local indigenous people and settlers from Germany, India, Afghanistan and Japan, reflected through the eyes of an English woman. One of the first female accounts of a strange, foreign and unfamiliar Western Australia during the goldrush of the Roaring Nineties, it is a record of historical significance.

Maggie's own experiences ran parallel to those of her main character Violet who is shown as a wistful alter-ego of the author. Violet's features are described as 'too small and sharp', her 'tender' mouth showing 'wilfulness' and an 'almost childlike, wholly pathetic expression'; the description matches the only known drawing of Maggie in the English magazine *Queen*. Violet leaves 'a certain little room where she tasted the elixir of London life, and drained the cup of domestic unhappiness' to escape to Australia and finds a place filled with canvas structures. She initially lives in a tent fixed to the ground with string, lying on a bed constructed of sacks on poles and secured in place by wooden logs. This is an isolated place where many miners lack identity, except as generic 'diggers' who are considered merely 'a pair of hands and a stomach' by goldfield folk. During the rush to make a quick fortune it is where miners 'left their bones in the sand, through thirst, fever, and sunstroke'. 'Alone' is the tragic epitaph on their graves.

The grim realism of her writing depicts the monotony, tedium and hardship of life on the goldfields, the xenophobia (with an archetypal Jewish villain), the fear of suffering unwanted male attention and 'disgusting language' from men in a land where few women ventured at that time. As Violet explains: 'A goldfield is meant for men; and women are *de trop* upon it. No man who cares for his wife will subject her to its danger and discomforts, much less bring his children to a place given over to fever and malaria'. This leaves a disparate group of women divided by their occupations as barmaids and nurses. As time passes, some are transformed into drinkers or 'champagne ladies' who 'graduated at the bar, that is to say they were barmaids' before marriage. Her aversion to nursing, naturally formed by her own youthful experience, is apparent in stories of government nurses who care for the sick in hospital tents where a miner's death invokes a search for gold stitched into men's clothing and the question: 'How much did he leave, and where is it?'.

Maggie named her imaginary goldfield town Fiery Cross after one of the papers Champion ran in Aberdeen to support his political ambitions, the name chosen because the Scottish Highlanders' Crann Tara (or burning cross) was used to summon clans to battle. Obviously referring to the real mining town of Southern Cross it was a place featured later in Katharine Susannah Prichard's Western Australian goldfield's novel, *The Roaring Nineties* (1946). A socialist character in her first chapter is known as Oram the Democrat, 'a man of the stars and gutters' which is an allusion to Oscar Wilde's oft-quoted line from *Lady Windermere's Fan*: 'we are all in the gutter, but some of us are looking at the stars'. The harsh reality of life on the goldfields is therefore contrasted with a dream of a higher vision or purpose, with stars dividing the old world (England) and the new world (Australia).

Maggie also used Champion to shape her major character Bertram Ore, cognisant of his pseudonym, 'Leslie Orde', his ironic reference to 'Tory gold'. Champion's Norman-French ancestry was detailed as part of her description: 'There is no mistaking the man's station in life, it is stamped on him as indelibly as the broad arrow on a convict; he is an English gentleman, not of three generations or six, but of the Norman Conquest'. Her character Violet was also shaped by Maggie's youthful desire for independence: 'I remember the time when my prayer would have been for change and excitement'. She reflected her early sentiments: 'She knows that no other woman of her sex would have had the courage to break away from society'. However, after Violet has 'smashed her own shell, and stamped on it', she is touchingly nostalgic: 'Oh, to get back to one's environment, to the shell that was given one as a child, to the cradle that grew to one's back. Do the new women ever think of it?'. Beatrice's reference to her old shell cast off through marriage was common to their student experience when studying natural history and Roget's observations. Beatrice may have cast off her shell to assume a new one but Maggie destroyed hers and was still mourning its loss.

Under a new name, Marguerite, Maggie opened her typewriting office in Coolgardie and began advertising on 28 September 1895. She also threw herself in the town's festivities helping to prepare a Christmas dinner for about 60 Coolgardie aboriginal people at St

Andrew's Hall while another 500 people lined up outside of the Post Office waiting to claim at least one of the 8,000 Christmas letters and 25,000 newspapers.364 She moved her typing business to 9 Imperial Chambers in Hunt Street and six months later expanded to 2 Bayley Chambers in Bayley Street where she prepared share and scrip forms, prospectuses and foreign correspondence for people in the mining industry, promising her clients complete privacy and referees. General information on the goldfields was supplied to Champion for his columns 'The Age of Gilt' and 'The Golden Fleece' and for Jerome K. Jerome's *To-Day* reports on Great Boulder and other mines. Her introduction to *Imperial Credit* (1899) details this period:

> I was intimately connected for more than a year with a large circle of English, French, German, and Russian speculators and company promoters ... I cannot say where I knew these gentlemen, for to do so might give them annoyance, and to hurt of the feelings of those from whom one has received nothing but kindness would be a bêtise. They were exploiting a place for the money market, and were all connected in one way or another with the Money Ring in London (p. 38).

Maggie had been forced by time and expense to become familiar and competent with a typewriter in London when many in her circle were embracing new technology to make journalism and writing easier and quicker. Advertisements promoted 'Prints like a Press', shorthand and typing courses while Jerome's *To-Day* promoted North's and Williams typewriters. Shorthand classes were readily available and advertised for socialists in the *Commonweal* in December 1887, while Henry Sweet's new book, *Current Shorthand* was popular. When Alice Hamlyn married Morley Roberts, she typed as he dictated to shorten the overall process from imaginative invention to manuscript and he completed a story in one sitting with little revision. Most of Eleanor Marx's business letters and reports were produced on her new typewriter and in 'Sweating in Type-Writing Offices' she discussed the intense pressure of work that was far longer than eight hours a day.365 Clementina Black's essay suggested unions seek a remedy for the common practice of starting typists on nominal salaries only to sack them and employ another learner to save money. As editor of *Book Lover* Champion complained 'it is a cruelty to ask people in these busy days to read hand writing' and he also carried advertisements for typewriters.[366]

Maggie's typing skills were vital for her new occupation and with the expansion of her business she needed typists and shorthand experts. As a result, Champion arranged for an advertisement in his newspaper for someone to share her 'lucrative' Coolgardie typewriting business for £300. In fact, a few months later her offer was accepted and then declined by Miss Florence Bingham who had been the owner of a Sydney typing business. She sued Maggie 'as the takings were not up to her expectations' and wanted the return of her initial payment of £25. Argued by the parties to be a deposit during negotiations for the establishment of a branch office versus rental for Maggie's house in the settlement of Montana, Bingham failed in her law suit, and a new person instead took over her typing practice.[367]

Armed with new schemes, Maggie and Mrs O'Kelly opened a 'residential club' in Montana. This club consisted of a group of detached light-framed buildings made of sacks that provided miners with the choice of furnished, green, lined and floored tents called 'hessian tenements', purchased from the government and sold for a guinea each. Workers with resources could procure bedspreads made of opossum and linoleum or Turkish rugs to cover their floors and the club also offered miners a cooked breakfast, games and current newspapers. Less than six months after Maggie established her club, a fire broke out on New Year's Day.[368] The uninsured club was totally destroyed and her practical attempt to help mine workers was at an end. The fire had begun at 3 o'clock in the afternoon and took people by surprise because of its intensity and speed. There was no water close at hand in a region where water cost sixpence a gallon and beer or lemonade were cheaper options and when the local fire brigade arrived nothing was left but smoking ash. Fire was a frequent occurrence in mining towns, whether deliberately lit because of personal grievances or merely accidents from cooking, smoking or using candles. Flames were quick to ignite and spread through the makeshift sites. Improvised fire buckets were, like the mining buckets on windlasses, made of animal hide and Maggie recalled haunting images:

> ... the wild fears of the women, the suppressed excitement of the men, the emptying of offices, the piling up of things in the street, the hacking down of walls, the hoarse shouts and foolish orders, the wild demands and mad requests, the seething, joking sightseers, and the dispassionate police.[369]

Ironically, only six months after watching her business burn to the ground, Maggie was called as a witness in an attempted arson at a neighbour's house while she shared a home with Mary Bradley at 2 Toorak Terrace, Coolgardie. An investigation reported that an incendiary device in a simple tin packed with hessian and a lit candle was employed.[370]

As early as 26 October 1896 Champion had told Morley, 'if I was a wise man I should clear off to Western Australia ... But I can't just because I can't do without the sight of her' [Adelaide]. With his liaison rapidly winding down, Champion sailed to Freemantle two months later on 19 December, just prior to Maggie's devastating fire at Montana, while his newspaper continued without obvious pause. Only a few papers on the goldfields noticed his short visit undertaken as an 'advocate of the claims of labor'. One local newspaper saw a 'political freelance' who hadn't 'caught on' with members of the Trades' Hall at a time when John Forrest and John Winthrop Hackett (father of General Sir John Hackett) were being assessed as political delegates for the Federal Convention. 'Champion was said to despair of catching on in Melbourne' and thought 'to move West', another announced.[371]

By the end of January Champion was back in his office after travelling to 'places where no men, or few, abide', a reference to small outback settlements and coastal districts.[372] His return by sea was described using a satirical pen-name taken from a Scottish medieval philosopher 'Duns Scotus'. Knowledge gained from his visit allowed Champion, as a Melbourne SDF founder and secretary, to organise John Lane's 1901 schedule of visits with Thomas G. Taylor, an SDF member who had firm ties to the Coastal Trades and Labour Council.

John Lane, brother of William Lane, was recruiting people from the goldfields and the south-west district who were interested in Cosme, a breakaway colony of the New Australia movement. Champion advised him to visit the area around Cape Leeuwin, an untamed and beautiful region he admired as 'the original site for the Garden of Eden', though Lane reported the trees had grown too dense to proceed.373

As Maggie readied her goldfield's serial for publication in the *Western Mail* her chapter on 13 August 1897 described the pain of losing a close friend: 'a resurrected friendship is phoenix; one has its ashes always before one's eyes, one remembers all the pain of its cremation'. This beautifully crafted image had its roots in a prior decade when she made a decision to never again see Champion. Her character Violet talks about the 'cruel irony, a refined torture, in our having been thrown here together' although she 'would not for all the world have missed this friendship'.374 Now a woman in her early forties who was starting again, Maggie took temporary work as Mary Jane Harkness. She was remembered by a Perth journalist as the woman who ran 'a bob-a-knob' lodging house, a female journalist, and a worker in a pie shop in Piesse Street in Boulder.375

A couple of months after the serial's conclusion, Maggie was in Adelaide and her departure from the west could only have been a relief. She called the goldfields 'a land of sand, sin, and sorrow' both in her letter to the *Champion* and her serial the following year. 'Those who come here are stamped for life, no one leaves the field the better in character for its experiences', her serial warned, with the goldfields a symbolic construct of 'an octopus, drawing into its maw good, bad and indifferent'.376 She started a new novel about cycling, her keen interest generated by Champion's obvious excitement and enthusiasm about a competition for the best report of a cycling tour. Champion bemoaned the 'disappointing' entries he received: 'Either those who ride bicycles have not much literary talent, or those who have the writing talent are too busy riding bicycles to display it'. As there were cycling enthusiasts and racing clubs on the goldfields such as one joined by the Duchess of Newcastle's brother, Maggie developed a 'knowledge of everything pertaining to those who cycle'.377

The invention of the Dunlop pneumatic tyre changed both ease and range of social interaction and a bicycle factory opened in April 1896 near Prince's Bridge. The factory offered riding instruction, storage, a bike mechanic, and membership of a new cycling club. Demand was so great the Carbine and Collier Two Speed Company bought them out while a history of their expansion (with photos) was told in the *Champion*. With great passion Champion wrote about the 'cycling craze' consuming London and Paris with bikes well-priced at £30. Beatrice and Sidney Webb bought three bicycles while John Burns conducted bicycle interviews around Battersea for such papers like the *Guardian*. A bold new comfortable cycling attire was invented with the *Champion* focused on 'wheelwomen' wearing 'knickers', a 'divided skirt' or 'trarsers [sic]' to cycle on lanes that wreaked havoc with old fashioned attitudes; an illustration showed three straps on both sides of the cycling skirt forming a modesty 'apron'; when rebuttoned it was transformed into a walking dress.[378]

In Adelaide, Maggie published *Imperial Credit* (1899), a political tract printed by Vardon and Prichard of Hindley Street, part of the Co-operative Printing and Publishing Company. In the book she farewelled the Labour Movement for 'other work' and became a journalist for eighteen months on the Adelaide weekly trade union magazine, *The Herald: The Official Organ of the Trades and Labor Council, United Labor Party, and Democratic Societies of S.A*. Another journalist uncovered Maggie's involvement in the Docker's Strike and her time in Coolgardie and Adelaide:

> After visiting all parts she settled at Coolgardie, investing her savings in an uninsured Travellers' Rest, which was completely destroyed by fire. When Mr. Wedd resigned the editorship of the Herald, the committee of the paper was asked to appoint the lady to the office, but in a spirit of half-informed democracy they declined to employ women labor! Mr. Roberts took the position and offered her a portion of his salary to become a contributor. She accepted the terms, and though Messrs. Batchelor and Robinson conjointly now fill the chief chair, she continues to do the bulk of the writing. According to my informant Miss Harkness is exceedingly well connected and possesses very great ability, but she suffers from the prejudice of sex,

which seems destined never to be killed, or scotched, even in the enlightened circles of advanced liberals.[379]

In response eight days later, management claimed Maggie was asked to be editor but 'declined absolutely' and that she should have been consulted before open discussion of her 'private business'. In fact, she was happy to be a contributor under three different editors over her time at the newspaper where she wrote numerous items for columns such as 'Passing Notes' (a prelude to 'Passing Hour' in the *West Australian*). She wrote short pieces on the Independent Labour Party, as well as old labour friends such as Mann, Tillett, Hardie, Cunninghame Graham, and also William Lane who had recently returned from Paraguay. 'Western Australian Notes' were written by the 'The Wanderer' and her British Museum experience was drawn upon for her column 'This and That' by 'Ra'. She was still in touch with Champion and used information from him to write 'Our Melbourne Letter'.

Maggie also reflected on the loneliness of an Anglo Australian, equating a new arrival with 'amphibious animals, animals snubbed and misrepresented because misunderstood. So we draw into our shells, and being outsiders, we see more of what is going on than do the Australians'. Wondering whether a Federation could create a unified nation, she wrote:

> We worship the constant sunshine, the royal blue sky, the lovely, if scentless, flowers, the gorgeous birds, butterflies, and insects. The big yellow moon, the stars that turn night into day, even the crepitating frogs win our hearts, while the grand scale on which Nature shows herself to us here, expands our intellect, England, dear little England, is very dreary and dark, is very like a bandbox. Our places there are filling up, our relations and friends are gaining new interests. Those thoughts act and counteract upon us; and just as English flowers transplanted here, gradually change their form and color [sic], so do we slowly become Australian.[380]

As an outsider, Maggie was attracted to Australia but not fond of the people escaping from or in search of something elusive. Two weeks later she wrote sad snippets about unhappy people caught between two worlds in 'Some Anglo-Australians I Have Met'.[381] She questioned: 'Why should disappointed men like [Adam Lindsay] Gordon and Francis Adams have carried Weltselimerz [melancholy] into the land of the sun and the golden wattle?'. One tragic cameo centred on the son of an overbearing nobleman who ran away at an early age and found his way to the goldfields as a cook in a miner's camp. He often came to the hotel where she stayed and she saw his lack of a toothbrush, an item thought to be a precaution against typhoid on the goldfields. When he received an inheritance on his father's death, he asked her to join him in England, a tale that may relate to her poem 'Ideals' about a man who 'offered his title and fame'.[382] Returning to the west briefly to examine attitudes about Federation in 1900 Maggie produced articles such as 'The Westralian "Uitlanders"' for London's *Daily News* capturing the mood of the goldfields as 'a curious haggis of hopes and fears, of bluff and menace'. She also filed interviews with the Premier, Sir John Forrest, about the separation movement.[383]

During her sea voyage home to England Maggie finished *George Eastmont* and Australian newspapers reviewed the novel in May and June 1905. Commenced in 1890 immediately after the London Dock Strike, she put it aside for fifteen years and now it was framed almost as a farewell tribute to Champion. Her disappointment with Champion's new marriage effectively transformed her vulnerable female character, Miss Mary Cameron, into a cipher, as Maggie swung between her position as an author and her own desire. Tensions are also obvious in the author's portrayal of the hero of the 'People' and his 'experiment', distorted by Maggie's own close friendship and admiration of Champion. The ending reads like an author searching for expediency, his inheritance an easy contrivance. Her experiences in Sydney lingered in George's tale but her focus was clearly on Champion's early character and life in London as she intentionally placed him in a romantic crusading role. As a boy he 'admired above all things the Crusaders', attending the Knights Templar church near Fleet Street. Moreover, he experiences something of an epiphany in his grandfather's vast library when studying a painting depicting Saint George and the Dragon, realising the 'saint had thrown up his commission in the Army, and stood before Diocletian as the champion of the despised Christians'. Richard Johnson's history of the *Seven Champions of Christendom* was probably the book of saints Maggie read while waiting for Cardinal Manning during the Dock Strike and it was full of martyrs and knights-errant. Saint George in particular was defender of the innocent and embodied courage in the face of adversity.

Maggie's novel situated George in Arthurian romance as a gallant knight, a role Champion himself embraced with enthusiasm, having named his own Australian magazine the *Champion* and placed a drawing of a knight with lance, seated on a horse with an inscription 'Tenax Propositi' below the title banner. Translated as firm of purpose (or resolution) this was a classical reference from Horace's Odes. A lone gallant man with an individual quest, this had no brusque masculine connotations of dragon-slaying but rather of high romance, of journeys into dangerous and unexplored territories defined by 'Here be dragons' of ancient terrestrial globes. One Australian friend, Bernard O'Dowd, in his poem 'Young Democracy' included two stanzas that mirror Champion's experience as one of the 'Knights-errant of the human race'; individuals who are described 'as mad or traitors' by a world where knights exist only in tales.

Despite returning to England, Maggie couldn't break her attachment to Australia, staying as an overseas correspondent for the *West Australian* for 'The Passing Hour' and 'A London Letter'. Her last articles for the *West Australian* were written in February 1905 about the Salvation Army soup kitchen and General Booth's new project, a farm at Hadleigh Castle ruins in Essex where participants were trained for labour settlements in the colonies.[384] Having run into Annie Besant at a London Theosophy Congress in October 1904, Maggie left England on the *S.S. Golconda* with her on 17 February 1905 for Colombo then took a steamer to Madras (Chennai) in Southern India. It was perhaps fitting that Maggie's journey took her to Champion's country of birth and also to a place where her own relative, Earl of Ellenborough, had been governor.

This was a time of cultural, social and educational transformation for Maggie as she joined Annie's community to implement reform through the organised spiritual framework of the Theosophical Society headquarters at Adyar where she attended and reported on their annual convention. Annie had spent over a decade involved in Indian education and in Delhi she founded a school for Hindu girls. She and Maggie travelled extensively to Madras (Chennai) and Calcutta (Kolkata) and they motored to Benares (Varanasi) in central north India to visit a college Annie established in 1898.[385] The scene of a massacre by British troops at the beginning of the Indian Rebellion, Benares was significant in Champion's father's history and, during the 50th anniversary, historical extracts from the uprising were included in her *Glimpses of India* (1909) published in Calcutta and revised as *Indian Snapshots* (1912). *The Horoscope* (1914), published in Madras, was her story of Buddhists and Christians in Ceylon (Sri Lanka).

The date of Maggie's return to England is uncertain although she came from France. Either way she returned home to help her unmarried sister, Katharine, nurse their aging mother Elizabeth who died on 26 October 1916 at Fareham, Hampshire. It was a standard expectation of the time for an unmarried woman to be responsible for the care for an aged parent and Maggie helped and cared for Elizabeth and tended her father's grave. She resided in London until her mother's probate of £1051 was settled in December and returned to France during the tumultuous period of the First World War. Although alienated from family by her past activities, distance, religion and politics, she took on arrangements for an endowment of a stained-glass window inside the church of Wimborne St Giles in Dorset which eventually would be completed in 1934.[386] One of two small lights near the entrance to the south porch was a memorial to Reverend Robert Harkness but also a purposeful remembrance for both parents, buried thirty years apart.

After the burial, Maggie reconnected with the Salvation Army, an organisation working on the English and French battlefields and published another novel, *A Curate's Promise: A Story of Three Weeks, September 14–October 5, 1917*. Now approaching 83 years old, General Booth wrote a short foreword, as he did for her earlier book, *In Darkest London* (1891). A nostalgic return to Booth's work in the East End slums, the book is set against the bombing of Whitechapel. Seen through the eyes of Reverend Benjamin Digby of the Salvation Army, its narrative praises concepts of 'social work', 'rescue homes' and 'life-saving', all terms familiar today. The novel received little attention, although *Times Literary Supplement* found the author wrote with 'power and brevity' and her character sketches were 'vivid and moving'.[387] No novel from her years spent in the harsh, alien and isolated environment of the Australian goldfields was ever printed in England and, in line with this, 'Called to the Bar' remained a local serial because either she or her publishers lost interest.

Maggie died in Italy at her room in the *Pensione Castagnoli*, via Montebello 54, close to Florence's Arno River on 10 December 1923. She was buried in the foreign resident's section ('Ossario Comune' or Common Ossuary) of Cimitero Evangelico degli Allori near the city's centre, the resting place of artists and writers as well as Australian aviator, Bert Hinkler. While tempting to think Maggie visited Percy Frost in Perugia, not far from Florence, or he attended her winter funeral, the fact remains she was buried hastily in a second-class grave for the poor, the day following her demise.

Maggie's identity was always bound up with her writing and hidden for the most part behind a man's name. As she tried to find her place in the world, she saw herself as an Englishwoman, an Anglo-Australian, perhaps later an Anglo-Indian, but always an 'outsider'. Brought up in a family of Anglican ministers and rectors, she was buried in an evangelical cemetery although she loved Catholic cardinals and nuns, the Salvation Army's chief and officers, and the spiritualism of Indian religion. Like Champion, she died just short of her 70th birthday and whether he knew of her death from mutual friends is not known. Certainly, there was no obituary for a woman who had spent her life pursuing social and political activism.

Love in a Warm Climate
Adelaide Hogg (1854–1930)

> *But when you and I were parted*
> *There were neither sighs nor tears.*
> *The sighing and the weeping*
> *Came in the after years.*
> E. Pariss Nesbit (trans.)
> (Heinrich Heine, *Champion* 9 May 1896)

Following his SDF expulsion, the Brunner libel threat, the Dock Strike and rumours about deals to keep the *Labour Elector* viable, Champion needed a break. He closed the doors of the newspaper in April 1890, went to Scotland for May Day, then Germany and Holland for three weeks in June, before sailing to Australia. By early July Champion was on the high seas with his friend Percy Frost, intending to study labour conditions in 'the Workingman's Paradise'. The trip to Australia was partly to improve his health concerns; like many friends, he was 'rather knocked up' and his doctor's advice was dire: 'he would not live until he was forty' unless he slowed down.[388] This prediction contained some truth and later, at the age of 42, he suffered a paralysing stroke.

Although Champion travelled to Australia for a lecture tour, the long sea voyage had added benefits, allowing escape for both Champion and shattered friend Percy Frost, newly released from prison and facing public humiliation. Convicted at the Old Bailey in October 1888 Percy spent a gruelling eighteen months in gaol because of a scandal associated with Mrs Gordon Baillie, an 'adventuress' he met in 1884 in Scotland. He sailed to New Zealand intending to join Baillie and arrived at Hobart on the *Doric* on 28 July. A few days later the pair sailed to Melbourne as Mr and Mrs Bromby Frost where she sought grants of land for the emigration and settlement of crofters from

Ruins of Castle Craig, Comarty Firth, Scotland
In author's possession. 2018.

General Manifesto from Central Committee, Wade Arms resolutions
Public domain.

Henry Hyde Champion
Source: H. H. Champion, *The Great Dock Strike in London, August, 1889.*

John Burns
Source: H. H. Champion, *The Great Dock Strike in London, August, 1889.*

Keir Hardie
Public domain.

Ben Tillett
Source: H. H. Champion, *The Great Dock Strike in London, August, 1889.*

Henry Hyndman
Source: *The Labour Annual* (1895).

Tom Mann
Public domain.

Adelaide Hogg (Adelaide Elder)
Photograph courtesy of the State Library of South Australia, PRG 1495/1/8.
Source: John Fergus studio photograph. 1877

Elsie Belle Champion
Photograph courtesy of the State Library of Victoria.
Source: Falk studio photograph. 31 December 1896.

Vida Goldstein
Photograph courtesy of the State Library of Victoria.
Source: T. Humphrey & Co. photographer. 1912.

Margaret Harkness
Source: *Queen: the Lady's Newspaper.*
31 May 1890.

Katharine Susannah Prichard
Photograph courtesy of the National Library
of Australia. Source: *Milady Magazine* (Perth)
12 November 1949. c. 1910.

Morley Roberts
Source: Portrait by E. M. Jessop.
31 December 1893.

Norman Lindsay (bookplate)
Courtesy of the Newspaper Collection,
National Library of Australia.
Source: *Australasian*, 24 April 1926.
Early design c.1899.

Skye. One journalist was told she was Mrs Frost although kept her former name as 'a lady by birth does when she condescends to unite her fortune with a commoner'.[389] On return to London, Percy rented a furnished house in Westminster, with a reference from Champion who later appeared at his trial. Transformed from Mrs Gordon Baillie into Mrs Annie Bodley Frost, she set about defrauding tradesmen with dishonoured cheques and, to obtain a loan, she pledged valuable items belonging to the house owner. She was sentenced to five years in gaol and Frost received a year and a half.

Ballie left a legacy behind that today would delight Hollywood. Born Miss Mary Ann Bruce Sutherland, daughter of a laundress, she started her life of crime in Dundee defrauding tradesmen and served prison time in 1873 in Perth. She assumed various names over a lengthy period: Mrs Gordon Baillie, daughter/niece of the Earl of Moray, Lady Carn, Lady Gladys Campbell, Lady Cochran, Lady Dundonald, Lady Stewart, Lady Williams and Lady Hill. In November 1876, as Annie Ogilvie Bruce, she rented a mansion near Inverness, married Thomas Ashton White (Knight Ashton) before divorcing him in Australia. She then married Captain John Hill of the British Army and after that a Scottish solicitor, Allan Carn.[390] After her conviction, she again offended by attempting to relieve deceased Sir George Duckworth King of £100,000 and received another seven years for stealing pictures, before her release early in January 1899. Known to have at least five children, she reappeared in 1902 in America to impersonate aristocratic women and served six months in Blackwell's Island prison.

Champion and Frost arrived in Melbourne at the beginning of the Maritime Strike in August 1890. Three months later he and Percy were mocked as 'dual entertainment' for fictional lectures on *Labour Problems* and *My Prison Life*.[391] In just over six months Champion would gain the enduring hatred of executive members of the Melbourne Trades Hall Council and fall deeply in love with a married woman, Adelaide Hogg. For her love he 'was willing to give up home & country, friends & careers, everything that a man can give including sense & honour', he told Morley Roberts on 15 August 1897. He was completely smitten and hopelessly trapped by his attachment and prepared to abandon his previous life. His drivers were love, sacrifice and his own need to 'save' her from her marriage.

In the midst of the Maritime Strike he gave his first speech at Melbourne's Trades Hall.[392] Then, on 24 August he met Adelaide Lashbrooke Hogg at a Sunday supper. Born on 11 April 1854 in Dysart, not far from Edinburgh, Adelaide was a member of the newly established Austral Salon that organised a discussion of Jerome K. Jerome's 'Stage-Land' at Buxton's Art Gallery. Champion was invited to stay for a couple of weeks at Adelaide and Henry Hogg's St Kilda house and here their relationship sparked. Under her first name, 'Adelaide', she had published a successful children's book, *Jemima: A Story of English Family Life* (1879). Her book received favourable press in the London *Times* during Christmas 1879, her main character 'full of energy, resource, and generosity', a 'ringleader in mischief' with her brothers and sisters. Reviews were good in South Australian papers, one journalist called her 'a native of South Australia, and connected by many strong ties with the colony'.[393] Champion told Morley Roberts on 26 October 1896, 'She can really write & if she had married any reasonably intelligent being she would have made a great storyteller'.

Adelaide's wealthy father was Alexander Lang Elder who came to Australia and returned to England as the owner of Campden House in London's exclusive district of Kensington. Campden House was an imposing mansion, extensively remodelled by Elder and its vast scale is evident in a London survey for Northern Kensington. At the age of 27, Adelaide married an older man who studied at Cambridge, Henry Roughton Hogg, who lived close to her father's home at 36 Cheniston Gardens. Later they named their Australian country residence in Upper Macedon 'Cheniston', as well as a new species of spiders that Henry discovered and catalogued as 'Chenistonia Maculata'.

Henry Hogg was the son of Francis Hogg who, together with his brother-in law Robinson, established the firm of wine merchants, Hogg, Robinson and Company, still a major business today.

From their Marlborough College years, Champion and Frost knew his brother William Edward Hogg[394] and a relative, Augustus Frederick Robinson. Henry Hogg was an introvert who liked close research and scientific study, his hobby of natural history leading to his early membership of the Field Naturalists' Club of Victoria, the Royal Society of Victoria (sponsors of the Burke and Wills expedition) and a role as president of the Zoological Society. Champion called him a 'little man'.

Adelaide's uncle Sir Thomas Elder was responsible for colonial exploration of the interior using Afghan camels. Never married, he was associated with the Elder Conservatorium of Music as benefactor from 1883. When his sister Joanna married Robert Barr Smith, the two men established Elder Smith and Company, one of the largest sellers of wool in the world, owners of vast tracts of Australian pastoral holdings and mines. Adelaide's husband became a director of the Campaspe Deep Lead mine early in 1896 when he joined a syndicate with her uncle Thomas, after application for 80 acres of land at Boggy Creek in the Yarra Ranges. Aunt Joanna was considered to be one of South Australia's primary hostesses and her city mansion 'Torrens Park' in Mitcham and summer house 'Auchendarrock' at Mount Barker were adorned with art and furnishings imported from London. These included designs from William Morris, gifted to the Art Gallery of South Australia. Four years after marriage Adelaide received an inheritance from her father's estate, valued at £317,000 (at November 1885), divided between over a dozen of his children. Adelaide's inheritance money flowed to Henry Hogg who controlled all her property. She also had expectations of inheriting from her wealthy and aging uncle, Sir Thomas Elder, who died in March 1897, leaving her £1500 to £2000 per annum.

Adelaide was cultivated, wealthy and well-read and, unlike Juliet Bennett, was not one of 'the People'. She spent her days receiving visitors and visiting wives of people met in the social cliques of Melbourne. Used to the finer things in life they were frequent attendees of Government House social functions, 'at homes', and official functions at the Melbourne Zoo while a nurse looked after the day-to-day supervision of their only daughter, Shirley Roughton Hogg. Shirley was born in New Zealand on 1 December 1884 and there are indications that she was the daughter of Adelaide's youngest brother Austin Elder. Alexander Lang had bought the 6880-hectare estate in

1878 near Masterton and when Austin arrived at 'Langdale' in 1883 to help manage the farm he was single and only 19 years old.[395]

Adelaide's residence on Alma Road at St Kilda was full of valuable made-to order English furniture and contained a substantial library. She surrounded herself with the best money could buy including lavish carpets and curtains, crystal, Wedgwood dinner services, Venetian and Japanese ornaments, a large oak dining table for entertaining and a grand piano made in Paris. 'Cheniston', their country residence, built in 1890 to escape the stifling heat and odours of Melbourne summers, was a charming brick villa set on 23 acres in the Macedon Ranges. The house boasted four bedrooms, a maid's room, stables, coach-house, and gardener's cottage when auctioned on 28 October 1911. The area was popular with the wealthy Melbourne population, various state governors resided at Macedon's Government Cottage and newspaper proprietor David Syme and singer Dame Nellie Melba bought second homes there.

For a short time, Champion lived at the Yorick Club in Collins Street where the honorary secretary was former *Age* journalist and artillery officer, Captain John Stanley, a colleague of Joseph Goldstein. From this club, Champion wrote a preface to the pamphlet by Samuel Rosa, *The Truth about the Unemployed Agitation of 1890*, on 10 September. He defended agitation for the unemployed and implored Australians not to ignore a growing social problem. A former SDF Executive member, Rosa emigrated to Sydney where he edited and wrote for the *Truth* from 1901. The Yorick Club was regarded as 'a poor man's club' whose 'members were much more remarkable for brains than money'.[396] Originally founded in 1868 by editor of the *Argus*, Frederick Haddon, at his rooms in Spring Street, the club moved to Nissen's Cafe in Bourke Street and then Collins Street. The Yorick Club was noted for a bohemian atmosphere and the earliest known members were literary people, Richard H. Horne, Marcus Clarke, Adam Lindsay Gordon, Henry Kendall, George Gordon McCrae (father of Hugh McCrae) and Henry Byron Moore. Champion believed Marcus Clarke 'would have been in his element in the Bohemia of Fleet-street and the Inns of Court, or even more suitably circumstanced on the Parisian Boulevards'.[397] Through this club he discovered the literary and artistic heart of Melbourne, recording the type of society he loved:

> I had dinner the other evening with some friends at their rambling and genial house, round the table of which a miscellaneous collection of Bohemians is wont to assemble. They are really Bohemians hearty and lively, men bound more by the facts of life than by rules of convention.[398]

The hosts of this dinner may have been the McCubbins who were famous for holding Sunday night suppers and many believed it was 'a great privilege to be invited to the Bohemian suppers' in their 'quaint old home on the banks of the Yarra'.[399] Although he also enjoyed the company of Brighton surgeon who lived in a house called 'Bohemia'. Dr [Stephen] Mannington Caffyn was a medical officer at the Kew Asylum in 1884 and close friend of George McCrae.[400]

The day after Champion's letter to an editor from the Yorick Club, a scathing attack was launched from Geelong, listing Trades Hall Council grievances about Champion in the Maritime Strike:

> He dined at the Australian Club off dainty dishes prepared for capitalists and their friends, and was made a member of the Yorick Club, where literary men of all shades of opinion and large experience discuss the burning questions that stir the souls' thinkers the world over ... He may have brought, indeed did bring, the highest credentials from the socialist party in England, but yet he left Victoria to act as a conciliator at the Sydney labor convention, and was not accredited from our Trades Hall. No wonder he has advised the leaders of the party in London that the Australian strike has been grossly mismanaged, and that even the solicited loan of £20,000 cannot avert its absolute failure.[401]

Obviously, these were the complaints that the Aberdeen Trades Council found ridiculous later, and the writer was not a fan of either the Australian Club or the Yorick Club. Champion's love of fine dining and intelligent conversation, his appreciation of literature and his aristocratic background seemed to many a contradiction of his advocacy for socialism and social change for workers. The Australian Club, on Williams Street's corner with Little Collins Street, was an exclusive and opulent club with a marble staircase five metres in width and baroque oak fireplaces; later it was registered as Hugo Throssell's address prior to his marriage in 1919. Two members of this club were at Marlborough with Champion and sons of Sir William Stawell; one was a barrister and the other a Collins Street's doctor.

The relationship between Champion and Adelaide intensified after his return from the Gippsland town of Walhalla while her husband was on a fortnight expedition with the Field Naturalists' Club to the Grampians National Park in mid-November. He was boarding around Brighton and recalled: 'I wanted, before I left Australia, to read Gordon's poems, and to read them at Brighton Beach ... I was staying just outside Melbourne, and within a mile of the place'.[402] Aberdeen-born Adam Lindsay Gordon, one of Australia's favourite poets at the time, committed suicide in the ti-tree scrub at Brighton Beach in June 1870. Champion later reviewed the poet's 'melancholy life' and said his verses represented 'the sweet dying swan-song of a sick soul and a heavy heart'.[403] On a fine summer's day Champion visited a friend's home wishing to borrow Gordon's poems from Alma's mother. Finding the mother to be unwell, he offered to take Alma to the Brighton seaside with her two young neighbourhood friends. Alma was Champion's surrogate character for Adelaide, her name a reference both to her home on Alma Road at St Kilda and to Adelaide's sister (Mina Constance recorded as 'Alma C.' in the 1881 census).

In a quietly humorous piece, Champion admitted that his fondness for Alma developed during his stay at the family home. Published in the *Leader* and later for the *Aberdeen Standard* and *Labour Elector*, the two versions of the piece show the latter version to be more sexual in tone, enriched with subtle overtones of secrecy, concealment, guilt and conspiracy. While the tale is about the daughter, the tone suggests his fascination with the mother. The first version was published just before he left Adelaide Hogg and returned to England while the second version was released just before he returned to Australia to be reunited with Adelaide.

> She had taken my measure very accurately in the early days of our acquaintance when I was staying in the house. I began it, I admit. I let her see that I was fond and foolish. She grasped the situation at once. I became her slave ... I used to carry Alma round the garden on my shoulders, so that she could reach the lilac blossoms, pick the roses on the higher trellis of the verandah, and inspect the growth of the loquats ... Alma took to stamping at my bedroom door to wake me at unearthly hours in the morning, so that I might give her rides before any one was up and about to detect her or protect me. I tacitly assented to this arrangement, which both of us knew to be wrong and underhand. It established a secret bond of iniquity between us. She always referred to me as 'my friend'. [404]

'That was how the trouble began', he complained, and while men with tales of similar 'experiences have sometimes kept me up very late at night in order to recount them', he naively believed 'the fault was in themselves'. Later, another of his romantic attachments, Katharine Susannah Prichard, referred in her autobiography also to 'my friend' and wrote of the secrecy and guilt of her relationship with a married man.

Champion's original intention was to be back in England by Easter and he was in Trafalgar Square after sailing to England on 28 February 1891 on the P&O steamer, *Valetta*. On his return he bumped into a journalist who saw Champion was now a different person after a sea voyage and rest. Bronzed and happy, he reported feeling ten years younger.[405] It is apparent that he was smitten by Adelaide and looking forward to seeing her secretly in London.

In the middle of March Henry auctioned their furniture, carpets and crystal from their city house, displaying the items at St Margaret's Church on the corner of Alma Road and Hotham Street in St Kilda. A month after Champion's departure, Adelaide, Shirley and Miss Elder sailed for London on the *Ormuz* on 4 April 1891. Adelaide's intention was to nurse her very ill sister, Mary Anne. While Adelaide's husband was also on board, he left the ship at their first port of call in South Australia (presumably to conduct some business there) and returned to Melbourne.

Champion obviously saw Adelaide very discreetly while her sister was in decline. Meanwhile, Adelaide had the opportunity to view her lover in the social setting of London. Now working for the prestigious *Nineteenth Century* journal his insertion into her smart world was probably impressive, a sharp contrast to her later insistence he 'achieve', in his newspaper, 'something'. As assistant editor to James Knowles, Champion was considered important socially although he admitted that he could only 'devote' himself for 'a couple of years to that kind of business'.[406]

Champion had met Knowles in the House of Lord's lobby in 1886, introduced by Maltman Barry. Knowles had been an architect for the Park Town estate of Battersea from 1863–66, an organiser of the Paris Food Fund for relief of the besieged population in 1871 and associated with the Sanitary Laws Enforcement Society. Needed for three hours a day, five days a week, Champion was busy during the early stages of his affair with complex editorial work for a highly regarded journal. Knowles needed an assistant editor confident enough to approach many people of different attitudes and political persuasions who were leaders in current opinion. An astute, smooth facilitator was required, a discerning person who recognised insightful argument and engaging content, who provoked discourse across political boundaries or social parameters. Writing tasks were challenging for practical activists like Burns who needed heavy editing but whose advanced radical ideas attracted other observations and debate. In addition, from late December to March 1891, while Knowles was ill with typhoid, Champion stepped in as editor for four to five months. Champion worked at his Queen Anne's Mansions home overlooking St James's Park. Champion's own 'top flat' at 142 Strand was in the heart of the publishing world, home to book seller and publisher, John Chapman, owner of the *Westminster Review*.

When invited to dinner at Knowles's home, Champion showcased his intellectual and political value to the journal within a formal social setting. At a spring dinner party for two dozen people around a large circular dining table, Champion met Gladstone and his wife, Sir William Howard Russell (war correspondent for the *Times* during Crimea, the Indian Rebellion, Egypt, and the American Civil War), Robert Lincoln

(American Ambassador and son of Abraham Lincoln), Lord Allendale Wentworth Beaumont and his wife Lady Pomeroy-Colley (sister of General Sir Ian Hamilton and now married to Beaumont), and Dr Charles Waldstein (American archaeologist known for uncovering the site of ancient Troy with Schliemann and Dörpfeld in Hissarlik). Waldstein was 'the man of the moment' because of his discovery of Aristotle's Athenian Constitution; he was invited to write an essay for the October edition of the *Nineteenth Century* on excavations at Eretria that were believed to hold Aristotle's sarcophagus. Champion sat next to Lady Edith Pomeroy-Colley who blamed Gladstone for the death of her first husband at Majuba Hill and gave Champion a 'most vitriolic summing up of Mr Gladstone's colonial policies'.[407]

Because of his notoriety from the Trafalgar Square Riots and the Dock Strike, social invitations proceeded from all directions. Champion later recorded receiving an invitation to Grosvenor House by the Duke of Westminster to meet Professor Henry Drummond, a favourite of Lady Aberdeen. At another dinner he met 'a lady well-known in social and literary circles' who wrote under a pseudonym for the *New Republic* and her friends were well-known English authors and eminent politicians.[408] This was Lady Mary Montgomerie Currie, poet, writer and wife of a future British Ambassador to Constantinople who counted amongst friends Charles Kingsley, Robert Browning, Oscar Wilde, Swinburne and Gladstone. She wrote as 'Violet Fane' and Champion reviewed her book in 1896, praising the author for 'some very fine poems'. She was also a childhood friend of David Urquhart who was one of Champion's ancestors.

Without doubt, Adelaide moved about London more freely during breaks from her nursing duties, and while her daughter was either at school or in the care of relatives or staff. Champion's flat at the Strand was close to her mother's home in Kensington although for the first few months of 1892 a friend lived with him. John Evelyn Barlas, a Scottish poet known also as 'Evelyn Douglas', was arrested as an anarchist on Westminster Bridge on New Year's Eve 1891 after firing six shots from a revolver at the House of Commons. Barlas was an old acquaintance of Champion, Morris, Carpenter, Salt and Cunninghame Graham from early SDF days; they knew Barlas after he entered Middle Temple to study law in 1882. At the time he was writing poetry and exploring political and social theory as he moved from socialism to anarchism and Wilde's biographer told of Barlas living in a Lambeth slum with a 'red-hot' anarchist, a girl who wore 'underclothing of a blood-red hue to denote the colour of her convictions'. A contributor to William Morris's *Commonweal* and Charlotte Wilson and Peter Kropotkin's *Freedom: A Journal of Anarchist Communism*, Barlas wrote of two opposing classes 'the *haves* and the *have-nots*', a term well-known today.[409] He also contributed to Maggie Harkness's *Novel Review* where she placed him in the company of friends Olive Schreiner and Edward Carpenter, as a visionary socialist. Involved with Cunninghame Graham in 'Bloody Sunday' at Trafalgar Square, Barlas was 'battoned and floored', the probable origin of his ongoing mental illness.[410]

Through another Oxford graduate, Robert H. Sherard, great-grandson of William Wordsworth, Barlas was a friend of Oscar Wilde. Together Wilde and Barlas attended Douglas Sladen's 'at homes' that Champion described as hosting 'some of the shining lights of the Author's Club' as well as 'hangers-on to the skirts of literature'.[411] Wilde engaged Barlas as his tutor and advisor for his 1890 essay, 'The Soul of Man Under Socialism', after Wilde heard Bernard Shaw give an address on socialism in 1888 (published in *Fabian Essays in Socialism*).

After the Westminster arrest, Sherard wrote from Paris to the editor of the *Pall Mall Gazette*, pleading his case. Barlas was 'a young Byron, handsome as a demi-god, a scholar, and a gentleman' with a fortune of £20,000 now living destitute in a Salvation Army shelter because of his generosity in helping starving people.[412] Nearly a week later Sherard added that his friends were surprised by the moment of 'insanity' because Barlas had not exhibited any signs before. However, his obvious signs of distress were evident as early as mid-1883 when Barlas introduced his anarchist girlfriend to Wilde. Barlas believed she had not been treated with the correct amount of attention, according to the latter's biographer:

> ... when they all left the house together he was excessively put out because Wilde did not offer an arm to the lady across Grosvenor Square. He therefore hailed a hansom, shoved the girl into it, and

after expressing his sense of grievance in forcible terms gave the Lambeth slum address to the cabby, who seemed unwilling to drive to such a place.[413]

As Sherard implored people to help in the aftermath of the shooting incident, Champion actively searched for another person of means:

> His defence at the police court was that he was an Anarchist and had determined to usher in the year 1892 by firing off five barrels of a revolver at the clock-tower of the Houses of Parliament 'to show his contempt for Parliamentary institutions!' ... I discovered that his relatives had abandoned him, that he was penniless, and unless someone interfered would infallibly be committed to a pauper lunatic asylum, and never get out again. The only alternative was to get two responsible householders to give security for his future constraint.[414]

Champion called at Wilde's Chelsea home and found him responsive and sympathetic. Though Wilde was off to a rehearsal he came at once, dropping the stage play, *Lady Windermere's Fan*, on the courthouse floor and imagining this to be 'a bad omen' that his play may 'fall flat'. To reassure him, Champion pointed out the rolled manuscript had landed on its side. They provided £100 each to the court to guarantee that Barlas would maintain good behaviour and the magistrate was 'pleased' that two eminent citizens were caring for him.[415] Champion was made personally responsible for the well-being of a delusional Barlas, bringing him into his flat for a couple of months.

With Barlas's 'tottering intellect' directed to 'weaving mad anarchistical plots', Champion was initially amused until the problem escalated. Burdened by delusions of being the Messiah, Barlas conducted an endless Biblical search looking for proof while waiting for Judgement Day, seeing Champion as a reincarnated prophet on good days or as an anti-Christ on others. Coupled with the sharpening of razors in a locked bedroom, this behaviour made Champion admit his task of looking after him was 'arduous'. This was a lengthy time as carer, especially when he was busy with editorial work, although by late February he recognised Barlas needed specialist assistance. At midday on the morning after the premier of Wilde's *Lady Windermere's Fan* at St James's theatre, Champion visited Wilde at the Berkeley, an expensive West End hotel. To Wilde he described their friend's increasing hallucinations and frantic Bible searches. In his 'pyjamas of wondrous hue' Wilde suddenly mumbled: '"Ah, the Bible?" and sitting up to rub his eyes he went on sleepily: "When I think, Champion, of the harm that book has done, upon my word, I despair of writing anything to equal it"'.

When writing later of Wilde, Champion also pointed to the identity of Dorian Gray claiming 'the original of the hero was a youthful barrister, who was living a few years ago in the Temple' and he called him 'a minor poet, whom it would be unfair to name since he still lives'.[416] Many critics believe Dorian was modelled on John Gray, another poet and friend of Barlas. However, Barlas, with his 'demi-god' looks and mental illness, may have served as better material for the journey of a 'young man of extraordinary personal beauty' who was 'wonderfully handsome'. *The Picture of Dorian Gray* was published in *Lippincott's Monthly Magazine* in July 1890 and scholars point to Wilde's composition as prior to December 1889, a period coinciding with Wilde's employment of Barlas for his essay, 'The Soul of Man Under Socialism'. Admitted to Gartnavel Royal Asylum near Glasgow for over 20 years, the death of John Barlas prompted Champion to recall the final time he saw him at a London slum 'lying on the floor, surrounded by his books extracting from his disordered brain those beautiful thoughts'.[417]

The wheel of introductions for like-minded people of a literary, artistic, and political persuasion turned swiftly in inner London and Champion must have introduced Adelaide to many interesting people. Early in 1892 John Davidson (author of *Fleet Street Ecologues*) called at Champion's place to talk with Barlas until four in the morning, the two poets exchanging criticisms of each other's work after a night at a music hall. Champion remembered Barlas 'seemed to know other poets by the score'. Morley Roberts called to see how he was progressing and introduced himself to Champion.[418] From their first meeting Champion and Roberts developed a long-lasting friendship based on their love of literature, travel and relationships.

Both men were hopelessly in love with married woman so each felt safe to share secret, painful experiences. Their lengthy and enduring correspondence was always frank and open with Champion's letters to Morley becoming the only record of his tumultuous love affair with Adelaide. Their friendship was so strong Morley entrusted Champion with the task of taking his lover, Mrs Alice Hamlyn, to Australia in 1894. Affectionately called Glory or Glo, because Alice's hair was white in her twenties 'an ivory tint which was a glory', Champion followed Morley's lead. They in turn called him Hyde.

At the time Morley was a poor writer unable to afford bed sheets. His early years in a Chelsea artist colony close to the Kensington School of Art were featured in his story 'The Artist' in the year following his marriage to Alice. He wrote vividly of inhabitants 'living on a course of high ideals' and 'writers learning their business on a little oatmeal, as George Meredith did' in *The Private Life of Henry Maitland*. Morley knew many bohemian artists and studio workers and introduced his own bohemian lifestyle to readers through *In Low Relief, A Bohemian Transcript* (1890) and *Immortal Youth* (1902). Morley was also responsible for introducing Champion to Felix Moscheles, a socialist and painter whose Chelsea studio was Mazzini's 'favourite haunt',[419] and whose article 'In Bohemia with Du Maurier' for *Century Magazine* was turned into a book. Invited to look at a painting by Moscheles, Champion met Robert Browning.[420]

Years after reading George Gissing's novel, *The Unclassed*, Champion claimed he met the model (Morley Roberts) for Osmond Wayward who was a good-humoured writer with a 'heavy moustache' aged 26. Wayward's bohemian lifestyle led him to a state of 'semi-starvation alternating with surfeits of cheap and unwholesome food' of Australian tinned mutton.[421] Even Morley's letter to Champion recognised: 'Ten years of starvation and misery at the best time of life tell upon a man if he lives to forty: I begin to feel rather old, and don't like the prospects of annual novels for indefinite years to come. If one could take a year or two of rest! One can do little that one ought.'[422]

Morley's lover, Mrs Alice 'Glory' Bruce Hamlyn (née Alice Selous), lived with her stockbroker husband and three children in Holland Villas Road, Kensington, and she and Adelaide struck up a strong friendship. This guaranteed easy access for secret meetings of both couples. With Morley and Alice's affair in full bloom, the two women probably used each other as convenient excuses for a call on a friend, for shopping trips, exhibitions and visits to the British Museum while Morley's rooms in Bloomsbury and Champion's flat were only a brief walk away. Morley's short story 'Panic', a year after his marriage to Alice, sketched a story of 'a sweet-tempered, calm, and dignified woman who everyone liked' and a lover of Shakespeare. She has a close relationship with a trusted male companion (who resembles Morley)[423] although the couple do not attract gossip: 'the very people whose ardour in taking away others' reputation robbed them of their own left her untouched in the social mud-slinging which gives half society its sole virtuous and intellectual amusement'.

Wedded the same year as Adelaide Hogg, Alice was extremely unhappy. In *Hearts of Women* (1920), published nearly ten years after Alice's death, the novel depicts a woman trapped in the prison of a soulless marriage to a cruel man and paints her husband's psychological brutality with raw emotion. While both Alice and Adelaide were neglected by their husbands, there were differences. Alice's husband was abusive, Adelaide's meek and compliant; Alice was joyless and miserable in her marriage, Adelaide could live amicably with her husband although her guilt made her unhappy. During an interview with Blathwayt for Maggie Harkness's October *Novel Review*, Morley discussed the 'tragedies' of unhappily married women whose 'remorse is endless', capturing the mirrored experience of Alice and Adelaide during their affairs.

When Henry Hogg sailed to England to see Adelaide, secure in the knowledge that his wife was with her family, Champion was not visible because he was in election mode in Scotland and busy as the proprietor of two Scottish newspapers (the *Aberdeen Standard* and *Fiery Cross*). Realising her sister's illness was lengthy, Henry returned without his wife and daughter via Marseilles early in June 1892. Champion returned to London around Mary Anne Elder's death which occurred on 22 November. With her funeral and the intended sale of the Campden House, Adelaide had excuses to delay a return to Australia until the house went to auction in the middle of the following year.

Around Christmas Champion was laid up in bed for a lengthy period with a serious knee injury forcing him to miss the ILP Conference at Bradford in January 1893. The nurse who left him at eight at night and returned at nine the next morning was probably Adelaide who, like Morley, sat with him to 'cheer him up'. Morley also probably read to Champion since his powerful new short story 'The Man-Eater' was to be unveiled on 10 January 1893 at a public reading at the Authors' Club. They also quietly planned their departure from England.

The two men quietly left for the Continent for six months' travel and this departure in March surprised Morley's friends, especially Gissing who queried his sudden and secretive disappearance although there was not much speculation about Champion's withdrawal from public and political life. The two friends went 'rambling' through Europe with a few weeks in Paris, then on to Italian places like Livorno (Leghorn), Corsica, Rome, Terracina, Formia, Fondi, Naples and Vesuvius. Morley wrote in *A Tramp's Note-Book* (1904) about sailing from Leghorn to Napoleon's birthplace of Corsica with his friend and their arrival at Bastia where Nelson had been repelled. They took a train to Corte, drove to Ajaccio and thought 'a great epidemic' had swept through the region because so many women wore black, only to discover it was the custom for females losing any relative to wear mourning for three years. Published as 'Mournful Corsica' for *Westminster Budget* it reappeared in his collected tales in 1904, while Champion casually mentions he was Morley's 'fellow traveller in Corsica' in a letter on 23 December 1898.[424]

The two men went on to Switzerland where in Zurich they attended the International Socialist Workers' Congress held between 6–12 August. The British delegation numbered 65 members and Champion was one of four Independent Labour Party delegates with Arthur Fields, L.A. Glynn and Shaw Maxwell. There were five women, Eleanor Marx, 'Ad' Smith [Mrs Adolphe Smith?], May Morris, Margaret Irwin and Miss Ogilvy; the Fabians included Bernard Shaw and Sydney Olivier; SDF members were H.W. Lee who wrote their report, Belfort Bax and Hunter Watts, while Adolphe Smith was translator. Champion saw German socialist Wilhelm Liebknecht (met early in the Dock Strike with Paul Singer), and August Bebel.[425] The anarchist Charles Mowbray was one delegate excluded from the Congress and all the noise and frequent disorder was recounted by Morley in *A Tramp's Notebook*. At a social boat trip on the lake at Zurich, Bax described Champion's jubilation and called him 'the life of the party of English delegates' with his 'personal magnetism' captivating political comrades.[426] Champion was certainly in a euphoric mood, the result of decisions about their collective futures to set up house in Australia. He wrote a couple of letters to the *Pall Mall Gazette* and a light-hearted piece for the *Labour Elector* in September about an eight-hour day report and the struggle to keep delegates on track.

Alice, her mother and sister Emily were conveniently enjoying a family holiday at Vevey. The popularity of the lake had increased after Lord Byron stayed at Villa Diodati in 1816 where he, Percy and Mary Shelley scandalised tourists; this prompted the Hotel d'Angleterre to erect a telescope and charge fees to watch Byron's window. Mary's story of *Frankenstein* and the scandal encouraged tourist interest and so trips to Switzerland by stage-coach from London were increasingly popular. Although Morley could not afford it, he was staying in accommodation at the expensive Grand Hotel de Russie, a plush hotel facing the Mont Blanc Bridge on Lake Geneva, so it is assumed Champion accompanied him to that town in 'the shadow of the Grand Salève'.[427]

At Vevey, Emily discussed the distressing cruelty of Alice's marriage, after which their mother 'sent' for Morley and *'gave'* him his future wife.

Morley admitted the conversation in his *Hearts of Women* was 'a near report' of his actual discussion with Alice's sister. Whether Adelaide travelled with Alice's family to Vevey after her family home was auctioned and before her return to Melbourne is unknown and certainly was never mentioned. Campden House was passed in without sale after failing to secure an asking price of £25,000,[428] although the following year a lease was procured and the estate subsequently demolished for a new development.

After Switzerland, Champion travelled to Belfast and then on to Scotland to wrap up his newspaper and plan the next stage of life, a wonderful new life with Adelaide. Morley and Alice went back to a hotel in Livorno and requested Gissing to forward a note to Alice's sister at Hyde Park Mansions. However, Rodney Fennessy, Alice's brother-in-law, who Morley believed 'feared scandal more than sacrilege or cruelty', insisted they separate and travelled to Genoa to convince them to return to England. The couple parted at Aix, north of Marseille and, for a time at least, Alice remained married.

After Alice's aborted attempt to escape, a new scheme was devised involving complicated subterfuge. On 30 November Morley invited Gissing to dine with him and other friends at the Authors' Club where Gissing finally met Champion who surprised him 'favourably' enough for warm and lengthy correspondence between them to be established. Morley outlined the plan in his unpublished manuscript: 'Emmie sent Alice under a friend's care to a friend in Australia. This was heartily backed by Fennessy who thought in his vain heart that with half a world between us I should surely forget all that I was'.[429] Indeed, Rodney Fennessy appeared happy for his sister-in-law to visit Australia, with Champion acting as Alice's travelling companion and to stay with Adelaide, a trusted companion now in Melbourne. If Henry Hogg didn't know about his wife's affair, he soon would, for the two couples were to be united and share a house.

Throughout the last two months of 1893 and the first two of 1894, Champion published short stories by Morley in the *Aberdeen Standard* and interviewed him for Jerome K. Jerome's *To-Day*. When Champion returned to London, Frederick Rolfe followed and for a couple of months the three men shared his Kilburn cottage at 37 Greville Road, St John's Wood. To celebrate Morley's departure Champion arranged a farewell dinner at the 'New Travellers' Club' in Piccadilly on 29 December 1893.[430] They were joined by Gissing and journalist W.A. Mackenzie ['A.D. Mack'] noted for the 'Rowton House Rhymes' (featured in George Orwell's *Down and Out in Paris and London*). With a suitable time-period between departures, Champion left London, accompanying Alice on the P&O *Orient* on 23 February 1894; Morley left for America in March. Before leaving Champion and Morley secured Frederick Rolfe's story 'An Unforgettable Experience' for publication in *To-Day* and, after reading his homoerotic stories, 'Toto Tales', arranged for his introduction to William Colles, Gissing's literary agent.

Champion was later inspired to emulate Colles during the formation of the Australasian Authors' Agency, in particular the practice of publishing books in different countries. He also took advantage of the agent's expertise for a translation of Henri Murger's *Bohemian Life* under the name he used for the *To-Day* interview. His work was completed on the ship to Australia and published by Edmund Downey, originally an assistant on *Tinsleys' Magazine* and responsible for publishing Morley's Crimean War book *The Circassian* (1897). Boasting his translation was notable for the 'clearness, rigour, and vivacity, of this rendering, and its success in preserving the spirit of the original', Champion's selection of scenes was published in his newspaper.[431] Champion's book was also reprinted in New York in 1900 by Brentano's, a firm specialising in French literature.

Travelling via New York on the *Lucania* and then to San Francisco, Morley also stopped in Samoa to see Robert Louis Stevenson.[432] He recognised Stevenson in the town centre on his horse and spent three hours with him in the steamer's saloon sipping lemonade and gave him a copy of *The Western Avenus*, a book detailing Morley's travels from Texas to British Columbia. From Auckland on the *Monowai* Morley arrived in Sydney at the end of May while Alice, who arrived earlier in April, was to stay with Adelaide at Cheniston and then to meet Morley in Melbourne.

What looked like a wonderful new beginning for each of them was in fact the end. Adelaide left her husband and daughter to live at a cottage a couple of hours outside of Melbourne, near the Beaconsfield train station. Here Adelaide and Champion thought to construct a home with their friends. It was an insubstantial facade with Morley making his way to Melbourne by mail train only to be greeted by Champion with a cablegram from London that demanded their immediate return. Alice and Morley had a grand total of ten days before they surrendered to Fennessy's demand, leaving on 9 June as a married couple and travelling to Naples where Morley expected to access money to equip them for the rest of the journey to London.

In the absence of any return fare, money from a friend [Adelaide], income gained from Champion's lengthy interview with Morley on 4 June 1894 for the *Age*, and anything of value the three could sell, secured the fare to Italy. His interview was one he would 'always treasure', Morley wrote in 'Round the World in a Hurry' for Jerome K. Jerome's *Idler* in November 1895 (and republished in *A Tramp's Notebook*). In the article, Champion wrote of Morley's familiarity with Australia from his visit in 1877–78, working on the Victorian railways, as a station hand on an Upper Murray sheep station, the Dora Dora and sinking tanks in the Riverina on Robert Rand's *Mahong* station. The article was massaged by Champion to look like his new visit was part of a planned tour: 'Mr. Roberts is at present in Melbourne for a few days on his way to Europe, having come across America and on *via* Auckland and Sydney'. Champion praised his 'stories about the marriage question [that] have earned him the deep gratitude and admiration of the best friends of women in the old country and in America'. Much to the obvious chagrin of the THC Executive, the article led to David Syme's appointment of Champion to the *Age* as a leader writer the following month.

Costing Morley a total of £99 in fares and taking just under four months from March to June, his Australian trip consisted of ten days of domestic happiness in Melbourne with Alice and a stop-over of two days in Adelaide. The couple headed to Columbo through the Suez Canal to Naples and then overland for four days to London. The holiday on the ship was a treasured time before Morley and Alice were forced to part for a couple of years until the death of her husband. Champion admired the fact that, the year after this, Morley's obsessive writing at Lake Ullswater in Cumbria produced 'a novel of 90,000 words in five weeks, and revised one of 58,000 words, and in six succeeding days [he] wrote six short stories containing a total of 22,000 words'.[433] Morley continued his networking with writers of the New Vagabonds Club, such as Jerome K. Jerome, Anthony Hope and Israel Zangwill and often reported to Champion amusing speeches at the Club, such as an address to Lord Roberts of Kandahar that Champion added to his literary notes for the *Age*.

After Alice's now invalid husband suffered a heart attack in February and was buried at Brighton, the couple quietly married on 16 May 1896 and moved to Fulham. Morley released *Maurice Quain* the following year with Champion speculating the author had 'grown more than ordinarily serious and problematic' and warning his friend of his reputation as a melancholic writer. The novel 'showed flashes of humour of a rare kind' and Victor Urquhart (modelled on Champion) was casually noted as 'a caricature of one of his best friends'.[434] He originally titled it *John Romer*, a name drawn from *Piers Plowman* to suggest another wanderer although Morley renamed and revised the novel with the concluding chapter pointing to Australia as the place of escape from London's sordid life. Morley also tried his hand at a one act play, 'The Plot of His Story', produced at the Garrick Theatre on 15 December 1899 that became one of George Alexander's curtain raiser plays at St James's Theatre the following year.

With Morley and Alice's departure, the house of cards collapsed. Champion and Adelaide enjoyed nearly three months together, renting a smaller place at Clifton Hill, an upmarket suburb close to the city. Adelaide soon realised she had much to lose by her relationship with Champion, including placing access to her daughter in jeopardy. By August 1894 they separated, with Adelaide quietly reconciling with her husband and returning home to live in 'apparent amity' with him. Henry Hogg quietly sanctioned her ongoing affair with Champion, whom she continued to see and holiday with, including one trip to the mountains. Champion told him on 6 April 1896, 'the position is hopeless & can't be either ended or mended'. He was completely smitten and hopelessly trapped by his attachment and prepared to abandon his previous life – his drivers were love and sacrifice, not dissimilar to those for socialism.

Champion informed Morley on 3 July 1898 of the roller coaster of emotions following Adelaide's decision to move back to her husband. A number of formal conditions had been set by Champion for her return to Henry. The marriage would remain intact, husband and wife maintaining a separation within the marital home, while Adelaide was free to have a lover as long as no gossip emanated from the association:

> I made her promise, and get *him* to assent in writing to several things as conditions of her return. Among these were that (1) she should have her own rooms and live apart from him (2) that she should see me openly when and where she liked so long as no scandal was created

(3) that she should keep separate control of her own money & do as she pleased with it (4) that she should devote her time to writing or anything she pleased and not have to waste it calling upon his friends. There has never been any attempt to keep any of these promises. She has shared his room exactly as before & she never made the smallest attempt to create her own money & own time.

However, it appears that Adelaide wanted to placate both men so the affair continued along with the marriage. On 23 December, Champion argued that Adelaide 'was deceiving *everybody*'. She 'could tell no one the truth … but wanted us to be lovers still'.

Adelaide was increasingly a bundle of contradictory needs, demanding she and Champion meet frequently, despite the fact many people recognised him in the street. In addition, she was unhappy if he did not demonstrate his love for her in public displays of affection. These overt actions proved his love for her, showed their relationship was important to him and provided Adelaide with some sort of relationship security. Champion was clear when he said, 'she was miserable if I did not show her all the outward signs of passions' and may highlight a lack of physical intimacy within her marriage. Adelaide was plagued with guilt for deserting their adopted child and fretted about causing her husband's suffering. Her child-like refusal to see beyond her own emotional needs can be seen as projected through Adelaide's surrogate (Alma) in his tale of Brighton Beach: 'She was of a generous disposition, and, unless it promised her an irresistible amount of pleasure would generally refrain from any course likely to give pain to others'.[435] In essence, Adelaide could not end the affair, needing to see Champion regularly and appearing to really love him, but she couldn't leave her husband for fear of hurting him further. Adelaide had 'the whip hand' with both men but it was her 'infernal softheartedness that ruined us', Champion declared to Morley on 26 October 1896. 'I don't think I should love her so if she had been different', he confessed, so she remained a 'paragon'. He would continue to see her as 'most utterly angelic' forever, despite her vacillation and reluctance to leave.

Adelaide's return to her husband was a catalyst for Champion to try politics again even though he admitted to Morley on 14 June 1896: 'Politics only means worry. You can't get anything done without working like a slave. I want money, enough to be free forever & a day of this cramping poverty & to do a heap of things for A.' His failure in Scotland was now regarded as a rehearsal for success. Not long after she moved out Champion changed his address to 64 Hawksburn Road, South Yarra, in preparation for his run for the seat of Albert Park. At the same time, Henry Bournes Higgins was a candidate for the seat of Geelong, George Prendergast for North Melbourne, and William Trenwith for Richmond; the first of these three men became a friend and the others enemies.

Champion attracted good audiences with Herbert Brookes establishing a committee to support his political venture, paying the deposit for his candidature, and assisting to launch his newspaper. He told Morley that Brookes shared a similar belief in Champion's abilities as George Gerrie during the Aberdeen election. Brookes was an admirer of Champion's stance against the big banks and his personal papers hold one of Champion's 1895 'Open' letters 'To the Directors of the City of Melbourne Bank Ltd'. In fact, he urged Champion to place a land values tax high on agenda when addressing members of Strong's Australian Church Literary Society. As a result, Champion argued in a speech that Victorians paid a 'crushing tribute' of £6 million on mortgages from which the colony would not recover unless an unimproved land value tax was introduced to reduce debt.[436] His success as a candidate seemed guaranteed when a Town Hall meeting overflowed with supporters, as well as 'a sprinkling of opponents, chiefly big brawny workers from the Melbourne Gas Works'. Champion's talent for public speaking and sense of public theatre were on display for all and Brookes watched him at the hall speak forcefully and with clever humour, calling him 'a very plucky man'. The *Bulletin* also saw Champion in a favourable light as 'a plain, straightforward talker':

> Champion says nothing without giving a reason for his doctrine, and at answering every kind of question from both sides of it at once, he is a much smarter man than Deakin. He makes 10 words go farther

than 50 from the ordinary platform spouter ... Champion's style lacks the features that most impress an audience, especially a working man audience. He is a slight, young-looking speaker, with a voice unlike a bull's – no fire, gesture, or air of 'deep sense of responsibility' about him. However, he has been a revelation in fluent democratic argument to the denizens of Albert Park, and if they don't return Champion in preference to the late member (an ex-night-soil contractor) his failure will be entirely owing to the lateness of his arrival on the scene.[437]

It was decided nothing would be lost in working with an arbitration panel to select one candidate from the four nominated: Champion, Harry Meadows, Ernest Joske and William Mountain. A timber surveyor, Mountain refused to participate, so a high-profile panel was chosen in mid-September consisting of Alfred Deakin, supporting Joske, a barrister; Prendergast, supporting Meadows, a tailor; and Sir Graham Berry, regarded as a member of the 'snobocracy', supporting Champion, a gentleman. Prendergast's nomination won while Champion and Joske retired gracefully from the contest to back Meadows who failed to win the seat. This trust in arbitration was a miscalculation, erupting into a deep enmity later between Champion and Prendergast. Subsequently, Champion formed the Victorian Progressive Democratic Party (VPDP) as an Albert Park branch with a committee composed of Champion, Brookes, Joske and Meadows. The intention was to stop the decade of political instability that occurred around candidates running for seats. At the inaugural address in October 1894 Champion was first speaker, followed by lectures from Dr Charles Strong and Professor Tucker to promote the VPDP and its objectives.

In the aftermath of the arbitration that led to Champion's withdrawal from the 1894 election, he looked around for something to capture his imagination and perhaps make money. His ambition in the political area had been stymied for the time being and a gold mining adventure was a lure. Invited by Herbert Brookes to Glen Wills in the Alpine mountains above Omeo in East Gippsland, Champion accepted an offer of an option to peg a lease. His hope was that gold would lead to his fortune and secure a future so Adelaide could leave her husband. A couple of thousand feet above the township, Brookes had a house looked after by 'Old Harry', a Londoner who had emigrated to Australia. William Brookes, Herbert's father, originally had purchased four leases in a claim called the 'Smile of Fortune' with Isaac Wheeldon (a partner in the Madam Berry West mine at Creswick) and Thomas Daniels Merton. They were secretly exploring the alluvial area in the Alps for gold although later it was discovered Merton had been involved with a fraudulent mining venture called 'Taranganba' in New South Wales in 1889. Nothing came of Champion's foray into gold mining and the lease for Glen Wills was sold two years later.

Although Brookes and the gold claim were never mentioned, Champion documented his trip a couple of years later, writing on road conditions and the surrounding area for the *Champion*.[438] One of the holidays he and Adelaide secretly took together, this was an opportunity afforded in the spring after she returned to her husband in August. Champion's first article discussed the mining town of Bonang in East Gippsland accessed by coach from Orbost. The second presented the whole experience as a cycling tour of the Alpine Region, detailing the route taken to the Brookes's house above Glen Wills. After travelling by train to Bright there was a trip of 16 miles through the Ovens Valley between Bright and Harrietville by horse-drawn coach, then an ascent of the Alps for another 11.5 miles to *Bousted's Hospice* accommodation, a refuge for tourists and the mailman, as depicted in a painting by Tom Roberts, 'The Mailman to Omeo (Snow Shoes)'.

According to Champion, also on the road at that time were eight people including one woman who were on a tour between Bright and Bairnsdale and took more than four hours to ascend to the *Bousted's*. This was the perfect place to act on the stipulated condition for Adelaide to see Champion openly and without 'scandal'. Holiday excursions were often advertised by Victorian Railways in 1894 and special trains were scheduled from South Yarra or Caulfield to mountainous areas. Trains left the Princes Bridge station at 7am to reach Bairnsdale at 1.15pm for journeys to Bright, Ovens Vale or Beechworth, with the ability to book return journeys several days or weeks later.

Brookes reminisced about Champion leaving his Alpine house early one morning for a day's ride by horse, ostensibly to explore around *Boustead's* on the road to Mount Hotham. He wrote of his friend getting 'bushed' and being forced to camp alone overnight in the 'wild region' and was amused Champion wasn't perturbed by his adventure in the lonely bush, but 'rather thrilled about it'. This ex-artilleryman, trained as a proficient horse rider, who rode to Quetta as well as up the steep Khojak Pass, was definitely not bush-wacked and his spirits were rising. No wonder Champion was 'thrilled' to be in a region where an individual could contrive, in his own words, to be 'lost amid the immensity' of the mountains. In all probability, the road to Mount Hotham was a journey to the 'lady' on a tour who boarded at the hospice. Staying with Brookes further up the mountain, Champion certainly knew the exact half-a-crown tariff at *Boustead's* where guests were well looked after.

It seems highly likely Adelaide joined him and travelled back with him visiting remote country places where neither of them was known and they could travel as husband and wife. Indeed, quite a few other places with accommodation are mentioned on his journey back to Melbourne as he travelled slowly through Parslow, crossing Tambo and through Bruthen, before catching a train from Bairnsdale to Spencer Street. Although he wrote of the area in the guise of a wonderful cycling tour amongst magnificent scenery and suggested places along the route for cyclists to stay, he didn't inform readers that he saw this region three years before and not on a bicycle. At a time when communication with Adelaide was cut off for six months, he was able to remind her of their shared experience.

Adelaide threw herself into her new religious movement and both she and Champion joined the Theosophists.[439] Champion became president and founding member of the Ibis Lodge at 8 Garden Street in South Yarra, giving talks on 'Theosophy in Practical Life' at their annual convention in 1896; Alfred Deakin joined and was secretary. As part of her plan to show him in a good light, Adelaide now avidly encouraged him in public work, including visits to places such as hospitals and prisons, and arguing for women to hold positions in these institutions. Champion raised concerns that hospital administrators prioritised hospital routine over the comfort of patients and was critical of the fact that women had been denied places on the hospital committee in Omeo. Critiques were made on the treatment of nurses in the Women's Hospital where their 90 hours work per week was seen as sweating, his past association with professional nurses such as Maggie Harkness probably adding to in-depth knowledge. Involved with the Melbourne University's Historical Society, Champion made excursions to places such as the Prison Gate Brigade's Home, the Women's Industrial Home and Shelter, as well as a Salvation Army farm and gave lectures on favourite topics such as 'The Old Chivalry and the New'. He tackled an assertion by an Oxford professor that university was only a place for men, drawing attention to the vast sums donated by prominent women in receipt of no benefit.[440] He also visited the Children's Convalescent Home at Brighton Beach which had the added benefit of various trips to the area with Adelaide. Writing to Morley on 3 July 1898, he claimed that Adelaide kept pushing his 'advocacy of purer morals' until he was forced to abandon some activities because of 'shame'.

As Adelaide's commitment to Theosophy grew, so did Champion's scepticism. Throughout 1897 he informed Morley that she was 'deeper into the Theosophy maze in a vain endeavour to find out what the object of it all is' (1 January), believing 'our misfortunes were managed by a Divine Purpose to improve the texture of our souls' (11 July) even though it was 'the thinnest sort of nonsense ... for the study of the occult' (22 August). Adelaide continued throughout 1898 to leave Macedon for Tuesday sessions in Melbourne or, as Champion labelled it, 'to fool about with the Theosophists' (28 March 1898). In London Champion had witnessed a number of organisations springing up in the wake of Darwinism, many attracted to spiritualist séances and psychic research, popular because of their novelty and entertainment value for parlour games. They often served as drawcards to engage an audience searching for an alternate belief system or something metaphysical. Adelaide's husband was a member of the Society for Psychical Research enlisting prominent academics, politicians and poets to study the phenomenon. SDF treasurer, Herbert Burrows – who claimed in the London *Daily Chronicle* that Annie Besant astral travelled from America to see him – resigned his own membership of the Theosophical Society, alleging the Society was 'an open door to superstition, delusion, and fraud'.[441]

In March 1895 Champion's father died at home of pneumonia after a bout of influenza. The event would have more commercial implications for Champion than emotional ones, as suggested the following year in his dispassionate pronouncement of the fact that both his father and mother had died. His sister Louisa was married with children so Annie Beatrice was his father's nurse as well as executor of his will, along with a wealthy barrister and part owner of Vale Press, William Llewellyn Hacon (who married another sister, Mary Leslie, before her early death in 1887). Champion's father left an estate worth £13,000 and his mother Henrietta died only six months later on 8 September in Leicester. With £500 bequeathed to him through his father's will, he collected a group of shareholders and commenced publication of the *Champion* newspaper in June 1895 to provide a platform for political, social and literary issues. The following month Champion founded and was appointed secretary of the Social Democratic Federation, with W.J. Lorimer J.P. (chairman) and J. Cook (treasurer). They met at the *Champion* newspaper office and the SDF Manifesto was drafted and printed on 20 July 1895.

Champion was motivated, organised and innovative at this time, putting his inheritance to work to make a better life for Adelaide. Using his practical skill from the publishing business and his forward thinking as a campaigner and activist, he was eminently qualified to take on an opinion shaping role. He established many organisations in the year following his father's death, always as either secretary or director, and threw himself with frenetic energy into a network of political and social association, advocating for various causes. He purchased the Champion Printing and Publishing Company with £750, giving him equivalent shares and, as manager and editor, drew the substantial salary of £300 per annum. Registered on 19 November 1895 with shares of £1 each, the company raised capital of £2,500 in a fashion similar to the establishment four years earlier of Twentieth Century Press, where Hyndman became chairman of shareholders for *Justice*. Able to issue shares to replace wages, by 18 January 1896, Champion told Herbert Brookes he owned 825 shares.

The newspaper title, the *Champion*, was seen as a display of his 'frank egotism' and one journalist used Gilbert and Sullivan's *The*

Gondoliers (1888) to refer to Champion's use of the Limited Liability Company Act to restrict any loss to capital investment, not personal assets: 'The Duke of Plazza-Torro hit upon the expedient of floating himself as a limited liability company, and joining the board of directors after allotment. H.H. floats himself as a paper, and will sell himself in penny numbers'.[442] While *Champion's* reputation grew in a niche market, the paper was well known for topical issues, and was recorded in parliamentary debates by *Hansard.*

Three directors, Percy Frost, Herbert Brookes and Ernest Carey, worked with four other shareholders, John Whichells Cutting (later printer of *Book Lover* at 270 Post Office Box, the address for Spectator Publishing Company), W.J. Lorimer (SDF Chairman), Edward Tierney and Walter Vizard. Carey was the newspaper's principal financial backer and also secretary of the Northern District Starr-Bowkett Building Society, which provided loans on mortgages free of interest, a sign of a bubble economy. Later, two businesses – Carey, Frost & Co., a consulting firm of accountants and auditors selling real estate in Queen Street, and Victorian Registry Offices, an employment agency in Russell Street – were established although the partnership was finally dissolved on 9 January 1899. In April 1900 a newspaper, the *Outpost,* was started with Walter Vizard as editor and Ernest Carey as manager, at the same address as Northern District Starr-Bowkett Building Society at 237 Collins Street. Champion told Morley on 14 June 1896 that, similar to his experience owning and editing the *Labour Elector,* a bid was made 'to seize the paper & crush me – when it became known the thing [*Champion*] was on its feet and worth stealing'; he was forced to dispense with the 'other fellows' as 'autocrat'. Brookes recorded that Carey left for San Francisco early in 1905 'after robbing the Building Society of a large sum of money' while a South Australian paper reported the manager was 'a flighty man who afterwards ran away to America with a wife that didn't belong to him, bringing ruin to the whole concern'.[443]

Another interested party was the Spectator Publishing Company Ltd. registered on 8 March 1889, before Champion arrived in Australia, and an owner of the *Spectator and Wesleyan Methodist Chronicle.* Both a shareholder and a trustee of the company, Elisha

Clement De Garis was born in the Channel Island of Guernsey where a well-known branch of Champion's family still resided. A friend of Alfred Deakin, De Garis was a prominent advocate of irrigation, a founder of a farmers' distribution co-operative and a commissioner of the Melbourne Centennial International Exhibition. His own niche newspaper had merged with the *Weekly Times*. A passionate hater of both De Garis and Champion was Grant Hervey, blacksmith turned journalist for the Sydney's *Bulletin* and *Truth*, Perth's *Sunday Times* and Kalgoorlie newspapers. De Garis was instrumental in exposing Hervey as a swindler and forger during an irrigation swindle in Mildura in mid-1919, while the proprietor of *Truth* reported Hervey to police for forgery involving the editor's wife. Champion had attacked him as a poet in 1914 for 'shocking rhymes, bad grammar, absolute nonsense, and false feeling' and this induced a virulent tirade in the *Truth* later that month, with Hervey calling him an imported 'English failure' who was 'not fit to lick the boots of any recognised Australian writer'. Hervey earlier poured his vitriol on Tom Mann after his speech at Fitzgerald's Circus and aggressively slammed him as an import to the country with 'nothing in the man – save noise'.[444]

The *Champion* had 'a short, a merry and an exciting life', according to Brookes, even though it was a 'gloomy' office accessed by a flight of wooden steps, positioned next door to busy kitchens pumping out cooking odours of oysters and steak. The editorial office was centrally located on the first floor at 7 Queen's Walk near the Melbourne Town Hall. Queen's Walk, newly constructed only half a dozen years before, travelled east from Swanston Street before turning north onto Collins Street and in the same arcade was the Melbourne Savage Club, founded for the appreciation of music, art, drama, science and literature.

Champion's main creative contributors on his newspaper were John Buckley Castieau ('Paul Mell') editor of *Free Lance* until October 1896 and Bernard O'Dowd ('Danton'). Political cartoons were supplied by a Scottish-born artist for the Cannibals Club, Max Meldrum, responsible for revamping the front-page drawing of *Champion* and Ambrose Dyson (the first to draw the 'larrikin', said to be a Melbourne constable's mispronunciation of an Irish word) and one of his cartoons depicted Sisyphus in fruitless labour rolling the Legislative Assembly uphill.

Walter Vizard, whose inflammatory writing for *Outpost* showed his distinctive libellous style, was responsible for some early contributions that, at a public lecture at Footscray Workingmen's club, Champion had to defend himself, claiming he did not write a nasty paragraph about John Hancock on 27 July 1895. Carey was probably responsible for portions of the 'World on Wheel' column (he later represented himself in 1899 as a cycling journalist for 'Cycling News'), Ernest Buley concentrated on sport, while Jeffrey Macpherson (Melbourne Grammar School teacher and Dandenong lawyer) wrote pieces under 'Crites'. As a newspaper editor and contributor, Champion kept up to date with politics, society and entertainment and voraciously read overseas and local newspapers and journals, parliamentary debates, speeches and *Hansard* proceedings. His 'crusading' paper took up the cause of everything he saw as wrong or corrupt. However, he admitted to Morley that there was no money to be made by the newspaper, 'a bare living only'. While admiring his friend's courage, the gentle William Gay gave an early and wise warning to Champion that 'zeal has dangers'. Gay was not the only person to see significant and powerful enemies lined up against Champion. As Champion caused consternation with his trenchant criticism of those in parliament and society, even a small country magazine could see the risk to both newspaper and proprietor:

> 'We confess that we are watching the career of the CHAMPION with deep interest. It is a novelty, if not an experiment. Mr. Champion is engaged in probing the bowels of our social system with a red hot poker. He knows that he is perilously near a powder magazine, but the work is so dare-devil and exhilarating that he probes on. Some day the poker and the powder will coalesce and then we shall have cause and effect!'.[445]

In his political writing in England Champion had assumed *nom-de-plumes* of ancient philosophers, a tradition he continued in Australia and one Morley Roberts termed Freudian 'alter ego-es'.[446] 'Diogenes' (a Greek philosopher who believed in action, rather than theory) was a favourite in *Justice's* 'Letters to Revolutionary Agents'. In one article on financial institutions in the *Champion*, he explicitly pointed to the Lamp of Diogenes, a dramatic prop carried in daylight by the philosopher in his search for an honest man. The Scottish medieval philosopher 'Duns Scotus' who debated the number of angels on the head of a pin featured along with 'Philalethes' the lover of truth. The Latin phrase, Fortes Fortuna Juvat, or 'Fortune favours the brave', became the quirky 'F.F. Juvat', then 'F.F.J' and a shortened 'F' used for theatre articles 'Murmurs about Mummers'. 'The Golden Fleece' on finance, share markets and gold mining, cunningly merged George Sala's visit to 'The Land of the Golden Fleece: Marvellous Melbourne' in 1885, with an allusion to the legend of Jason and the name of the claim owned by William Brookes. In addition, H.C.C. was used for writing creative verse or stories although, like his correspondence, this sometimes served as a conveyer of cryptic messages to Adelaide.

Occasionally Champion's columns got him into serious trouble. On 11 February 1896 he faced prosecution for criminal libel for his comments on a horse owned by Charles O'Halloran, solicitor and member of the Turf Club, pulled from a race because of blindness in one eye. His paper's comments about the stewards having 'blindness in both eyes' resulted in court action with James Liddell Purves QC announcing Champion's 'paper had been started on the principle of extracting money from the public by publishing infamous and scandalous matter concerning private individuals'. Days later *Table Talk* laughingly explained the antagonism between Champion and Purves QC, claiming this went back to a meeting in Dion Boucicault's Melbourne dressing room after a performance at the Princess Theatre.[447] Boucicault (Champion's old class-mate from Marlborough) had been talking to Champion, now a critic for the *Age*, about the performance of Pinero's *The Second Mrs Tanqueray* in July 1894. Purves wandered in, interrupted and commented brashly on Boucicault's production (with deleted expletives): 'why the devil do you waste your company on a [–] trashy play like this?', to which Champion, on introduction to Purves, mentioned its success in London. Purves blustered: 'Oh, so you're Champion, are you? Well all I can say Mr. Champion is that you may know something about Socialism, but you know [–] little about the drama.' Champion's cold and casual response: 'I might easily say, O you're Purves, are you? Well, you may know something about the law, but you know [–] little about manners'. The story was repeated endlessly, much to the amusement of people in Melbourne.

Champion was vindicated, accusing Purves of making 'wild and totally unfounded charges' in calling him 'a blackmailer who extorted money under threats' and making use of legal privilege in his 'cowardly' assault. He also happily printed Edward Pariss Nesbit's public support against the bullying tactics of Purves: 'If I had my way his silk gown would be stripped off his back, and he would be drummed out of the ranks of the Bar'.[448] Nesbit QC, known as the 'Prince of Bohemia' was a highly intelligent man with ideas for social reform and a drafter of many significant parliamentary laws. He wrote *Lunacy Laws and Procedure in Victoria* (1896) after his admission as an inmate to Kew Lunatic Asylum. Champion published his poetry and translations and also reviewed and promoted the verse and tales of country life of his cousin, Edith Bland (née Nesbit). When Purves described Chief Justice of the Supreme Court, George Higinbotham, as 'punctilious and narrow-minded', Champion labelled his slur as 'tinctured with malice, indicating that the Purvesian vanity had at some time or other collided with the Higinbothamic dignity', calling Purves a 'bullying barrister' who was fair game because intimidators were 'always cowards'.[449]

Champion read and promoted many Australian poets, including his friends William Gay and J.B. O'Hara, the latter a trophy-winning cricketer and popular headmaster of South Melbourne College. In addition, he highlighted the works of Adam Lindsay Gordon, Henry Kendall and Henry Lawson. Kendall's love of nature he found engaging but 'such a throat with its sweet notes should have sung for the democracy'. Champion insisted that, like Ezekiel, Kendall had a responsibility to warn humanity of approaching danger: 'Had he no watchman's warning to shout, saw he none of the old evils in their newer forms, heard he no cry of the dispossessed?'. Champion preferred the radical bush poet Henry Lawson, 'the singer' of Australia's 'hope and joy, and the psalmist of her wrath and woe', and envisioned a 'crucial crisis' in Australia's future after Lawson released *In the Days when the World was Wide, and Other Verses* (1896). Champion surged with admiration for a 'universal genius stamped with the hall-mark of Australia' and he passionately proclaimed that 'Brotherhood and Love and Honour!' was universal. Later, in '"Pursuing Literature" in Australia' Lawson lamented that his two 1896 books represented 12 years of literary work and earned him a mere £200 after he sold the entire publishing rights and he warned aspiring writers to go overseas 'rather than stay in Australia till his genius turned to gall, or beer'.[450]

However, it was not all sad and serious and Brookes was correct that the *Champion's* life was sometimes 'merry'. With a lively and vital air, in a press which was constrained by old conventional ideas, the wit and fun of writing shone through. One delightful example came from an article on rational dress for women where Champion observed that veils for both sexes existed since Homer:

'Ulysses, taking a large purple veil in his sturdy hands, drew it over his head and covered his beauteous face, for he was ashamed before the Phocians, shedding tears from under his eyebrows. But when the divine bard had ceased singing, having wiped away the tears, he took the veil from his head, and, taking a round cup, he made libations to the gods.' The manly veil thus seems to have been, as it were, a sort of portable tent, into which emotional men could retire to escape observation when they wished to indulge in the luxury of weeping (*Champion*, 14 September 1895).

The snapshot displayed a mischievous sense of humour. Similarly, his facetiousness showed in Champion's quiet summary of an English author's absurd description of a woman's sexual attraction to a country gentleman who was

> ... a superior rustic, being of gentle blood but not of gentle nurture. He is nothing if not strong and passionate. He takes her literally by storm and violence. And she, delicate and cultured woman though she is, finds it not unpleasant. There is a misunderstanding to be worked out, but finally everything is straight, and she quotes: –
> Why care by what meanders we are here
> I the centre of the labyrinth? Men have died
> Trying to find this place which we have found.

His reading of *The Failure of Sibyl Fletcher*, a novel he never expected to finish, was blamed on the need of rest after bicycle riding. He obviously found the book hilarious as he read about a girl who was 'faded, jaded, jilted, and eight and twenty all at the same time'.[451]

A month after Champion's new publishing venture burst into life, one newspaper's satirical piece anticipated two new rival newspapers would spring into life: the *Hancock* and the *Prendergast*. Champion attracted commentators who revelled in the effect Champion's paper would have on his THC enemies:

> Every member of the Trades Hall will buy 'The Champion.' They will buy it to see if the conductor of it pitches into any of them; and if he does (such is the jealous state of feeling existing in that delightful body) it will give the keenest delight to every man not attacked, and everyone will be anxious to see who is going to get it next. The Trades Hall will think a penny very cheap for a paper Champion, if only for the reason that they couldn't on any account consider him 'dear'.[452]

With a deep-seated suspicion and loathing of the military and with his hatred still resounding from the Maritime Strike, in 1896 Hancock labelled Champion 'a treacherous fellow, who would dine with the Labor [sic] party in the morning, and with their bitterest opponents in the evening'. Four months later, Champion highlighted Hancock's likeable traits of 'the genial, beery, pot-house variety' but pointed to his manners in the Assembly as those of 'a stupid boor', complaining that some members lacked 'the pluck and wit to speak some obvious truths to this incompetent, blustering and ill-conditioned buffoon'. Such plain speaking exposed his own anger and was never guaranteed to win over enemies who had long memories, remained intractable and were not subtle in revenge.

George Michael Prendergast, joined the list of enemies who delivered virulent hate speeches. As a man of great ambition, considerable resentment and little remorse, Prendergast opposed Champion's aspirations and seriously threatened his personal life with Adelaide for a few years. Widely known in Melbourne as 'Windy Mick' because he could speak at great length on any subject, the *Champion* placed Prendergast on its 'list of the most inflated gasbags', designed to cause much amusement for readers. After school in regional Stawell, Prendergast had been an apprentice printer on the *Pleasant Creek News* then secretary of the New South Wales Typographical Society from 1881, before moving to Melbourne prior to the Maritime Strike in 1888. An enthusiastic member of the United Irish League and Celtic Club, from 1891 he joined the Progressive Political League, a short-lived party (established by Hancock, Trenwith and Bromley) that focused on electing men to represent labour. Some also believed the party's intention was to keep people like Champion out. Only months after Champion's arrival back in Australia, Prendergast and Edward Findley established (in late August 1894) the democratic weekly, *Boomerang*, which ran to eight issues before going into liquidation 14 months later. After newspapers refused to print Prendergast's response to Champion's Open Letter to Michael Davitt,[453] Prendergast was invited by Champion to publish the reply in his own failing newspaper.

The THC remained firmly opposed to Champion and were well organised in their dissent and opposition, especially once Prendergast assumed office as THC president. Described as 'a fierce, violent demagogue' and 'too rough, too violent and too bitter', one journalist believed:

> He is ideal when speaking from a lorry at a street corner, his face lit by murky kerosene torches, his voice loud and raucous, roaring out bitter invective, and launching the most sweeping accusations against his opponents ... Intemperance of thought and language are fatal blocks to success in politics, and that is the flaw in Mr. Prendergast's make-up as a politician.[454]

Alfred Buchanan, novelist and journalist for the *Age* and the *West Australian*, used the volatile Prendergast for his fictional character McNeill, a platform speaker and 'a voluble one'.

> There was no doubt that he could talk. With more ballast and more training and more self-control he would have been an orator of the very first rank. As it was, he talked too much and too often. He

never knew when to stop. And his creed outran the majority even of those who voted the Labour ticket. It was the creed of many landless Irishmen; it was the creed of the outlaw and the renegade. Wherever there was a Government or any political institution of standing, he had a burning desire to pull it down – a desire amounting to a passion (*Bubble Reputation*, p. 272).

In the lead-up to May Day there was increasing tension. In February 1895 Prendergast and Hancock watched approvingly as Edward Findley and Frank Anstey were selected as candidates for South Carlton amidst rumours of intrigue in the selection process. Nearly two months later Prendergast led the charge against Champion at a THC meeting, brandishing replies to letters sent by Anstey to Keir Hardie and H.W. Lee, to argue for his refusal to stand on any platform with Champion. Hancock also expressed his outright disdain for Champion. A few members (Walter Hurrell, John Billson, Robert Solly) disputed the allegations, arguing Prendergast exhibited ill feeling towards Champion over many years and that some members had not been in agreement with the sentiment against Champion during the Maritime Strike. The boot trade (Solly) supported Champion, claiming his lectures brought in large amounts of money for their cause across the country. As a THC delegate to the May Day committee a week later, Findley was also sent to read aloud letters from Hardie and Lee published in the *Worker* on 16 February, while the May Day chair pointed to an obvious personal quarrel between THC and Champion.

Now that Champion was the owner of a newspaper, he had founded the SDF and published their manifesto, he turned his attention towards helping with the formation of the Anti-Sweating League of Victoria. Formed on 23 July 1895 in Bourke Street Champion was vice president and Samuel Mauger was honorary secretary.[455] At this time, with a committee that included Mrs Isabella Goldstein, Professor Gosman, Dr Charles Strong, Alfred Deakin, Marshall Lyle, Henry Dalgish and Mrs Sarah Muir, the Factories and Shops Act 1896 was prepared and drafted for the Legislative Assembly. It would provide the first statutory minimum wage in the country.[456] Elections loomed and the pressure was turned up as Adelaide 'urged' him stand for a seat and Brookes provided the £20 fee.

Now an elected member for North Melbourne, Prendergast ratcheted up his verbal assault on Champion with a re-run of stories from the Maritime Strike days. At an Anti-Sweating meeting at the Town Hall, where the speakers were Deakin, Hancock and Champion, Prendergast constantly interrupted with invective about Champion's 'forged credentials' to some amusement within the crowd. Provoked by references to cowardice, Champion finished his speech labelling a coward 'someone who ignorantly led his forces up a blind alley to destruction' telling the crowd that if the 1890 strike had been successful there would not be those still 'pleading in their weakness for what they should have been able to insist on'.[457] In lengthy commentary on the incident particularly over a drunk Prendergast shouting inflammatory lines about gaol, a disgusted editor suggested either proof or apology should be provided or Prendergast would be 'branded as a liar and a coward':

> If there be anything calculated to transform the pity felt for the Trades Hall Council into contempt, it is the completely childish and despicable conduct of some of its leading members. One of the worst instances of this occurred at the anti-sweating meeting, when Labor [sic] Member PRENDERGAST, in coram publico, hiccoughed out, in maudlin fashion, insulting and slanderous interjections while H.H. CHAMPION was speaking. The ordinary foolish interruptions of a public meeting are not deserving of notice. But the mudslinging indulged in by PRENDERGAST was not ordinary. It was a deliberate and dastardly act, which the FREE LANCE believes it would be difficult to extenuate by any solid justification.[458]

It was a vain request. What part of Prendergast's personality suggested he would ever act on such a proposition?

However, the 1890 strike had raised the ire of the THC leaders and Champion was obstinate, never apologetic for his actions, advice or his famous phrase 'lions led by asses'. He had denounced the leaders as vain and inept and would never be forgiven nor his comments forgotten.

Old enemies formed a united front and concerted campaigns were waged to discredit Champion after 26 societies elected him president of the May Day Committee. In one of his speeches, Champion saw the crux of the issue as 'the twin evil' facing workers being 'over-work and want of work'.[459] Hancock, Prendergast and Murphy refused to be on the same platform for May Day 1896, Murphy declaring the THC should have stayed out of the Anti-Sweating League because Champion was involved. Their own counter demonstration on May Day was called 'a fizzle' in the *Champion*. One journalist noted 'the asses have never forgiven him' and 'the magnates' (Hancock and Murphy) called him a deceitful traitor and 'a wolf in sheep's clothing'. Champion continued to be the lightning rod for past grievances.

At a meeting on 7 May at the South Melbourne Town Hall Champion proclaimed he was against future arbitration for the seat because of political dishonesty during the 1894 election. A couple of weeks later he explained:

> He had since ascertained that one at least of the umpires was committed to vote against him before consenting to act as arbitrator. He would therefore not resort to arbitration again unless there was security for fair play (*Champion*, 16 May 1896).

Politics required people who were 'not afraid to make enemies, who have no private interests to gag them, no personal cliques to serve, who are prepared to speak the truth unflinchingly until this truth is accepted by the country as a whole'. Assailed on the political front Champion positioned himself on a metaphorical ledge of truth-telling, subject to slander yet continuing his fearless fight against opponents. His attack on prominent men in the THC, together with his propensity to push hard from an independent position as a non-unionist, a gentleman and an outsider, caused deep anger and was emotionally draining not only to Champion but to all those who admired him, including Adelaide. Now up in Macedon for the winter, she was 'dreadfully lonely' and 'very melancholy'. She turned back to writing and had completed 25 chapters, Champion told Morley on 14 June that year.

Alfred Buchanan's main character in his novel, *Bubble Reputation*, was modelled on Champion during this time of his life. The author chose the title from Shakespeare's play, *As You Like It*, referring to a soldier who defends his honour, is quick to fight and risks his life for fame.[460] Buchanan caught the mood of Champion's address to a meeting when he spoke to Victorian electors.

> He believed in the absolute necessity of letting in the strongest searchlight of criticism upon existing administration; he believed that the blood and toil and money of the workers of the country had been used constantly in the past and were being used now to fatten parasites who were the most contemptible creatures on God's earth (p. 279).

Buchanan also captured an attitude and purpose, strikingly familiar to one Maggie Harkness described when she wrote about Champion.

> 'So far as I am personally concerned, I am here because my lot is cast, now and always, with those who have suffered from social, moral, and political wrong … It seems to me that the only real satisfaction, the only lasting happiness in life is to be found in working for a cause to which you are pledged, for which you are prepared to make some sacrifices, and in which you thoroughly believe' (p. 280).

Increasingly exposed to Prendergast's personal attacks Champion developed his own needle of hatred, keeping up his defence while pointing the finger at Prendergast as the probable source of 'poisoned darts' that aimed to discredit him politically and personally. His newspaper claimed,

> … certain lying slanders are being used by adherents of the Trades Hall and others as a means of discounting his candidature. These slanders do not take definite shape, they are the lies, original or second-hand, of desperate political opponents, many of whom possibly believe some of the things they disseminate so sneakingly … If PRENDERGAST is in earnest he will perhaps assume the virtue (even though he has it not) of courage – and will make his charges clearly and in the open, as he has over and over again been invited to do. The public will then

have a chance of deciding whether he is a liar or not (*Champion*, 23 May 1896).

Free Lance declared their opposition to Champion's detractors, calling them 'common scandalmongers' with 'venomous intent' who issued their 'whisperings in preference to open denunciation'.[461]

The toxic war of words was relentless and stressful. The onslaught of political upheaval and personal assault after Prendergast and the THC's attack caused Champion to be 'mildly threatened' by one or two 'seizures' from working too hard or when he was under 'an acuter attack of utter despair than usual', he told Morley on 14 June 1896. By October he was beginning to feel the frost of advancing years, his hair was turning white and 'dyspepsia' (indigestion) added to his health issues, all of which Adelaide thought was caused by excessive work. In addition, he was still smoking tobacco in a time of excessive pressure. His old classmate from Marlborough, Anthony Hope [Hawkins], president of the Oxford Union in 1886 where Champion honed his speaking skills and author of *The Prisoner of Zenda*, was now 'a bald-headed man of grave middle age'. On seeing his friend's photograph, Champion confessed on 6 June to feeling 'senile and decrepit'. While writers still used Champion as a model for their fictional characters, he felt the stirrings of irrelevancy in the political arena.

Before the onset of winter, Mrs Isabella Goldstein (who was working on the Factories and Shop Act 1896) permitted Champion and Adelaide to meet secretly at her office five days a week for an hour or two in the afternoons, before they walked through the Botanical Gardens, he explained to Morley on 14 June 1896. When Adelaide came to town from Macedon for a few weeks, they were forced 'to be very careful', he confessed on 26 October. Unlike London, Adelaide was 'pretty well known to all the well-to-do people' while he was 'known by sight to 9 out of 10' people. Months before this, Mrs Goldstein had been 'warned' by an anonymous letter that the pair's meetings at her office would generate 'a scandal' and Champion too had then received a letter. Gossip was circulating in Society that he had been '*en ménage* at Clifton Hill' and so Champion endured 'nasty' comments made to his face about Adelaide that were designed 'to see how I would take them'. He abandoned going out in public. Mrs Goldstein now was implicated in 'arranging secret meetings' between the couple and so was placed in the firing line.

By the end of the year, Champion believed he knew the identity of his accuser. To Morley he explained on 1 January 1897: 'one of my enemies (I know who it is – a chap who beats his wife – a friend of A's the wife is – whom I compelled to sign a deed of separation, after which the wife of course went back) has taken to bombarding us with anonymous letters'. In all probability Adelaide shared snippets of personal information with her battered and beaten friend, repeated back to her husband during the couple's reconciliation. Champion's use of artillery terms such as 'bombardment' suggests correspondence became a sustained, targeted and deliberately planned campaign, a continuous offensive designed to undermine and weaken him using the fear of disclosure. Champion was also able to pinpoint the same man as responsible for a personal campaign against him.

> Then it came to my ears that he (or some one else) had put about the same sort of thing that time I stood for Parliament at South Melbourne & got so few votes last May. Of course in this little place any beast like that who knows a bit may any day run up against one of the two or three people who know that I was living with some one at Beaconsfield & Clifton Hill. For myself that does not matter. If ever challenged I could just brazen it out or say it was my private affair. But the truth is that this beast will know & say that A is the person involved & that won't do. You see the position is impossible.

Questioning why 'an act which requires two people for its commission should be considered necessary and right for the one and wrong for the other',[462] he nevertheless recognised Victorian morality would consider Adelaide a fallen or ruined woman.

As William Gay advised 'zeal has dangers'. Champion's secret relationship with Adelaide was also dangerous. Aware that his lover was residing happily with her husband, Champion acknowledged his frustration at being morally hamstrung, his ingrained urge to do battle inevitably curtailed by worry about the effect of scandal on Adelaide.

He could only snipe at people such as Prendergast 'from behind the journalistic hedge,' he confessed, although in his newspaper he always sounded confident and strong, an image a political leader needed to project. Effectively his love of an unattainable woman meant any political career he thought to achieve was self-sabotaged. With language rich in negatives, Champion's letter on the first day of a new year bemoaned his failure to 'manage to take any interest in two consecutive issues', a fact that impacted the pathway to making the *Champion* 'a paying property'. He was hobbled in his ambition and his interest was 'mortgaged'. He was without 'zest for any kind of public work' or 'any hope, object or interest in life'.

Champion saw his relationship with Adelaide as doomed because of her temperament and his nature, he told Morley on 23 April 1897. He added, 'I don't love her any the less for her failings, her indecision, her ostrich-like propensity to persuade herself that the unseen does not really exist, her ability to inflict torture on me whom she loves'. However, he recognised that Adelaide was 'intricately posed between grief that my "career" is adrift and delight that it is my love for her that has done it'. Not interested in taking Morley's advice to 'come home & do something in politics and not "rot like a potato in a cellar"', he waited in limbo. Many letters were written to his friend about his frustration at being paralysed with dread, fearful of the discovery of their affair would make her a target for public scandal and social ostracism. Powerlessness was devastating to his imagination and he lamented on 15 August 1897: 'Picture me knowing who wrote those letters & not being able to lift a finger on him because it could only pillory her publicly if I did. Fancy me afraid to go on a platform or to stand for Parliament'.

In a retrospective review of the affair, he told Morley on 3 July 1898 of Adelaide's desire for his overt displays of affection even while he tried to protect her reputation, and so being torn between these two imperatives. Pointing to the stories that circulated during the election campaign about their liaison Champion confided, 'in the contest my enemies taxed me with fag ends of the true story as it had leaked out which I had to listen to with shut teeth'. Although initially she had handled the onslaught with a 'philosophic calm' of the spiritually certain, Champion noted that as the campaign of toxic 'darts' continued Adelaide became 'miserable' and 'distraught'. Ignoring the immense political and personal strain, Adelaide believed Champion was 'ill & unsuccessful' as a sort of karma or destiny because his 'love for her could not be of the proper sort'. As Champion worked out who was behind the attack, Adelaide became 'suicidally melancholy'.

A time of great vulnerability, the threat of exposure was imagined in all its ugliness, horror and gossip. Communication between the pair was effectively cut off for nearly six months from November to the following May 1897, as caution became their ally and public shame a close enemy. Of course, this lack of contact exacerbated Champion's own bleak mood. A week before Christmas 1896, a poem appeared in the *Champion* by 'The Bookman' titled 'Victor and Vanquished', finishing with the lines: 'Each had grasped the gift of fortune, each had counted up the cost, / And the vanquished was the victor, and the winner he had lost.' Even more telling was his mournful piece after Christmas 1896, 'The Yellow Rose: A Memory of a Little Girl'. Written at the time when all communication had been cut off with Adelaide, it is another story ostensibly about the author and six-year-old who are 'fast friends' and '"Lovers" they often called us'. The child's name, Queenie, in all probability is a pseudonym for Adelaide and is drawn from the town of Adelaide (named after Queen Adelaide) where Adelaide's father, Alexander Lang Elder, made his fortune. The story is couched as a memory of a children's game, requiring an appeal to a tall yellow rose growing under a large tree, that 'climbed higher than the others'. Queenie has 'golden hair', her prognosis of 'no hope' from ill-health means she returns home and he is left with 'a terrible sorrow pressing tightly upon his heart'. The final sentence is cryptic: 'But the rose never comes down, for all his calling – and he would not have it otherwise, because he loved her'. A symbolic representation of love and loss, the tale recalls his Brighton Beach story of helping Alma (a pseudonym for Adelaide) to reach roses outside her verandah.

On Boxing Day Champion turned to a poem by John Barlas, with his powerful images centred on love, life, sacrifice, death, loss and remembrance to encapsulate his emotional state. This was a beautiful and mournful love sonnet urging a lover to carry roses to his grave where, 'Living, with selfish love the loved-one's lot, / Nor, dead, would have my dear love live forlorn, – / Yet would not wish my own love quite forgot'. His nostalgia for old friends was also evident in 'A Christmas Meeting', a poem that recalls people who had died, including Juliet Bennett, James L. Joynes and William Morris, and featuring female friends, Maggie Harkness in the west, Vida Goldstein with her dreams of women's suffrage and Adelaide Hogg. With formal rhyming patterns, the poem's focus was clear: the author's 'higher aims' for a better world and desire for the vote for women.

Vindex, a pseudonym recalling an intelligent, ambitious and military-skilled ancient Roman governor, urged Champion to see the 'gravity' of his situation, the degree to which his fight against corruption made him the target of hostility and gossip:

'… don't be bought off or choked off like the rest. If you make your paper, as it might be made, the inspirer and educator of this movement, you must be prepared for what will happen. You will have against you the bitter and unscrupulous animosity of all the money-bags and their hangers-on. Every bribe and every threat in their tremendous armoury of such things will be used against you. Your character, public and private, will be assailed, your credit ruined, your fortunes shattered, your very life endangered' (*Champion,* 19 December 1896).

The call to arms demanded the newspaper 'take its coat off' and fight, noting the editor was rumoured to say he had 'taken care to have nothing to lose' and pointed to courage in the face of adversity. On Boxing Day, Champion apologised for some inattention during his absence and announced that 'all gossiping paragraphs in the irresponsible press to the contrary notwithstanding, [he was] going to remain in Victoria and give to this experiment all his energies'. He would not run for political office but intended to nourish his dream of helping a well-informed political movement by supporting others for parliament.

The first signal that the *Champion* would close its doors was the elimination of the banner of his charging knight and motto 'Tenax Propositi' in the first issue of 1897 and his cryptic line in reply to one correspondent 'A. H.' [Adelaide Hogg] on 30 January where he intimated their relationship was finished: 'Have made what we could of it'. In a farewell to the newspaper holding his name he stressed his appreciation:

> This paper has reason to feel great gratitude, amidst a good many discouragements, at the growing evidence that its influence is a real power for good in this community. It is easy and common for the journalist, when anything happens, to strike an attitude and exclaim, in leaded type, 'Alone I did it!' and then go off into raptures about the Power of the Press, the Force of the Fourth Estate, and quote the remark that the last Lord Lytton but one puts into the mouth of a stage-hero, that 'the pen is mightier than the sword'... But it is easier and commoner for people to think that the printed word is not a living, generating force. A man conceives an idea and it is his own possession. When it gets into print it falls seemingly on unheeding ears. But if it be a true thought, and re-iterated with the persistence that will take no denial and a little freshness of utterance, the germ, though it be small as a grain of mustard seed, will develop to its appointed end (*Champion*, 3 April 1897).

One of the last stories in the *Champion* was by Morley Roberts. 'The Artist' pointed to 'the popular novelist who ends with a wedding when by all natural right he ought to have ended with quite another catastrophe'.

To help with Champion's increasing debt, Adelaide offered to ask her husband for some of her inheritance because she wanted him to continue the *Champion* so that he 'might "achieve" something'. She had refused to assert her right to her own money and had passively accepted the convention of a husband's control of his wife's money. Two years before, Champion argued that the New Woman 'desires, whether married or single, to be pecuniarily independent of man'.[463] Receiving financial assistance through her husband's graces was now seen by Champion as a final indignity. He chose the path of liquidation. One journalist ran through the numerous liabilities and creditors of the *Champion* that April and the next day Champion fired last shot at Prendergast, just under a month before the newspaper closed. He labelled the MLA's work as one of hollow promises and slammed Prendergast's blustering, ranting performance for its lack of substance, summed up as 'a velvet hand in an iron glove'. Workers, he asserted, didn't want 'protestations of undying affection for the cause of the poor but active and intelligent work in furtherance of it'.[464]

When Champion shut his newspaper at the end of May 1897, *Table Talk* suddenly announced Prendergast's new paper. From a series of names (*Clarionet, Foghorn, Trumpeter, Sunrise, Call, Gazette, Leader*) *Toscin* was chosen from Victor Daly's new poem. Prendergast picked Edward Findley as compositor and lured writers, poets and artists who previously contributed to the *Champion* and *Free-Lance*, both now defunct. Suspicion remains about the identity behind the attempt to snatch the *Champion* and break the hold of its editor, around the time *Tocsin* was being founded and anonymous letters were being sent 'to all & sundry'. Evidently the plans were underway from late 1896 with Prendergast financing and organising plant and premises belonging to *Free Lance* at 181 Little Collins Street (near Russell Street). From the first issue on 2 October, Prendergast was identified as instigator and manager of *Tocsin* which proudly announced it was printed and published by a co-operative society and 'owned and maintained by workers and their unions'. President of the THC in 1896–97, Edward Findley originally made a loan to the business of £25 and 25 shares were issued in lieu of repayment.[465] *Toscin* was marked clearly as a publication of workers and unions to identify it with Trades Hall. However, in 1901 the secretary of the THC stated *Toscin* was not an 'official organ' of Trades Hall 'or any other labour organisation' and newspaper policy was run by a committee 'independent' of the THC Executive with nothing to do with Trades Hall.

As Prendergast's new paper was announced in May, Champion discreetly bought another paper and merged the *Champion* (now £350 in debt) with the *Sun: the Society Courier* that 'was going bung at the same time', he told Morley on 22 August 1897. Champion deeply felt the shift to editing a society paper when he wrote to Morley on 11 July, bitterly announcing, 'it is a nice paper isn't it for a fellow like me to be connected with? A noble mission for the man I once was.' Eighteen months later he explained his situation in detail: 'Personally I was in a miserable position. Heavily in debt, an utter mystery to all the public from my erratic bursts of energy and then effacement, ill & dreadfully poor and doing the most ignominious kinds of ink slinging for a bare crust.' This signalled his quiet withdrawal from politics, an escape plan freeing Adelaide from gossip and himself from the pain of loving her. The new newspaper operated on a commercial basis through an affiliation with an advertising agent and Champion himself performed basic office work to pay down debt, leaving much of the editing to 'a man who smells of whisky'. Interestingly, the postal address for the *Champion* as well as the *Sun: the Society Courier* and later the *Book Lover* was 270 Post Office Place, Melbourne.

In *Toscin's* second issue, Prendergast couldn't help but gloat, elated that Champion was 'shining as the proprietor of a shoddy society paper, run for the edification of the toffs of Toorak'. After Prendergast lost his seat in the Legislative Assembly in 1897, he wrote that 'this exquisite bescented ex-army popinjay' was now considered worthless 'by the real representatives of the workers' which added to 'perennial laughter' over Champion's fall.[466] This overblown caricature by a political enemy would cement an erroneous public assessment of Champion over generations with the eye-catching statement repeated as a deliciously salacious barb. When Ben Tillett came to Australia on a lecturing tour in April 1898 and drew attention to 'the noble self sacrificing work' of Champion for the English labour movement, it was to his audience's stunned amazement. People had been fed a consistent diet of adverse propaganda about Champion for eight years. A vindictive tirade appeared in Walter Vizard's *Outpost*, much in the style and content of *Tocsin's* earlier rants, berating Champion as a traitor, 'a spy and an informer' and a man with two failed newspapers, the last 'a chronicle of the small beer and skittles of Toorak'. In March the following year this same author called Vizard's former employer 'autocratic'.[467]

In the future Prendergast would have his own troubles caused by a series of irresponsible acts. Having lost his seat of North Melbourne, Prendergast was charged with loitering, obstruction and refusing to move on during an altercation with two men. His defence in September argued he was not on the footpath but in 'a dust bin near by'. A decade later he was named as a co-respondent in the divorce of a publican in his constituency and throughout May 1908 lewd allegations were reported in Ballarat newspapers of his drunkenness and attempts to secure a new hotel licence for the publican's wife in Castlemaine. While Champion believed these were 'possibly exaggerated reports of his semi-private acts', he slammed Prendergast as 'not the sort of man to be trusted with the government of Victoria'. Many years later, trade unionists subscribed £500 to fund Prendergast's six months' trip to London via Japan and China so he could have surgery on a nose injured in a boxing mishap.[468] He became premier at the age of 70.

Dejected and rejected after a long cycle of indecision, Champion was examining his seven-year relationship with Adelaide and, in a letter to Morley on 11 July 1897, he told of his decision to 'clear out of politics', insisting he would 'not stand again' and might head to Western Australia with his toothbrush. With the West recently devastated by typhoid, he speculated that if he caught this illness (again), death would spell an end of the affair. A 'change of scene might do me good', he considered, but it was a self-aware Champion who, in the midst of turmoil, realised the predicament: 'I fancy she [Adelaide] *really* would be glad if I were away. In her secret heart she knows quite well that I am in a pretty bad way down this particular blind alley'. Champion was losing his political road map or what he called his 'faith' in his 'star'. Meanwhile, Adelaide was 'cheerfully' regarding her return to England for Shirley's education as her 'duty' but had not untangled whether Champion was 'expected to stay & rot here or to slink to England & do a few years rotting there'. He highlighted the essential difference between romantic fiction where heroes 'in books would live a noble life & do heroic things' and his own reality where 'noble life can only take the shape of the drabbest suffering – to no earthly purpose'. The narrative template of romance where his role was as a chivalrous knight of Arthurian legend was effectively discarded as it became painfully obvious Adelaide would never leave her husband.

Champion informed Morley on 15 August 1897 that he had

dispatched a letter to Adelaide 'that practically ends the whole thing'. Almost a relief at a time when both parties were worn down by emotional pain and suffering caused by the ongoing intrigue, he admitted he had been 'willing to give up home & country, friends & careers, everything that a man can give including sense & honour on the offchance of someday her finding a use for me. And she has no use for me. I can do nothing for her except say I don't mind'. He was now 'cured' of his romantic obsession and released from the 'shame and misery' of the affair and had abandoned 'any notion of putting the world to rights'. A few days after his letter to Adelaide, her '*angry*' reply accused him of 'fickleness' in discarding her. Again, he remembered on 3 July 1898 that in the midst of her plans to return to England, Adelaide's letter concentrated on 'complaining of *my* desertion of *her* in terms which killed dead any affection'.

Adelaide and her husband carried on with their lives as if nothing had happened. Champion admitted that he 'really knew that it was all up' when Adelaide returned to her husband after Clifton Hill. Her guilt forced an impasse where it was 'impossible to keep her against her real wishes and to have done so by artifice would have been hideous misery for both of us'. So, a woman who didn't want to hurt anyone but couldn't help but deeply wound two men for years had the decision made for her. Henry Hogg was obviously a passive and patient man who had waited quietly in the wings over the seven long years it took for the affair to finish.

The relationship finally ended with a feeble whimper not an explosion. Early in 1897, Adelaide had 'adopted' another New Zealand baby, Alison Austin Elder, born on 15 November 1895 after her favourite brother's death from pneumonia. With a sick baby she 'tied herself up tighter than ever', Champion complained to Morley on 15 August; by 27 March 1898 she was 'altering and improving' Cheniston, with daughter Shirley 'packed off to a convent having proved more troublesome the older she grows' and a new baby to fill the void. In subdued fashion everyone moved on with quiet resignation after all the dithering, with matters brought to a head by the whisperings and rumours of a third party who circulated damaging letters.

And that's when the deepest despair arrived. Only a week after Champion ended the relationship, his letter to Morley talked about the 'ruins' of his life and his understanding that he was 'a hopeless failure'. He lamented on 10 October 1897 that he expected and 'wanted the best of every thing'. It was the simple things in life that mattered. 'I could not learn the ABC of it while my blood was young & I was not so very tired – that's all.' Life was empty and humdrum and held 'no ecstasies' although perhaps it was 'the absence of acute pains' which provided 'the common happiness' not 'bursting your heart over tasks beyond your strength'.

Meanwhile, Adelaide turned her attention to a program of children's holidays in the Macedon district near her country house. She was the originator of a scheme for poor and delicate children to have three weeks holiday in summer in fresh country air. Funded through subscription, the Children's Country Holiday Fund was also supported by cottage owners who provided board for poor children. The United Council for Women's Suffrage also gave assistance. Adelaide soon became known as a 'philanthropist' and her husband Henry was the honorary treasurer of the fund.[469]

As Champion 'brooded over wasted enthusiasms [and] lost chances', by 14 November 1897 'aspiration and the despair' were discovered to be just 'a habit'. The suite of traits that he had cultivated (confidence, courage and tenacity) were stripped away and his political ambitions and work for a cause abandoned. Seeing the shrinking horizons of his personal and emotional ambitions, his resolution was now to have health, some money and a couple of local friends to play tennis with or watch cricket. Such simple pleasures were with people he knew such as Mrs Goldstein's daughters (Vida and Elsie) who played tennis and Herbert and Norman Brookes, the latter a world-famous tennis champion looking to practice at his family's mansion on Queens Road and nearby courts on Lorne Street. Champion was a welcome addition as a partner and attended Saturday tennis parties. Living close to the Albert Cricket Ground, St Kilda Cricket Ground and Melbourne University fields, he frequently sat in the press box throughout the summer cricket season and, as 'The Willow', had composed the *Champion's* 'Snick-Snacks' column for matches at the

Melbourne Cricket Club. He wrote to Morley on 27 March 1898 that he was 'comparatively content, in a low soul destroying way'.

Adelaide's plans were now in full swing for their return to England. An auction was organised for December 1898 to sell their modern and expensive furnishings, household effects, silverware, grand piano, books and artwork, with no reserve placed upon the 'clearing sale'. Adelaide, Henry and Shirley together with Alison (Austin Elder's young child) and a maid left on the *Oriental* on 14 February 1899 directly after the sale of their effects. On 12 December that year, Champion reviewed his past as the 'Slough of Despond', a swamp of despair drawn from *Pilgrim's Progress*. Although Adelaide had written to Alice regularly, Champion believed she would 'avoid' the Roberts on her return to London. Henry Hogg came back to Melbourne alone for four months in April 1900 to wind up his affairs. A couple of months later, in a book review about John Ruskin, Champion argued that the biography of a man 'who wrote so much for and about women' gave an impression that Ruskin 'had no "feminine interest" in his own life' and ignored 'the painful story of his marriage and divorce, his Quixotic treatment of an unsuitable wife, or of the love affair which still more deeply affected his life'.[470] Perhaps Champion caught a glimpse of his own personal history.

On the family's return to Kensington, Adelaide's elderly mother lived with her for some months. Shirley was sent far away as a pupil boarder to the small town of Shanklin on the Isle of Wight where, in the St Blasius parish, she attended a small private school run three Hayward sisters.[471] Alison Elder, now five, lived in Berkshire with the eldest of Adelaide's brothers, Thomas Edward Elder. In 1907 Shirley married childhood Australian friend and barrister, Norman Hamilton-Smith, and after a stint in Melbourne, the couple moved to Berkshire in England where her uncle Thomas resided.

Adelaide's future was secure and she was no longer mother and carer. She seems to have found contentment living at Vicarage Gate and later 23 Hornton Street in Kensington, throwing herself into work at her local branch of the London Society for Women's Suffrage, the same organisation where Beatrice Potter's sister was a member. Adelaide's name was listed as a participant at a three-day conference in 1908 with over 300 other representative women in Aberdeen. In May 1911 she opened her house to 35 people for a debate that even included Anti-Suffrage League members; a meeting that her husband Henry chaired.[472] She also organised events for the Women's Convey Corp Hospital in February 1914.

On 2 November 1911, the auction of their country residence Cheniston, for 'immediate possession', severed any remaining material ties Adelaide had to Australia. Adelaide would go on to outlive her husband, chairman of Sunderland District Electric Tramways and of A.L. Elder and Company, who died in 1923. She also outlived Champion by two years and died on 11 September 1930. A month later the *Times* recorded her estate being worth £35,699 with her executors also selling a number of corporations and long-term leases of houses and shops, as well as significant investments owned across London and her premises near Kensington Gardens at 3 Douro Place, Victoria Road. It is unknown whether Champion tried to see Adelaide on either of his overseas trips in 1908 and 1912 or whether Adelaide saw Vida Goldstein when she came to London for the suffragette marches.

A year after their breakup, Champion lamented Adelaide's 'fatally weak' nature and his role as romantic saviour. 'I was obsessed with a vain hope of rescuing' Adelaide, he confessed to Morley on 3 July 1898, 'though I know it was wickedly weak not to pack up and clear out at once, I did so want to save her and to have my chance of helping her'. It remains pure speculation from what circumstance or unhappiness he thought Adelaide needed saving. On 26 October 1896 Champion talked about Adelaide's improvement in mind and body: 'She was in a terrible state of mind about getting fat once but to her immense relief got thinner'. There are references in his letters to Adelaide's 'melancholy' (caused by her brother Austin's death, her loneliness at Macedon, her lack of friends and her husband's suffering) and Champion thought her 'suicidally melancholy' about the anonymous letters. However, there was no mention about whether she had depression. When writing in retrospect about his 'loyalty' to Adelaide over seven years he made this sad observation to Morley: 'She will wake up one day, of course and when she does see it as it is, I think she will kill herself. But I cannot help it. The whole episode has made me know what the word "*impossible*" means and when one learns that it changes one's whole point of view.' Adelaide didn't commit suicide but died at the age of 76.

A Mild Affection
Elsie Belle Goldstein (1870–1953)

Great sense of humour and much literary taste. Lots of faults and foibles but a very good generous nature. An eminently companionable person and the least blasée girl of her age you ever saw.
(Letter H.H. Champion to Morley Roberts 3 July 1898)

In the last week of June 1898, before the public announcement of his engagement to Elsie Belle, Champion wrote to Adelaide to inform her. He was very aware that Adelaide might learn of this news 'suddenly in some crowded room'. There is no doubt Adelaide's departure for England 'closed up the past', as he told Morley on 12 December of the following year. In addition, the sale of the *Sun: the Society Courier* newspaper meant Champion was now able to cast off his former life and craft another. The contrast could not have been starker between his former love and his new partner. Adelaide was placed on a pedestal as a 'paragon' whereas Elsie Belle had many 'faults & foibles'.

Reminiscent of the silence surrounding Champion's first wife there is not much known about Elsie Belle. Recalled in various articles as a librarian because of her ownership of Melbourne's Book Lovers' Library, she is defined primarily by her relationship to other family members who were prominent in social and political issues. Appearing to stand in the shadow of her mother and her slightly older sister Vida, she was far more fulfilled when engaging with theatre and literature than with social reform, public forums, debates, and political ideas.

During the difficult financial years after 1892, when Australian bank crashes affected the family income, the Goldstein sisters opened a preparatory school and kindergarten for boys and girls. Initially they taught at a church schoolroom at Inkerman Street in Balaclava while living at Tivoli Road in South Yarra. Champion reported to

Morley on 14 June 1896: 'Mrs Goldstein has gone broke – mostly owing to her domestic tragedy and has taken to working for her living & has an office near to my newspaper offices'. After his trip to Western Australia, Champion informed Morley on 23 April 1897 about moving from his two-roomed 'garret' to the Goldsteins' home 'to help them a bit – & also to escape the unwholesomeness of solitary means & silent evenings'. He noted her daughters were 'very true trusty, & companionable'. Selwyn, who was just over 20 years of age, was now in Western Australian having taken a metallurgy position and so Champion moved into his room. Though the household was to break up shortly, it was a temporary but welcome place of sanctuary in his volatile life. On 10 October 1897 he explained: 'The lease of the G's house is up & they can't carry on. The girls have a school which practically keeps their home together & giving up this house means starting elsewhere which is beyond their means, so they will probably go out as governesses at Xmas'. Situated at East St Kilda, 'Ingleton', was a large brick residence fronting Alma Road and consisted of 12 rooms, kitchen, scullery, pantry and stables.[473] Their residence was also a school that could cater for boarders.

Born on 27 June 1870 in the Victorian rural town of Warrnambool, Elsie Belle was the second of five children; her siblings included Vida, Lina, Aileen and Selwyn. She attended Cornelia Ladies' College in Toorak and matriculated to Melbourne University where she studied from 1890–93. She and her siblings met Champion through their mother and, after a four-year friendship and a short engagement, Elsie Belle married an 'old literary friend' who was nearly forty. Champion's previous relationships were mostly with older women; the late Juliet Bennett, Margaret Harkness and Adelaide Hogg were between four and six years his senior. His friendship with Elsie Belle, he claimed, had grown 'naturally' into love over the fifteen months he lived with the Goldstein family.

Elsie Belle was an intelligent woman and a lover of plays and literature. She was described in a local newspaper as 'bright-eyed' and 'a pretty, fresh-complexioned girl'. Her niece, Leslie Henderson, later styled her as 'an extrovert', 'popular', 'impulsive', 'full of bubbling enthusiasm' with her 'child-like innocence' and 'personal needs [that] were very modest'.[474] When Champion explained to Morley about his engagement on 3 July 1898 and then marriage that December, he represented Elsie Belle as a 'well educated' woman who had a number of fine qualities: 'Great sense of humour and much literary taste', 'a very good generous nature', 'companionable' and 'about ten years younger in health spirits & appearance' than her 28 years. She was 'fond of books, dancing, tennis, bicycling walking. Bright, clever, shy, quick tempered and *good*'. He promised to make her happy: 'I love her very truly & deeply, and though she has plenty of faults she has not got a bad streak in her'. The idea of a companion informed much of the record of their marriage. Later she was depicted by Katharine Susannah Prichard in *Subtle Flame* as the wife of a middle-aged newspaper editor, a woman 'so lovable and ineffectual', with their marriage providing an 'undemanding companionship' to both parties.

Elsie Belle etched a bright flicker of hope across Champion's dreary life that surprised and delighted him and he quickly recovered his equilibrium. He was not only engaged by the whimsical and spontaneous temperament that made her enjoyable to be with on a daily basis but relished her unorthodox free-spirited way of seeing the world, precisely because it was unhampered by tradition. She was 'a young wife of mercurial disposition & unconventional ideas'. Affable, good-natured and sympathetic, she made friends easily because of her natural hospitality and outgoing personality. With her uncomplicated and undemanding nature Champion found himself on a steady, effortless path where he discovered life to be plain-sailing. Neither person made great emotional demands and the relaxed nature of their camaraderie suited both. It was a quiet, comfortable and happy relationship, coloured by Champion's tumultuous experience of a failed love affair. He readily embraced married life and his letters to Morley are full of wonder about his improving health and sense of well-being, the return of good temperament, as well as a general sense of relief from his debt-filled past. On their first anniversary at the seaside, he wrote:

> Since I really closed up the past & ceased repining, I have steadily got fitter & fitter and since my marriage I have been quite as hale & hearty

as any man of forty who has spent 20 years trying to kill himself, has any right to expect and temper & nerves & insomnia are all over & done with.

My marriage has been a great success and is going to be one right along. She's really a *good* girl and so happy that I suspect I must, after all, be a husband worth having. We have settled down to a very delightful companionship which has no symptoms of staleness about it and I don't want anything better than to get away alone with her for a holiday, as we did this week.

According to Herbert Brookes, around the time of his marriage Champion 'lost his dynamic drive and his desire to reform the world'. Brookes never knew about his liaison with Adelaide, and marriage to Elsie Belle was blamed for his friend's loss of motivation.

Herbert Brookes recalled Champion reading his book, *The Root of the Matter*, to people congregating at the Goldsteins' Balaclava place in 1895. Both the serial (published in Strong's *Australian Herald* from December 1894 to March 1895) and his book attracted a wide audience. The Kilburn residence (where he lived with Morley Roberts and Frederick Rolfe) served as the setting for the opening paragraph. The main character was George Blake, a name Champion used previously in the *Nineteenth Century* for dialogue between the 'thin disguises' of John Morley MP, the Marquis of Northampton and Sir Blundell Maple.[475] A supporter of the advancement of women, George's 'neat, sober dress and quiet, self-possessed manner' belied his activities as an agitator. His other characters included Dr Frederick Burton (Morley Roberts), a young feminist, Ida Burton, a graduate of Girton College in Cambridge and a New Woman (Morley's sister Ida) as well as a Tory barrister, Mortimer. George's argument on married women subjected to 'neglect or ill-treatment' by husbands seemed to point directly to Adelaide and Alice and perhaps also Mrs Isabella Goldstein:

But is there anything much more utterly detestable and flagrantly immoral than a continuance of marriage between two people who are divorced in thought and sentiment, and merely kept together by a fear of what their neighbours would say if they parted? (pp. 133–34).

The Goldstein daughters knew about Champion's affair with Adelaide and about the anonymous letters implicating Mrs Goldstein as an accessory in arranging clandestine meetings for the pair; the exception was the married daughter, Lina, who had married banker Charles Henderson in 1892. There is no doubt that the Goldstein women were observers of the collapse of his failing romance and their emotional support was invaluable; particularly the support of the 'brave' and sympathetic Mrs Goldstein. He divided his leisure time between the three girls, taking one of them to the theatre each week and one on a bicycle ride each Saturday. He admitted that Elsie Belle had been his favourite; she contributed her literary skills for his newspaper during his two trips to Sydney in October 1896 and to Western Australia the following December. A formal studio portrait of Elsie dated 31 December 1896 and signed in her own hand, 'Yours Ever', is held in the State Library of Victoria.

Nine months after his breakup with Adelaide, having had 'no communication direct or indirect' with her, he was reduced to being a spectator on a tram and saw Adelaide on the street walking with her husband 'in a most Darling and fond like manner'. He floated the idea of pursuing a romantic relationship to Morley on 27 March 1898:

> Of course I'd like to renew my youth & get some savour into my life by starting afresh on a more romantic basis but even if everything were all different I think that would be impossible. One could not chain an educated Englishwoman down to the sort of life one must live here & the colonial article would have to be taken with a full appreciation of her inevitable deficiencies.

As a supporter of the concept of the New Woman, his letter was jarring and carried a general feeling of self-centredness, intellectual arrogance and self-despair. However, he had just been taunted by the sight of Adelaide's affection to her husband while they were walking along a street. He was jaded and adrift. Only a few days after this, he and Elsie Belle, an active supporter of Melbourne's dramatic and literary societies, together attended 'A Marriage of Convenience', a comedy by Dumas adapted for the Bijou Theatre that focused on a man, his former lover and the woman he contracts to marry.

A few weeks after the play, a rumour ran like bushfire through Melbourne that lifted Champion's social profile and forced him into some contemplation of his future. London's *St James's Gazette* announced his unexpected inheritance of £7,000 per annum from his maternal grandfather's Scottish estates and this was quickly picked up by Australian papers who labelled him the 'swell socialist'. His cousin, Captain Beauchamp Colclough Urquhart, who less than two years earlier inherited the title of Meldrum and Byth after his father's death at a battle at the Atbara River, was killed in the Sudan where he fought with the Queen's Cameron Highlanders. With the death of two Urquhart heirs (father and then son) in such a short space of time, genealogists probably poured over Burke's peerage, and ancestral lines are no less complicated today. In the absence of a direct male heir, people speculated about Champion's substantial claim to valuable estates. Instead, the estate passed to Beauchamp's sister, Annie Isabel Urquhart, one of Champion's close childhood friends. His aunt, Henrietta Champion's sister, Douglas Isabella Maria Urquhart, had married the 9th Earl of Hatton. Their son then married his cousin, Annie Urquhart, and Annie cared for Henrietta's brother at Hatton Castle until his death in September 1896. This added weight to an argument to merge the two estates. Still privately owned by the Duffs, Hatton Castle was not transformed into a hotel, a fate suffered by Meldrum and Byth, and Craigston, as well as many other estates in England and Scotland.

Doubting the veracity Champion paid £3 for an overseas telegram that corrected the false rumour about his inheritance in mid-April. The newspaper hype was controlled after he explained the entail had been broken and the estate passed to another relative. Campaigning for an election in 1900 he was far more open and claimed he was disinherited because of his socialism. A 'change the world' event to fund activities for socialism or a hindrance requiring untold commitments to estates and family duties? Whatever the money meant to Champion there was no personal conflict for there was no money. He received 'much condolence from his lady friends (and they are legion)', one paper wrote after he missed out on the inheritance.[476] However, he still retained the 'fascinating and magnetic' persona that a journalist enthused upon.

Champion discovered his 'chance of happiness' lay with Elsie Belle and, in June 1898, suddenly asked her to marry him. Only then did he discover that she was in love with him but 'had hidden it so well'. Champion told Morley on 3 July, 'I don't think I've made any mistake this time my friend. I shall make her happy & have a happy home myself'. *Toscin* news-hounds got wind of their engagement and Prendergast was quick to snipe about the engagement: 'Rather amusing the engagements of H.H. Champion and Bernard Shaw – both critics of the matrimonial system, and not moderate ones either. Another illustration of "not what I say, but what I do"'.[477] Two days before Christmas, Champion wrote to Morley explaining his sudden attraction and trying to dispel any notion his friends may hold that it was 'a rash act' or that he just switched his 'affections to the nearest nice girl'. The Goldstein household was to split up, so they married sooner than they planned. He spent many letters reassuring Morley and Alice of his happiness, even though he acknowledged that Alice 'must resent it'. Instead, he saw it as an opportunity for a happy life 'after all the storms' with his 'chummy companion', Elise Belle, even though local gossips had thought he would marry the 'extremely pretty and very "advanced"' Vida.

His precipitous engagement seemed related to his disinheritance although there were other reasons feeding into his sudden decision. Three of Champion's close personal friends, Morley Roberts, Bernard Shaw and Percy Frost all married around the age of forty to women ideally suited to them, and Champion was now the last to marry. Morley quietly married his long-time lover in May 1896 following the death of her husband. Upon their marriage Champion quoted Samuel Johnson's opinion of second marriages as 'the triumph of hope over experience'. After years as a confirmed bachelor and philanderer, Bernard Shaw surprised everyone by marrying a rich widow from Dublin, their June 1898 wedding ceremony reported humorously by Shaw as registry office confusion as they sheltered from rain. Percy Frost was married the following August by E.S. Hughes at St Peter's Church Eastern Hill, another surprise given Percy's disastrous affair with an 'adventuress'. Champion told Morley in October 1896 that Frost had been 'on the tank' but found deliverance from severe and lengthy bouts of drunkenness with a nurse, Violet Richardson. The Frosts sailed with the McEacharns for England in July 1904 after Percy received an inheritance from his mother of £15,000.

The wedding of Champion and Elsie Belle was held on 8 December 1898 at 'Ingleton' schoolhouse, only weeks before Adelaide Hogg and her husband left the country. The school became the backdrop for Dr Charles Strong's Australian Church marriage service and Champion gave his wife his share in the Book Lovers' Library for a wedding present, or as he termed it, a 'marriage settlement'. Champion's interest in libraries had been evident in his analysis for the *Age* on the 16 May 1896 of Melville's Public Lending Library, Mullen and Slade's, and Cole's Book Arcade. As a result, Champion and Mrs Goldstein decided to form a library. Elsie Belle often worked in the Book Lovers' Library as gradually Champion became part of both her home and working life. On a 'first come, first served and no favouritism' basis for loan, the library increased its stock and moved from a ground floor shop at 15 Queen's Walk (off Collins Street) to new premises on 215 Collins Street opposite the Town Hall. The Book Lovers' Library finally settled at 239 Collins Street (next to the *Age*), located not far from the Women's Political Association at 229 Collins Street in Arlington Chambers where Vida Goldstein's various election campaigns for parliament were run.

One of the couple's well-wishers was John Burns, whose letter on 30 December recorded his 'heartiest wishes' for the pair's 'mutual health, happiness and prosperity'. When Annie Beatrice Champion who lived at Bickenhall Mansion, Marylebone, heard the news she made a will leaving him 'half her spondulics' (money). His sister died on 10 November 1929 at London's Mount Vernon Hospital, her estate worth £40,084; a sum he never inherited. The newly married couple had a fortnight's honeymoon with a week at a secluded seaside spot near Lorne and another week staying with squatter friends near Colac. Two days before Christmas 1898, Champion was relaxed and happy and told Morley he was considering writing a couple of novels.

A month later Champion sold the *Sun: the Society Courier*

newspaper at a loss and it was a final break with his turbulent political and romantic life. After the sale, he was still in debt to the tune of £850 but experienced 'a most refreshing feeling' because he was approaching solvency with every week. The paper was sold to Catherine Hay Thomson and Evelyn Gough, two women he knew well through Isabella, Vida and Elsie Belle Goldstein. The new owners were in the right position to buy the newspaper and operate it from their professional chambers in the newly constructed six story Pleasance building in Collins Street (just a small walk from the Book Lovers' Library). The two women intended to use the paper as a platform to reshape the cultural, social and political landscape and, although regarded as a society paper of interest to ladies, it supported women's suffrage as well as reform work for female prisoners and institutional welfare.

Both new owners were founding members of the Austral Salon (established March 1890) which sought to cultivate a sisterhood with creative and scientific women in order to expand their intellectual horizons. Scottish born Melbourne University graduate Catherine Thomson, like the Goldsteins, conducted a boarding and day school at 11 Spring Street before she joined the *Argus* and then became a literary agent. Previously, after securing employment in the Kew 'Lunatic Asylum' in 1886, Catherine wrote for the *Argus* about the conditions of thousands of female inmates, including epileptics incarcerated as 'mad'. Canadian born Evelyn Gough wrote articles for the *Argus*, *Australasian* and occasionally for the *Champion* and was on the National Council of Women with Vida. Evelyn also spent a number of nights in a Russell Street cell to further the appointment of police matrons and improve prisoner accommodation for women.[478] The co-owners operated the *Sun* only until February 1903 when it merged with Charles H. Chomley's *Arena*, changing its title to *Arena-Sun*. Evelyn Gough then joined Vida Goldstein as a candidate for Federal Parliament in August 1903.

With his marriage Champion gained an intelligent and likeable family. Isabella Goldstein was the daughter of a Scottish pastoralist, S.P. Hawkins; he was the owner of Melville Forest Station and member of the Portland Benevolent Asylum Committee. After marriage, Isabella and her husband Jacob moved to Warrnambool where Elsie Belle was born and finally to Melbourne where they were involved with the Convalescents' Aid Society for Men at Cheltenham. Dr Charles Strong was vice president, Elsie Belle's father secretary and her mother a council member.[479] Champion often worked alongside Mrs Isabella Goldstein, Herbert Brookes and John Buckley Castieau on Strong's Executive Committee of Australian Criminology Society to oppose capital punishment. After experience with John Barlas and private mental patients who exhibited panic attacks, anxiety, phobias, depression and stress, Champion was naturally drawn to such an organisation. The flogging of a man whose paralysis appeared an issue of social disorder were primary concerns to the Society and Champion was part of a deputation to Victorian Cabinet to protest the flogging of two prisoners in December 1912.

Champion gained an 'excellent' mother-in-law, known to be courageous, supportive and affected deeply by slum misery. An ardent supporter of social reform and enthusiastic advocate for women and children, Isabella was involved in establishing the first working women's creche in Collingwood (1891) and prominent in attempts to raise the age of protection for children. She often took her older two children, Vida and Elsie Belle, as helpers at stalls for fetes and fundraisers for neglected children in Collingwood. She escorted Strong through the Collingwood slums to show him the insanitary conditions and 'the vice and misery'. One journalist revisited some of the houses with Isabella to write a heart-felt story 'How the Poor Live'.[480] Like her own father she played a role in a Benevolent Asylum Committee and was involved with Champion in the anti-sweating movement. Champion was also involved with Dr Strong's Workingmen's Club in Collingwood, lecturing in politics and economics and in Footscray to aid funds. In the *Champion* he had pointed to her role with Mrs Bear Crawford and Dr Constance Stone, in establishing the Queen's Jubilee Fund for the Queen Victoria Hospital for Women and Children.[481] On Isabella Goldstein's death in 1916 the *Socialist* newspaper, where Champion held executive positions, sent Vida a letter of condolence.

Champion was also fond of his father-in-law, Jacob Goldstein, who in 1898 retired with the rank of Lieutenant Colonel and was cared for later at his home in Bank Place until his death in 1910. A Jewish immigrant from Poland, Jacob was involved from 1886 with projects including the Convalescents' Aid Society for Men, the Leongatha Labour Colony, the Charity Organisation Society, the Hospital League of Mercy and the Women's Hospital Committee. He spoke fluent German and the *Champion* published his translation of the poet Heinrich Heine on 28 December 1895. As a major in the local militia at the North Melbourne Battery, Jacob was friends with a young army officer and Melbourne University student of Jewish/Polish descent, John Monash, whom he later recommended for membership of the Yorick Club. In October 1885 Monash's mother died of abdominal cancer; his diary entries were silent for nine months and his university course was placed on hold. Monash joined, in January 1886, the Deutscher Turn Verein for social life and attended balls, dances, picnics and the theatre. His biographer noted Monash embraced 'the social whirl and went in for some dissipation', his diary between 1886–87 recording the 21 year old's interest in over 'fifty girls'; the 'accomplished flirt' honed his skills in 'romantic dallying and snatched kisses' and gained sexual experience.[482] His biographer is quite explicit about Monash's sexual experimentation as well as his ability 'to play upon the delicate keyboard' of a girl's 'soul'. One girl in his diary was Vida Goldstein who was still at school; her family believed Monash was interested in marrying her. Monash openly considered Vida a challenge and believed that if he could 'get an uninterrupted half-hour with her' he could overcome her disinterest.[483]

Vida was older by a year than Elsie Belle and attended the Presbyterian Ladies College with John Monash's sister, Mathilde. Early in 1886, while she was still 16 years of age and a student, she was 'heavily handicapped by a physical breakdown owing to the strain of study', although Monash's pursuit of Vida may have been the reason. Vida's breakdown forced her withdrawal from a school concert in July although she matriculated, telling told an Adelaide interviewer in September 1903 that if 'her health had not broken down' she would have pursued a degree. According to *The Life and Work of Miss Vida Goldstein* published (and perhaps partly written) by Champion later for her campaign in 1913, Vida actively threw herself into a reckless 'period of great gaiety, during which she tasted all the sweets of society', attending balls, parties and functions, playing lawn tennis, driving 'spirited horses' and rifle shooting at a gun club. Champion's small pamphlet on Vida had a lot in common with his bold publishing strategy to inform the public of achievements and character, while reclaiming potentially damaging information useful to opponents. As a result, the discussion of Vida's collapse as a schoolgirl and social activities were presented in a straight-forward manner.

Vida then turned her life around and dedicated herself to social reform and suffrage, taking a leading role with her mother in Strong's anti-slum crusade and the anti-sweating movement. She joined her mother on the Women's Suffrage League and became president of the Women's Political Association, later recalling her early canvassing for women's suffrage in 1891:

> They were told that 'woman's sphere is in the home,' 'man is the sturdy oak, woman the clinging vine,' that 'the hand that rocks the cradle rules the world,' and 'women's brains are not as big as men's.' They even had to face the sinister accusation 'It was Eve who tempted Adam,' and were warned that 'the Bible says women must submit to their husbands'.[484]

Champion's position as secretary of the United Council for Women's Suffrage in 1894 was soon held by Vida and her strong endorsement of Champion during his election to the May Day committee of 1895 was sent to Rose Scott, secretary of the Women's Suffrage League in New South Wales: 'Our success is largely due to him. He is always brimful of ideas and a splendid tactician'.[485] Vida later introduced her brother-in-law to Rose, and Champion wrote to thank her for 'the good she had accomplished in the course of her short stay' in Melbourne, in what Rose termed 'the kindest and most complimentary' language.[486]

On 4 August 1899, eight months after her sister married Champion, Vida gave her first public speech for a Woman Suffrage meeting at the Prahran Town Hall. She was on the same platform as H.B. Higgins. The rough and tumble world of interjections and personal comments faced by many platform women was now Vida's arena and she learnt to perform, although there were adverse comments by some who disapproved of Champion's influence and advice. When asked for her thoughts on the notion that 'the hand who rocked the cradle ruled the world', Vida replied, if males accepted the axiom as true 'they would have been rocking the cradles all the time'. One of her witty retorts to a man's shout 'Wouldn't you like to be a man?' was a quiet 'Wouldn't you?'.[487]

Vida was engaged in reforms to raise the age of consent from 16 to 21 years of age and insisted, 'the age of consent should be raised to 21. Who is the victim of sexual outrages? The girl, in 99 cases out of 100. Who suffers by seduction? Not the man.'[488] When she first tried to enter politics, Vida recalled: 'As soon as my candidature was announced the enemy prophesied a physical breakdown'.[489] Like Champion, Vida chose to stand as an independent in politics. She ran for the Senate in 1903 (the first election for Commonwealth Parliament where women could vote) and again in 1910 and 1917, as well as for the House of Representatives in 1913 and 1914. She later detailed some disadvantages of her first campaign, including press antipathy, gender prejudice, her lack of funds, and Labour's suspicion. She expounded on the latter:

> The Labor [sic] party, too, issued a leaflet warning electors not to give her a vote; First, because she was a woman, and therefore not qualified to sit in the Senate; and in the second place, because she was not a pledged labor [sic] candidate.[490]

Having promoted many activities of the women's movement and worked actively for the enfranchisement of women, Champion came to his marriage with good credentials and much to recommend himself to the Goldstein family. As mentioned, they thought enough of him to issue an invitation to reside with them during his romantic crisis with a married woman. The network of intelligent women expanded with new clubs and salons, and Champion forged strong connections with many friends of Elsie Belle's family, influential suffragettes who often were professional freelance journalists, such as Evelyn Gough, Catherine Thomson and Alice Henry. The latter was warned by

Champion, 'If you don't take care, Mrs Webb will do the interviewing', when Beatrice and her husband visited Melbourne in 1898. The same building at Queen's Walk that housed Champion's newspaper was home to a women's employment agency for governesses and domestics run by Alice Henry for four years from 1895, as well as the Warrawee Club. Although Elsie Belle attended meetings of the Warrawee Club, her mother and sister sought more active roles on the committee.

Based on Champion's lecture to the Prahran branch of the Victorian Women's Franchise League on 4 April 1895, Champion's essay on *The Claim of Women* was developed into an article for *Cosmos* and immediately published as a pamphlet by Pitt Street firm Gordon & Gotch. Throughout 1895 he sold Alice Stone Blackwell's *Twelve Reasons Why Women Want the Vote* and other such leaflets from his newspaper office, advertised dates of women's suffrage lectures and reports from the League where he was one of three vice presidents. Champion was against 'unjust marriage laws' arguing that 'marriage should be recognised as a partnership in which both parties have an equal right to their joint earnings', believing 'most women would prefer an ounce of justice to a pound of that sentiment which makes it possible for them to be left homeless and destitute'.[491] He also published Catherine Helen Spence of the South Australian Woman's League, promoting her speech on 'The Democratic Ideal' and her articles on proportional representation. When he proposed a mock election in his paper to encourage voting in an alternate fashion, Spence offered suggestions for a competition to select Victoria's ten federal delegates for the June issue.[492] Spence was the first woman to write a novel about Australia that was published in 1854; her portrait was placed by Champion in the frontispiece of the *Book Lover* in July 1908 as a tribute.

The newly married couple, together with Elsie Belle's mother, her two sisters and Lizzie Kavanagh, their long-time family domestic, shared a large modern flat with a suite of six rooms on the fourth floor at 88 Oxford Chambers in Bourke Street. A telephone was installed with direct access to the *Age* office. At their residence, the Goldstein women held lively meetings, conducted debates and accessed a room large enough to conduct their social and literary enterprises, including

Vida's new newspaper, the *Australian Woman's Sphere*. Significantly, Champion was now part of a close extended family after an isolated bachelor existence.

Once Elsie Belle was the owner of the Book Lovers' Library, she took on new business and managerial roles. The library was 'quite a literary club' where people could be found browsing and seeking advice from her and by August 1899 Champion believed she had 'her finger on the pulse'.[493] With Elsie Belle's love of Browning's poetry an animating concept for her work, she followed the principles espoused in his poem 'Shop':

> Because a man has shop to mind
> In time and place, since flesh must live,
> Needs spirit lack all life behind,
> All stray thoughts, fancies fugitive,
> All loves except what trade can give?

Empowered by ownership and an income, her role was to 'create a bank balance and save your soul into the bargain', she claimed in an October 1900 interview 'How Women Can Succeed in Business' for Vida's new *Australian Woman's Sphere*. With a photo of Elsie Belle in one corner with her books, the interview clearly pointed to discussions with her husband on the higher purpose of the Book Lovers' Library and the ideal of 'mental nutrition'. Her love of literature was embraced and her role as an independent woman was validated. In addition, she gained experience in business management in her role as proprietor and manager of the library. It was not surprising Champion immersed himself in a literary life with his new wife.

Husband and wife soon became involved in a spinoff journal, the *Book Lover: A Literary Review* with much cross marketing and promotion between the library and the review. With subscriptions for 3, 6 and 12 months to the Book Lovers' Library, the review initially advertised the best very literature not 'dull' books. The first issue of the *Book Lover* (May 1899) continued a pattern Champion pursued in both England and Australia, with one newspaper closing and another opening. He wrote to Morley on 29 May 1900 using Browning's concept to admit he 'never thought to become a successful shop-keeper'. After Champion's death, Nettie Palmer described the *Book Lover* as 'midway between a critical "forum" and a booksellers' catalogue' and noted its editor 'gathered round him a few Melbourne writers who held genuine opinions on literature, and gave them a place where they could express themselves'.[494] His literary review sought and published book titles read by prominent Victorians such as Professor Morris, Professor Baldwin Spencer, Sir Edmond Barton, Sir Samuel Way, Lady Madden, Mrs Henry Gyles Turner, Mrs McEacharn, Ethel Turner, Alfred Deakin and H.B. Higgins. A variety of competitions were run, including one in January 1900 asking readers to choose four men and four women who, 'in your opinion, make up the most interesting dinner party' and three conversational subjects that 'would best "draw out" your chosen guests' while in September he suggested reading circles be established.

By the end of March 1900, *The New York Times* were likening the *Book Lover* to their own 'Saturday Review'. Champion's close relationship with Coles Book Arcade meant the 'Publishers' Circular' was forwarded to the *Book Lover's* editor. By Christmas Champion was formerly invited to become a committee member of the Australian Literature Society with its aim to help authors protect authors and their copyright in a fashion similar to the Society of Authors in London. The letterhead of the *Book Lover* in 1905 proclaimed the review had 'the largest circulation of any Australasian literary organ' and its subscription increased from 1 shilling 6 pence to 3 shillings 6 pence per annum. What impressed many readers and critics was the reviewer's daring use of the first person in his writing.

As an affectionate gift to his wife, Champion arranged for a young Norman Lindsay to create a bookplate (or Ex Libris) with the owner's name, 'Elsie Belle Champion'. Titled 'Her Book', the bookplate reflected Elsie Belle's intellectual pursuit through its design of a pastoral scene. Lindsay's black and white pen-drawing was decorative and romantic, featuring a woman in a field of flowers with a man reading a book to her and represented the newly married pair with their literary passion. This was an intimate and carefully selected gift for a lover of books, utilising the names of both library and review for his commission. Norman Lindsay was 'destined to be famous', Champion wrote.[495] The artist was only in his teens when Elsie Belle displayed both his and his brother Lionel's bookplates in her library to encourage interest. Norman Lindsay had been experimenting from the time of his first bookplate etching for John Lane Mullins in Melbourne and he and Lionel used a studio in Swanston Street for their work. Later, another member of the Bohemian set, Dr John S.C. Elkington, also published a small book of Lindsay's first plates, *Ex Libris*, and commissioned bookplates for himself and his wife.

Lionel Lindsay was also a student assistant at the Melbourne Observatory in the Royal Botanic Gardens under the chief astronomer Pietro Baracchi who was responsible for establishing the Mount Stromlo Observatory. Weather forecasts regularly appeared in the *Argus* from Baracchi and Champion later arranged for him to lecture on his passion to socialists in August 1907. The Lindsay brothers, including Percy, also received early praise in the *Champion*, Lionel for his black and white 'Brander's Ferry' at Swan Street and Percy for his landscape painting, and in November 1909 the *Book Lover* reproduced a photo of Norman, Lionel and Hugh McCrae. Lionel and Percy's drawing teacher at his Swanston Street studio was George Coates who Champion described as 'a thorough Bohemian' when he won the National Gallery travelling scholarship to Paris and Rome.[496]

Under 'the influence of a very happy home life' Champion rejoiced in regaining health and good temper. He was a member of the exclusive Melbourne Wallaby Walking Club, founded by Dr Louis Henry in 1894 for exercise and an 'interchange of ideas' for prominent doctors, professors, professionals and men in public office. Other members included David Syme's nephew, H.B. Higgins, Pietro Baracchi and Frederick McCubbin, the latter pointedly naming his painting 'On the Wallaby Track' (1896). Champion saw opportunities through membership to expand his networks around the publishing arena and the political sphere. Appointed secretary from 1896–97 Champion remained a committee member until 1902. (Alfred Deakin joined when he was an *Age* journalist in 1899, supporting women's suffrage and giving Vida Goldstein his private home phone number.)

Champion's charm and a habit of wide reading, as well as his relationships with overseas and local authors, assured him a place amongst academics, writers, artists and the literati in Melbourne while Elsie, a well-educated graduate of Melbourne University, was readily accepted as an intelligent and engaging partner. Although he had complained to Morley on the first day of January 1897 that he was 'quite friendless' and 'gloomy & dyspeptic & non-gregarious', now Champion energetically re-engaged and sought bright friends and lively conversation. He enjoyed Melbourne's bohemian lifestyle, surrounded himself with its leading creative figures, and relished his new found enjoyment and pleasure of a vibrant city whose population had grown rapidly because of the gold rushes. There had been an influx of many foreign nationalities to Melbourne and even THC members like W.E. Murphy, an auctioneer in real estate for half a dozen years, gained from the land boom.

Champion appreciated restaurants with a bohemian flair and the *Maison Doree* (Golden House) run by an elderly French woman served tasty, cheap and popular food which the *Champion* frequently advertised. As Champion rediscovered life and purpose in the aftermath of his failed romance and political aspirations, one of his favourite places became Fasoli's a popular Melbourne Italian restaurant and wine bar in Lonsdale Street. Opened in 1897 by Vincent Fasoli in a cottage with prints of Garibaldi, it recalled his Aberdeen friend, John Morrison Davidson of 'the old Brigade of Liberty'. Managed by a gentleman named Tony, affectionately called 'St Antonio' or 'The Professor', the restaurant could seat 60 or 70 customers, with cabaret and music accompanying the dining. No reservations were needed and diners of both sexes and many different nationalities took any vacant chair in the hall to eat at an enormous dining table. The delights of the restaurant were recorded in many newspapers, some as far away as Kalgoorlie.[497] With its cheap European meals, wine and easy bohemian atmosphere, the place attracted those who loved to intermingle with artistic and gifted people. Louis Esson's poetic celebration of Fasoli's food for the *Bulletin* in 1906 caught the atmosphere: 'Oh! that bottle-laden table! Oh! the mixed and merry scenes! / And oil and garlic mingled with that salami and beans'.

It was a vibrant place drawing impressionist artists, writers, musicians, professionals, astronomers and politicians. Good friend George Marshall-Hall (Professor of Music at the University of Melbourne) and Champion became regular patrons and, according to Lionel Lindsay, they dined together on Sundays at Fasoli's. The flamboyant Professor also dined there on Wednesdays with members of the Ishmael Club, symbolically named after the outcast son of Abraham. The club included Norman, Lionel, Percy (and later Ruby) Lindsay, Edward and Will Dyson, Blamire Young, Max Meldrum and Randolph Bedford. Two of these artists were commissioned by Champion; Norman Lindsay for Elsie Belle's Ex Libris gift and Max Meldrum for the *Champion's* nameplate. Elsie Belle also commissioned Ruby Lindsay for her Book Lover's Library poster in October 1907.

Other writers and artists who, together with the Wallaby Club members were patrons, were well known Australians, Louis Esson, C.J. Dennis, Hugh McCrae, E.J. Brady, William Moore, Leon Brodzky, Dr Maloney (a candidate for McEacharn's seat) and Randolph Bedford. Pietro, a diner who argued with 'The Professor' about the meaning of the word for thief in Turkish, was Pietro Baracchi, the astronomer. The waitresses, Kate and Virginia Fasoli, dressed in costume to give an authentic atmosphere and in 1905 Kate and her husband Nerino Maggia took over management to open *Hotel Fasoli* in King Street and its famous patrons followed.

Champion thrived on the cosmopolitan atmosphere, intellectual conversations and debates on politics, music, art, acting, language and literature and, like Morley Roberts, loved the working men who included foreign seamen. Fasoli wholeheartedly encouraged female patrons and Champion obviously took Elsie Belle to his favourite restaurant, given she was social, gregarious and an extrovert although she wasn't reported in tales by male writers about the restaurant. Over time Elsie Belle may have been more comfortable at home, perhaps happy with the opportunity, as one of a small group of educated women employed outside domestic sphere, to relax after work, read quietly and develop ideas for her library.

Champion had been consistently 'pounding out leaders at a clerk's salary' at the *Age* for five years, ever since his first article on Morley in June 1894. Shortly after his engagement, he had approached

Syme for employment and was placed on a salary of around £400 a year. Champion wrote to Morley on 23 December 1898 that he was cautiously optimistic Syme would select him to succeed the current editor who was ill and intended to retire after nearly three decades. While it is not known how Elsie Belle felt about her husband's aspiration to secure the *Age's* editorship, she probably gave her support. Nearly nine months after officially joining the staff, Champion did not want to rock the boat and was willing to appear 'steady & reliable' and play by Syme's rule book. It was well known Champion had been owner of two Melbourne newspapers, unhindered by conventional media power and that he revelled in the freedom of writing for his own newspaper rather than joining the ranks of the newspaper hacks of Grub Street or becoming an ink-slinger, as he called press writers. Champion's journalism was 'much duller' but he was happy to knuckle under in order to gain Syme's confidence. This reflected a different man to the one who took aim at Syme in his first edition of the *Champion* and who used Voltaire's 'with great power comes great responsibility' to argue the *Age* had the 'power' and 'influence' to dominate the information flow:

> It has no competitors. It can make any person or policy popular or unpopular. It can fail to report any man or thing, and for four-fifths of the citizens it is as though that man or thing were not. It can misrepresent any speech or movement and the printed lie alone will reach the electors. It could teach the people anything you choose. It has ruled the country for a couple of decades. It rules the country to-day (*Champion*, 22 June 1895).

Now he summarised Syme's fears to Morley on 15 March 1899:

> He is afraid (1) of my socialistic proclivities (deuced well cured by now) (2) my independence (3) ambition for public life (which is dead) (4) of my putting too high a price in bawbees [Scottish for low value coins] on my services.

Having struck off two out of four objections, Champion was left with the matters of a journalist's freedom and value. In fact, the other two characteristics – his socialism and desire for a public platform – were lying dormant in Champion's post marriage contentment. All four of Syme's fears about his employee remained drivers for much of Champion's subsequent behaviour and actions. However, Champion's articles were receiving praise.

> The fine philosophical leaders (with a tinge of religion in them) which the Melb. Age has been publishing for a few weeks on Saturdays, are from the pen of Alfred Deakin. What with H.H. Champion's biting epigrammatic style, and Deakin's fine nervous English, the Age leading columns are sometimes as brilliant as anything in modern daily.[498]

By August that year he was complaining, 'the duller and more apathetic I get the more I suit the people of this parish'.

On 12 December 1899, one year into his marriage, Champion angrily explained to Morley about his withdrawal from the political game: 'I am finished with being sacrificed, to no purpose, by aggregates of fools & sneaks who call themselves democracies. I'm doing more to govern the country at this minute than if I were Premier & I can do it without moving from my comfortable study or addressing crowds & being insulted & envenomed'. Unfortunately, as the new century ticked over, the editorship went to a long-term chief of staff. Facing the tedium of leading articles about mundane issues Champion often quarrelled with Syme – who also clashed with Alfred Deakin – and it was widely known that the arguments concerned topics Champion wanted to write about. Finally, the following year Champion was allowed some freedom of subject matter and was engaged to write book reviews for Saturday's *Age* (often thanking the Book Lovers' Library for his copy). With his aspirations now dashed, he lost interest with the steady boring *Age* journalism. His fascination with the political arena smouldered and he was drawn back to the fray.

Champion's role as publicist, convenor and chair of a meeting about reform of the Upper House on 26 August 1900 seemed to reignite his interest in politics. Attended by around 120 people, many of them women, this meeting's aim was to get the 'machinery' of reform to the forefront of the public's mind and to garner the support of those who genuinely believed in women's suffrage. At the meeting a motion was moved to insert a clause into the Federal Electorates Bill for women of 21 years of age to receive the franchise. As the chair, Champion had the satisfaction of watching Edward Findley, Prendergast's compositor on *Toscin* and THC aspirant for the Victorian Legislative Assembly, talk himself into a corner. Findley's rhetorical question was one mistake made early during the meeting: 'Who was it that ran Victoria? Forty-eight old women at the top of Bourke Street'. Objections came swiftly from long-time suffragette Annie Lowe because of this 'slight' against women and she was cheered by the audience. Findley dug himself into another hole by amending the phrase to 'old women' in male clothes and the clamour continued. Attuned to the nuances of language and the clever use of a quick and timely press release, Champion helped highlight Findley's archaic beliefs (in sharp contrast to the mood in the hall) and his printed report helped journalists draw their conclusion: 'It shows how insincere the Labour Party is in their support of the Woman's Suffrage movement'.[499]

Champion told Morley a few weeks later of his re-entry into the political arena for the general election in October.[500] Perhaps it was encouraging for Elsie Belle that Champion seemed so relaxed: 'I don't care two straws about it now, so I suppose I shall romp in. It's the usual way. I shan't take it at all seriously or lose an hour's sleep or a penny over politics anyway'. Elsie Belle's cousin, Harry Lawson, later Premier, was in the Legislative Assembly after winning the seat of Castlemaine as a Liberal candidate at 24 years of age and perhaps this example was on Champion's mind. Only a couple of weeks later, Champion stood before crowds at Albert Park to tell them he had been 'disinherited' for endorsing the working-class cause.

He was again trying to topple the conservative John White, the sitting member for the 1896 election when Champion was forced to withdraw. The local labour leaders strangely threw their support behind White for Albert Park, 'a seasoned enemy of the working classes and consistent reactionary on every progressive movement' and the labour movement was accused of 'democratic dementia' in this decision. The leaders appeared to have either 'malignancy or idiocy' or were acting out of 'some insensate hatred' of Champion.[501] Once again his political aspirations reignited vehement claims made against Champion to discredit him. On the eve of the election, leaflets were passed around accusing him of being a 'blackguard and a liar' whom labour leaders in London had repudiated, and reports that he was forced to relinquish his commission in the British army because of his disloyalty. As this was a recirculation of old pamphlet claims, Champion seemingly knew the identity and motivation of the perpetrator and intended to pursue a case of libel for the 'false and malicious insinuation'. Meanwhile, a letter to the editor from a large number of trade union secretaries supported Champion.[502] He was electorally unsuccessful once again, losing by a margin of 51 votes with White securing 929 votes and Champion 878. In fact, the publisher of this propaganda was the secretary of the election committee of John White although no one seemed to know who was his source. Champion's intention was to seek damages of £1000 and to contest once more.

At the same election Henry Higgins lost his seat of Geelong and, during a meeting of 200 people on 7 November, Champion spoke of his dedication using Milton's words: 'We measure not our cause by our success, but our success by our cause'. Anticipating that in a federal consolidation of parties Higgins would be an important force, Champion moved a motion for a testimonial for his services to the Legislative Assembly, sending out letters to numerous Victorian newspapers as honorary secretary of the support committee of Higgins in order to raise money. Champion was to support Higgins in his bid for federal politics for the Commonwealth of Australia (scheduled for March 1901) and so he contributed articles on Federation to the London *Daily Express* to this end. Higgins was a close friend of Alfred Deakin and Alexander Sutherland (tutor to Syme's sons) and a member of both the Wallaby Club and the University of Melbourne Extension Board and Champion knew and liked him. Higgins was also a brother-in-law of George Morrison, journalist for the *Leader, Age, Times* and author of *An Australian in China* (1895) as well as life-long friend of Douglas Sladen, editor of *Who's Who*. Ina Higgins, his sister, was a close friend of Vida Goldstein, involved with her at the Warrawee Club and on the

Executive Committee of the United Council for Woman suffrage. In June 1901 Champion arranged a presentation for Higgins at Rubira's Café although Champion failed to attend because of sickness.

The first notice of Champion's health issues occurred at a meeting of labour parties held on 12 March 1901 in South Melbourne to select a candidate for the House of Representatives. On this occasion, the secretary apologised because he couldn't find a letter from Elsie Belle Champion indicating her husband's desire to serve the labour cause, along with his doctor's certificate excusing her husband for a fortnight because of illness. F.G. [Frederick Gordon] Knight, the chair, insisted a signed 'pledge' to the platform was required for consideration. Some members recognised this would debar Champion by default and requested time to collect his signature. Unconcerned Knight responded, 'Well, why don't you go?' provoking laughter and on return the secretary discovered the letter, causing someone in attendance to complain of a 'rigged' process. Due to this hostile environment, the meeting was described by the local newspaper as 'disorderly' with 'heated discussion' and 'great uproar' while Knight attempted 'to quell the tumult'.[503] Even in his absence Champion still remained a lightning rod for dissent in labour circles.

Champion's illness progressed from March through to August 1901 and initially it seemed like a debilitating bout of influenza. Not realising it was more serious, Elsie Belle expanded the Library's size during August to give browsers twice the space and provide room for more books and displays, envisaging ten days of renovations and normal business after a month. At the same time, the *Book Lover's* style suddenly changed, as Frederick W. Maudsley (of the Women's Federal Political Association) took up the writing and Elsie Belle the administration. Queen Victoria's death was blamed for the disruption to reviews. The flu-like illness, today linked with an ischemic stroke, meant the seriousness of Champion's condition went unnoticed in the lead-up to a sudden catastrophic condition. At the annual meeting at the Austral Salon on 25 November, Sumner Locke's sister Lilian, secretary of the United Council for Women's Suffrage, recorded their dismay at the resignation of both Champion and Vida Goldstein, a decision that reflected the family's focus to prioritise his health.

At that time medical assistance was limited because of a lack of knowledge, diagnostic tools, technology and specific medicine, as well occupational therapy and physiotherapy to assist recovery. Elsie Belle turned instead to Christian Science and the closeness of the church venue to their home presented itself as an opportunity to pursue something alternative. Christian Science services were conducted in Melbourne during the 1890s and by the turn of the century the organisation resided in Collins Street before relocating to the second-floor reading room of the Oxford Chambers in Bourke Street. 'Science and Health' classes advocated self-healing or faith-healing. As membership increased, services were held in larger centres (the Athenaeum Hall in Collins Street and later at St Kilda Road) while Mary Eddy's Christian Science book increased its popularity. Vida joined her sister as a regular attendee during this time with the *Age* noting on 14 December 1903 that her involvement was used against her in the election. Champion was obviously grateful to Elsie Belle and her sister but whether he accepted Christian Science because it helped them, or because it helped him, was not revealed. Over the years Elsie Belle's sisters would personally and collectively lean on Christian Science, with Vida becoming a faith healer and Aileen a first reader and president of the First Church of Christ in South Melbourne in the 1940s.

Between January and November 1902 Champion's illness became noteworthy for journalists and it was during his journey to Christian Science meetings that his paralysis became obvious. As 'the once smart and brilliant' Champion, he was seen now to be escorted by women to a church meeting and it was considered a 'sad end' to his career. There was also a suggestion about 'a number of misleading rumours' that circulated after his position at the *Age* ceased. Champion had been in very poor health for quite a lengthy period and was being treated by Christian Science members whose success with Elsie Belle meant she no longer required reading glasses. The assault on Champion's dignity and way of life in his early forties was not confined to the physical in his convalescence. When Tom Mann had arrived from New Zealand in September 1902 and spoke emotionally of his early years with Champion, the *Bulletin* saw 'the erstwhile dapper Hussar officer and Socialist, H.H. Champion, now paralysed and almost helpless, with the appearance of a very old man', being 'assisted to a seat by his wife and [Trades Hall] secretary Barker'.[504] Champion attended most of Mann's series of lectures and, although improved in health, was considered 'still far from well'. His own letter before Christmas told of 20 months of rehabilitation and he must have felt a different person to the man who strode forth confidently into the Maritime Strike 12 years before.[505] For a period after the stroke Champion's correspondence with Morley Roberts stopped before he returned to type with one finger.

While Champion's gait was crabbed by a paralysis of his right side there was no permanent brain or speech damage. On his pathway to recovery, Champion praised his wife in a letter to Morley on 8 January 1903 where, in an understated fashion, he admired her fortitude as 'a regular brick' who coped 'remarkably well'. Although it was a terrible time for both, Elsie Belle bore it with resilience and her husband with stoic resolve. He told of nine months in bed, five doctors, sleepless nights, no appetite or ability to swallow liquids and, reverting to his Scottish language, 'a chawing' or grinding at his heart (chest pain). The following year he spent recuperating. A letter from Champion to Hyndman on 27 April 1921 talked about Champion's arrival in Australia the second time 'with £3 capital' and reflected on his achievement, 'considering that I was sort of paralysed all down my right side, and have not written a line with my right hand ever since'.[506] Champion found different ways of performing tasks, teaching himself to write with his left hand, his spidery penmanship evident in a letter nearly four years later written to Nettie Palmer after he changed his writing hand.

While he was confined to bed, Elsie Belle continued the management of the Book Lovers' Library to support their income. However, her husband did not succumb to defeat and his intellectual presence was not confined by the physical boundaries of his disability. He poured his meagre energies into the literary solitude of *Book Lover*, a pastime that brought no anxiety, stress or personal abuse. Gissing wrote at the time: 'To tell you the truth, I could not name any periodical in English which treats of current literature so thoughtfully, moderately, genially, as does "The Book Lover". What specially pleases me is its constant reference to a standard above that of our time; without touch of pedantry, there is almost always the note of scholarship in its columns'.[507]

During Champion's recuperation, Elsie Belle took an immediate shine to eighteen-year-old Stella Miles Franklin's 'passionate revolt' in *My Brilliant Career* with Ethel Turner also admiring this authentically Australian novel.[508] In June 1903, the *Book Lover* became the first to report Miles's accident in a gas explosion, where she sustained facial injuries and, when she arrived in Melbourne in 1904, the Champions hosted her at their home where they introduced her to a wide variety of political and literary friends. Champion found Miles delightfully entertaining and wrote to Rose Scott on 26 February about her immense enjoyment of her visit.[509] Ever the literary opportunist, Champion placed advertisements in the *Argus* informing readers of his literary chat with her and announcing her book's sale at his office, while the *Australian Woman's Sphere* republished her 'portrait' from *Book Lover*. Elsie Belle was on hand to farewell Miles in April as she left in a carriage decorated with flowers bound for a ship to Sydney. From this time onward she became a lifelong friend of both Champions. Detailing her new career as 'Mary Ann', during which she daringly disguised herself for twelve months as a maid in Sydney and Melbourne, Champion commented on her photo:

> The waggish looking damsel, looking remarkably pleased in her 'get-up' as a parlor maid ... now is going to devote herself to putting down on paper what she has heard, seen, and learnt during that time. It would not be fair to state any of her discoveries before she makes them public in her own way. But it may be said that she will hit harder in these revelations than any writer of recent times, for she will speak with knowledge (*Book Lover*, April 1904).

Her book 'aroused England' and was so popular it was in its fifth edition and a column of favourable press criticism was added by Champion, including from the *Pall Mall Gazette*. One South Australian journalist called Champion's praise 'extravagant adulation'. Undoubtedly, he was responsible for sending Miles to see Bernard Shaw with whom she spoke for 'a lovely ten minutes' and to John Burns for tea on the terrace. Champion often provided introductions to John Burns, including Vida Goldstein, Walter Murdoch, Dorothy Mackellar (and her father) and Herbert Brookes.

Champion's recovery was slow and not sufficient to allow him to travel overseas to his brother, Arthur's London wedding.[510] However, Champion's health improved rapidly enough for him to accompany Elsie Belle regularly to the theatre where, because she was concerned by safety aspects, she wrote letters to newspapers about lack of theatre escape doors.[511] In their enthusiasm for plays, the couple now became central to the establishment of the Playgoers' Club, a name inspired by a London theatre club. Funded by annual subscription, a sub-committee was formed of regulars from Fasoli's including H.B. Higgins, William Moore and Walter Murdoch, with Blamire Young as president and Champion honorary secretary. Champion promoted the club's inaugural meeting at a concert hall with 'The Players', dramatic art students from Philip Lytton's acting school.[512] The aim was to stage plays and exchange ideas about important dramas and to use Turn Verein Hall in Lonsdale Street as a venue. As usual Elsie Belle assumed no public role but was happy to attend in support and to issue tickets from the Book Lovers' Library with their eye-catching stricture: 'Citizens in evening dress not admitted'. Such attire was termed by Clementina Black's socialists as 'badges of an effete aristocratic system'.

Champion and Elsie Belle were not only friends with literary and theatrical figures, artists and musicians but also strong advocates of their creative efforts. Elsie Belle saw the Book Lovers' Library as having an important community role and enjoyed selling tickets to theatre events, concerts, lectures and discussions, along with sales of framed paintings. (Her activities continued long after Champion's death for friends like Will Dyson.) Events promoted included various University Extension lectures on literature, the army nurses' ball and Vida's 1904 talk 'The Humour and Pathos of My Senate Campaign' with lantern slides of comical newspaper cartoons.

Not one to face the onslaught of public speaking, Elsie Belle enjoyed talking to individual library customers and enticing them inside by designing creative advertising displays in her windows and out on the side walk. In May 1907 she used an eye-catching theme centred on the colour red, advertising publications with red covers around a red bowl with red leaves that caused passing pedestrians to pause and admire. She often placed boards out the front of the library that illustrated both authors and magazines. She was also an early promoter of the sale of published plays – Bernard Shaw, Somerset Maugham, J.M. Barrie and John Galsworthy. During the First World War, box plans for Gregan McMahon company's theatre seasons were displayed and advertising notes sent to major Victorian newspapers to support the Melbourne Repertory Theatre. She also enjoyed social networks surrounding the theatre and, together with McMahon, his wife, and Annie McCubbin (who featured in her husband's famous painting, 'The Pioneer') Elsie Belle joined an organising committee for a large ball held at the Town Hall. Champion was an open admirer of McCubbin's painting and an early advocate of a permanent Victorian gallery where local artists such as McCubbin could display their works. A book club organised through the Consul for France, enabled Elsie Belle to lend books they purchased to their club members[513] and in September 1927 her library was a participant of Australian Author's Week.

The Champions used both the library and literary review to experiment with niche markets and in the early stages tested public response to unorthodox works like Charles Bogue Luffman's the *Principles of Gardening in Australia* (1904) and Paul Wenz's novella, *Diary of a New Chum* (1908) published by the Book Lovers' Library. French author Paul Wenz had been jackarooing in outback Australia in the nineties and Nettie Palmer's *Fourteen Years* described his 'broad square shoulders that made you wonder how the man had ever found a horse strong enough to carry him'. Wenz's advice to new chums was regarded as hilarious but truthful; some tips for survival in Australia were to take no offense at being called a new chum, listen to unknown adjectives and 'multiply the breadth by the length and divide by ten' for snake length and size of Murray cod.

As early as 20 July 1900 Bernard Shaw wrote to London publisher Grant Richards that Champion was 'a remarkably clever, resourceful, plausible, smart man, excellent company and authentically wellbred style' who would be an effective agent in Australia. Three days later he advised Richards to 'jump at him' for not only was he 'very clever' and 'a man fertile in schemes', but also his wife ran a library that survived the crash in Australia.[514] Champion's interest was always firmly on the side of the writer because authors historically signed away or sold copyright to publishers, including Henry Lawson. With two books translated into Dutch, even Ethel Turner had no financial benefit because of the lack of copyright law between England and Holland.[515] A public campaign by the English branch of the Author's Society tried to dissuade authors from a contract where they didn't retain copyright and, to secure his rights in 1896, Morley Roberts changed his agent to A.P. Watt who handled the literary affairs of Anthony Hope and Conan Doyle.

James Brand Pinker became Champion's British agent and they corresponded about authors from 1906 until Pinker's death in 1922.[516] A Scottish clerk on the Tilbury Docks in the 1880s and then a literary agent in London's Strand, Pinker's famous clients were George Gissing, Oscar Wilde, Frederick Rolfe, H.G. Wells, Henry James, Joseph Conrad and Margaret Harkness, as well as Australian authors such as Henry Lawson and Miles Franklin. Pinker was growing in influence in the new literary marketplace helping young authors and he sparked Champion's interest. Australia had 'really excellent stuff' although editors continued 'filling their pages with the twaddle' from England, Champion told readers of the *Book Lover* in June 1906.

While Pinker spent his time negotiating with publishers, Champion found a solution for emerging local writers – he would form his own agency and become publisher as well as influencer. The Australasian Authors' Agency was a natural extension of Champion's interest in books which their literary review and the library supported. Established to assist writers enter the market, the Australasian Authors' Agency began life in November 1906 at their home, an apartment in Bank Place (off Collins Street) where they lived until 1914.[517] Champion performed the role of agent, proof-reader and adviser for emerging new authors, with literary and dramatic agents situated in New York and London. By the end of 1908 Champion was forced to ask potential authors to pause for a period, adding a paragraph to his literary review titled 'Overwhelmed!'.

For over a decade, the Agency published dozens of authors, including William Chidley, Dorothea Mackellar, Ruth Bedford, Frank Wilmot, Alan Gross, Alex Somerville, Capel Boake, Mrs Norman Brookes and Marjorie Barnard. In addition, the Agency concentrated on World War I writers, such as Trooper Gerardy, Martin Boyd, Sydney Loch, Geoffrey Wall and T.G. McLean. Dorothea Mackellar's *The Closed Door and Other Verses* (1911) was a great success and received effusive praise from the Governor of Victoria who, in a letter to the *Book Lover* that May, requested copies to send home 'to teach British people, what to look for' in the Queensland bush. The *Book Lover* printed 'My Country', her verse that was popular with generations of primary school students. In addition, the Australian Authors' Agency published *The Life and Work of Miss Vida Goldstein* to publicise his sister-in-law's political campaign for the House of Representatives in 1913 after she was effectively ignored by mainstream press. The Agency continued publishing after the war, including in 1922, when Herbert Brookes's brother Norman, a former Australian Red Cross Commissioner in Egypt, looked to publish his wife Mabel's daring book *Old Desires*.

Increasingly, much of Champion's time from 1905 was consumed by socialist activities as he became an advocate and founder of political groups, many with meetings held at their Bank Place home. The Social Questions Committee (SQC), formed on 1 September 1905, was an attempt by Champion to 'persuade Tom Mann to stay in Melbourne and bring a real straightforward, active body of Socialists into being'. Nearly 60 members met at a music hall in the Royal Arcade in Bourke Street and decided on the collection and reporting of unemployment and housing issues for the following month.[518] Members of the committee were Champion, Mann, J.P. Jones, George A. Carter (cigar manufacturer) and F.C. Gray (former MLA in Prahran). In order to promote a sense of community fellowship, entertainment and education, Champion and Mann began Sunday lectures at the Bijou Theatre in October 1905 (later at the Gaiety and Zion) with Champion speaking on his experiences in the socialist movement 1880–89, ending with the Great London Dock Strike, while Mann spoke on pioneers of socialism. The following month the *Bulletin* saw Mann in the same light as Champion – an imported problem from England with ill-suited ideas for Australia: 'Why doesn't the dear old Mother Country keep its rabbits and thistles and Tom Mann?'.

The Socialist Party, a name suggested by Champion and quickly adopted, was reported subsequently in the first edition of the *Socialist* on 2 April 1906 and eighteen months after the formation of the SQC, membership numbered 1,800. Under J.P. Jones, Champion was one of the vice presidents of the Socialist Party from February to September 1906, Tom Mann was secretary and William Marsh assistant secretary. Rooms were secured at 117 Collins Street and the new propogandist party continued work on the eight-hour day and May Day celebrations. Writers such as Bernard O'Dowd, Louis Esson, Marie Pitt and Nettie Higgins were foundation members of the Socialist Party, with Vance Palmer joining in 1909. Dr Rudolf Broda (a member of the French Socialist Party) arrived in Melbourne and spent time at Trades Hall, speaking on the aims of international socialism. His parting letter expressed great admiration for the Sunday evening propagandist meetings at the Bijou Theatre, as well as his intention to copy their format on his return.[519] The same month Champion retold his story of the Social Democratic Federation's formation in England for *Steele Rudd's Magazine* and set up a Prahran branch of the party. Using a practice that he and Mann used in their agitation in London, meetings were held in the streets (one on the corner of Commercial Road and Cato Street). When a speaker was arrested in October 1906 it snowballed over weeks into a multitude of imprisonments (including Mann) and became a fight for free speech.[520]

The increasing attention attracted new members and galvanised an argument for a unified body under one national socialist umbrella. Travelling to Sydney, Champion and Marsh attended a meeting at 174 Castlereagh Street on 4 December 1906 where a Sydney branch of the Social Democratic Federation was established. They found themselves elected to represent the Sydney SDF at a Melbourne conference of nationwide bodies planned for 15 June 1907.[521] As president of the Socialist Party of Victoria from June to September

Champion chaired the conference and moved a motion 'to formulate proposals designed to bring all Australian Socialist bodies into the united body'. *The People: Weekly Organ of Australian Revolutionary Socialism* saw distinct parallels and remembered a similar dilemma during the Maritime Strike 17 years before this conference.

> Champion and Marsh shouldered the responsibility of the Social Democratic Federation, Sydney – a load under which both exhibited signs of painful distress. Neither knew whether such an organisation was living or dead, and frankly admitted it, the former delegate being understood to remark that he represented a body for which he had little respect. It was with difficulty we suppressed a smile; the circumstance brought vivid recollections of a past! History repeating itself: once as a tragedy and again as a farce![522]

Champion's brutal honesty, always a key to his troubles, inevitably caused antagonism and he moved back to the Executive in September. His Sydney trip also would gradually affect his later political activities when an attraction sparked between him and an aspiring writer, Katharine Susannah Prichard, 25 years his junior. Another secret liaison occurring while he thought he was happily married to Elsie Belle.

A Manifesto was issued in December 1908, stating the Socialist Party's intention to run two candidates for parliament and stressing 'these two seats shall be acorn whose outcome is the impregnable oak'. The explanation 'To the Electors', written by Champion, included a quote from August Bebel's *Women Under Socialism* (1879).[523] Together with John Curtin, Champion also served on a committee to enlarge the *Socialist* newspaper, becoming acting editor from April until the end of September 1908 and was later mentioned along with editors R.S. Ross, Frederick Sinclaire, Marie Pitt, and Maurice Blackburn on its anniversary.[524]

After his campaign in the *Age* in opposition to the Metropolitan Gas Company's charges, he formed the Gas Consumers' League (in August 1911) where he took on the role of secretary and Maurice Blackburn treasurer. The *Woman Voter* regarded his efforts to reduce gas prices as elevating him to 'a very St. George' and together with 'his able henchman' Blackburn, now active in the Socialist Party, they were fighters against exploitation.[525] Champion appointed Blackburn to take his place on an inquiry board in March 1912; he had also been his defence lawyer for legal proceedings over Champion's publication of what was regarded as an obscene book – William Chidley's book, *The Answer* (1911). In the trial, Blackburn defended Champion as publisher for the Australasian Author's Agency (and E.W. Cole as bookseller). Testimony was used from Archibald Strong and Bernard O'Dowd, sub-librarian at the Supreme Court library, to argue that it was not obscene and even Havelock Ellis had quoted Chidley's theory.[526] Blackburn later married Doris Hordern who was an assistant at the Book Lovers' Library and campaign secretary for Vida Goldstein in the 1913 election for the seat of Kooyong.

A Friday writing class was started at Champion's home to train journalists for the *Socialist* newspaper and a circulating library was added for educational purposes. Some organisations founded by Champion during the late 1890s, were re-established under the banner of Socialist Party with the Socialist Co-operative Trading Society (June 1906) for general goods and groceries, as well as the Socialist Co-operative Savings Bank (November 1907). Champion retired from the Executive at the start of 1909 though he continued to write articles occasionally.

Although Elsie Belle shared Champion's literary loves and publishing joys, she seemed not to share his intense political drive. Nonetheless, she bore all the invasion of enthusiastic and dedicated people into her home with apparent calmness. Champion was so busy in the thick of organising and planning for the Socialist Party, the time he had with Elsie Belle was certainly curtailed. Her involvement in activities was restricted mostly to the *Socialist* newspaper's family functions and their Christmas activities although she happily supported fairs with donations of books culled from the Book Lovers' Library. She did become a member of the Women's Social and Political Union in November 1912.

In the midst of his political activities, Champion continued to cultivate literary and artistic friendships. The Boulevard Cafe opened at Arlington Chambers, 229 Collins Street, near the Book Lovers' Library, and offered a bohemian dining experience. Run by a German, Ludwig Politzer, the place had an informal club lounge feel with cabarets and musical entertainment and staff wearing traditional clothing; it advertised 'intellect and spaghetti'. Champion often organised regular dinners at this venue with journalists, artistic and literary figures such as Frederick McCubbin, Frank Wilmot, Bernard O'Dowd, Louis Esson, Hugh McCrae, Rupert Atkinson, Peter (Roy) Newmarch and Percy Lindsay. The *Book Lover* and the Book Lovers' Library were promoting and distributing Hugh McCrae's poetry, so in June 1914 when McCrae left for New York, Champion chaired a farewell for him with 30 friends at the Boulevard Cafe. The following month Champion organised an invitation for A.G. Stephens, founder of the short-lived literary magazine *The Bookfellow*, who was lecturing on the lives of Adam Lindsay Gordon and Barcroft Boake. Inevitably, the restaurant was a victim of the times and the following year, prosecution commenced under the Health Act when someone reported one woman for smoking and one for buying a bottle of stout. By July 1916 Politzer's German background and the fact he served foreigners at his establishment caused one journalist to write that the authorities were aware of the place.[527]

The heightened awareness and level of suspicion was obvious throughout the First World War. Elsie Belle's youngest sister Aileen Goldstein experienced anti-German sentiment when she sailed via London to Boston in August 1914. Aileen's letters home, published in the *Woman Voter* in November, told of being rejected by a shipping line because of Aileen's 'suspiciously foreign name'. Thought to be German, the travel agency tried to reassure authorities that both she and her travel companion were British. After she arrived in Melbourne with great fanfare in April 1914, Adela Pankhurst was also forced to defend herself in the *Woman Voter* against criticism she was pro-German. She had withdrawn from the Women's Social and Political Union and her mother Emily gave her £20 to emigrate to Australia, together with an introduction to Vida Goldstein with whom she stayed as a guest.

In March 1916, only a couple of months after the death of her mother, Elsie Belle started proceedings to sue Hugh McCrae who had informed Rupert Atkinson that she and her husband were 'pro-German'. In the court case, McCrae argued Adela Pankhurst was pro-German and twice was 'a guest' at the home of the Champions. The association with Champion's club dinners at bohemian venues frequented by overseas nationalities had fuelled suspicion. Unlike her husband, Elsie Belle was unacquainted with McCrae but had aided distribution of his Sydney publication free of charge. Notice of the court action was placed in the *Book Lover* that March though Champion's name was not used; and no-one reported his absence at court or asked for his statements. Her sister Vida also stayed out of court which may have been a strategic decision to empower Elsie Belle. McCrae's remarks had been repeated to her by Rupert Atkinson's wife, Marie, a friend with whom she enjoyed motoring. Lionel Lindsay later gave an interesting insight into Atkinson's relationship with McCrae:

> Genial and kind-hearted, he had done much to help the perennially-penniless Hugh McCrae, who responded with a vast fund of malicious stories which mainly dealt with ridiculous escapades with Rupert's wife, Marie.[528]

McCrae's slander was passed on at a patriotic concert at Fairlie House as gossip spread.

Court statements showed McCrae believed the Champions wouldn't take the issue to court because of the effect on their business. In her defamation case Elsie Belle fought on principle, claiming £19 19s as a token sum for damages for what she desired was a 'refutation of the cruel and wholly uncalled for remarks of the defendant'. McCrae's comments were especially hurtful to her because her brother Selwyn was now a lieutenant fighting in France for the Royal Engineers and she herself was the daughter of an army officer. The court judgement, only a year before her brother's death, was sympathetic to Elsie Belle and legal proceedings cleared her name of German sympathies. Selwyn died in 1917 during the Battle of Messines in Flanders when he became another casualty of the war after shooting himself.

The Gallipoli campaign statistics had been shocking to Australians, with 50,000 troops at Gallipoli suffering over 26,000 casualties. Champion greatly admired *The Straits Impregnable* (1916) by Gippsland farmer, Sydney Loch and he published it through the Australasian Authors' Agency. The final report of General Sir Charles Monro (May 1916) illustrated to Champion how Gallipoli had been abandoned. Never a fan of Randolph Churchill, Champion was blunt about his son:

> 'He has shot his bolt, and will never have another chance. My brother, in the proceedings before the Battle of Omdurman, marched along the Nile at the head of the 21st Lancers with Mr. Churchill. He remembered one remark that the reckless future Cabinet Minister dropped: – "They now talk of me as Lord Randolph's son; in the future they will all speak of Lord Randolph as my father." More probably he will be forgotten in another couple of years, if the truth about the Gallipoli campaign ever sees the light'.[529]

Champion was wrong that Winston's career would soon fail although he entered his wilderness years after Gallipoli. Vance Palmer enlisted and later revisited of Gallipoli:

> An heroic force was allowed to wear itself out in the dispiriting task of holding on to a few lines of ridges along the coast, until sickness, heavy casualties, and the rain and sleet of early winter made withdrawal inevitable.[530]

Part of General Sir Beauchamp Duff's letter was released by Champion.

> 'There is a pretty influential party in England who is crying for my blood. I do not know if you realise that I am the last man of those who held high military positions before the war who has not been shunted elsewhere or broken. The crowd I spoke of has now got its knife into me. I do not think I mind much. I always did like a fight, and I rather think I can give as good as I get'.[531]

Duff overdosed on barbiturate in January 1918 after a Royal Commission censured him, Sir John Nixon and Viceroy Lord

Hardinge for their failed plan to capture Baghdad. Subsequently, Champion fondly recalled a simpler time of boyhood with Duff, 'the last of Kitchener's men'.[532]

As the leader of the Social Democratic Federation, Hyndman maintained 'an intensely patriotic attitude' to the war but Champion's attitude was different. With Champion's own military background informing his response, he gave a touching review of Frank Wilmot's 'To God from the Weary Nations', the poet's theme on humanity's culpability in war:

> 'To God' is a monument to the wantonness of it all, to the cheapness of life in war, the disregard alike of promise and performance, the elimination of personality. This is what war means – what it really signifies. One does not disregard the honour lists indeed, but realises more fully the exquisite bodies insulted by agony and death, the ineffable spirits devastated, the dire necessity that makes pitiable horrors ...[533]

Champion also included two other viewpoints in the same issue: one from Christopher Brennan, and one from his long-time friend Walter Murdoch. Murdoch's warm and teasing response extolled the virtues of Wilmot's poem and was addressed to 'My Dear Champion':

> Why all this mock humility? Why pretend that you do not know true poetry when you see it, that you must have someone else's opinion, &c.? You know as well as I do that Wilmot's poem is a poem in the best sense. It will be read long after the war is over ... Wilmot is to be congratulated – if congratulations were not in such matters a horrible impertinence – on the courage he has displayed in the invocation to the God who gave him a soul to be set on fire and a brain to find expression in noble and burning words for his vision of the truth. I have not been so moved by anything that has been written since the war came, and I am very much your debtor for sending it to me. If you are sending copies to the booksellers here I shall try to make people buy.

The *Book Lover* appeared irregularly from September 1916 for two years while Champion worked with Brieux's play across cities in eastern Australia and New Zealand. While travelling, Champion employed an associate editor, Peter (Roy) Newmarch, and a Boulevard Cafe member from 1914. Among the creditors listed when Newmarch became insolvent were Elsie Belle who was owed close to £400 for his board and lodgings at 462 Punt Road, and Rupert Atkinson whose summons assisted Newmarch's three-month imprisonment (when he was swindled by a so-called Newmarch, the son of an 'Earl'). By April 1920 his liabilities were nearly £5,000 and he added his fee as a journalist for *Book Lover* articles (£330/13/18 for ten months to June 1922). Elsie Belle's niece blamed Newmarch for the closure of the *Book Lover*. However, Speciality Press in Little Collins Street was the business that actually petitioned for Champion's bankruptcy for the amount of £192/11/3, his liabilities in 1922 exceeding his assets four-fold.[534]

Vida Goldstein later disclosed that the Book Lovers' Library was 'bled white' for Champion's expenditure and perhaps his habit of recording cash-only transactions disguised other payments. Business trips – as a theatrical and literary agent on behalf of the Australasian Authors' Agency and Brieux's play – were excuses for overseas travel, hotels, theatres and dinners, and a number of people contributed to Champion's various enterprises at different periods to enable these trips. Apart from Newmarch, Bertha Gross, sister-in-law of Percy Laidler, worked at the journal for 12 months researching and publishing for Champion's Gas Consumers' League. E.A. Sexton assisted the Australasian Authors' Agency correspondence, particularly with Jack London which spanned 1909 to 1915.[535] Elsie Belle also enjoyed corresponding with writers for the Agency and over a lengthy period became friends with many authors. A year after his bankruptcy, Champion talked wearily of saving for a visit to England and, as his 65th birthday loomed, he was still correcting manuscripts when he wrote to Morley on 20 April 1923: 'I am very happy and bullied to death by my wife, but she really loves me and I submit to it with pleasure'.

Momentum suddenly changed when Champion saw his first

performance of *Pygmalion* in late 1923. After the Tait family merged with J.C. Williamson they purchased the burnt-out Olympic Theatre at the corner of Lonsdale and Stephen Street. Suddenly a new spark was lit in Champion as his interest fixed on an enterprise needing financial backing. It is not known whether Elsie Belle was in favour of her husband's leap into another enterprise at a time when the *Book Lover* had just failed. Shaw wrote to Champion from his home in Adelphi Terrace on 31 January 1924, referring to Mrs Pitt-Rivers, daughter of the Governor-General of Australia, who performed in the role of Eliza Doolittle at Her Majesty's Theatre in Melbourne in November 1923. Shaw replied to Champion's obvious interest in the play:

My Dear Champion, –
Pygmalion succeeds everywhere. It does not seem to matter who plays it or where it is played; it always boils the pot. It has been going round the English provinces now since 1913, and it is still the touring manager's trump card. I am greatly alarmed by your proposal to start a theatre. Don't. It will leave you without soles to your shoes. If you can get any capital for the purpose get it for Gregan McMahon, who is comparatively young and in the business .... Obviously Mrs. Pitt Rivers must remain an amateur whilst she is officially connected with the British Empire unless she runs a theatre herself, like Marie Antoinette at the Trianon. Ask her to send me some photographs of herself as Liza if she has any taken.[536]

The letter was provided to the *Age* many years later by a man who claimed it was 'among many letters written by George Bernard Shaw, the dramatist, both to her late husband, Mr. Henry Hyde Champion, and Mrs. E.B. Champion'. Little is known of the person who held Shaw's correspondence and used the pseudonym Fabius. From around 1895 this person wrote letters to the Melbourne *Herald* and indicated his familiarity with Champion's newly released SDF Manifesto. In the *Age* in the 1920s he published short stories and articles and was a lover of literature, particularly poetry, drama and Thomas Hardy. An admirer of Hugo Grotus who was instrumental in defining laws of war and peace, the name was chosen, like the Fabians, from Fabius

Cunctator, and over the next twenty years his letters to the editor were on issues such as equipping the Second AIF for war in the tropics and the Northern Territory railway.

One candidate who may have held Shaw's letter to Champion is Herbert Brookes, an engineering graduate of the University of Melbourne and later active in the League of Nations Union. Norman Brookes (his brother) and wife Mabel were members of the audience along with the Champions on 13 November 1923. Only a few months before Shaw wrote to Champion on *Pygmalion*, Brookes's sister-in-law was published through the Australasian Authors' Agency, accompanied by a review for the *Herald* and a background to the novel's origin. Herbert Brookes also maintained a lengthy correspondence with Walter Murdoch (lasting over fifty years) however, Shaw's letter was not found among his papers.

He and Elsie Belle were planning to visit England, Champion told Tom Mann when he was no longer active in the Victorian Socialist Party.[537] Annie Beatrice Champion, who had seen her brother when he came to London, wrote to Miles Franklin on 28 October 1925 from Hatton Castle, informing her the Champions were planning a spring visit. When Miles visited the Champions early in March 1927 it was evident his health was rapidly declining.[538] Robert S. Ross provided another update that November: 'Champion keeps about quietly and alertly and is as much a treasure-trove conversationally as at any time in his remarkable career'.[539]

Four months after Champion's death, Elsie Belle undertook the mammoth task of assessing the library's material and selling surplus stock. It was systematic labour, conducted in a time of loneliness and absence; a task that Elsie Belle was fully equipped to tackle. Champion's immense capacity for reading, analysing and appraising books meant that a wide spectrum of works needed to be evaluated after the demise of both the *Book Lover* and her husband, and she probably needed the extra cash that came with down-sizing the collection. The Book Lovers' Library advertised and held a large sale on 2 September 1928, reducing prices of new fiction and clearing out books on travel, biography, memoirs, literature and political works, including Havelock Ellis and W.H. Hudson. While it is possible that all business records and Champion's letters were destroyed by Elsie Belle when she organised the clean-out or after she sold the entire library contents ten years later, Aileen Goldstein, as executor of both Elsie Belle and Vida's wills, may have completed this later.

A year after Champion's death Vida encouraged Elsie Belle to go with her to London for a lengthy holiday and they departed on 5 March 1929 on the P&O liner *Maloja*. In England they lunched at Sloane Square and met political and literary figures such as John Burns, Ramsay MacDonald, John Galsworthy and, of course, Bernard and Charlotte Shaw. Elsie Belle's letter to the editor of the *Age* recalled her visit to Shaw who prompted her to ask 'Old John' [John Burns] about the origin of the epithet 'The silver Thames' as he guided the Goldstein sisters around the city. John Burns recounted one tour with two American and Canadian visitors whose rivers in their own countries were extensive, telling them the Thames was 'liquid history'.[540]

The two sisters took the opportunity to visit Ramsay MacDonald who they last met in November 1906 when he spoke at Melbourne's Socialist Hall prior to his election as the first Labour Prime Minister of England. (In April 1896, Beatrice and Sidney Webb had refused to engage Ramsay because he was 'not good enough' as a lecturer for their new London School of Economics.) Elsie Belle and Vida also visited the novelist and poet, John Galsworthy, one of Champion's theatrical clients in Australia. Elsie Belle had struck up a lengthy correspondence in 1906 and remembered Galsworthy's 'tranquility' and 'large heart'.[541]

The sisters met Bernard and Charlotte Shaw at lunch and confirmed what Shaw probably suspected for years – there was not much money left in the household. Shaw always remembered his own lean years. The value placed on first editions of rare books and authors were noted many years before in the *Book Lover* and there were discussions now about letters and postcards being saleable, a helpful suggestion to the cash-strapped sisters as they faced the long years after Champion's death. At this time Australian papers were openly chuckling about a woman selling a sentence by Shaw because it had his autograph. In fact, one card from Shaw to Champion was brought by the sisters to England and he suggested that 'a rich American then in London would pay anything for his signature'. A New York book collector, Gabriel Wells, had bought Shaw's postcards, scribbled notes, fragments and letters in London and it was sensational enough to be reported in UK newspapers throughout October and November 1928. Wells later sold his whole collection to T.E. Hanley, a millionaire from Pennsylvania, who resold them in 1958 to Harry Ransom from the University of Texas. One of Shaw's post-cards carried by the Goldstein sisters was stolen prior to the London auction, although they insured it for a 'starting' price at auction of £50. Given they were auctioning memorabilia it is plausible that, as they became older and poorer, the Goldstein sisters quietly sold letters between Shaw and Champion, as well as other valuable manuscripts and memorabilia kept by Champion, to collectors. Certainly, Elsie Belle and Vida left London for a 'short visit' to New York and Boston before returning to Australia at the beginning of 1930. Elsie Belle continued to correspond with Shaw and facilitated a meeting with his Australian cousin. Shaw later contributed delightful acerbic introductory comments and corrections in red pen to Charles MacMahon Shaw's *Bernard's Brethren* (1939), his work tracing their ancestry from Scottish Highlanders given land in Ireland after the Battle of the Boyne, to explorer Robert O'Hara Burke who crossed from Melbourne to the Gulf of Carpentaria.

A decade after her husband's death and after nearly four decades of ownership of the Book Lovers' Library, Elsie Belle retired. Over two months from late July 1938 library stock was advertised and sold along with shelving and shop fittings. She was sufficiently attached to stay close to books and readers, working part-time at Robertsons and Mullens Bookshop until a few months before her own death at eighty-three. Elsie Belle died on 21 October 1953 and was cremated at the Necropolis Springvale which held Vida's ashes in August 1949 and Aileen's in August 1960 but not Champion's ashes. Champion's probate in England was finally released in 1946 giving Elsie Belle a tidy sum of £375.

After the emotional turmoil of previous relationships, it was Elsie Belle who provided Champion with gentle contentment during a marriage lasting 30 years. Despite Champion's yearning for 'some commonplace friendship or mild affection' in his letter to Morley on

10 October 1897 and his happiness in marriage, it seems he still felt something was missing. It was less than 10 years into his marriage when Champion revisited his romantic vision of wanderer and gallant knight, attempting to recapture a new romance with a young aspiring writer over half his age. His friend Brookes wrote of his sadness over Champion's fate as 'a cripple' early in his life although he 'passed his latter days happily with his wife and hobbling about the city he had adopted as his home'. In fact, he was much more active than anyone suspected when Katharine Susannah Prichard appeared to capture his attention. The narrative of romantic fiction, rejected in 1897 after his soured love affair with Adelaide, and recanted in the *Book Lover* in December 1900 as 'sentimental' fiction with 'characters who are capable of romance, honour and faithfulness' was about to be tested with a new liaison. He was to rediscover the mirage of a spring love after his stroke and dark days of recovery, and to dream of possessing what he felt was lost. As Morley Roberts wrote in *Immortal Youth* (1902): 'Monogamy properly understood means carrying on but one intrigue at a time'.

A Guilty Secret
Katharine Susannah Prichard (1883–1969)

Dear lips
That to me prove
My body
But a chalice, white,
For thy delight,
My love, my love!
Oh, I am faint
When thy lips hang on mine
And there is ecstasy
In their mute questing,
Easting, westing.
(K.S. Prichard, 'Lips of My Love', 1914)

There is a strong body of evidence to suggest Henry Hyde Champion was the 'Preux Chevalier' in Katharine Susannah Prichard's memoir, *Child of the Hurricane* (1963). The title of her autobiography supposedly referred to her tumultuous birth in a storm in Fiji on 4 December 1883 although it was more a rendering by an elderly writer of her turbulent life and loves. Breaking her silence on a liaison, she used Preux Chevalier (or gallant knight) to conceal the identity of an older married man who was a friend of her father and well-known in Melbourne. Champion's overt identification with the symbolism was obvious in his newspaper where, under the nameplate, there was a drawing of a medieval knight with a lance riding a war-horse. His friend Maggie Harkness, in her novel of a labour leader, explicitly called her hero a 'wanderer', a quest seeker in the true tradition of a knight-errant and defending warrior. Through his relationship with Katharine, Champion had a direct formative influence on her understanding of social and political issues, which led her inexorably to activism.

Despite her Preux Chevalier being mentioned in relatively few pages of her autobiography, Katharine's references are significant. A 'man of the world, elegant and assured, accustomed to authority' he was used to the finer things in life, enjoyed the theatre, concerts, art, books, fine dining and was 'the most considerate and fascinating of cavaliers'. Not only was he well connected in the political sphere, but also in the journalistic and literary worlds of both Australia and England.

He travelled extensively overseas, spoke fluent French, knew Paris intimately and encouraged Katharine to speak the language. He helped shape her reading, loaned her books and she was flattered by his interest in her early writing. He talked with knowledge about political issues of the day, international problems of peace and war, and the rights of women. His knowledge of poetry, history and politics was remarkable and impressive to a young inexperienced girl. Katharine went to the hotels he advised, his friends were organised to meet her when she travelled, and he had control of various itineraries when he joined her in overseas cities while on work-related trips. He was twice her age, her father's friend who also became her friend. As a trusted family friend, he was told when she would sail back from New Zealand and knew the exact date of her return so he could meet her at the Sydney docks. He arranged to meet her in secret around Melbourne and in Paris for a brief autumn interlude in 1908 where he took her to Montmartre and bohemian artists' studios. When she again returned to London, he joined her in the spring of 1912. Her tantalising trail of clues points to a man who was intellectually attractive to a young aspiring writer as she endured the traumatic events of her father's depression and death.

In the summer of 1890 when Katharine was nearly seven years old, Champion lived less than a mile away from Brighton Beach where her father Tom was teaching his children to swim in all weather conditions. Tom Prichard was editor of Frank Critchley Parker's *Sun: the Society Courier* from April 1889 to early 1892 while Champion was owner/editor from August 1897 until January 1899. Tom lost his job in 1892 and secured a new position with Launceston's *Daily Telegraph* and was welcomed as a new member of the local branch of the Australian Institute of Journalists in late August 1893. Because of management's 'tomahawk' wielding cuts,[542] Tom lost this job too and the family returned to Melbourne where he finally secured a position as editor-in-chief of Parker's *Australian Mining Standard* the following year. Apart from editorial work at the same newspaper (although years apart) Champion and Tom had a lot in common through journalism, travel, literature, love of theatre and enjoyment of friends.

Katharine's parents called on a number of friends, a rich intellectual community, to help further her education prior to the entry examination for South Melbourne College on her 14th birthday. A Parisienne teacher living in Prahran, Mademoiselle Irma Dreyfus helped Katharine with French lessons. Irma was an early member of the Austral Salon and the Warrawee Club with Mrs Goldstein and her daughters. In addition, she was a member of the Melbourne Shakespeare Society with Julia Sutherland who prepared Vida Goldstein for entry to the Presbyterian Ladies College; her sister, Jane Sutherland, was one of the Heidelberg School of painters and studied under Frederick McCubbin. Irma counted Champion as an enthusiastic supporter for her lectures on French literature in August 1895, his newspaper office even selling tickets. At the age of thirteen, Katharine admitted she didn't understand much of the content of Irma's lectures, however she would later point to Irma's book, *The Spring and Summer of French Literature* (1896), as responsible for her enthusiasm for French Literature. Katharine called her the 'most exquisite and charming of French women',[543] one who had arranged for her visit to Sarah Bernhardt in Paris after her performance in a play on the life of Napoleon II.

While Tom seems a dominant figure in his daughter's early life with his enjoyment of literature, drama, poetry and music, Katharine downplays the role of her mother, Edith Prichard. However, Edith was an intelligent and creative woman who lived with a sensitive husband whose nerves were stretched and strained and whose income was not steady or sufficient to maintain a household for a lengthy period. Edith had a strong friendship with Alfred Deakin in her youth and he frequently visited her grandparent's 'Clareville' home in Caulfield. Deakin also lived in South Yarra at 'Llanarth', named after his mother's birthplace in Wales, a town not far from Tom Prichard's birthplace Whitchurch in northern Shropshire.

Edith loved the theatre and playing the Broadwood cottage pianoforte, inherited from her mother, which she eventually bequeathed to Katharine. She gave wonderful dinner parties for likeminded people who discussed literature and art, with the children joining guests at the large table in the home's ante-chamber. Edith was also adamant that a friend of hers should teach Katharine sketching and water-colour, two areas in which Edith herself excelled even entering an exhibition while in Launceston. She chose Frank Brookesmith, a recognised artist with a studio at the Melbourne Chambers in Collins Street, and invited him to dinner parties. With other invited friends and neighbours, Brookesmith also attended a drama Katharine wrote, acted in and directed at the family home. An exhibition of his pupils' work at his studio in February 1898 included paintings by Katharine and Elsie Cole. The girls were school friends and both were editors (at different times) of J.B. O'Hara's quarterly school magazine, *The Collegian*, where Katharine had a short piece 'The Dance – A Memory' published. The two friends from South Melbourne College were delighted to find their paintings displayed although Elsie was more serious about water-colour painting and black and white illustration than Katharine.

Many paths in Katharine's early life seemed to lead to the city centre, particularly around Collins Street where Champion lived, worked and socialised.

J.B. O'Hara, Katharine's headmaster at South Melbourne College was a poet, mathematician and 'crack cricketer,' as Champion called him in 1895, and later in April 1901 both he and O'Hara were judges for essay and poetry prizes for South Melbourne Literary Societies. A majestically named 'Katharine Tudor', still aged 15, who gave her address as her grandmother's house 'Clareville', submitted her story to the Children's Page competition at Champion's newspaper, *Sun: the Society* Courier, via the postal address used for the *Book Lover*.[544] For 'originality and composition' Katharine won the newspaper's first quarter prize for a unique story of a waif, 'That Brown Boy', although she shared the prize of 10 shillings with another entrant because of her 'carelessness in grammar, writing and orthography'. What better place for an aspiring young writer than a newspaper where her father was once editor and where his 'Aramis' and 'Fijian Superstitions' contributions were well regarded. Finally published on 7 April 1899, 'That Brown Boy' was also republished eight days later in the *Federalist*, a short-lived political weekly in Launceston supporting Federation. Prior to the finalisation of his newspaper sale, Champion was still interim editor. Katharine recalled the 'kindly editor' who commented that her story held potential and his recommendation that she study life and people as material if she desired a career as a writer. Taking Champion's advice as a guide, her writer's notebooks testify to her attention to research, the study of characters and her expeditions to remote places. In her autobiography, Katharine wrote of his early literary support:

> My Preux Chevalier and I had not been much more than acquaintances before. He had been interested in my writing and lent me books. Then, too, he was one of the few people on whom I could practice French. He was married, of course, and had a daughter my own age, which I thought was why he was so courteous to me (*Child of the Hurricane*, p. 93).

At this stage, interest in her writing was limited to a small unpublished love story 'For Her Sake' (1896), her 5th form essay-writing prize in 1901 and two published short stories for competitions, 'That Brown Boy' (1899) and a romantic story of Katharine and Angus, 'Bush Fires' (1903) for *New Idea*. The daughter Katharine mentions in her recollection was probably Adelaide's adopted daughter Shirley who was six years of age in the summer of 1890. Champion was in the middle of his affair with Adelaide so it is possible (at least at that stage) that Katharine believed Shirley was his daughter. Strangely, in his biography of Katharine, her son recalled talk of three daughters, perhaps references to Elsie Belle, Vida and Aileen Goldstein.

In Katharine's last school year (1902), her brothers Nigel and Alan called her Jemima because of her apparent 'superior airs', an interesting nickname considering Adelaide's children's novel featured

Jemima. Katharine spent the following months at home looking after her mother who had sciatica and standing in for theatre trips with her father. As her parents were not in a position to afford Melbourne University fees because other siblings needed education, Katharine followed her mother's example and became a governess.[545]

Katharine spent time as a governess for an English doctor's two children at Yarram in the Southeast of Gippsland, the Garden of Eden of her story 'Diana of the Inlet' and the setting for *The Pioneers*.[546] After Dr Muir sold his practice in April 1905, Katharine spent another period as a governess travelling by coach to the opal fields of White Cliffs before returning south as summer commenced. Her own experiences were published as a *New Idea* serial from May–October 1906 and, while not about a city girl in the London slums like Maggie's first novel, her city girl in the outback received accolades. 'A City Girl in Central Australia: Her Adventures and Experiences at "Back o' Beyond"', a term for a remote and isolated region. Katharine's serial was set at Edward Quinn's Turella Station near Wilcannia and White Cliffs in shearing season. She was in famous company, standing shoulder to shoulder with a successful writer, Mary Gilmore, who had written for *New Idea* on her experience as a teacher in the bush. Katharine's homecoming coincided with the release of Maggie Harkness's *George Eastmont*, a work based on an English socialist from the Dock Strike. It is quite plausible Katharine heard gossip and learned more about her mentor.

Katharine's friends, Nettie Higgins, Hilda Bull and Christian Jollie Smith all entered Melbourne University. Nettie had her first literary success in the *Book Lover* in her first year of university, with Champion informing Nettie on 6 January 1905 that she was now 'covered with glory'. Katharine had no university degree and this remained a sore point as she tried to keep pace with her friends by reading widely and continuing her French and German study.[547] She borrowed books from a Public Lending Library and browsed Coles' Book Arcade in Little Collins Street although she studiously ignored any mention of the Book Lovers' Library. Champion was known to encourage 'younger people to bring their sandwiches to the upstairs' area of Collins Street to discuss ideas,[548] and into this informal circle he attracted intelligent young individuals with an interest in social reform. He entertained them with lively tales of writers, artists and political figures and challenged their ideas as he saw a generation to educate beyond their local environment, drawing in those seeking a change in conventional thought and practice. They knew Champion was a militant socialist, a major figure of the Great London Dock Strike and infamous in the Maritime Strike in Melbourne. He owned, operated and wrote for radical newspapers, and had started the *Champion* which upset the establishment. He wanted 'something better than the bottomless dullness of the local dailies', dared to attack the iconic *Bulletin* for 'prostituting its artistic side to its commercial' and castigated the owner for reliance on revenue producing advertisements that undervalued literature. He also had the temerity to reprimand the *Bulletin's* editor and cartoonist for publishing a tasteless illustration suggesting women attended a law court to hear 'spicy details' about a young girl and demanded a public apology for these members of a child protection society.[549]

Katharine registered as a primary school teacher on 30 June 1906. That month, Dr Rudolf Broda, who represented the French Socialist Party, arrived in Melbourne. Champion, as vice president of the Socialist Party, ensured both Katharine and Vida Goldstein received an introduction, probably at the Sunday night lecture at the Bijou Theatre. Katharine was asked to contribute to Broda's Paris journal, *Les Documents Du Progrès* and also the German *Dokumente Des Fortschritts*. Katharine wrote on women's suffrage, anti-sweating laws, literature and the education system, all issues of keen interest to Champion. Vida's article on women's suffrage and Katharine's on Australian literature were both published in the same issue of *Les Documents Du Progrès* the following year and Champion's fluent French would have assisted the proofing. Early Australian literature was one of 'imitation', Katharine wrote.

> It has reached the age of adolescence, it is ready to do great things, it grows day by day in power and in liberty. For too long its literature has fed on convict escapes, on droughts and on the death of sheep. With

the birth of national feeling we begin to examine with a healthy and vigorous mind problems that concern our social and political life, and under the veil of poetry and the novel we idealise the too cruel realities of our evolution. (*Les Documents Du Progrès*, pp. 124–25)

When Vida's 'Socialism of To-day: An Australian View' was accepted for *Nineteenth Century* in September 1907, Champion was full of praise: 'Getting an article in that review has been described as winning "the Blue Riband of the Turf"'.[550]

Vida 'tried all the 'isms and 'ologies, and found them all wanting, until she came to Socialism'.[551] So too, Katharine was investigating and reading Robert Blatchford's *Clarion* at a time when Champion was writing a regular column from January 1907 to December 1908 on the Australian socialist movement. In 'Why I am a Communist', Katharine wrote that the arguments of Marx and Engels 'satisfied my common sense', a phrase strongly associated with Champion. Katharine was also closely studying reports by Champion and Laura Bogue Luffman, both contributors to Clementina Black's *Sweated Industry and the Minimum Wage* (1907).[552] In 'Why I am a Communist' she later wrote of the Australian Anti-Sweating League reports detailing 'nervous wrecks' of girls subjected to lengthy hours. She also later interviewed Mrs Powell of the Anti-Sweating League and the Shirt and Collar Makers' Wages Board for the *Herald* in July 1910. At an afternoon tea Katharine and Hilda Bull were amused by talk of 'the red Tiger of Socialism' and the prediction that ordinary people would suffer under the system.[553] Voting at her first Federal election on 12 December 1906 she chose a Labour candidate (a soap manufacturer from Bendigo) although didn't tell her conservative father.

Meanwhile, Tom Prichard's depression had been building. His son Alan's acute illness and hospitalisation one October night in 1906 was believed to cause Tom's extreme anxiety and insomnia.

During this ordeal, Katharine told her father she wished it had been her and he replied 'I wish it were', a scene replicated in her novel *Working Bullocks*. Although Alan recovered, her father stopped going to his office and never returned. Katharine was aware of her father's short committal to an asylum, her autobiography recalling his obsessive praying, mental anguish and her mother's tears. Admitted in November to Cloverdale private asylum in Bruce Street, Toorak for just over a week he was sent home with a recommendation of rest and a sea voyage. With Katharine's money from her serial, Edith saw an opportunity for Tom to be taken in mid-December to his brother's farm at Canterbury in New Zealand.

One indicator of concern for Tom Prichard's state of mind was that, on Katharine's return from Canterbury, she had the phone number of a friend from Edith's youth, now married to a Sydney medical asylum administrator. Callan Park Hospital for the Insane was on the shores of Iron Cove, only a short ferry ride from the city. Like Edith's parents, Simon and Susan, who married at Chorlton-upon-Medlock, Joseph and Jane Pope were from the same Manchester city in Lancashire. Their daughter, Sarah, gained extensive experience as a matron at Rydalmere and Kenmore mental asylums and was appointed (in August 1900) matron at Callan Park where she met and married Medical Superintendent Dr Andrew Davidson, a graduate of Aberdeen University.

Known to rescue people with mental health issues, (John Barlas, Frederick Rolfe, William Chidley, and Edward Pariss Nesbit) Champion's circle included people with similar concerns such as Catherine Thomson and Evelyn Gough. Catherine Thomson's undercover position as an attendant at Kew Asylum enabled a number of ground-breaking articles on female inmates for the *Argus* in March 1886 and Champion was active in 1896 discussing asylums and promoting changes to Victorian 'lunacy laws'. Evelyn Gough was responsible for social welfare reforms particularly in prisons, factories and asylums.

Tom Prichard's mental illness issues were probably known amongst friends and colleagues involved with front-line institutions dealing with these issues. After watching with concern her father's further deterioration on the New Zealand farm, Katharine wrote 'The Kid' which she submitted to the *Bulletin*. This story must have sounded alarm bells in her family as they read 'the unreasoning human, passionate pain through which the child was laboring' over the death of a baby brother, an event sparking her own tragic end.[554]

A GUILTY SECRET

On her return from New Zealand early in January 1907, Katharine was welcomed at the Sydney dock by her father's friend who knew exactly when she would arrive alone.

Her autobiography indicates the information source was her family, probably Edith and/or her mother's youngest, widowed sister Aunt Lil (Mrs Lily Wilson-Williams) who knew Champion was in Sydney to confer with members of the newly established Sydney Social Democratic Federation and the International Socialist Club, currently holding a conference on socialist unity. Obviously, great family trust was placed in him and, while Katharine's autobiography tells of outings with the Preux Chevalier, she does not mention whether he escorted her to the director to discuss her father's mental health. A romantic lover who never 'hinted at anything but a distant respectful admiration and concern to help her over difficulties' later appears in *The Roaring Nineties*.

Inserting himself as a helper at this time recalls Champion's ready help of many friends experiencing emotional difficulties. Upon disembarkation he booked her into the Metropole. Inferred as a pedestrian or even downmarket hotel, in the heart of the city she had his reassurance: 'I'll be your *preux chevalier* and show you Sydney'. With electric lighting, luxurious furnishings and a frontage to Bent, Young and Phillip Streets leading to Bligh Street, this hotel was certainly not small, quiet or average and could accommodate over 300 guests. With a tiled mosaic entrance, lavish stained-glass windows and the roof promenade containing views to Parramatta it was a grand structure. 'No more magnificent structure of design or appointment of its type can be found in the colonies, and certainly not in Sydney' was the local verdict.[555]

The Metropole was favoured by Champion for his stay there in September 1890 during the Maritime Strike where he was interviewed in his rooms by the *Daily Telegraph* and the *Australian Star*. Rudyard Kipling stayed there the following year and Sir Henry Parkes celebrated his 79th birthday there in style. Margaret Harkness's character, based on Champion, also debated on his arrival in Sydney: 'Where should he sleep tonight? The Metropole? It would swamp his funds'; he chose the hotel later for breakfast and a bath (*George Eastmont*, pp. 193, 234). In her autobiography as she approached her 80th year, Katharine felt safe to name the Metropole, perhaps believing that the aging hotel, approaching demolition in 1969 as part of a changing inner-city landscape, would be inconsequential to modern readers. Moreover, close friends who knew the hotel in its original splendour were no longer alive. The bill for an overnight stay was advertised in the *Bulletin* on 5 November 1903 as 10s 6d and was certainly paid for by Champion. Katharine could not afford the exorbitant expense over a significant number of nights. Whether she hid the extent of her ramblings with him in Sydney, she certainly would never have disclosed to her family the extravagant hotel payment.

At this stage Katharine had just turned 23 and Champion was approaching 48. Her mother was only five years older than Champion, a similar age to both Margaret Harkness and Adelaide Hogg. The age difference was significant – six months before Katharine's birth in Fiji, Champion joined the Democratic Federation in England and was married. At the end of an affair with Adelaide Hogg, Champion wrote wistfully of a desire to recapture his youth through romance and this desire seems to resurface in his relationship with Katharine. He was still in the role he carved out in his relationship with Adelaide, one of champion and rescuer.

Dazzled by the heady experience, flowers, hansom cabs and the refinement and elegance of her surroundings, Katharine recalled in her autobiography:

> He, a man of the world, elegant and assured, accustomed to authority; and I in my home-made summer dress and floppy hat ... conscious of being a little dowdy and gauche in the company of this Preux Chevalier. Not that he seemed to notice it! He treated me, not as an immature and insignificant damsel, but, to my surprise, as an attractive and intelligent young woman whose escort he was delighted to be (pp. 93–4).

Together they wandered the city visiting the art gallery, the library, travelling on ferries around the harbour; nights were spent at dinner, supper, the theatre and a concert. She told of an awakening of her political and social conscience in his company as he 'opened my mind to political questions, international problems of peace and war, the rights of women'. He covered a gamut of subjects across 'politics, history and poetry' as he enthralled a mind hungry for knowledge. 'Gaily irreligious and iconoclastic', humorous, clever, charming and entertaining, he knew a wide range of writers and enchanted her with his 'witty observations and amusing anecdotes of politicians and writers he had known'. Her attentive companion was obviously well-heeled and had moved with ease in political circles.

This was a heady time for a young woman who, although no school-girl, was inexperienced. The autobiography pulses with excitement for a companion made even more alluring by the clandestine nature of their meetings.

Champion told her 'no one must know' so the 'flutter' in Sydney must remain 'a guilty secret', his name never to be divulged because of inevitable gossip. Champion was familiar with Alice's progress through Wonderland and had met Sir John Tinniel, artist for Lewis Carroll,[556] and so the White Rabbit's summary certainly echoes his attitude: 'A secret, kept from all the rest'. His attentions were well received and Katharine loyally kept to the agreement. Champion had changed from her father's friend, to her friend before transforming into her Preux Chevalier while she transformed into his *chèrie*.

Any chance to practice her French was seized and the Preux Chevalier graciously helped his young friend. His repeated phrase insisting on her future fame as a writer was so very appealing and, at a room secured at the Paris Café out of sight of other customers, he toasted her success as a writer in the city of Paris. At the time Café de Paris at the Victoria Hotel in Sydney's George Street was popular with French speakers and frequently advertised in *Le Courier Australien* although another Café de Paris also operated in Melbourne's Theatre Royal, retaining the name of a celebrated restaurant operated by Spiers and Pond for the first Melbourne Cup. Advertising a salon bar, coffee and smoking room with elegant and tasteful decorations, the Melbourne venue was said to rival the Paris venue. While her reminiscences suggest Sydney, her relationship with Champion continued in Melbourne and so the reference may have been to either.

In addition, her Preux Chevalier issued an invitation: 'Some day, I will show you Paris'.

On parting, her Preux Chevalier again took control, informing her she was 'too young and unsophisticated' to handle any 'malicious gossip' associated with their meetings. As Katharine pondered the motivation behind why he was kind, he declared: 'There are all sorts of rapprochements between a man and woman beyond reason or argument. I've wanted to get to know you better, *chèrie*'. These connections or 'rapprochements' flourished back in Melbourne where Katharine began to chaff at her lack of freedom and family constraints discarded in Sydney with her escort.

After Sydney, Katharine gained more freedom of movement. She found work as a tutor, with afternoons off to study at the library, meet friends and attend night lectures at Melbourne University. She often caught a tram to the university with one of the lecturers in English, Walter Murdoch. Murdoch's series of six lectures at the university was promoted in *Book Lover* and Champion recalled the large crowds drawn to these.[557] Champion was active as a member of the University Extension Committee with Blamire Young, Alfred Deakin and novelist T.A. Browne (Rolf Boldrewood) and lectures covered Champion's favourite writers Browning, Shelley, Rossetti and William Morris, in venues such as the Collins Street Assembly Hall. He believed university was 'an intellectual club' where 'intermarriage of ideas' created 'knowledge as offspring'.[558] Katharine's reading interests now included Champion's favourite literary authors (promoted in his columns and library) as well as Thomas Carlyle, and political tracts like John Ruskin's *Unto This Last* (1908), prefaced by Champion. In addition, as a keepsake, he gave her a small pamphlet by William Morris, *Under an Elm-Tree; Or, Thoughts in the Country-side*, printed in Aberdeen in 1891.[559]

A raconteur and great debater, known to expose injustice and oppression, Champion knew many of the authors studied at university and cared about emerging writers who were beginning their journeys. Katharine, Nettie and Hilda were members of the Melbourne Literature Society where Murdoch was president and a whole article was devoted to the organisation in the January 1907 issue of *Book Lover*.

Although Katharine admitted to never knowing Bernard O'Dowd well, she remembered meeting him at the Melbourne Literature Society at the end of May 1909. The occasion was one of her 'most momentous experiences' listening to O'Dowd speak with Murdoch as the chair. She was deeply affected by O'Dowd's passionate delivery of his legendary speech 'Poetry Militant' with 'his hair flaming to the white-hot intensity of his passion and faith that poetry, and all literary expression should be inspired by love and service for Humanity'.[560] Many young aspiring authors who Katharine met and engaged with during this exciting time were fascinated by O'Dowd's first collection of verse *Dawnward?* (1903) dedicated to 'Young Democracy' with ideas of the 'Knights-errant' and modern 'Quixotes', his sentiments also holding great appeal to Champion who had an inner belief in the importance of his own mission to 'right a wrong'.

Studying music under Professor Marshall-Hall, Henry Tate was introduced to Katharine by an unnamed friend. In turn, Tate introduced her to his friend, Frank Wilmot (Furnley Maurice), whose father, Henry Wilmot, was a socialist colleague of Champion who gave speeches with him on the Yarra banks on Sunday 10 August 1895 about a new party. Working at Cole's Book Arcade at thirteen, Wilmot published his poetry under 'Furnley Maurice', a pseudonym created by combining his two favourite places, Ferntree Gully and Beaumaris,[561] while the *Book Lover* published Wilmot's poetry from 1904. Along with Vance Palmer, Hugh McCrae and Herbert Brookes, Wilmot was a contributor for the *Trident* where Champion and O'Dowd were two of five members of Murdoch's editorial panel. Wilmot's 'To God from the Weary Nations' was published in 1916 and reprinted by the Australasian Authors' Agency as a pamphlet in July 1917. In *Child of the Hurricane* she called the poem, '... a cry of agony, incoherent but magnificent: invocation for mercy from an omnipotent being.'

Well before Katharine went to England the first time, she travelled with her friends to Olinda and probably stayed at the boarding house 'Lumeah'. In *Fourteen Years* Nettie Palmer wrote fondly of the Dandenong Ranges around Emerald, the road climbed to Mount Dandenong through the towns of Sherbrooke, Sassafras and Olinda and, on the return, the striking views of the Port Phillip Bay with the You Yangs in the background and Western Port Bay.

Katharine developed 'a deep affection' for Wilmot over many years and recalled 'an unforgettable weekend' with Elsie Cole, Henry Tate and Frank Wilmot (before his marriage in 1910) at Olinda in Ferntree Gully near Emerald. They walked and then went to Tate's room to drink wine. 'But Elsie Cole & I were far too inhibited damsels to make anything but a thoroughly virtuous occasion of it'.[562]

So, the network of friends continued to position Katharine close to Champion's circle. Katharine and Champion continued to bump into each other at various public meetings and venues, and so their relationship developed. Compared to Katharine's young male friends, the Preux Chevalier was a better conversationalist and it is easy to imagine the impact on any listener of his tales of international dignitaries and famous writers, his knowledge of literature and the arts, coupled with his effortless name-dropping of people he knew. This trait was annoying to some, a journalist ridiculing Champion as one of three men with overstated self-esteem: 'Australia's trio of champion egotists: Sir Henry Parkes, 'The Vagabond' [John Stanley James] and Socialist Champion. The latter, while the newer is the most pronounced member of the 'I' brigade'.[563]

Katharine's assignations with Champion, throughout 1907 and well into the following year, continued at Brighton Beach, the Botanic Gardens and the seaside around Black Rock at Beaumaris where Beach Road ran along the foreshore. They included dinners at seaside restaurants close to Brighton Beach's tram terminus and walks along the beach through ti-trees where Ricketts Point was a favourite scene for the Heidelberg School of artists such as Frederick McCubbin, Tom Roberts, Arthur Streeton, Charles Conder and Jane Sutherland. Katharine continued to see him frequently with 'accidental, and not so accidental, meetings'. These were not dissimilar to Champion's clandestine meetings at similar spots ten years earlier with another woman after her return to her husband, his meetings allowed as 'long as no scandal was created'. Preventing gossip was again foremost in his mind.

An undated, loose and handwritten page of jottings inserted into her early writer's notebook, holds vital clues to the places she met Champion. She writes of black swans, the beach, the sea and a yellow moon over a jetty that situate her near Black Rock's small marshy lagoon, a wild life sanctuary for flocks of these swans. Professor Marshall-Hall, Champion's close friend, was author of the controversial *Hymns Ancient and Modern* (1898) and one poem, 'Among the Ti-Trees', was filled with the romantic atmosphere of trees, 'kisses of blossoming ocean' with stars shining upon 'the souls of true lovers', verse that caused a public scandal and accusations of 'immodest', 'lascivious' and lewd images.[564] It is not difficult to imagine Champion and Katharine reading the verse and the impact of sensuous poetry, read amongst ti-trees and mana gums of Beaumaris. After her return from New Zealand Katharine's writings contained feelings of increasing despair and hurt. There is a glimpse of growing physical intimacy in her jottings that indicate a sexual encounter, desire and pain, and each ellipsis in Katharine's writings inserted a sustained pause:

> 'I want you. I want you – want you' – I hear you say – & see your eyes grow round, in the dark ... And then the fierce desire fails, & pain comes, the prayer in your eyes, the hunger of the mouth, the setting of my lips like a child that is going to cry ... Your kisses bruise & blacken my lips.

Private vulnerability was buried deeply and Katharine writes of succumbing to doubts or despair in the person's absence.

> When you are here, of course, I wear an invisible armour, deep plated.
> I am concerned in pleasing you ... only when you are not here
> I – surrender ....[565]

When Keir Hardie visited Australia in January 1908 people were thrilled to see Champion and his oldest friends Ben Tillett, Tom Mann and Keir Hardie all together on the platform. All were having liaisons with younger women. Keir Hardie was involved with Sylvia Pankhurst whose parents established political 'salons' at Russell Square. With Hardie's wife Lillie remaining in Scotland, the couple entered into a 'free sexual union contracted and terminated at will' with Sylvia's mother disapproving and ceasing her friendship with Hardie. The affair lasted until 1911 and the couple's unconcealed affection was obvious to friends. Like Champion, Hardie suffered a series of strokes that paralysed his writing arm, forcing him into a nursing home before he returned to his wife who nursed him in his final months of life. In April 1898, Tillett also met a girl, Eva Margaret Newton, an aspiring singer just out of her teens whose pregnancy forced her to leave for England on the *Oroya* on 1 October that year to join him. Although in the *Pall Mall Gazette* on 13 February 1891 Maggie Harkness extolled Tom Mann's luck in having a conflict free home and wrote about his 'sensitive, 'delicate' wife Ellen and four daughters, he lived openly with Elsie Harker, a Manchester girl met around the time of Dock Strike, who accompanied him in 1902 to Australia.

Only a few months after his return from New Zealand, in June 1907, Tom Prichard hung himself in the backyard shed. Although Tom had never threatened suicide, Edith told the coroner that her husband spoke of 'burdening' his family.566 Tom had previously suffered a nervous breakdown in Tasmania with the loss of his newspaper position and remained unemployed for over twelve months. As Katharine tried to find underlying reasons for her conversion to Communism in later years, she drew on early memories of their possessions hastily sold at auction for their return to Melbourne and her mother sewing into the night to earn money because of the loss of income. Tom's second breakdown was not employment related and his 'unsound mind' was explicitly linked by Edith to their son's illness.

Katharine escaped the confines of her home and the trauma of her father's suicide by travelling to England as a journalist for the *Herald* to cover the Franco-British Exhibition and interview the famous for *New Idea*. Before she embarked the *Runic* on 3 July 1908 she penned 'Our Homes and Altars', an article on women's role in the defence of their nation and received letters of acclaim from many, including the Prime Minister, Defence Minister and Premier.567 The following week in another article she discussed the 'Defence of Australia' and Deakin's concept of young men being trained for 16 days a year in the militia and volunteer regiments. This 'citizen-soldiery' was aimed at a

Japanese threat and, in passionate, jingoistic and racist tones, Katharine wrote of potential Asian invasion by 'a pagan and barbarian horde' as 'its teeming peoples stream across the adjacent islands into our great empty lands'. It is probable Katharine and Champion were both reading the same book as she embarked, though interpreting it a little differently. Champion commented in the *Book Lover* on *The Coming Struggle in East Asia* by Putnam Weale [Bertram Lenox Simpson] where Australia was warned of 'falling prey' to a Japanese threat.

Katharine arrived at Tilbury Docks and was one of millions of visitors flocking to London for the Franco-British Exhibition and the Olympian [sic] Games. Katharine's first article on the exhibition was sent back to Melbourne in late July where she highlighted the 'symphonies of color' of clothing, bejewelled shoes and various formal displays.[568] As well she sent home an article for the *Weekly Times* in early August about her stopover in Durban and Cape Town on the way to London.

Originally intending to stay at a London hotel where she was told Bernard Shaw and John Galsworthy had stayed in the past, Katharine carried a letter from her father's friend that enabled her to secure accommodation in an expensive boutique hotel in South Kensington, a place where Champion likely had many a discreet rendezvous with Adelaide. It was with 'rapturous excitement' Katharine wrote of locating famous places such as Nelson's statue in Trafalgar Square, locations where Champion, Burns, Hyndman and Williams once stood to address a crowd of unemployed before climbing on a statue of Achilles; she would keep a picture of Achilles with his shield and javelin on the wall of her Emerald cottage. Recording impressions of London, Katharine portrayed two women in her 'Exiles' Symposium': Agusta [sic], a pseudonym for herself, who 'rhapsodies about the history and poetical associations of the old grey city' of London as 'the stage on which the nation's history has been enacted'; and Bobbie, a 'rebellious red head', complaining about a lack of bathrooms in rentals. Katharine's cabin mate on the *Runic* (called Robbie in her autobiography) was an adventurous red-headed theosophist, and is probably Bertha Gillbanks, violinist and member of South Yarra's Christ Church. Katharine had little experience in where to look beyond the tourist sights of London. Nonetheless, by the August Bank holiday she found the slum-dwellers at Hampstead Heath, a few miles from Trafalgar Square.[569]

In November 1908, Katharine was in Paris where her Preux Chevalier turned up via Italy on business. Champion sailed to Italy after his 'Quorum Pars Fui: an Unconventional Autobiography' was finalised, his last interview appearing in the *Trident* in November. From May 1908, along with the other editorial staff including Archibald Strong, Murdoch and O'Dowd, he revamped the *Trident* at 226 Little Collins Street trying to turn it from a trilingual journal of education to an Australian review. This panel met at 'Munches', lunches held every Monday to confer on the magazine's contents for each issue. Champion's seven interviews were an attempt to create Champion's autobiography using his responses to Murdoch's questions. The venue chosen was a corner table in the 'grill-room', probably at *Mia Mia* close to his offices in Collins Street, a place for many such discussion groups and luncheons. The penultimate October interview was conducted on 11 September 1908 with Champion dressed to attend the third anniversary of the Socialist Party at the Town Hall that evening. As acting editor of the *Socialist* from April to early October Champion was writing wearily about time-consuming 'little squabbles' after an unsuccessful attempt to tender his resignation on 24 June.[570] A new full-time paid editorial position was advertised on 2 October and requested 'trenchant criticism' from readers to improve the newspaper. R.S. Ross thanked Champion for his service as honorary editor on 27 November.

Murdoch left on the German mail steamer *Gneisenau* which left Circular Quay on 3 October via Melbourne, Colombo, Suez Canal, Naples, Genoa and Southampton.[571] Murdoch reminisced later about meeting Katharine in London where they were unable to enter the House of Commons and instead went to the House of Lords.[572] As for many of his friends, Champion gave Murdoch a letter of introduction to John Burns who took him to 'an eating-house in West Ham', a contrast to a wealthy restaurant in Piccadilly. He also provided a letter of introduction allowing Shaw to receive Murdoch at his home to present him with six *Trident* issues containing Champion's 'Quorum

Pars Fui: an Unconventional Autobiography'. The last issue was missing because Murdoch sailed before printing, creating an illusion Champion was still in Melbourne. Murdoch also carried a letter of introduction from Deakin, just as Katharine did, to George Meredith at Flint Cottage. Their conversation was recalled in Murdoch's University Extension lectures and for the *Argus*. Meredith admired Deakin and listened carefully to Murdoch's talk about Bernard O'Dowd while he rhetorically questioned London's social inequality: 'how can you expect people to remain blind to the enormous waste of wealth, the excesses, the banquets, and what not? The working man has opened his eyes, and slowly and surely is coming to his own'.[573] Deakin's letter, dated 8 May 1908, also enabled Katharine as 'a humble worshipper' to pay 'homage' to George Meredith and Mrs Deakin also spoke of 'pilgrimages of homage' made with her husband when Katharine interviewed her for the *Herald*.[574]

Murdoch's perceptions of London (1 May 1909), Christmas Day in Florence (24 July 1909) and New Year in Naples (13 February 1909) were published later the *Argus* and he returned home from Italy in January 1909 on a small ship, *Posilipo*. Champion was well and truly back in Australia when on 1 May 1909 Murdoch wrote about a Dutch passenger on his voyage who was 'a professional sociologist and a man of exceptional intelligence'. At Colombo he discussed 'a new theory of Buddhism' and 'British Misgovernment in Ceylon'; at Port Said his discourse was on Disraeli, the Suez Canal Company, Moses, and Lord Cromer (a British consul-general during the occupation of Egypt); and at Naples when they arrived on 8 November, he was able to converse in the language. It is hard not to identify Champion in Murdoch's short portrait of a 'globe trotter' who studied a grammar book in preparation for his two-week Italian discovery. Why did Murdoch feel the need to disguise Champion as Dutch? Champion obviously studied the labour colonies in the provinces of Overijssel and Drenthe in Holland [Netherlands] for the *Age* in November 1890, but why protect Champion's departure from Australia unless requested? A modern observer is also left to wonder whether Murdoch later held suspicions about the identity of Katharine's Preux Chevalier.

In the European autumn of 1908, it was no surprise to Katharine that her well-travelled Preux Chevalier arrived from Italy. Their perfectly timed meeting in France ensured both anonymity and romantic ambience. But why sail to Italy and disembark if he was to meet Katharine in Paris? One probable answer lies with his old friend Percy Frost, who now lived in Perugia and was 'a Professor of English at a Foreign University' [Royal Italian University for Foreigners]. Widely reported in February 1908 was an innocent day-trip in Umbria when Frost and Evelyn Snodgrass (curate of St Mark's Church Fitzroy) were mistakenly imprisoned by Italian detectives looking for two robbers of Tiffany's jewellery store.[575]

Katharine's sojourn in Paris lasted a few days, with her Preux Chevalier taking her to famous restaurants and theatres, introducing her to writers and artists in their studios within the bohemian atmosphere of Montmartre so beloved by Champion. No doubt Katharine saw the cafe life and struggling artists through the eyes of Champion's translation of Henri Murger's *Bohemian Life*, as he guided her through the streets. A hotel was chosen for her near the opera in central Paris: 'He knew when I would be there, [and] had advised me to stay at the Hotel de l'Arcade'. They enjoyed performances at the Moulin Rouge and Comedie Francaise and afterwards suppers at places such as Maxims. On one afternoon, the Preux Chevalier's role as tourist guide for Katharine was interrupted for business and it is likely his meeting was with another close friend, Robert Hudson. The soap business was sold to Lever Brothers in May 1908 and Danesfield mansion sold after architectural photographers snapped a series of farewell shots for his wife Gerda in August that year. The Hudsons moved to France and in 1925 purchased a Riviera residence, 56 Villa Paloma on the Boulevard du Jardin Exotiques in Monaco. Champion's sister, Annie Beatrice, told Miles Franklin on 5 October 1927 that her brother pleaded with her to meet him in Marseilles and to join him on the Riviera until England was warm enough to visit.[576] During Champion's business meeting Katharine visited Montmartre Cemetery where Murger was buried and wandered around reading inscriptions of the graves of famous writers. She stayed until the gates of the city necropolis were closing and was surprised at Champion's anger over her remaining in the isolated, dark spot.

Katharine described wearing chic fashionable clothes – an Empire dress with its train and an ostrich plumed hat which made her feel like a *fille de joie* – to dine with her cavalier. It must have been a wonderful time for Katharine and, in a book review two years after Champion's death, she wrote wistfully of the author capturing 'perfect' images of Paris that stimulated her 'nostalgia' and a desire 'to see again that "pencil-greyness of Paris, now emphatic, now delicate as a cobweb"'.[577] She did return to Paris on her way to Russia in August 1933 where she signed another contract for *Coonardoo*.

Katharine's tale about her dining companion's attention to their celebrated soup served at the Café Royal demonstrated Champion's fastidiousness when dining out. Described as 'an aristocrat to the fingertips', he enjoyed the finer things in life and was recorded to have said: 'I prefer the poor man's politics and the rich man's dinners'.[578] Even Maggie Harkness described this particular trait via George Eastmont's character who eats with his wife: 'Having lived all his life amongst people who make eating a fine art, he found Julia's gymnastics with her knife and fork rather a trial to his appetite'. On the Preux Chevalier's second visit, they dined at luxury hotels in London, so the Café Royal in Regent Street near Piccadilly, may be the place Katharine recalled. Established by a French wine merchant and his wife in 1863 and immortalised in paintings by Charles Ginner and William Orphen, the venue was patronised at the turn of the century by Bernard Shaw, Oscar Wilde, Rudyard Kipling, H.G. Wells, Aleister Crowley, Cunninghame Graham and Morley Roberts.

After an exciting time in Paris, Katharine's articles took on a new direction and now she investigated Salvation Army activities and their soup kitchens. 'Life is Cheap: In Darkest England' reported on 'the crushed spirit of the masses', slum children and factory girls, concluding that 'Merry England' was a 'myth'.[579] A February visit to a Salvation Army Whitechapel shelter showed her destitute men and women and throughout March 1909 she wrote a series of articles as she joined one of their soup kitchens on the embankment in Westminster. With her dramatic heading, 'A Night in Slumdom', she wrote about London's doss-houses where she quoted John Burns who called their work 'indiscriminate charity' and Bernard Shaw's opinion it was 'a national disgrace'. The conditions of the homeless were seen as containing potential seeds of 'Revolution' as she saw bodies 'that should have been strong and straight, were bent and weakly; hands were limp and clumsy that should have had workmanlike grip; feet were bruised and sodden that should have stepped briskly and proudly'. How different after Paris were her articles as she abandoned the naive 'Agusta' role of enthusiastic observer of sights.

After her return from Paris, an arrangement was made for Katharine to interview Christabel Pankhurst at her residence, Clement's Inn. Christabel formed the Women's Social and Political Union in 1903 with her mother whom Champion knew from the ILP. The interview was titled 'A "Shrieking Sister" at Home', a variation of a term by Eliza Linton. Katharine's article called her a 'womanly woman' to dispel the derogatory connotations of a 'New Woman'. Katharine's passion for the subject and her enthusiasm as a journalist was at its most fervent as she wrote about the position of women as 'helpmates' in 'the purification of public life in Australia'. She cited Joan of Arc, Florence Nightingale and Elizabeth Fry as comparable to Christabel Pankhurst who believed in 'reform for the welfare of the human race'.[580]

Suffragettes imprisoned during this period of upheaval were presented at the Albert Hall on 29 April 1909 with Holloway brooches that were based on the portcullis symbol of parliament and designed by Christabel's sister, Sylvia. The gate was wrought in silver with an enamel overlay of a convict symbol – a broad arrow and in purple (dignity), white (purity) and green (hope). An example of this broach is on display in the British Museum today. Katharine also interviewed British writer Beatrice Harraden, close adviser of the Pankhursts, for the July edition of *New Idea*. As mentioned, another sister, Adela Pankhurst visited the Champions' home in Melbourne after her mother gave her an introduction to Vida Goldstein. Adela subsequently became a member of the Victorian Socialist Party and the Women's Peace Army, marrying unionist Tom Walsh in 1917; together they joined the Communist Party.

Katharine had changed during this period. She was gaining confidence as a journalist and interviews were rolled out for March 1909 with Madam Marchesi, actresses Alice Crawford and Sarah Bernhardt who was in Paris.[581] After the last interview, Katharine sailed in March from Marseilles to Melbourne, her occupation registered as 'reporter'. Although her nationality was listed as French, the Preux Chevalier knew of Katharine's specific travel arrangements and timings, and probably even suggested the passage as a chance to practice French onboard. Champion knew she was leaving on 'Messageries Maritimes Paquebot' of the *Australien* from Marseilles via Port Said, Bombay and Colombo, the ship's blank note paper kept as a permanent keepsake. Writing to Morley Roberts just after his 50th birthday on 17 February 1909, having resigned from executive posts on the *Socialist*, he seemed disinterested. 'Things matter less and less', he told his friend.

Champion also knew she would arrive in Fremantle on Friday 9 April and organised an old acquaintance to meet the ship in Western Australia on its brief stop-over. The acquaintance, Alfred John Buchanan, a close friend of Alfred Deakin, was receiving good reviews in Australia and England for his new book, *Bubble Reputation*, based on Champion's run for election. Buchanan was a barrister, drama critic and journalist at the *Age* with Champion, and a dramatist for Gregan McMahon's Melbourne Repertory Theatre with Louis Esson and William Moore. He had visited England with letters of introduction from Champion to overseas publishing contacts and as an overseas correspondent for the Sydney *Daily Telegraph* wrote 'Literary Life in London: How Australians Fare'. Champion argued, there were journalistic and literary openings 'for Australians of talent' and published Buchanan's statement: 'I never worked so hard in my life before, but I like it'.[582] On return to Perth, he was lead writer for Hackett's paper, the *West Australian*. Knowing Katharine and Alfred Buchanan shared mutual interests, Champion obviously arranged for him to meet her at the Fremantle docks. In her autobiography Katharine wrote of her irritation that this man was in competition with a French officer from the ship for her attention.

Back home Katharine received two letters in August and November 1909 from Aleister Crowley, an expelled member of the Rosicrucian Order studying mystical philosophy. Her story was finally published in Crowley's *The Equinox: The Review of Scientific Illuminism* in March 1912 although Katharine was disappointed when his promised £10 cheque was only a gift of the magazine. The lengthy, esoteric short story, 'Diana of the Inlet', was centred on a couple of 'renegade souls' in a modern Eden. 'He was the Adam, purged of memory, she "new-waked" to woman's primitive innocence and purity' was the Eve who becomes the 'wild witch-woman of Inlet superstition'. The sensuous overtones are obvious: 'The great hungry heart of the sea yearned for the river. And I – I yearned for the lips of my love', imagery refined for her 1914 poem, 'Lips of My Love'. Her Preux Chevalier specifically warned Katharine away from the magazine, dismissing it as 'neurotic, tommy-rotic and abominotic', his phrase echoing Hugh Stutfield in *Blackwood's Edinburgh Magazine* in June 1895 that modern fiction was 'erotic, neurotic, and Tommyrotic'. The latter was a phrase used in the *Champion* in August 1895 and Katharine may have deliberately steered away from the obvious implication of the word 'erotic' when she quoted him.

Having encountered various political groups and sought conversations with radicals in London, Katharine's interest in unconventional organisations began to blossom:

> In the studios and literary coteries of London, I had come in contact with Fabians, Guild Socialists, Syndicalists, Theosophists, Anarchist admirers of Kropotkin, Futurists, Surrealists, and the disciples of Aleister Crowley – without becoming attached to any group.[583]

She also specified, in *Tribune's* 'Why I am a Communist', her interest in Fabians, especially Shaw and the Webbs as well as Kropotkin and Anarchism, and while examining different theories and philosophies, admitted she 'committed to none' and was 'never a member of any organisation' until the Communist Party.

She secured a position on the woman's page of Tuesday's *Herald* (with its offshoot the *Weekly Times*) and took as her editorial pseudonym, 'Pomona', suggestive of a Roman goddess and wood nymph identified with fruitful abundance. She interviewed Muriel Matters, Catherine Spence, Annie Lowe, Mrs Powell, Rose Scott and Mrs Alfred Deakin, while tackling issues such as a home for unmarried mothers and England's law regarding marriage to a deceased wife's sister.

The delightfully named Muriel Matters, a suffragette and Christian Scientist Katharine admired, left Australia for London to lecture, study art and literature and give readings of Ibsen and Bernard Shaw. Establishing the League of Light to support women, particularly stage actresses, Muriel was both seen and heard as she shouted in the House of Commons for women to be given the vote and was imprisoned for a month in Holloway gaol after chaining herself to a grille in the Ladies' Gallery at the House of Commons on 28 October 1908. She identified the grille as a 'cage' and 'symbolical of man's conventional attitude towards women'.

Vida Goldstein was in agreement about the grille that separated women from parliamentary debates, seeing it as a symbol of 'slavery and degradation'.[584] As early as 1894 the Ladies' Gallery was represented by Mrs Humphry Ward in *Marcella* as a confining and stuffy cave for animals with its 'grating' covering 'the front of the den into which the House of Commons puts its ladies'. Millicent Fawcett called it 'Oriental seclusion' to invoke the veil-like isolation of a watcher, adding:

> One great discomfit of the grille was that the interstices of the heavy brass work were not large enough to allow the victims who sat behind it to focus it so that both eyes looked through the same hole. It was like using a gigantic pair of spectacles which did not fit, and made the Ladies' Gallery a grand place for getting headaches.[585]

Finally removed on 23 August 1917, a piece of the grille was loaned to the South Australian Parliament for display in 2010. Muriel also helped in London later during the performance of Katharine's play, *For Instance*.

Strangely, there was little mention of Vida Goldstein in Katharine's journalism at this time, although she wrote that Victoria was home to 'many clever women workers in women's causes, but no distinctive non-party leader'. Vida rarely received more than passing mention in Pomona's columns, generally brief notes or short entries on meeting dates. The exception was one interview after Vida polled 54,000 votes in the federal election. After 20 years of educating women for the vote, she reported that Vida's strategy was now to educate them about the importance of women representing women.[586] Katharine wrote in her autobiography of a clash with her editor about her personal opinions on Vida's campaign. Maybe this was as close as she could come to aligning herself openly with Champion's sister-in-law.

After working for the *Herald* for a year and a half, Katharine handed over to Maisie Maxwell [May Moorhead] and took a short holiday to Sydney from where she sailed for Vancouver on the Canadian Royal Mail steamer, *Zealandia*, on 24 October 1910. As an added incentive, the ship had a stopover at her birthplace of Fiji and a rail trip to the United States. On her way to New York, Katharine abandoned any idea of staying there and made plans to travel to England. Two months later, Champion wrote to Morley Roberts on 21 December about his desire to take an overseas holiday:

> ... I really wish I could make up my mind to turn up in London and crawl round the old places for a month or so before taking a tour on the Continent. You must understand that I am no longer a beggar and am really almost cured of my old habits of floating around with a large floating debt and a couple of sovereigns in my pocket, full of schemes for the bettering of mankind and omitting any regard for my own financial capacity. It has been a pretty tough job for me, and you must know that I nearly gave it up more than once. However, I have pulled through and maintain a pretty lively equilibrium and still am able to laugh at most things in the world, including myself.

At the time, Vida Goldstein was planning to leave Melbourne on 14 February 1911 with her first speech to be delivered at Albert Hall. In the lead-up to the demonstration of 40,000 suffragettes on 17 June 1911 Katharine listed Australian women marching in her article for the *Herald*.[587] A Melbourne artist, Dora Meeson, designed the suffragette banner under which the Commonwealth contingent marched, with Australia addressing Britannia: 'Trust the Women Mother As I Have Done'. Katharine's autobiography focused on the Women's Social and Political Union although she did not seek Vida out for interviews despite the fact that she led a contingent of

Australian women bearing iconic small kangaroo models on sticks; she also ignored Vida's speech in August at a function attended by Bernard Shaw, despite being there to listen to him speak. Discretion may have kept her apart from Champion's high-profile sister-in-law although she briefly mentioned Vida in London in reference to the effect of woman's suffrage in Australia since Federation, adding: 'The world has not stood still; the stars have not fallen from the Southern skies ... no happy homes were wrecked'.[588]

Katharine's cousin, James Fraser, lived at 'The Elms', Houghton in Huntingdonshire and unsurprisingly this area was chosen for Katharine's first public debate on women's influence on history. She spoke at the Primrose League of St Ives, arguing that women 'have other means than their beauty and charm for influencing public affairs' and that their votes aided society's improvement. She also attended Freewoman Discussion circles exploring the concept of marriage as a contract in which women abdicated their sexual rights and also contributed a letter to their newspaper.[589] Her articles for the London *Daily Herald* throughout April and May 1912 concentrated on schemes of co-operative housekeeping.

Katharine's first play, *The Burglar*, performed in Melbourne in early October 1910 focused on the theft of precious gems to protest against social inequality. The socialist governess describes a society divided into the haves and the have-nots and Katharine's dramatic skills were now honed with two one-act plays on social and suffragette themes, produced by the Actresses' Franchise League as a satellite of the Women's Social and Political Union.

Her Place (1913) juxtaposed 'selfish and idle women' of English society with a 'charwoman' while *For Instance* (1914) was based on Katharine's interview with Mrs Powell of the Shirt and Collar Makers' Wages Board.

The latter play was set in a 'white blouse factory' and depicted a female English factory worker who emigrates to Australia and discovers better working conditions. Throughout much of her writings, Katharine exploited ideas of romance, politics and contrasting economic circumstances.

On this second trip to London, there was a circle of friends around Katharine, many of whom knew Champion very well. Katharine recalled Robbie and Sumner Locke, whose sister Lilian was a Christian Scientist, socialist and close friend of Vida Goldstein. On Sumner Locke's tragic death Katharine was honorary secretary of a memorial that sought donations for a collection of her verse and she also wrote the preface in 1921.[590] Will Dyson was now a cartoonist at London's *Daily Herald* where he attacked social injustice, unemployment and poverty, and depicted the working man as youthful and militant. Dyson's war cartoons were on display at Leicester Galleries early in 1915 with his catalogue containing an introductory note by H.G. Wells. Later Katharine told of how he 'swept England with a sirroco of scorn for its stuck-up-ishness and absurd prejudices, and his cartoons on the English attitude to women's suffrage had a considerable influence'.[591]

The spring arrival in 1912 of her Preux Chevalier was casually noted in her autobiography, marked by another series of visits to theatre and expensive dinners. From February to September 1911 Champion had been secretary of the *Socialist* and his plans were well underway for a trip to England. Writing fondly of memories of a Thames boat trip with William Morris and friends after Katharine's departure, he stated wistfully: 'If I have the luck to get back to England, I have made up my mind to do the trip again in the earlier part of the year'.[592] His 'promised' trip to England to see Tom Mann showed his trip was never a spur of the moment decision and he even organised for Blackburn to take his place on an inquiry board into gas prices in March 1912.[593]

In early April 1912 a break-in and theft occurred at Mrs Isabella Goldstein's house 'Wyebo' on Como Avenue, South Yarra. While Vida, Elsie Belle and friends played cards on the Saturday night, an intruder entered through an unlocked window and stole the bedroom drawer in which Elsie Belle stored her jewellery and private papers, the contents estimated at £30. Having locked the drawer, she placed the key in her bag on the bed and discovered the whole drawer missing at the end of the night. It was later found abandoned and covered with leaves on vacant land with Elsie Belle's two lockets and her papers still inside.[594] What the intruder was looking for remains a mystery, although one reporter suggested the objective was suffrage material. Perhaps the real target was information about Champion. Newspapers explained Champion's absence – he was 'enjoying his long-deserved, and well-earned vacation, and may soon return to harness again' and he intended to have 'a month or so in Sydney' with his wife.[595] In fact only Elsie Belle stayed in Sydney, attending a program on 11 June on Celtic writers at the Sydney University Women's Union club.[596] (The club was founded by Louisa Macdonald, principal of the Women's College, member of the Women's Literary Society and Womanhood Suffrage League of New South Wales.)

Champion was away spring and summer. He had written 'The Antipodean Repertory Theatre: Ibsen and Some Others' for the *Pall Mall Gazette* on 13 January 1912, in anticipation of discussions with Shaw for Australian performances of his plays. Shaw continued to correspond with Champion about his possible appointment as theatrical agent for his plays performed in Australia. Champion's article in the *Socialist* on 23 August showed detailed knowledge of companies touring England with Shaw's plays, as well as their box office returns, and he recalled their early friendship:

> I knew Shaw very well during his hardest years, and never knew of him losing his temper. This gave him an unusual advantage in debates, when he invariably got the laugh on his side, and his opponent lost both his temper and victory at the same time. This gives him much of his fame, exclusive of his writings and dramatic pieces, which is now very great, although he does not eat any meat, wears no clothes made from animals' skins, smokes no tobacco, drinks no intoxicants, and thinks very hard things of medicine. Yet he gets a great deal of genuine fun out of life.[597]

As Shaw's theatrical and literary agent, Champion had excuses for overseas travel on business and it appears as if the Book Lovers' Library was paying his travelling expenses.

Champion certainly saw his sister Annie Beatrice and may have felt impelled to visit Morley after his adored, frail wife died of fever in London's extended summer heat wave of September 1911. Two months later her mother Emily Selous died in his arms. Alice's death was an incredible shock where Morley withdrew, played chess all day and into the night and barely spoke to anyone. Champion would have seen a skeleton-thin person, a pale imitation of the tough, weather-beaten man he once knew.[598] Indeed, their correspondence has a large gap from December 1910 to 1923 although this may have been caused by Morley's decision to burn painful letters.

The grief experienced over the death of individual friends was mirrored on a grander scale with the world reeling from the sinking of the *Titanic* in April 1912. On its maiden voyage from Southampton to New York, the ship hit an iceberg south of Newfoundland. The impact of such a tragedy on people living at the time caused worldwide shock because of the enormous loss of life and the crew's evacuation of so few. Bernard Shaw and Conan Doyle appeared in print in the London *Daily News* to argue the effect of the accident on their nation, with Shaw seeing the protocol of taking women and children as first priority from the ship as 'romantic formula'. Champion called Shaw's comments on the Titanic, a 'display of good humor and invective like a shower of fireworks'.[599] Two weeks before Shaw's comments, Katharine wrote an emotional letter to London's *Freewoman* on 2 May about the death of people 'who "did what they could," and went into the shadows', an echo of the Melian dialogue of Thucydides. She argued against the chivalry of 'women and children first', a regulatory rule for lifeboats. Having travelled on passenger liners across various oceans, recently to Canada and from America to England, Katharine experienced the event in an immediate and personal way. Her Preux Chevalier was to join her in London in spring, as was her uncle Frederick Prichard and his daughter Winifred who departed on the *Orama* for London and Europe for an extended six-month holiday in late April. Her letter to the feminist newspaper gave an insight into the imagery of whirlpools and wreckage embedded in Katharine's writing, as a symbolic representation of her relationship struggles and, in a larger context, her desire to help humanity. Many years before her death Katharine conceived a straightforward epitaph to pay tribute to her life's work, obviously drawing on her remembrance of the Titanic: 'She did what she could'.

Champion's arrival coincided with Katharine's trip to Clovelly. In an article for the *Daily Herald* on 15 May, she apologised that, because of 'a few days absence from London', she was late with a response to the claim that house-keeping was 'the natural avocation of all women'.[600] Katharine's week-long holiday in the small Devonshire fishing village was an inspiration for her slim book of verse, *Clovelly Verses* (1913). The tiny village of Clovelly was accessed by a train running via Exeter to Bude in Cornwall and to Barnstaple junction, after which transportation was needed for twenty miles to a small dirt track and a further three miles to the woods surrounding the bluff. The 170 steps were steep and cobbled and led straight down to a tiny winding high street with the village's white cottages perched cliffside. (Katharine's personal papers contain a postcard sized photo of the steps looking upwards.) The only way to arrive at a cottage (especially with luggage) was by donkey and sledge and in her poem, 'Clovelly', she writes of 'Donkeys with clicking feet'. Her short story, 'A Wandrin' One', written in England at this time, showed her familiarity with the local area. Centred on the treatment of a young girl living in a fishing village with 'rows of ancient, irregularly-built houses to the path that twists off the sides of the hill to the white cottage', it reveals her knowledge of the surrounding areas of Bideford, Buck's and Barnstaple.[601] Serialised in the *Age* between March to June 1916, her novel *Windlestraws* also included a fishing village with a seawall near 'heather-clad hills' and woods, 'a sleepy village on the south-west coast' that becomes a retreat for 'Peter, Anything-Else-You-Like Windlestraws', the latter reference drawing on Kingsley's *The Water Babies*.

Only a couple of lines in her autobiography were devoted to the week at Clovelly but the result, *Clovelly Verses*, speak eloquently of a wonderful experience. Dismissed as 'an inconspicuous murmuring' and 'naive' her small book alluded frequently to a spring love. With names such as 'The Lover Sings', 'A Wanderer's Song' and 'Pink Campion', the poems burst forth with happiness and give a sense she experienced more than just a restful holiday. Her title poem 'Clovelly' has a concluding line 'I love, love, love you!', 'A Wanderer's Song' ends with 'When together, / My love and I / Sleep on the heather!', and in 'Hedgerow Blossoms' the author has 'a haze of love'. A 'diminutive booklet', her verse was printed in April 1913 by McAllan General Printers at 3 Ludgate Circus and sold for sixpence. Champion was familiar with the firm as they published Tom Mann and Ben Tillett's pamphlet, *The 'New' Trades Unionism: a reply to George Shipton* (1890). The printery was positioned near to Thomas Cook and Sons, direct agents for P&O Liners, and probably indicated an opportunity seized by Champion for a special present while organising return travel arrangements to Australia. Given Champion's ability to align an affectionate gift (a small print run of her verse) to a particular person's passion (such as Elsie Belle's library and her bookplate), combined with his printing knowledge, this gift acknowledged Katharine's writing aspirations and was a fitting souvenir of time spent together. Her sensuous poem 'Lips of My Love' in all probability was written during the Clovelly experience, although not included in a book dedicated to her mother. Later published by Austin Harrison in his *English Review* in April 1914, a year after the release of *Clovelly Verses*, the poem was included in *The Earth Lover* (1932). Katharine's poem certainly evokes an ecstatic, romantic and/or sexual response, with her 'body' a symbolic 'chalice' for her lover's 'delight'.

Picturesque, quiet and difficult to access, why was the village chosen for her short holiday? It is not a stretch of the imagination to suppose that Katharine went to this private area when the hedgerows were in blossom and the wild flowers blooming because Champion organised the holiday. He placed much importance on the writings of Charles Kingsley; he had been a new lieutenant posted to Plymouth on Devon's south coast; and Morley Roberts had a connection with the area. (In May 1897 Morley stayed at the Devon country house of novelist Charles Garvice and they took at a day trip to Clovelly; Morley also had lived at Barnstaple as a boy.) [602]

Charles Kingsley was a social reformer who spent time as curate and rector at Clovelly and left this isolated community to become a canon at Westminster Abbey in 1873. Champion claimed that, as a schoolboy, he met Kingsley prior to his death.[603] Kingsley's youngest daughter Mary (later known as 'Lucas Malet') married her father's Westminster curate, Reverend William Harrison, later a parish minister at Clovelly. *The Wages of Sin* was based on Malet's experiences after her marital separation as she toured Naples, Rome, Perugia and Vevey and Champion greatly admired her fiction, advertising her family connection to Kingsley. Kingsley was readily identified as an inspiration to young Champion in *George Eastmont* and Maggie Harkness restated his *Christian Socialist* message from Kingsley its first issue in June 1883. Champion also repeatedly quoted the romantic concept from Kingsley's *Letter to Ladies* at the top of his 'The World of Woman' newspaper column, 'Your business is to go to him and say, 'Here is a wrong. Right it!'.

In fact, Katharine used *The Water Babies* in her journalism, imagining herself as Kingsley's 'Mrs Do-as-you-would-be-done-by' and 'Mrs Be-done-by-as-you-did' when she wrote about the Children's Welfare Exhibitions held at Olympia and the toys of slum children in December 1913. With good intentions directed to the poor, she assisted the drop-offs for 'The Farthing Bundle' for the *Daily News and Leader* on 16 December. A plan she suggested for the 'Forgotten Child' was accepted, launched and culminated in a dinner. Katharine achieved a massive response with patrons/donors, including two queens (wives of Edward VII and George V) and a best-selling writer (Marie Corelli).[604]

Katharine's opportunity to pursue a writing career arrived in the middle of 1913 with Hodder and Stoughton's announcement of a literary competition stipulating some connection with the land and giving a closing date of 31 March 1914. Katharine spent the last three months of 1913 and the first three months of the following year at her flat at 64 Chelsea Gardens, Chelsea Bridge Road, bringing together her ideas into the novel, *The Pioneers*, and eating little food to emulate the lives of bohemian writers. Early in the life of the *Book Lover*, Champion told writers their hand written submissions were 'a cruelty' for publishers and Katharine cleverly engaged two typists, delivering her professional manuscript in person on the final day of the deadline.[605]

Anxiously waiting for the result of the competition, Katharine decided to visit Lady Dudley's Australian Volunteer Hospital at Wimereux to write about their work. In 1908 she had visited Witley Court in Worcester, six miles from Stourport by horse-drawn coach, to interview Countess of Dudley who later sailed to France on Lord Dunraven's yacht to open the hospital at Wimereux on 26 October 1914.[606] Katharine accompanied Sister Leonara Allender, an Australian nurse from a private hospital in South Yarra, who was stopping there briefly on her way to a Serbian hospital with the Red Cross.[607] The Australian Volunteer Hospital, situated at the Grand Hôtel du Golf et Cosmopolite in the seaside town of Boulogne, had been accommodation for Robert Hudson and his wife Gerda before the war; their granddaughter, Dorothy Hudson was also at Wimereux as a Red Cross nurse.[608]

The following year Katharine won the coveted prize, departing her publisher's office in Paternoster Row around Ludgate Hill, perhaps glancing towards the area where her first tiny collection of verses from Clovelly had been printed. *Everylady's Journal* printed two articles on their journalist in quick succession.

In April 1915 Sumner Locke gave readers a picture of Katharine's 'daily wandering around the exclusive east' with her 'slender, restful, brown-bonneted, brown-eyed figure, guiding the unlucky ones among the mazes of mediocrity into the open, breezy channels of a beautiful and great simplicity', her philanthropy with the children 'an excuse for her shrinking bank balance'. The day after the announcement of her prize, William Moore called on behalf of the June issue and asked for advice on breaking into Fleet Street, even though he had been in London as a journalist since 1912.

Katharine readily admitted her inspiration was Frederick McCubbin's triptych of 'The Pioneer' and her own memories of South Gippsland were used to imaginatively recreate the story of people in his painting. The work was painted in 1904 over his previous canvas; McCubbin's wife was in the triptych and the couple was well-known to both Katharine and Champion as enthusiastic patrons of Fasoli's and for their bohemian suppers. Katharine used the names of Mary Gilmore's parents, Donald and Mary Cameron for her characters.

At the end of March Katharine told Nettie Palmer that old friends had sent her flowers from Clovelly but this merely disguised the real sender's identity.[609]

Now a mature woman making her way in the world at a time when many women depended on the support of a husband or a family,

Katharine was now richer financially (the prize was £250) and in experience. Her success, not only in the challenging arena of Fleet Street but also the literary world, was no mean feat. An independent woman and acclaimed writer, she could now return to Australia as an internationally recognised author to be feted as a celebrity. In triumph she sent home a charming photo to Champion for the *Book Lover* and a profile for the December 1915 issue. She claimed praise from Professor Frederick Delmer (who married her teacher Miss Hook) for her 'sketch' in *The Collegian* motivated her to become 'a famous writer some day'. Meanwhile, mourning the loss of his youth after editing the *Book Lover* for seventeen years, Champion told his readers in the October 1915 issue, 'it is impossible to pretend one is still young'.

Katharine commenced her return from London on the *Omrah* on 23 October 1915 bound for Colombo to see her newly married and pregnant sister Beatrice. Their brother Nigel was engaged earlier in the year so, with Katharine's literary success, there were reasons for family celebrations. Stopping in Sri Lanka at Ratnapura, about 100 kilometres south-east of the capital, Katharine stayed with her sister and husband Patten Smith Bridge, the son of family friends who lived at Newbridge, who was now employed by a rubber company. A day visit to a Buddhist temple and library holding ancient manuscripts caused Katharine to enthuse about Sir Edwin Arnold's *The Light of Asia* (1879), a poem of eight books in blank verse on the life of Budda. Edwin Arnold was principal of an Indian Government Sanskrit College from 1856 at Poona, a place of Champion's birth, and his first book review for the *Times of India*.[610]

Katharine had not seen Champion since 1912 and now she was heading home, their long-distance relationship about to be renewed. Boarding the ship in Colombo was Guido Baracchi, son of the Victorian Government Astronomer. Katharine saw him dressed in a pith helmet and thought he was another plantation owner exploiting the local population although at the time he was a second-year Arts/Law university student and a member of the Victorian Socialist Party since 1912. Another knight-errant, Guido received even fewer words in her autobiography than her Preux Chevalier, merely described as 'a wealthy young man', a friend, and someone with whom she discussed theories of Marx and Engels. In fact, Katharine described the voyage home as uneventful in her autobiography. However, she and Guido were 'kindred spirits' and moved quickly from friendship to 'love-affair'.[611] Katharine's relationship with Champion would falter as one with Guido began to blossom.

Katharine arrived home on the *Karmala* on 12 January 1916 and was at the centre of celebrations accorded to a successful Australian author who had impressed England. A special dinner with each menu painted with scenes from *The Pioneers* was organised by Maisie Maxwell at the Melbourne Café Français in the Royal Exchange Hotel, a dinner venue popular with people such as Alfred Deakin, Edmund Barton, John Monash and Champion.[612] On Wednesday night, Katharine was seated between her two editors J.E. Davidson from the *Herald* and W.A. Somerset Shrum from *New Idea*. Undoubtedly, Champion attended because two days after this he organised and chaired another dinner at the same venue for the British war correspondent and graduate of Marlborough College, Ellis Ashmead Bartlett who was lecturing on the Anzacs at the Dardenelles. A month after her return, on the final day of February, Katharine's novel was proposed as a film to be directed by Franklyn Barrett and screened as a trial at the Hoyts Olympia.

Whatever disappointment Katharine experienced at this time, she believed, was interpreted by Edith as signs of heart break. A few days after the celebratory dinner, escaping both public attention and relationship turmoil, she rented a little white weathered cottage near the bluff at Black Rock with a print of a black swan in a lagoon. As mentioned previously, at this time Elsie Belle Champion was preparing for her imminent court case against Hugh McCrae, so if Champion believed it was possible to join Katharine, he couldn't. Katharine's jottings about the special place, with suggestive ellipses, was entered in her *Notebook: Australia I* on 22 February 1916:

> I hiked almost to Beaumaris yesterday. I wanted to find my 'little green parlour' down by the sea. Do you remember when we went there together. The ti-tree was in blossom […] & above us the great blue roof of the sky. I walked & walked intending – to find it … was tired long

before I got there – & then I went straight to the place ... It was just as we left it – I sat down outside – & thought of you – & of the time when we used to come, plodding arm in arm through the sand together.[613]

As she worked her way through her dilemma, she personified the water as 'a disturbed & jealous lover' while she felt 'out of her depth in the power of the sea'. The waves throw her on the beach 'in a frenzy of rage & grief' leaving her 'almost dead with grief that the sea sh[ould] want me no more'.

On 25 February she wrote about the 'jeune gars' [young guy] having fun: 'Does he feel as I do? Is he plagued like this? Is there rest & peace for him?' Near the end of the holiday, with a palpable sense of frustration as she complained:

For two nights & two days I thought that you are the wild, adventure love I've dreamed of – but here you are now behaving like any other, respectable commonplace, young man with no passion & dream in his soul to carry him out of his depths in the ocean of fire.

After this personal and introspective note, the following page tallied the pros and cons of relationships: 'The great love – passion' versus 'a nice working comradeship & affection'. Her summation was a simple one: a passionate love was 'completely destructive of mind, body & soul' while the second one enabled most people to 'breed' and 'to live peacefully together'. On the 4 March 1916 her jottings were intense as she responded to her aloneness:

I have no soul to-night. I have given it to the wind & the sea & the ti-tree. The wind tore it out of my body & threaded it & some fell into the sea & some onto the ti-tree! Dark. Dark it was under the trees – & good to be mad for awhile. To stretch my arms over the sea & swear that I belong to it & the world – & to no man'...

Written only six days before she left the seaside, her notebook entry on 14 March was obviously about Champion, his ambition and female relationships. She scribbled a telling character appraisal as she pondered her future:

> It was because he was a strong man – & feared the strength of his emotions that he avoided women, he told himself. He did not permit himself the temptations which might mean the wreck of ambition. But other strong men had come to grief on the rocks of women – or women had come to grief on the rock of them. Caesar, Napoleon, Parnell (–). He really tremendously admired Parnell as the strong man. He w[oul]d have hated to think of himself as anything but the strong men he appreciated – his square jaws – & eyes that gave him the gleam of iron. If he had not tried so constantly, to be the strong man his natural rugged strength of character w[oul]d have had a chance; as it was, his strong man pose was his weakness.
>
> All the glory of her – all the majesty of her nursing him! He envisaged the prospect. Drunken with it, with the unbelievable imaging of the dream, his mind swepted [sic] over the precipice of Temptation.

Champion always portrayed himself in public as a strong, calm, rational man who was emotionally in control, essentially a person 'of will and action'.[614] Evidence from his letters to Morley instead shows him to be extremely vulnerable and sensitive. Katharine astutely wrote of Champion's temptations, particularly after his disastrous affair with a married woman. Did the metaphor also contain a classical allusion to Sirens, dangerous figures of temptation who lured sailors to their death on rocks? Is he envisioned as Odysseus bound to the mast of his political ship fighting against alluring songs?

The three figures greatly admired by Champion were Caesar, Napoleon and Parnell. Katharine points to these men in her jottings and each was involved in romantic liaisons that caused scandal. From boyhood Champion had read adventure novels about Napoleon who he saw as a 'magnetic' leader; he even visited Napoleon's birthplace in Corsica in 1893. Champion also had great admiration for Charles Stewart Parnell, leader of the Irish Nationalist Party in the House of Commons, believing he was 'the greatest factor in influencing the destiny of the British Empire', a great man with 'courage that rises in adversity' and 'the ablest man' he had ever met.[615] They had a two-hour meeting in 1888 about the Independent Labour Party and his admiration for the leader was widely known in London, with Mrs Ward's character in *Marcella* pondering the question of leadership: 'Can I – like Parnell – make a party and keep it together?'. Champion accused Michael Davitt on 3 August 1895 of bringing down 'Ireland's only possible saviour', and hounding Parnell to an early death. Davitt was blamed for not standing by Parnell after his adulterous affair with Mrs Katharine O'Shea although Parnell and Prendergast would not 'be snuffed out of political existence by a *decree nisi*'; a denial that their affair and her divorce did influence political opinion against Parnell.[616] Prichard's notebook entry showed she felt Champion's personal stance was a facade and a failing that would prohibit any personal happiness.

Katharine's seaside holiday was a solitary time of much reflection and marked the beginning of the end of her longstanding relationship with her Preux Chevalier. The whirlpool of emotions involved breaking off a previous lengthy and secret attachment to Champion, while concealing a new evolving and intimate relationship. She wrote mournfully of a love stifled and a song silenced, on a handwritten sheet she dated 14 March 1916:

> All day – all the days, all the nights. My Being murmurs like an [?] harp to the wind of my love for you. But all I can do for you is to silence the singing – to muffle the music so that You do not hear it.

She returned home to another round of invitations, including a lunch in her honour as a guest of the Premier at State Parliament House, attended by Champion's old enemy, Prendergast MLA. She travelled in July to the Flying School at Point Cook with the Premier, and Prendergast, the Assistant Minister for Defence. In addition to the volatile mix of feelings about Champion and Baracchi, now Hugo Throssell popped in from Adelaide via Bairnsdale to visit her very briefly at the start of August 1916. Awarded a Victoria Cross in December 1915 for his bravery at Hill 60, now Throssell was involved in a recruiting campaign prior to re-joining his unit in Gaza. In London, Katharine had met the Light Horse officer and son of the West Australian premier on 14 September

1915 after his evacuation from Gallipoli. She said goodbye to him as she returned to Australia, having dismissed their emerging attraction as a short-lived 'bushfire flare'. There were now three competing relationships, Champion, Baracchi and Throssell. All of them were uncertain attractions and two of these were newly formed.

Using her free railway pass for Victoria and New South Wales, Katharine escaped at the end of the first week of August to East Gippsland and onward to Sydney, Walgett and Lightning Ridge. She stopped to visit E.J. Brady and also Hilda and Louis Esson at Mallacoota.[617] 'Hiding from the general interviewer Katharine passed silently through Sydney', pausing there on her way to the opal fields, according to Mary Gilmore.[618] 'Hiding' was a strange word to use, suggesting Mary recognised Katharine in the street. The front entrance of the *Australian Worker* where she interviewed Katharine faced Pitt Street and was only a couple minutes from the Criterion Theatre and the Metropole.

At this stage Champion was in Sydney, a city he had introduced Katharine to nearly ten years before. He was working on a campaign for J.C. Williamson's play *Damaged Goods*, after Shaw suggested to Eugene Brieux that he used Champion as his dramatic agent for Australia. Brieux cabled Champion from Paris to ask him 'to look after his drama'.[619] *Les Avariés* (1901) had been translated from French into English in 1914 with Bernard Shaw's preface and Charlotte Shaw's foreword. It was an important social play about venereal disease and in a fashion reminiscent of modern health programs of intervention, the doctor in the play claims:

> 'Syphilis must cease to be treated like a mysterious evil the very name of which cannot be pronounced. The ignorance in which the public is kept of the real nature and of the consequences of this disease helps to aggravate and spread it.' (Brieux, 1914, p. 59)

Well before the first performance of Brieux's play Vida Goldstein worried about compulsory notification of venereal disease would create 'a danger of differential treatment' of women when she spoke at a Town Hall meeting on 27 May 1912. Vida and Adela Pankhurst both were involved in raising the awareness of venereal disease amongst soldiers in 1915.[620]

Brieux's play appears in Katharine's autobiography when she describes the disapproval of her mother and Aunt Lil because the subject was venereal disease. The play was acclaimed by audiences in London and Boston and, on 9 September 1916, scouting work was undertaken for an opening at the Criterion Theatre in Pitt Street. Realising the significant potential for a large theatre company wishing to become national, Champion conducted an effective advertising campaign for the performance and proved to be a mastermind who today would be applauded for a creative, attention seeking and educative approach. The theatrical world was changing and needed individuals who were adventurous and not afraid to think in different ways. An added benefit was that Champion was enjoying himself in his role as a theatrical agent. A private reading was organised for 22 September at Sydney's Queen Victoria Club, home of the Women's Reform League, and the play 'submitted to a jury of Sydney women with a view to obtaining their ideas of its value in national education'. Scenes were read by Champion's friend, Laura M. Bogue Luffman.

A letter writing campaign was generated with letters of support from doctors, clergymen and women, to address the play's importance. Participant feedback, in the form of quotes, was used as advertising. One comment applauded the author for having 'visualised the tragedy of sowing wild oats' and his ability to unveil 'the hideous possibilities of evil to the innocent'.[621] The next day the *Daily Telegraph* announced the passing of a National Women's Movement's resolution advocating the production, with parliamentarian Richard Arthur, Chairman of the Federal Committee on Venereal Diseases and Dr Matthews, Chairman of the State Committee examining health issues.

It was a dramatic start to an Australia-wide season with the first performance staged on 2 November. Copies of the play, printed by a Sydney firm through Champion's contacts at Cole's Book Arcade, were sold at the theatre. The performance was introduced by George Barnum with assurances that scenes would not 'provoke scandal or arouse disgust, nor is there in it any obscene word: and it may be witnessed by everyone without fear of offence, unless we must believe that folly and ignorance are necessary conditions of female virtue'. There were a number of clergymen in the Sydney performance and it was likened to Tennyson's 'Charge of the Light Brigade', 'canon to the right of them, and canon to the left of them', while the audience 'volleyed and thundered' in appreciation.[622] As popular interest grew, slips were issued for each performance to make it easier for playgoers to provide immediate comments, with names and opinions published from various doctors, clergy, chaplains and prominent women. It was a brave leap into a taboo subject and a big gamble for all involved but audiences flocked to performances.

Brieux's play and Champion were off to Melbourne, Adelaide and New Zealand, the latter leg starting in Wellington at the Grand Opera House in February 1917 and proceeding to Christchurch, then Dunedin before returning to Australia in April. Certainly, Champion's journey to New Zealand at the end of the month was to 'look after things there, for Brieux wants a little careful handling before his plays are performed' and he called this 'very pleasant sort of work, which suits me very well'.[623] The season ended in Brisbane in mid-September with returned soldiers admitted at half price. The following year, Champion's sister-in-law, Vida Goldstein, led a deputation from the Women's Political Association to the Minister of Health to propose amendments to the Venereal Diseases Act, arguing that a more effective remedy would be to educate young people and insisted the age of consent be raised to 21.[624]

Damaged Goods was performed on 2 December at Melbourne's Theatre Royal. The reaction of her mother and aunt to the play allowed Katharine to tell a very personal and tragic tale about a girl who, at the age of 16, was seduced by her father's friend and eventually confided in her brother-in-law who arranged long term specialist medical treatment. The girl's behaviour had become 'reckless' after her diagnosis, at a time when there was no cure and much stigma. Shocking to Katharine's Edith and Lil, the story pointed to a very close and trusting relationship Katharine had with someone about her predicament. Certainly, Katharine's conversation is cast within her discussion of Brieux's play and strongly suggests a connection with Champion. Katharine doesn't state who told her the tale, only that the girl told her brother-in-law. Much of what we know about Champion's relationship with Katharine raises speculation that he may have related the tale to Katharine. She never named her Preux Chevalier in her polite and nostalgic reminiscence in *Child of the Hurricane*, so she was never going to name this girl.

Mary Gilmore in her August interview had reported Katharine's intention of returning to England in November. Katharine was back in Melbourne by late September 1916 but didn't leave Australia. Champion was still busy interstate with Brieux's play and Katharine was shaping her new novel *The Black Opal*. Her character, Arthur Henty, has elements of Champion's characteristics, described as 'heroic and quixotic', an outsider leading a separate existence between station bosses and working men, 'drifting between two races and belonging to neither'. Reminiscent of the depiction of Champion in *George Eastmont*, he shares a similar boyhood admiration of medieval knights: 'He had thought sometimes of a medieval knight wandering through flowering fields with the girl on a horse beside him, in connection with Sophie and himself. A reproduction of the well-known picture of the knight and the girl hung in his mother's sitting room'. His love interest, Sophie, as she matures develops 'a subtle, unconscious witchery' and is strongly identified with Katharine's poem 'Lavender'. Memories of the Preux Chevalier surface with Sophie's youthful love, 'in Sydney ... summer time ... with the harbour there at your feet'. A description of Sydney Harbour at night was later described as resembling black opal in *Home Annual* (October 1936). Tellingly, her female characters in *The Black Opal* are caught between conflicting responses to three males with the married Arthur shooting himself after Sophie refuses to run away with him.

Attending a monthly meeting of the newly formed Melbourne Literary Club on 15 February 1917, Katharine delivered a paper for Vance Palmer on the art of the short story at a studio in Oxford Chambers, Bourke Street; she probably supplemented his three short paragraphs with her own experience on the opal fields at Lightning Ridge. The club was founded in June 1916 by three main people, Frederick Macartney, Frank Wilmot and Henry Tate, with other members (including Baracchi, Champion, O'Dowd, Marie Pitt, the

Palmers, Elsie Cole, Mary Fullerton, Frederick Sinclaire and Percival Serle). With this address to the club, Katharine reconnected with Guido.

She finally made a decision to break off her relationship with Champion while he was overseas in New Zealand for some weeks with Brieux's play early in 1917.[625] Katharine's autobiography records that she promised the Preux Chevalier that she would not marry and that he intended to shoot himself if she did. She seemed almost surprised at the response: 'There was no disastrous repercussion to the message I sent overseas. A promise was broken, but no fatal shot fired'. Similar to Champion's former love affair, the end was not dramatic and there was no gun. Champion had been in that situation before, although he had been the person who initiated the break-up.

How did she frame the scene? The young lover isolated by distance and tired of her older married man; his sadness growing into anger while she looks towards a new lover and a new future. Katharine's later play *The Great Man* (1923) was played as a light comedy and told of a man 'imploring' his lover to see him in person and 'threatening to kill himself … blow all their brains out'.

In operatic fashion he extended the threat from his shooting himself to killing several people. Performed by Louis Esson's Pioneer Players at the Melbourne Playhouse the year following Champion's bankruptcy, the play must have dealt a blow to his ego. There is a lingering idea that her Preux Chevalier turned from chivalrous escort into a possessive and 'jealous lover' with 'his demented threats to shoot himself when she attempted to leave him'. Also, that her lover was 'intensely self-centred' over the years, with her reluctance to break off the affair explained as her 'deep horror of being the cause of pain and suffering'.[626]

Although highly dramatic, it is possible Champion's emotional response expressed a lover's bitterness and despair at the age of 58 over love lost. Certainly, the *Book Lover* was published sporadically throughout 1918 and not at all from February 1919 for over a year after she married Captain Hugo Throssell VC early in 1919. However, Champion's actions and letters to Morley Roberts when he broke with Adelaide Hogg, show no indication that he was someone who threatened or used emotional blackmail to secure a woman who wanted her freedom.

He had surrendered the one thing he desired the most, life with Adelaide, and 'to keep her against her real wishes and to have done so by artifice would have been hideous misery for both of us', he explained to Morley on 3 July 1898. On 10 October 1897 he admitted: 'And my heart is not broken. I am simply 'an older & a wiser – if a sadder – man'.

By the time she terminated their relationship Katharine was no ingénue. Instead, she was a professional, well-travelled woman in her mid-thirties who was trying to unravel her own feelings, including guilt. Her commitment never to marry was given to a man who never looked like leaving his wife. The pain inflected on Elsie Belle should Champion's relationship be uncovered was never mentioned, even though Katharine hated being responsible for hurting another. Adelaide Hogg also had a paradoxical attitude about inflicting hurt on her husband while never considering the suffering imposed on Champion by keeping both lover and husband. Katharine's affair was sporadic and enjoyable, flaring in the wake of her father's death and afterwards mostly long-distance, conducted through letters from overseas and occasional exciting but brief visits. However, the narrative of a jealous, manipulative, controlling, unbalanced and unnamed lover, finds traction in research work on Katharine's life to this day.

The essential reason for Katharine's desire to dissolve her relationship with Champion was her expectation of deeper involvement with Guido Baracchi. They reconnected after her return from Lightning Ridge in 1916 and before she retreated to Emerald to complete *The Black Opal*. Katharine introduced Guido to the Palmers and he frequently 'spent some unforgettable week-ends' at their Emerald cottage where guests visited to share wine, fruit and conversation. Formerly a residence of the Essons until they departed for Mallacoota, the cottage was taken over by the Palmers in 1917 and then by Katharine in January 1918. Known today as Rose Charman's Cottage at 77 Monbulk Road, the place was a couple of kilometres from Emerald and described by Nettie as:

> ... a four-square little cottage, well away from main road and railway, twenty hilly acres, some in forest and some in grass, a landscape almost

as idyllic as that of Brittany or southern England. With its intimate fern-gullies, grassed hillsides and patches of forest, it was country to love and explore.[627]

In May 1917, only months after ending her long-time affair with Champion, Katharine wrote to Nettie about the restorative effect of Guido's arrival at the cottage while the Palmers were away on holidays. She admitted to Nettie that she was worried that news of their two days together would travel back to her mother through another resident of the area, Lily's aunt.[628] The following month Guido became one of the founding members of the Victorian Labor College in June 1917 and commenced an affair with the poet Lesbia Harford (Keogh) who fell 'deeply in love' with him. A writer who lived with Guido in the thirties, claimed 'Guido shared his favours equally' with Katharine and Lesbia during this period and his sudden marriage to another woman 'had lasting repercussions on both the other women'.[629] Katharine's poem in her notebook, written in June at Emerald to Nettie Palmer after the birth of her daughter, highlights the loss of a departed lover. At the same time, with its biblical symbolism, her words illuminate self-sacrifice that overrides biological imperative:

> You – little mother
> You have your home
> Among the trees:
> You have your mate
> And your baby.
> I have only
> The ache of my heart;
> The windy way –
> The breeze:
> And a will of thorns
> For lover.

Her short story 'Wild Honey', published that August, was set in the bush amidst nests of bees and birds calling 'mate to mate'. The story is heavy with sexual symbolism with a romance blossoming between a young pair who 'tasted the wild honey' and continue to desire it, although the price was 'always a bitterness' after the tasting.[630] In the aftermath of her break with Champion and probably with some idea about Guido's love affair with Lesbia, there were now rumours circulating in the press that month about his upcoming marriage to another woman, Kathleen Tobin.

Katharine left Melbourne and went to stay with her brother in Pyramid Hill, about a hundred kilometres from the goldfields of Bendigo. Nigel had been invalided after a lengthy period in France during the war while another brother Alan, a journalist on the *Argus*, had recently enlisted. On 17 November 1917 the daughter of the owner of Perry's Circus, Miss Lizzy Perry, fell head first to the ground at the Leitchfield grounds, dislocated her lower spine and was taken to Nigel's surgery where Katharine comforted the trapeze performer. The incident later formed the basis for her depiction of Gina, a crippled circus performer in *Haxby's Circus* (1930).

Guido married Kathleen Tobin on 17 January 1918 and around this time Katharine took a night train to join Nettie at Emerald, announcing she had been ill and needed to retreat to the countryside for a break. Over the long weekend a plan took shape and she decided to move there, think about purchasing the cottage; the decision made she would arrange for a van of furniture to the cottage and the Palmers could then use this van to return to Melbourne with their belongings.[631] Six weeks after his marriage, Guido delivered a speech on the banks of the Yarra River and was arrested for two offences against the War Precautions Regulations: 'making statements likely to prejudice recruiting' and 'attempting to cause disaffection among the civil population'. He was fined and paid £100 but refused to provide 'security for good behaviour' so was sentenced to three months gaol at Pentridge where he became assistant librarian. A deputation was made to the Attorney General for his release and Champion's sister-in-law Vida Goldstein represented the Women's Political Association, along with various members of labour, trade unions and socialists. Years later Katharine used his Pentridge experience and library work in her last novel, *Subtle Flame*. Unable to face Guido, who toasted Vance Palmer in front of Will Dyson, Henry Tate, Frederick Macartney, Frank Wilmot and

Mary Fullerton, Katharine was described as 'indisposed'. Both she and Christian Jollie Smith had organized Palmer's send-off at a cafe in Oxford Chambers after he enlisted in the army.

Guido's marriage was over by the end of 1921 after his affair with another woman. He married again that March and continued numerous other affairs. However, even in November 1926 Katharine was still emotionally fragile about Guido and expressed her feelings to Hilda Esson who obviously knew more about Katharine's early history. Katharine's letter was composed when newspapers announced Guido's return from Europe to be his father's executor. Later, Guido saw her at Greenmount in the thirties with Betty Roland and although Katharine stayed with them in Russia, she ended her friendship with Guido when he chose Trotsky politics. Years later they restarted correspondence after Nettie Palmer's death and she expressed her eternal gratitude to him for his role in introducing her to Marxism.

Teaching and attending lectures at the University of Melbourne, she also studied Labour's policy. Later, when attending the Victorian Labor College, she found 'a new world' in the arguments of Marx and Engels, as she described in 'Why I am a Communist':

> At last, I told myself, I had found a logical explanation of the poverty and injustices in the social system under which we are living: a complete tracing of social development through the ages; a philosophy derived from scientific investigation into the nature of actual, observable material from which the earth and everything on it, evolved.
> 'Then I felt like some, watcher of the skies. When a new planet, swims into his ken.'[632]

On 17 October 1918 Hugo Throssell returned and a whirlwind relationship developed with their engagement announced in early December. He was 'really a deliriously exciting and romantic lover' with flowers and love notes, Katharine wrote:

> It was his tempestuous wooing, physical strength and beauty, I adored at first. Then as we grew to know each other better, his sweet nature,

all the fine qualities of his great character held me so fast that no man ever again had any chance with me. There was nobody comparable with my Jimmy. Nobody, I felt could ever take his place – although of course, there were candidates.[633]

One of the 'candidates' who was quickly dispatched was the Preux Chevalier although this had happened over a year and a half earlier. Katharine linked her note breaking her commitment to the Preux Chevalier with Hugo's return and wooing, implying her engagement prompted her decision to break-up. On 28 January 1919, two years after her split from Champion and one year after Guido's marriage, Katharine married Hugo Throssell in a Collins Street registry office. They honeymooned at the cottage, purchased and gifted to her by Edith with Alan's 'legacy' after his death in France in December 1917. Even though her relationship with Champion ended long before her marriage, the picture of Achilles was still in her 'workroom' at the cottage.

On 23 August 1920 Edith Prichard died quietly in her sleep at 9 Kooyong Road Armadale, having seen the death of a son, two sisters (Christina Dickson and Lily Wilson-Williams) and her husband's Tasmanian brother, in her last few years. Katharine returned without her husband to Melbourne late the month before because her mother wasn't well although much of Katharine's stay was spent in a private hospital where she underwent 'a severe operation'. Whether this was related to Katharine's headaches and ill-health is unknown but she received news of Edith's death while she recuperated in a hospital bed and 'suffered keen mental distress'.[634] Shortly after, Hugo arrived from the west to take her home while Nigel sorted out Edith's affairs and sold her two houses in Normandy Road Caulfield, her piano was bequeathed to Katharine and the final estate was valued at £1421. Only a couple of months later, on 30 October 1920 the Communist Party of Australia was founded and Katharine was one of the first to join. Many would leave the Party over the years but she remained a committed member for life.

Throughout the twenties, Katharine embraced a creative period and secured income, accolades and even prizes, starting with 'The

Grey Horse' that won £50 in the 1925 'Art in Australia' short story competition. After journeying to the Karri timber forests of Pemberton in the south-west corner of Western Australia, not far from the area Champion called a Garden of Eden, she completed *Working Bullocks* (1926). Like Champion, the crusading protagonist, Mark Smith, a Marxist with 'subtle, imperious magnetism', is identified as an outsider, one who stands alone. In advance of the filming of *The Pioneers*, directed by Raymond Longford, she was able to holiday for three months at a cottage at Black Rock with her sister. She caught up with old friends and attended a meeting of Melbourne's Quarterly Club where guest speakers were Alice Henry and Muriel Heagney. Katharine found herself alongside Vida Goldstein and Evelyn Gough at the New Cafe managed by Annie McCubbin whose husband's paintings hung on the walls. During this time she caught up with friends such as Will Dyson, Louis Esson, Henry Tate, Frank Wilmot, William Moore and Max Meldrum.[635]

Katharine's solo trip in the middle of 1926 to Robert McGuire's Turee Creek Station in the Pilbara region in north-west Western Australia resulted in two acclaimed *Bulletin* stories, 'The Cooboo' and 'Happiness'.[636] *Haxby's Circus*, started in early spring 1927 after a short tour along the north-west coast with Wirth's Circus, was entered in Jonathan Cape's novel competition and an American competition in the hope of prizes. Returning to Melbourne in September 1927 during Australian Author's Week, Katharine attended a function with the Australian Literature Society where E.J. Brady sang her praises.[637] She also hosted a party at the Green Mill dancing academy for circus folk with Tom Roberts and Will Dyson. Chasing prizes and lured by money she entered competitions at a frenetic pace. The Tait brothers announced the *Triad* three-act play competition as they searched for an Australian playwright for their theatrical productions. Katharine submitted *Brumby Innes* under the pen name of 'Meroo' and won £50 in November 1927. One of the play's judges Gregan McMahon, a long-time friend of Champion, thought it 'one of the finest things' he had read. Only a few weeks prior to Champion's death at the end of April 1928, McMahon was announced as director of a permanent company touring the capital cities and New Zealand. Ten years after

Brieux's play, Champion's dream of a national Australian theatre was on the right track.

Katharine's holiday visits in 1926 and 1927 included catch-ups with friends and acquaintance from her youth, and these people must have alerted her to Champion's worsening health. He was now living quietly after bankruptcy. Miles Franklin visited Punt Road after arriving from Sydney on 9 March 1927 and wrote a lengthy report on Champion's condition to Annie Beatrice Champion who had last seen her brother in England. Annie responded on 5 October 1927 to Miles while visiting cousins at Hatton Castle that when she had seen her brother, though 'partly paralized [sic] still his *speech* was quite clear'. The fact that he was now 'a good deal worse & more helpless' made Annie suspect another stroke.[638] At the time of his first stroke, the *Bulletin* had commented on his paralysis that made him look like 'a very old man' while Herbert Brookes saw him transformed into 'a cripple at a comparatively early age'. A nasty article in the *Truth* on 25 April 1914 had described him 'like a disabled crab'.

A few days before Champion died, the *Bulletin* announced a prize novel competition with a deadline of 30 June 1928. Katharine wrote furiously, dropping *Haxby's Circus* (three-quarters completed at that stage) and writing *Coonardo: The Well in the Shadow* (1929). Only months after Champion's cremation, came the announcement of Katharine's award of the *Bulletin's* first prize and £500 and the serial was published between 5 September and 12 December 1928.

Katharine returned to *Haxby's Circus* (1930) and within the novel's sub-text she continued to explore the aftermath of Champion's crippling stroke. She must have seen Champion's strength in the face of adversity or physical 'deformity' as well as the hurtful insults about his appearance. Katharine's crippled circus performer, Gina, with a broken back, is transformed into a 'grotesque and hideous' hunchback clown. During a period of reckless behaviour, she is depicted as 'running amok'. Billy Rocca's counsel could have been drawn straight from Champion's own experiential playbook:

> He said to me once: 'Life's a three volume novel, Gina. The first's the book of ideals and illusions; the second's the book of realities and

noble resolutions; the third's the book of the senses and breakdown of the will.' (p. 342)

Many years before, when expressing the effect of despair on his drive and ambition to Morley on July 1897, Champion contrasted the narrative template of heroes who 'live a noble life & do heroic things' with his own truth where 'noble life can only take the shape of the drabbest suffering – to no earthly purpose'. In March 1898, Champion admitted he had 'definitely given up all hope of realizing any of my illusions', and was now 'facing the inevitable road down the hill of life'.

At the end of Katharine's novel, there is a declaration from a minor character summing up an attitude of reckless self-damage in the wake of personal difficulties: 'I'd like to crock up and run off the rails. It'd be a relief somehow; but I won't let life beat me that way. I've got to stand up to it, somehow'. Her novel presented human triumph in the face of adversity; a philosophical stance shared by Champion to underpin survival: 'You have got to stand up to things. You must not let life do what it likes with you. You have your brain. Make the most of it. You can make it pull you out of any hole you are in'. The exploration of why one person fights to overcome obstacles while another succumbs was complex, and Champion had seen that in Dr Strong's struggle for social reform and the pressures he was under to 'break-down', 'give up' or keep fighting.[639]

Her Preux Chevalier who loaned her French books and loved Paris was also an admirer of Victor Hugo's *The Man Who Laughs*.[640] Hugo's character, Gwynplaine, a man whose face is shaped into the 'rictus' of a perpetual grin, is described clearly: 'One corner of the mouth was raised, in mockery of the human race; the other side, in blasphemy of the gods.' He is taken into a carnival as a child, 'a creature grotesque', to become a clown and freak, provoking laughter for crowds at fairs. His role is to suffer and amuse: 'His face laughed; his thoughts did not'. Like Gwynplaine, Katharine's Billy is described as a 'caricature of a man', performing to an audience who 'laughed till they wept, shrieked helplessly. All the stolid red faces split in half, mouths gaping and bellowing, emitted strange helpless cries of glee and exhaustion' as he manipulates the crowd's laughter for the show's benefit. At the conclusion, circus life is shown to be a reflection of reality and Gina's appearance as a 'grotesque and hideous' clown with a 'plastered face and rouged mouth' exposes the audience in all its deformity. Gina joins in to laugh 'at the order and harmony of a world to which the circus held the dim surface of its mirror'.

Not long after Champion's death, Katharine sent her poem 'Lavender' to the *Australian Woman's Mirror*.[641]

> I'll send you lavender
> To lay among your thoughts of me,
> That I for ever in your dreams
> May dwell with fragrance,
> Subtle, mysterious and sweet,
> Of the herb flowers I love so well.
>
> Lo, I am a witch,
> And weave the spell!

One line from 'Lavender' is missing in the early version of her poem, with 'Breaths undying', but this is inserted into the poem in *The Earth Lover* (1932). This poem was associated in Katharine's mind with joining the local dramatic club with a leading role in 'Sweet Lavender', Pinero's popular play, as a young governess in Yarram. Later in summer time she wrote on the banks of the River Ouse at Huntingdon about basket weavers, the willow harvest and the old lavender-man, his son and his dog. When she won the competition with *The Pioneers*, the *Everylady's Journal* pictured her with a huge bunch of lavender and Sumner Locke wrote: 'During the lavender season in the good old fields of England Miss Prichard finds respite. A bunch of sweet lavender sprigs culled from the sweeping winds of the early morning are her dearest possessions; and a mind of lovely, happy thoughts, taken likewise as incense from a weary-eyed, weather-beaten old gardener, make for her a day of absolute pleasure.' Katharine had a strong self-identification with the fragrant herb.

Attached to the inside cover containing cuttings of newspaper reviews of *The Wild Oats of Han* (in Katharine's manuscript papers) is the poem 'Lavender' from the *Australian Woman's Mirror*, linking the novel with the poem. Katharine released her children's book as a serial in July 1926 for Leon Gellert's Sydney *Home* magazine, and as a novel in 1928. An early attempt at a sustained writing from England in 1908, the book was deliberately withheld for over twenty years, according to her preface. Penned the year following her father's suicide, a young distraught girl is told that life is full of hurt, pain and the unexpected: 'You've just got to shake your fist at Life and say: "You can't break me. You can't!"'.

Knowledge of her intimate relationship with Champion allows passages in *The Wild Oats of Han* to be re-examined, the central character's youthful experiences overlayed with Katharine's personal liaison. Tellingly, Han admits: 'She scarcely knew the world of the real from the world of the unreal'. She is convinced that a goanna, with 'a tongue as blue as the skies', is 'an enchanted prince' trapped in a different form: '"If only I knew the magic word – or who bewitched him," she assures herself, "I would change him to his proper shape and we'd live happy ever after."' However, this fairy tale wish remains unfulfilled and 'instead of changing into a knight-at-arms – although his coat was of as burnished mail as any hero's in history or a fairy tale', he was 'the source of all Han's misfortunes'. In her serial and first edition, one line is altered 'burnished mail like the coat of any *preux chevalier*'. Because she used the pseudonym in her autobiography to disguise the identity of her married lover, it was a necessary change when her children's tale was republished in 1968.

Han's transformed prince, lying lazily in the sun near to her and some 'white stone steps' is evocative of Robert Herrick's iconic poem, with its images of gathering rose buds:

> The air was full of rose sweetness and a hum of bees. Nearby, an enchanted prince basked. She watched him, and from time to time, mischievous imps provoking, threw handfuls of petals at him. They broke over him, but did not disturb his sun-dazed reverie (p. 20).

Herrick's line 'To Anthea, who may command him anything' was popularised in 1897 by songwriter Colin Bingham's 'Bid Me to Love' and sung at Melbourne's Austral Salon gatherings in September/October; Katharine also used that phrase in her unpublished play of the same name in 1927. Han's gathering of rose petals 'crimson and deep-hearted … with golden-bodied bees in them' is suggestive of Katharine's visit to 'The Elms' where the Frasers' gardener warned her, 'whom the bees love, is a bit of a witch'. As their manor house was only a few miles east of Huntingdon and a short distance from the Champion family's country house at Buckden, there is an apparent connection to Katharine's interest in the Ouse, where she lay on the riverbanks.

Later scenes, revolving around Han's lack of a childhood sweetheart, echo Champion's gait as he recovered from the stroke. The preying mantis who 'walked in a stiff twiggy way' is transformed into another enchanted prince who has been punished and needs 'release from his ungainly shape'. Unusual is the focus on 'a yellow rose which smelled exactly like castor-oil' growing outside of Han's room, altered from 'an enchanted rose' because it too was 'punished for something'. This suggests Champion's previous liaison, symbolised by a 'faded but still fragrant yellow rose' kept lovingly pressed in his book. Katharine's foul-smelling yellow rose represents chastisement for a past wrong-doing. Did Champion confide to Katharine his emotional turmoil once Adelaide returned to England? Is Adelaide the yellow rose who bewitched the Preux Chevalier and is now replaced by a magical good 'witch'?

It is also quite plausible Katharine read Margaret Harkness's novel, which conveyed 'the career of a man who will be readily recognised by those who are in full touch with literary and journalistic circles in Australia'.[642] Katharine's own title seems to play upon Lord Cashel's commentary in *George Eastmont* about 'George's crop of tame oats' sown in early adulthood and Katharine's preface speculates on a sequel, *Cuckoo Oats*, sown in spring when the cuckoo or 'rain bird' calls that will show Han's development. Wild oats develop 'in unbroken ground' in her children's novel and attempts are made to break the spirit and mould young ones into 'tame creatures'. However, it is 'spirited children that are always the great and good men and women, rebels and heroes, reformers'. For Katharine, rebellion and reform are intertwined concepts and the driving force behind her work. Many years before, in August 1895, the *Champion* warned that 'the sowing of wild oats means the reaping of a bitter harvest for the innocent to the second and third generation' and a contemporary described Brieux's play as embodying 'the tragedy of sowing wild oats'. By the time Katharine wrote her short story 'The Cow', wild oats had become 'empty sheaths' and her female character has had enough of fecundity.

Han's green fern-covered 'little rockbound parlour' is a reminder of the green parlour of Katharine's notebook jottings. While away at Black Rock, in February 1916, she reflected on earlier journeys along the beach to a secluded, isolated 'little green parlour' where she sat outside and thought of an unnamed person. 'It was just as we left it'. Champion's colleague, Henry Byron Moore, with his many roles (secretary of the Victoria Racing Club, former Assistant Surveyor-General, writer of fairy tales and cricket lover) suggested in 1890 cutting a maze of pathways through the dense ti-tree of Beaumaris. Two years later he argued for accessible picnic areas with scenic views and steps in the cliffs to the shore below. When this was achieved, there was access to isolated areas well away from public notice and these were areas of seclusion provided by the thick ti-tree.

If Han represented Katharine's relationship with Champion, what do readers make of her 'White Kid Gloves' for the *Bulletin* on 9 May 1928, written only days after Champion's death? The first in a series of short stories advertised by the *Bulletin*, it garnered a powerful campaign in local country papers that sensationally advertised 'the seductive glamour', the heroine's 'sex controls' and 'a furnace of passion' ignited by 'a fever that could not be subdued by time, distance nor reason'. The story centred on an affair in Egypt during World War One between the fastidious, married Colonel Anthony Bridges and nurse Emilia, intent on playing Cleopatra to his Anthony. Seeking him in Australia fifteen years later, she is served tea at his home by Mrs Bridges and feels 'he belonged to her, Emilia, really, but by some accident, shipwreck or misadventure in his early life he had been lost, cast away and fallen into this woman's hands! She had been kind; taken care of him. Emilia was grateful.' Mrs Bridges is described in a series of bland statements, as 'very healthy and good-humoured' exhibiting 'an expression of patience and perpetual smiling' and 'kind and conscientious' but she doesn't stop Emilia's future plans to establish residency nearby, with an inference that Anthony will be reclaimed by her.

Katharine spent three weeks on the Larkinville goldfields with her husband in late 1930. Here she wrote 'The Bride of Faraway', a short story set around Coolgardie and began planning a new novel, *The Roaring Nineties*. No-one would recognise the period as the one Maggie Harkness described in her 1897 serial 'Called to the Bar', set in Coolgardie at Fiery Cross. Katharine's trilogy tells the story of an industry through those who travelled to the Coolgardie area in 1892. A boarding house is opened for goldminers and a sexual attraction develops between Sally and Frisco:

> She was conscious of a secret understanding between herself and this man. It had been there when their eyes first met, although she was determined to deny it: afraid of what such a subtle intimacy might mean.
> To be sure, never in words, before, had Frisco hinted at anything but a distant respectful admiration and concern to help her over difficulties. It was his eyes that had done the damage, disturbing her with their gay recklessness, and forcing some response from the depths of her. It was not permissible and must be repressed, that altogether disgraceful feeling, Sally told herself ... Of course he was a fine figure of a man, handsome and powerful, with a dash of that romantic gallantry which would be attractive to any woman. And he had been very kind and thoughtful (pp. 212–13).

Sally is shocked 'this wild fire had flamed in her, kindling every nerve and fibre', his seductive 'virile devilry had overwhelmed her!'. In the sequel, *Golden Miles*, Frisco is a debonaire, childless, twice-married man of the world who, though bankrupt and blind, still has 'his old reckless gaiety'. By *Winged Seeds*, the last novel of the trilogy, their sexual passion has cooled, acknowledged as transitory: 'a stormy sunset ... which had flamed and vanished'.

Katharine returned to Victoria for her last novel *Subtle Flame* that recalls places from her youth: Beaumaris, the Dandenong Ranges, Emerald and the banks of the Yarra (scenes of Sunday political speeches). She recalled her 'portraits were drawn from life, though some from memory of people I had known' and her protagonist, a middle-aged newspaper editor, David Evans, was regarded as 'a very complex character'. Katharine's novel argued for peace and disarmament[643] and drew on classical references about Prometheus from writers such as George Herbert, Percy Bysshe Shelley and Christopher Brennan. Her main character was envisaged as 'mounted on an invisible steed charging hosts of the invisible enemy', complete with pen and typewriter as weapons available to 'a hard-working ink-slinger'. As he grapples with the issue of disarmament, he is no 'lone Prometheus' positioned 'on the same rock'. David's wife displays qualities Katharine saw in Elsie Belle Champion; she is 'so lovable and ineffectual' and in their marriage the Evans pair 'jogged along happily enough' in an undemanding companionship. David's encounters with other women during his marriage led to 'casual fornications' that did not require 'any overwhelming passion' although he 'missed the glory and glamour of a love'.

This changes when he meets a young teacher, Sharn, Welsh for Jane but also suggestive of the medieval village of Sharnbrook located on the Ouse where the river loops back to Buckden. With her 'elderly swain' who, like Champion, is married, twice her age and 'better informed and more far-sighted', they walk together along the tea-trees along the cliffs of Black Rock:

> Crushing the small rounded leaves of their foliage, which cast such deep shadow, she inhaled thirstily their acrid fragrance.
> 'It's the breath of the trees, David,' she cried. 'Something ancient and immortal. Isn't it wonderful this tea-tree scrub! Have you seen it in blossom? Snow, tinged with pink, that throws a garland round the sea' (pp. 100–01).

The narrative celebrates his belief in both the lone crusading impulse and the collective political effort. His future is perceived as 'an adventure: a glorious adventure in thought and experience' that involves a decision to leave his wife, to walk out and abandon his employment as a journalist and retreat to the forest.

> He had no fear that his wit would desert him. He could use that 'brilliant ironical style' of his more effectively. Not find himself limited and leg-ironed by the policy of a newspaper. He would make a name for himself as an independent writer of courage: turn out special articles exposing political skulduggery, religious hypocrisy, economic chicanery (p. 19).

His desire to communicate on a deeper level and influence opinion through his fearless writing is also indicative of the very qualities that made Champion a successful agitator and an uncompromising figure in newspaper and political circles. Her character is a one-man crusade, like George Eastmont, as he attempts 'to rouse them out of their apathy and ignorance, and give them hope'.

> 'I want to reach the people,' David explained. 'I want to know them better, in order to talk to them: write for them. Stimulate their courage, so that they won't allow themselves to be driven like sheep to the slaughter. There, you see, I'm talking like a demagogue ...' (p. 41).

David's wife, valued for 'her devotion to him', is dispatched by the author without emotion in a contrived death as he searches for a higher purpose with a promise of a new partner. A wish fulfilment, the novel concludes with Sharn's offer to live with David, to care for him, become his secretary, housekeeper and cook, 'be whatever you want me to be, child, mother, lover – or just a comrade'. Katharine's notebook from 1916 spelt out a caring role as a powerful temptation: 'all the majesty of her nursing him!' and was a far cry from concepts espoused in *Bid Me to Love* (1927) and *Intimate Strangers* (1937).

David's stroke appears to be a projection of Champion's stroke, slowing many of his ambitions but not halting his activism. It also reflects Katharine's own debilitating heart attack in August 1961 after a long period of cigarette smoking. With quiet courage, similar to Champion, she learned to write again, believing 'perhaps one should be content to count blessings and watch the world go by'.[644] Following the assault on her way of life, Katharine now took the inevitable path to her own lonely conclusion, writing with difficulty from her isolated haven at Greenmount outside Perth. Her autobiography and last novel seem entwined as she revisited her youth and tried to understand her life. Three years after her autobiography had revealed her youthful liaison with the Preux Chevalier, she completed *Subtle Flame*.

Despite being paralysed in her right arm she was driven to sort out her personal papers while working on the *Child of the Hurricane*. As she read and discarded certain personal papers, she relived and remembered her life, one letter or document at a time, and could not bring herself to throw away jottings in notebooks from her youth. It is interesting to speculate whether her reminiscences about the Preux Chevalier grew fonder as she looked back to the time after the stroke paralysed his right side, remembering the strength required to conquer pessimism.

The reception of her autobiography with details of her affair with a married man, four decades after Champion's death, showed a lack of reaction that could only have surprised her. In a modern world the New Woman helped shape, it raised no eyebrows and no-one even suggested a possible candidate. Writing of her mysterious married man was perhaps cathartic and, in a different social period from her youth, readers seemed not to care about a confession from a woman in her eighties. Her mother, father and husband were no longer alive to make any comment or judgment, nor was Elsie Belle Champion. As an elderly woman looking backwards to her youth, Katharine's desire was to explain to herself and others the reasons for the decade-long affair.

The question remains, why did Katharine feel the need to record this affair so late in her life? She wrote her story 25 years after Hugo Throssell's suicide on their verandah when he shot himself with his revolver while Katharine was in Russia, leaving his Lazy Hit Ranch with debts of £10,000. She was nearly eighty-six when she died, outliving people who knew both her and Champion: Henry Tate (1926), Furnley Maurice (1942), Louis Esson (1943), E.J. Brady (1952), Elsie Cole (1953), Hilda Esson (1953), Bernard O'Dowd (1953),

Miles Franklin (1954), Hugh McCrae (1958) and Vance Palmer (1959). Many of these people may have recognised her middle-aged intellectually stimulating married man. She never found the need to mention her affair with Guido although he popped up and surprised her with a letter only months after the release of her autobiography. Their correspondence restarted and his pen was slightly flirtatious in a letter on 15 March 1968.[645] It must have been intriguing for him to speculate on the identity of her *chère amie*.

No critic could connect her to a man who edited the *Sun: the Society Courier* a few years after her father's time at that newspaper, a man who was the 'swell' socialist and flamboyant journalist of the literary world and the socialist movement. Who would remember Champion, the revolutionary agitator or 'firebrand' who came to Australia in 1890 and was later the owner of a self-titled newspaper? A man whose caustic pen and audacious opinions set Melbourne on fire and made him so many enemies at the turn of the century. Who would know that he found 'the glory' of an affair with Adelaide Hogg and that his friend Morley Roberts found this with Alice? It is obvious Katharine read Storm Jameson's book on the difficulties facing writers in the Twentieth Century in *The Writer's Situation and other Essays* (1950) because she refers to Storm in an essay in *Southerly* and a series of Storm's quotes were recorded in her notebook.[646] Did Katharine read Storm's book on an eminent Victorian Morley Roberts in 1961 as she wrote her autobiography? The indications remain strong that Champion confided many personal details to Katharine that perhaps included his past affair with Adelaide, Morley's affair and his sister-in-law's troubles.

Katharine was an independent, experienced and capable journalist and writer and, despite the tendency of some to believe she was an ingénue, she wasn't. Katharine protested to her son that her autobiography 'tells too much and not enough' but was 'true enough'. Not long before her death in 1969, Katharine said that 'her work would be forgotten within ten years'.[647] This indeed was the experience of many of her contemporaries. Morley Roberts, in an article for the *Virginia Quarterly Review* in October 1930, wrote a simple but very true sentence: 'What we call "literary immortality" is but the remembrance of a few, who in a little while will themselves be nameless dust'. Katharine believed 'unpretentious' characterised her writing. 'The wit and gaiety I admire so much in other writers, I have lacked', she wrote with some regret and sadness in her essay for *Southerly*. 'Perhaps I have not made readers dream and laugh enough'.

A Remembrance

In the years before his death Champion was content to live a peaceful domestic life in South Yarra retirement, with Elsie Belle continuing to look after him while she still managed the library. A man of the world, he finished life quietly in his garden, the crusading knight, now bankrupt, retired from political life and was an 'elderly gentleman'. Although he spent half of his life in Melbourne and died there, Champion was regarded by many as a toff and an English interloper, although he reminded socialists: 'I am "an immigrant" too'.[648]

He died of a stroke at the age of 69, Sunday morning on 30 April 1928 at his Punt Road home in South Yarra, just ten minutes' walk to the Royal Botanic Gardens. His younger brother Captain Arthur Champion had died one year before in Bawtry, Yorkshire. Over thirty years before his death, Champion wrote of his aversion to 'burying and embalming' as 'barbaric' and announced his intention to 'patronise a crematorium'.[649] Elsie Belle oversaw Champion's wishes at 7am the following day, before newspaper notices hit the streets. The *Australian Worker* reported simply that Champion was 'a pioneer of the new Unionism and of Labor political action', the *Herald* called him a 'writer' and 'librarian', and James MacDonald shared memories of him in the *Social Democrat*. Morley Roberts was living on Civil List pension of £75 and was in Jamaica on a holiday.

In a return to his old religion, his ashes were deposited in the Church of England section of the Fawkner Crematorium. Perhaps this should be no surprise since he was brought up with a strong religious background although he carried his religion lightly. Though he was never afraid to criticise the clergy, he often worked closely with ministers and ex-clergymen. Maggie Harkness spoke of him in 1891 as 'having no prejudices against religion' for he was 'a deeply religious man, intensely sensitive and practical'. Generations of his Urquhart relatives were buried around Banff in the Scottish Episcopal

Kirkyards near Old Meldrum (Bethelnie Old Kirk from 1236) and also at Craigston (King Edward Kirk), while his Buckden relatives were buried at St Mary's church. He married his first wife at St George's in Bloomsbury and his second marriage was performed by Dr Charles Strong of the Australian Church, a breakaway from the Presbyterian Scots Church. In addition, Champion was close to Cardinal Manning of the Catholic Church and an admirer of General Booth of the Salvation Army, precisely because they provided practical and immediate assistance.

Henry Hyde Champion was able to keep many of his secrets till the end, entrusting Morley Roberts with his affair with Adelaide Hogg, as his friend trusted him with his own affair with Alice Hamlyn. If not for letters to Morley Roberts and Prichard's autobiography nearly four decades after their affair ended, Champion's secret liaisons with at least two of the women would remain hidden. Having denounced 'that buzzard, the collector of letters, who picks out the eyes and souls of dead lovers' and having burnt most of his own letters, Morley gave Storm Jameson the task of publishing a book about him without revealing important details. Ironically, by keeping Champion's letters, it was Morley's fate to provide clues and details of his own affair and to assist in the telling of another's tale. In perhaps a tongue-in-cheek statement, Morley Roberts described Champion as: 'ever a good talker and good at everything but his own affairs; the staunchest friend and wisest'.[650] Perhaps there was a *double entrendre* in 'affairs'.

A controversial figure throughout his life, Champion was a thorn in the side of both conservatives and radicals. To everyone who admired or loathed him, openly or quietly, he was unpredictable and unfathomable. He was too fraught with contradictions and controversies to fit neatly into any conventional role model for labour politics. Disparaged, insulted and ignored as the wider labour movement achieved success and influence, he was essentially forgotten. His enemies were delighted that he was written out of the history of the labour movement both in England and Melbourne. His friend, William Morris in one of his 1895 lectures, 'What We Have to Look For', anticipated 'all the miseries that go to make up the degrading game of politics'. Clementina Black's 'prophecy' that her agitator hero was 'one of the men who die brokenhearted, [sic] and get statues built to them afterwards' would never eventuate. Robert Browning's 'The Lost Leader', often quoted in Labour newspapers, perhaps his best epitaph: 'Blot out his name, then, record one lost soul more.'[651]

Endnotes

Introduction

1. *Weekly Herald* (Adelaide), 18 May 1895. All quotes by Herbert Brookes are from Brookes Papers, MS1924/7.
2. Clayton, 1926, p. 69.
3. *Trident*, April 1909 and September 1908.
4. *Trident*, August 1908.
5. *Champion*, 3 August 1895.
6. *Champion*, 13 July 1895.

Destined to Serve

7. Adam Urquhart was Sheriff of Wigtown in 1813 and Advocate of the Scottish Circuit Courts from 1852 till his death in 1860. Elizabeth's sister, Frances Susan and husband John George Green (related to the Bishop of Lincoln) lived at Buckden and their grandson was Captain John Leslie Green VC.
8. *Book Lover*, February 1918.
9. *Cambridge Independent Press*, 11 September 1869; *Lincoln, Rutland, and Stamford Mercury*, 17 September 1869.
10. *Book Lover*, March 1900.
11. *Champion*, 7 September 1895. Only his father and sister were in the 1891 London census while his mother does not appear elsewhere.
12. *Champion*, 30 January 1897. John P. Lauden who was 19, born in Goa, India and employed as a 'page' was the only male in the household census of 1871.
13. *Book Lover*, February 1909. His brother Lt Colonel John George Champion fought in Crimea and died in 1854 at Florence Nightingale's hospital in Istanbul.
14. *Book Lover*, July 1912, June 1899, February 1911.
15. *Champion*, 12 September 1896, confirmed in *Who's Who*.
16. *Table Talk*, 3 October 1890. Farrar was a friend of his housemaster's brother E.S. Beesly.
17. *Bulletin*, 3 February 1921. *Independent*, 26 May 1995.
18. *Trident*, May 1908.
19. *Times*, 9 August 1880.
20. *Socialist*, 9 November 1907. Lieutenant A.C. Daniell was probably the Woolwich subaltern. He commanded the Victorian Artillery at Queenscliff from 1888–93. *Trident*, June 1908.
21. *Justice*, 14 March 1885. *Champion*, 8 February 1896.
22. *Mail* (Adelaide), 13 January 1917.
23. *Book Lover*, October 1915. *Trident*, May 1908.
24. Morley Roberts Papers, University of Pennsylvania. All textual references refer to these letters.
25. *Aberdeen Standard*, no 1, September 1893.
26. *Trident*, June 1908.
27. Diack, 1939, p. 23.
28. *Table Talk*, 3 October 1890. *Champion*, 24 April 1897.
29. *Socialist*, 12 September 1913.

30 *Champion*, 24 April 1897.
31 *Register* (Adelaide), 21 December 1916.
32 *Age*, 1 November 1900. Another cousin, Beauchamp Colclough Urquhart, fought at the Battle of Tel-el-Kebir.

Activism
33 MacKenzie, 1979, p. 35.
34 *Socialist*, 23 February 1907. *Social Democrat*, August 1897.
35 Hyndman, 1911, pp. 279–80.
36 *Socialist*, 25 July 1913.
37 *Socialist*, 3 September 1920.
38 *Book Lover*, February 1900. *Trident*, June 1908.
39 Hyndman, 1911, p. 345.
40 *Christian Socialist*, February 1884.
41 MacKenzie, 1979, p. 42.
42 *Mail* (Adelaide), 13 January 1917.
43 *Daily Telegraph* (Sydney), 31 August 1912. Sold at a shilling, 2,500 copies were printed, see Weintraub, 1986, p. 132.
44 *Champion*, 10 October 1896. *Trident*, June 1908.
45 Kelvin, 1987 Part A, pp. 200, 206, 231.
46 Mackail, 1968, ii, p. 110.
47 *Weekly Herald* (Adelaide), 4 March 1899.
48 *Book Lover*, July 1899.
49 *Book Lover*, July 1899. See also *Worker*, 6 May 1911.
50 MacKenzie, 1979, pp. 47–9.
51 Williams, 1914, p. 2.
52 *Justice*, 23 February 1884.
53 Draznin, 1992, pp. 157, 169, 191.
54 Kapp, 1976, p. 35.
55 *Justice*, 11 October 1884. *Worker*, 6 May 1911.
56 *Justice*, 6 December 1884.
57 *Book Lover*, August 1899.
58 *Trident*, April 1909.
59 Kapp, 1976, p. 61.
60 Kelvin, 1987 Part B, pp. 363–70.
61 Hyndman, 1911, p. 328.
62 Draznin, 1992, p. 141.
63 *Socialist*, 12 September 1913.
64 *Justice*, 17 October 1885. Draznin, 1992, p. 402.
65 *Gadfly*, 13 March 1907.
66 Kelvin, 1987, Part B, p. 533.
67 *Champion*, 8 February 1896.
68 Blatchford, 1931, p. 198.
69 Burgess, 1911, p. 20.
70 *Times*, 16 June 1938. A friendship sprang up with the Morris family with Janey visiting Robert and Gerda in Wales throughout November 1889, see Kelvin, 1996, p. 123.
71 Burgess, 1911, p. 20.
72 *Weekly Herald*, 18 May 1895. Burgess, 1911, pp. 16–20.
73 *Trident*, August 1908. *Justice*, 14 August 1886.
74 Hyndman, 1911, pp. 282–83.
75 Mackail, 1968, ii, p. 175.
76 Whitehead, 1987, p. 24.
77 *Common Sense*, 15 September 1887.
78 *Book Lover*, September 1915.
79 *Daily Telegraph* (Sydney), 15 November 1887. Reprinted in *Common Sense* on 15 October 1887.
80 *Geelong Advertiser*, 29 November 1887.
81 *Trident*, August 1908.
82 Whitehead, 1987, p. 27.
83 *Socialist*, 6 July 1907.
84 Black, 1894, p. 58. *Christian World*, July 1888.
85 Koss, 1970, pp. 157–58.
86 *Trident*, August 1908.
87 *Justice*, 1 February 1890.
88 *Labour Elector*, 16 November 1889.

89 *Justice*, 28 September 1888. *Labour Elector*, 15 November 1888.
90 White, 1886, p. 184. *Champion*, 3 April 1897.
91 *Labour Elector*, 1 November 1888.
92 Kapp, 1976, p. 300.
93 *Examiner*, 28 June 1873.
94 *Labour Elector*, 1 November 1888.
95 *Age*, 22 April 1895.
96 Bax, 1918, pp. 54–55.
97 *Justice*, 28 February 1890.
98 *Worker*, 16 February 1895.
99 *Star*, 20 September 1889.
100 *Daily Telegraph* (London), 17 February 1934. Rolfe helped Lewis edit a periodical for eighteen months.
101 Benkovitz, 1977, pp. 60–66.
102 *Times Literary Supplement*, 6 February 1969.
103 *Times*, 13 November 1925.
104 Sladen, 1913, p. 63.
105 Tsuzuki, 1991, p. 25.
106 *Labour Elector*, 22 June 1889.
107 *Age*, 29 March, 26 April 1890. Years later one report was still using the information, 'John Burns: Denounced by Democrats', *Truth* (Sydney), 16 August 1896.
108 *Star*, 16 January 1894.
109 *Star*, 23 January 1894. Humphrey, 1912, p. 137.
110 *Justice*, 28 September 1889. *Table Talk*, 3 October 1890.

His Place in History
111 Hyndman, 1911, pp. 307–8.
112 *Trident*, April 1909.
113 Diack, 1939, pp. 21–23.
114 Mann, 1923, pp. 87, 42.
115 Bax, 1918, pp. 101–02. *Melbourne Punch*, 17 October 1918.
116 *Standard*, 7 April 1886.
117 *Trident*, July 1908.
118 *Register* (Adelaide), 21 December 1916.
119 *Trident*, July 1908. In Shaw's play, *Major Barbara*, Undershaft expounds on the growth of Mansion House Committee funds for the poor after Pall Mall clubs were smashed. *Echoes of the 'eighties*. Kelvin, 1987 Part B, p. 520.
120 *Age*, 22 March 1886.
121 *Herald*, 26 March 1886.
122 *Champion*, 8 February 1896.
123 *South Australian Register*, 18 August 1888.
124 Ward, 1894, p. 282.
125 *Champion*, 8 February 1896. *Table Talk*, 17 January 1896.
126 *Trident*, August 1908.
127 *Champion*, 20 March 1897.
128 *Trident*, August, September 1908.
129 *Times*, 9 September 1889.
130 Champion, 1890, pp. 3, 18.
131 *Nineteenth Century*, February 1891. Champion, 1890, p. 30.
132 Smith and Nash, 1899, pp. 62, 78.
133 *Labour Elector*, 7 September 1889.
134 *Socialist*, 18 May 1907.
135 *Pictorial Australian*, 1 September 1889.
136 *Champion*, 27 June 1896.
137 Smith and Nash, 1899, pp. 140, 178–82.
138 *Age*, 30 September 1899. *Labour Elector*, 31 August 1889.
139 *Australian Star*, 16 October 1889. *Telegraph* (Brisbane), 19 October 1889.
140 *Pall Mall Gazette*, 13 February 1891. Reprinted in Australia see *Bacchus Marsh Express*, 3 April 1891.
141 *Justice*, 3 October 1885.
142 *Times*, 31 August 1889. *Champion*, 8 August 1896.
143 *Pall Mall Gazette*, 31 January 1891. Reprinted in Australia see *Telegraph* (Brisbane), 25 February 1891.

144 *Labour Elector*, 7 September 1889.
145 *Labour Elector*, 31 August 1889.
146 Whitehead, 1987, p. 28.
147 *Champion*, 16 May 1896. *Bulletin*, 14 July 1921.
148 Reprinted in Australia see *Observer*, 17 June 1905.
149 *Pictorial Australian*, 1 March 1892.
150 Reprinted in *Fiery Cross*, 27 June 1892.
151 *Trident*, April 1909.
152 Bellamy and Kaspar, 1987, p. 28. Others included Bishop of Bedford, Dr Richard Billing, Lady Somerset and Lady Margaret Sandhurst.
153 Clayton, 1926, p. 69.
154 *Toscin*, 14 April 1898.
155 *Bunyip* (Adelaide), 28 April 1899.
156 *Age*, 8 January, 26 April 1890.
157 *Nineteenth Century*, February 1891.
158 *Trident*, August 1908.
159 *Age*, 14 August 1890.
160 *New Review*, June 1890.
161 *Age*, 28 June, 5 July 1890. *Socialist*, 13 February 1913.
162 *Nineteenth Century*, February 1891.
163 *Champion*, 16 May 1896. *Bulletin*, July 1921.
164 *Age*, 13 August 1890, 29 September 1893. Champion used the pass three times in September, October 1890 and February 1891.
165 *Nineteenth Century*, February 1891.
166 *Age*, 23 February 1891.
167 *Argus*, 30 August 1890.
168 *Age*, 8 September 1890.
169 *Evening Journal* (Adelaide), 22 September 1890.
170 *Adelaide Observer*, 17 September 1890.
171 *Australian Star*, 16 September 1890.
172 *Australian Star*, 13 September 1890. *Herald*, 11 September 1890.
173 *Daily Telegraph* (Sydney), 12 September 1890.
174 *Champion*, 22 June 1895.
175 Spence, 1909, p. 135.
176 *Daily Telegraph* (Sydney), 15 September 1890.
177 *Age*, 20 September 1890.
178 *Argus*, 8 October 1890.
179 *Reynold's Newspaper*, 5 July 1896, quoted in Burgess, 1911, pp. 128–29.
180 *Bulletin*, 18 October 1890.
181 *Age*, 11 November 1890. *Melbourne Punch*, 20 November 1890.
182 *Herald, Sydney Morning Herald*, 6 November 1890. *Age*, 13 December 1890.
183 *Age*, 8 November 1890.
184 *Worker*, 16 June 1894.
185 *Table Talk*, 22 May 1891.
186 *Aberdeen Free Press*, 27 November 1890. Reprinted in *Age*, 13 April 1891.
187 *Australian Workman*, 21 February 1891.
188 *Express and Telegraph*, 11 March 1891. *Daily Telegraph* (Sydney), 29 June 1891. William Gladstone, Charles Bradlaugh, Sir Charles Dilke, Lord Dunraven, Henry Broadhurst, Charles Parnell, John Burns, Tom Mann, Ben Tillett, William Morris, Cunninghame Graham, Michael Davitt, Stepniak, Annie Besant, Bennett Burleigh, John Morrison Davidson, George Shipton, Samuel Storey and Lawson MP.
189 *South Australian Chronicle*, 7 March 1891.
190 *Evening News* (Sydney), 17 March 1891. *Daily Telegraph* (Sydney), 19 March 1891.
191 *Nineteenth Century*, February 1891.
192 *Nineteenth Century*, March 1891.
193 *Pall Mall Gazette*, 24 April 1891. Reprinted in Australia see *Daily Telegraph* (Tasmania), 8 June 1891.
194 *Workman's Times*, 1 May 1891.

[195] *Evening News*, 24 March 1892.
[196] *Melbourne Punch*, 25 April 1895.
[197] *Age*, 22 April 1895.
[198] *Athenaeum*, 3 February 1912. Reprinted in *Socialist*, 29 March 1912. Clayton, 1926, p. 69.
[199] Hardie, 1908, pp. 9–10.
[200] *Age*, 6 December 1890.
[201] *Bulletin*, 17 February 1921.
[202] *Times*, 18 April 1888.
[203] *Nineteenth Century*, July 1888.
[204] Humphrey, 1912, p. 120.
[205] *Mail* (Adelaide), 13 January 1917.
[206] *Pall Mall Gazette*, 18 February 1891. Reprinted in Australia, see *Southern Argus*, 22 October 1891.
[207] *Daily Free Press*, 15 June 1891.
[208] *Aberdeen Journal*, 17 June 1891.
[209] Henderson, 1976, pp. 133–34.
[210] Humphrey, 1912, p. 131.
[211] Burgess, 1911, pp. 149, 145.
[212] Diack, 1939, pp. 21–23.
[213] *Fiery Cross*, 25 June 1892.
[214] *Evening Journal* (Adelaide), 7 September 1892.
[215] *Evening News* (Sydney), 4 October 1892.
[216] *Echo*, 17 August 1892. Laurence, 1965, pp. 356–62.
[217] *To-Day*, 6 January 1894.
[218] *Workman's Times*, 10 September 1892.
[219] Burgess, 1911, p. 151.
[220] *Derby Daily Telegraph*, 13 February 1893.
[221] *Workman's Times*, 26 March 1893.
[222] *Workman's Times*, 1 April 1893.
[223] Lowe, 1919, pp. 150, 152.
[224] *Champion*, 6 June 1896.
[225] *Brisbane Courier*, 31 October 1893.
[226] *Labour Leader*, October 1893.
[227] *Edinburgh Evening News*, 29 September 1893.
[228] Burgess, 1911, p. 161.
[229] *Aberdeen Standard*, 6 December 1893.
[230] *Manchester Guardian*, 2 February 1894.
[231] *Champion*, 9 January 1897.
[232] *Age*, 21 November 1896.
[233] *Clarion*, 3 January 1907.
[234] *Labor Call*, 22 November 1906. *Socialist*, 23 March 1907.
[235] *Times*, 8 January 1894.
[236] *Socialist*, 16 June 1911.
[237] *Socialist*, 14 November 1913. Gould, 1928, p. 280.

One of the People: Juliet Bennett

[238] Ellis, 1919, pp. 292–94.
[239] *London Gazette*, 6 January 1882.
[240] Black, 1894, pp. 155, 128–29.
[241] Kelvin, 1984, pp. 41, 63–64. Mackail, 1968, pp. 175–76, ii, p. 87.
[242] *Champion*, 26 October 1895.
[243] *Times*, 17 November 1886.
[244] *Table Talk*, 17 January 1896. *Trident*, April 1909.
[245] *Justice*, 31 October, 26 December 1885.
[246] *Letter* dated 11 October 1883, quoted in Barnes, p. 39.
[247] Black, 1894, pp. 14, 105.
[248] *Southern Cross*, 23 March 1900. *West Australian*, 15 August 1903.
[249] *Pall Mall Gazette*, 25 April 1892. Reprinted *Geelong Advertiser*, 3 June 1892.
[250] Laurence, 1965, pp. 801–03.
[251] *Champion*, 4 January 1896.
[252] Weintraub, 1986, p. 166.
[253] *Socialist*, 2 September 1909. Champion called himself a 'man of education'.
[254] *Argus*, 25 September 1900.
[255] Weintraub, 1986, p. 174. *Book Lover*, September 1915.
[256] *Champion*, 10 October 1896.

257 *Champion* 19 October 1895.
258 Dent, 1952, p. 28.
259 *Socialist*, 23 August 1912.
260 Henderson, 1973, pp. 160–65.
261 *Book Lover*, March 1900.
262 Albert, 1968, p. 139.
263 *The Woman's Signal*, 5 April 1894. *Champion*, 2 January 1897.
264 *Age*, 12 October 1940.

Salvation and Socialism: Margaret Elise Harkness

265 *Coolgardie Miner*, 24 February 1897. *Quiz and Lantern*, 4 May 1899.
266 *Pall Mall Gazette*, 29 March 1889.
267 All quotes are from Beatrice's digitised diaries, London School of Economics, unless referenced in the text.
268 MacKenzie, 1982, p. 139.
269 *Pall Mall Gazette*, 26 July 1892.
270 Bellamy and Kaspar, 1987, p. 103.
271 Nord, 1990, p. 738.
272 *Macmillan's Magazine*, May 1888, p. 374.
273 Bellamy and Kaspar, 1987, p. 104.
274 *Western Mail*, 30 July 1897, p. 43.
275 *Champion*, 27 March 1897.
276 *Nineteenth Century*, September 1881, pp. 369, 381.
277 *Woman's Journal* (Boston), 10 February 1883.
278 Passfield Collection quoted in Bellamy and Kaspar, 1987, p. 105.
279 *Southern Argus*, 9 March 1882, p. 4.
280 Republished in *Herald*, 1 February 1881.
281 *Champion*, 3 October 1896.
282 Rive, 1988, pp. 41–42.
283 Draznin, 1992, p. 104.
284 Ellis, 1935, p. 184.
285 Draznin, 1992, pp. 199, 373.
286 Kapp, 1976, p. 261.
287 Pearson, 1944, p. 123. Weintraub, 1986, p. 400.
288 *Reynold's Newspaper*, 10 April 1898. *Justice*, 30 July 1898.
289 *Table Talk*, 1 July 1898.
290 *Pictorial Australian*, 1 September 1889.
291 Maggie probably accompanied members of the British Museum to Berlin whose museum had an extensive collection of Egyptian artifacts.
292 Rive, 1988, p. 84. Draznin, 1992, p. 419. *Book Lover*, September 1915.
293 Beith, 1931, pp. 20–21.
294 Cronwright-Schreiner, 1924, pp. 101, 111.
295 *Evening News and Post* (London), 17 May 1890. *Queen*, 1 May 1890.
296 *Star*, 25 September 1889.
297 Bellamy and Kaspar, 1987, p. 106.
298 *Aberdeen Journal*, 17 June 1891.
299 *Socialist*, 6 July 1907.
300 *Trident*, August 1908.
301 *Pall Mall Gazette*, 18 February 1891. Reprinted in Australia, see *Southern Argus*, 22 October 1891.
302 *Herald* (Adelaide), 4 March 1899.
303 *Champion*, 9 November 1895. *Book Lover*, May 1899.
304 *Evening News and Post*, 17 April 1890.
305 *Justice*, 20 April 1889. *Captain Lobe* was subsequently republished as *In Darkest London* (1891) to echo General Booth's title.
306 *Justice*, 24 March 1888.
307 *Nineteenth Century*, July 1888.
308 *Champion*, 7 December 1895.
309 *Justice*, March 1888.
310 Weintraub, 1986, p. 469.
311 Weintraub, 1986, p. 482
312 *Justice*, 20 April 1889.
313 *Herald* (Adelaide), 20 May 1899.
314 *Pall Mall Gazette*, 18 January 1892. In his late twenties, Champion had

lengthy discussions 'full of the wisest advice to a young man from a sage 50 years his senior', *Bulletin*, 14 July 1921.
315 MacKenzie, 1978, p. 68. Passfield Collection quoted in Bellamy and Kaspar, 1987, p. 110. Barnes, 2005, p. 116.
316 *Pictorial Australian*, 1 September 1889. *Daily News* (London), 1 September. *British Weekly*, 6 September, 13 September 1889.
317 *Labour Elector*, 31 August 1889.
318 *Pall Mall Gazette*, 29 October 1809, 18 January 1892. Reprinted *People* (Perth), 27 February 1892.
319 *Bulletin*, 14 July 1921. The manifesto is printed in Tsuzuki, 1961, p. 67.
320 *Labour Elector*, 21 September 1889.
321 *Star*, 20 September 1889.
322 *Blackburn Standard*, 12 July 1890.
323 *West Australian*, 15 August 1903.
324 *Southern Cross* (Adelaide), 29 June 1900. Later an orphanage, a home for 'invalid ladies' and a school for girls working in factories was established there. Catherine's eldest brother, Eyre Stuart Bathurst was a priest, the youngest, Algernon, was a Hammersmith barrister.
325 *New Review*, February 1893.
326 *New Review*, October 1891.
327 *Labour Elector*, 15 March 1890.
328 Diack, 1939, p. 23. *Aberdeen Journal*, 17 June 1891. *New Review*, June 1890, October 1891.
329 *A Hand-book for Travellers on the Continent* (1838) provided essential advice about steamer passages from London to European ports like Rotterdam, Antwerp and Hamburg and information on Holland, Belgium and Germany.
330 *Pall Mall Gazette*, 23 June, 28 August, 9 September, 18 September 1890.
331 Webb, 1979, pp. 281, 407.
332 *Pall Mall Gazette*, 21 October 1890.
333 *Pall Mall* Gazette, 29 October 1890. Quoted in Bellamy and Kaspar, 1987, p. 108.
334 Lonsdale, 1884, pp. 409, 415.
335 Quoted in Tsuzuki, 1991, p. 83.
336 MacKenzie, 1978, pp. 256–58. Correspondence between Beatrice and Sidney Webb confirmed this tale.
337 *Pall Mall Gazette*, 7 February 1891. Reprinted in Australia see *Geelong Advertiser*, 20 March 1891.
338 *Pall Mall Gazette*, 7 February 1891.
339 Nearly 30 years later he admitted having 'tried' Mann frequently, *Bulletin*, 22 January 1920.
340 *Aberdeen Journal*, 17 June 1891.
341 *Windsor and Richmond Gazette*, 24 March 1894.
342 *Champion*, 1 February 1896.
343 *Pall Mall Gazette*, 1 September 1891.
344 *Argus*, 30 December 1893.
345 *Daily Telegraph* (Sydney), 15 October 1891.
346 *Age*, 29 November 1890.
347 *New Review*, October 1891.
348 *Women's Herald*, 5 December 1891 to 27 February 1892.
349 *Argus*, 20 February 1892.
350 MacKenzie, 1978, p. 430.
351 *Pall Mall Gazette*, 26 July 1892.
352 After meeting Beatrice again in London when an advisor to the Imperial Economic Conference in 1923 she invited Brookes to her flat and he found her 'actually rude in voicing her views', deciding 'she was an intellect and devoid of the average quota of feelings and emotions'.
353 *Pall Mall Gazette*, 31 May, 25 April 1892.
354 *Trident*, October 1908.
355 *New York Times*, 4 November 1894.
356 *Champion*, 2 January 1897.

357 *Woman's Signal*, 31 January 1895.
358 *Illustrated London News*, 9 February 1895.
359 *West Australian*, 15 August 1903.
360 *Australasian*, 14 April 1894.
361 *Coolgardie Miner*, 26 May 1899.
362 *Cosmos*, 29 June 1895.
363 *Western Mail* (Perth), 30 July 1897.
364 *Sydney Mail*, 25 January 1896.
365 *People's Press*, 5 June 1890.
366 *Fortnightly Review*, November 1889. *Book Lover*, December 1899.
367 *Champion*, 11 January 1896. *Coolgardie Miner*, 21 May 1896.
368 *Coolgardie Mining Review*, 29 August 1896. *Coolgardie Miner*, 2 January 1897.
369 *Western Mail* (Perth), 24 September 1897.
370 *Goldfields Morning Chronicle*, 1 June 1897.
371 *Kalgoorlie Western Argus*, 7 January 1897. *Melbourne Punch*, 14 October 1897.
372 *Champion*, 13 March 1897.
373 *West Australian*, 11 December 1901.
374 *Western Mail* (Perth), 13 August, 17 September 1897.
375 *Sunday Times* (Perth), 26 February, 4 June 1905.
376 *Champion*, 21 November 1896. *Western Mail* (Perth), 30 July 1897.
377 *Champion*, 30 January 1897. *Goldfields Morning Chronicle*, 11 January 1898.
378 *Champion*, 7 November 1896. *Guardian*, 2 October 1900. *Weekly Times*, 12 December 1896.
379 *Bunyip* (Adelaide), 28 April 1899.
380 *Southern Cross*, 9 March 1900.
381 Such as *West Australian*, 15 August 1903, 2 January 1904.
382 *Herald* (Adelaide), 9 March, 23 March, 20 April 1900.
383 *Daily News* (London), 17 April, 10 May 1900.
384 *West Australian*, 14 March 1905.
385 *West Australian*, 16 February 1907.
386 Bellamy and Kaspar, 1987, p. 113.
387 *Times Literary Supplement*, 1 September 1921.

Love in a Warm Climate: Adelaide Hogg

388 *Queensland Times*, 18 September 1890.
389 *Ovens and Murray Advertiser*, 27 August 1887.
390 *Age*, 7 April 1888. *South Australian Register*, 18 August 1888. *Times*, 3 November 1891, 2 June 1894. *Aberdeen Daily Journal*, 12 October, 7 November 1902.
391 *Australian Workman* (Sydney), 29 November 1890.
392 *Clarion*, 17 April 1906.
393 *Adelaide Observer*, 22 May 1880.
394 *Sydney Morning Herald*, 30 December 1921.
395 Kinnell, 2008, p. 82.
396 *Melbourne Punch*, 6 March 1890.
397 *Age*, 18 April 1896.
398 *Champion*, 10 April 1897.
399 *News* (Adelaide), 22 August 1928.
400 *Book Lover*, September 1900.
401 *Geelong Advertiser*, 18 October 1890.
402 *Labour Elector*, December 1893.
403 *Champion*, 5 September 1895. He was related to Gordons of Esslemont estate near Turriff.
404 *Leader* (Melbourne), 7 February 1891. *Aberdeen Standard*, 16 November 1893. *Labour Elector*, December 1893.
405 His intention was reported in *Daily Telegraph* (Sydney), 13 September 1890. *Pall Mall Gazette*, 24 April 1891.
406 *Book Lover*, 6 March 1908.
407 *Book Lover*, May 1899, May 1911, May 1916. *Socialist*, 23 February 1907.

408 *Champion*, 20 March 1897. *Trident*, November 1908.
409 *Freedom*, March 1890, p. 9.
410 *Chelmsford Chronicle*, 27 July 1894.
411 *Champion*, 4 April 1896.
412 *Pall Mall Gazette*, 7 January 1892.
413 Pearson, 1946, p. 90.
414 *Champion*, 13 February 1897.
415 *Trident*, October 1908. *Book Lover*, June 1909, February 1913.
416 *Champion*, 13 February 1897. *Book Lover*, July 1899.
417 *Book Lover*, December 1914.
418 *Book Lover*, February 1913.
419 *Champion*, 20 June 1896.
420 *Trident*, October 1908.
421 *Book Lover*, April 1903.
422 *Book Lover*, July 1900.
423 *Champion*, 24 April 1897. Alice's sister Emily and her husband Rodney Fennessy were also introduced to Gissing while hosting a Shakespeare reading on 24 October 1889, Coustillas, 2012, p. 195.
424 See also interview in *Daily Herald* (Adelaide), 19 December 1916.
425 *Socialist*, 22 August 1913.
426 Bax, 1918, pp. 101–02.
427 *Champion*, 23 January 1897.
428 *Daily Telegraph* (Adelaide), 8 July 1893.Champion would have charmed Adelaide's mother with his Scottish connections. Campden House was associated with Champion's ancestor Queen Anne (Hyde) married to Charles I.
429 Jameson, 1961, pp. 20–23.
430 *Book Lover*, February 1913. His letter to Morley on 12 December 1899 talks of their 'memorable evening at Gravesend'.
431 *Champion*, 12 September 1896.
432 After Stevenson's death Morley wrote a poignant article for the *Saturday Review* (January 1895), identified as Morley in *To-Day* a month later.
433 *Champion*, 2 November 1895.
434 *Book Lover*, July, August 1899.
435 *Labour Elector*, December 1893.
436 *Age*, 5 September 1894.
437 *Bulletin*, 22 September 1894.
438 *Champion*, 5 September 1896, 15 May 1897.
439 *Melbourne Punch*, 22 November 1894.
440 *Champion*, 3 August 1895, 26 September 1896. Blainey 1957, p. 97.
441 *Champion*, 23 November 1895.
442 *Melbourne Punch*, 13 June 1895.
443 *Gladfly*, 29 April 1908.
444 *Book Lover*, April 1914. *Truth*, 24 April 1914. *Bulletin*, 17 November 1904.
445 Quoted in *Champion*, 17 August 1895.
446 *Book Lover*, July 1900.
447 *Age*, 8 February 1896. *Table Talk*, 14 February 1896.
448 *Champion*, 15 February, 4 April 1896,
449 *Champion*, 7 March 1896.
450 *Champion*, 3 August 1895, 29 February 1896. *Bulletin*, 21 January 1899.
451 *Champion*, 10 October 1896.
452 *Melbourne Punch*, 13 June 1895.
453 *Champion*, 3 August 1895. Champion was highly critical about Davitt's abandonment of Parnell 'in his hour of need' and leading the men who 'hounded him to his death'.
454 *Melbourne Punch*, 25 September 1913.
455 *Age*, 30 July 1895.
456 *Toscin*, 19 June 1902. Sarah Muir had been vice president of the Tailoresses Union, *Prahran Telegraph*, 26 October 1895.
457 *Daily Telegraph*, 14 April 1896.
458 *Free Lance*, 30 April 1896.
459 *Prahran Chronicle*, 4 May 1895.

460 In Act 2 Scene 7 Shakespeare uses 'All the world's a stage' to separate life into seven acts; in man's fourth act, he is a soldier 'seeking the bubble reputation'.
461 *Free Lance*, 21 May 1896.
462 *Champion*, 17 September 1895.
463 *Champion*, 17 August 1895.
464 *Table Talk*, 16 April 1897. *Champion* 17 April 1897.
465 *Argus*, 24 June 1901.
466 *Toscin*, 4 November 1897.
467 *Outpost*, October 1900, March 1901.
468 *Ballarat Star*, 21 September 1897. *Socialist*, 13 November 1908. *Worker*, 21 August 1913.
469 *Melbourne Punch*, 18 November 1897. *Age*, 21 September 1898.
470 *Age*, 14 July 1900.
471 Census 1901. The school's proprietors were daughters of Robert Baldwin Hayward, mathematician, fellow of St John's College, Cambridge and also of the Royal Society; he died in 1903 at Shanklin, Isle of Wight.
472 Aberdeen *Daily Journal*, 13 October 1908. *Common Cause*, 29 June 1911.

A Mild Affection: Elsie Belle Goldstein

473 *Age*, 5 September 1896.
474 Henderson, 1973, pp. 169, 173. She was the daughter of Lina Goldstein who married Charles.
475 *Trident*, November 1908.
476 *Melbourne Punch*, 16 June 1898.
477 *Toscin*, 4 August 1898.
478 Evelyn's daughter, Doris Gough, became a Christian Scientist and married fellow potter (William) Merric Boyd, brother of novelist Martin Boyd. The latter was published by Champion through his agency.
479 *Age*, 10 August 1889.
480 *Leader*, 23 December 1893. *Herald*, 30 April 1891.
481 *Champion*, 13 March 1897.
482 Serle, 1982, pp. 50–51, 70–72.
483 Serle, 1982, pp. 71–3.
484 *Argus*, 28 October 1937.
485 Quoted in Bomford, 1993, p. 26.
486 *Australian Star*, 16 July 1903.
487 *Argus*, 17 March 1910. *Bunyip*, 17 July 1932.
488 *Sun* (Kalgoorlie), 26 February 1911. See also *Woman Voter*, 2 December 1913.
489 *West Gippsland Gazette*, 9 February 1904.
490 *Mount Alexander Mail*, 25 December 1903.
491 *Cosmos*, 31 May 1895. *Champion*, 6 July 1895.
492 *Champion*, 23 May 1896, 23 January 1897.
493 *Arena*, 13 September 1900.
494 *Illustrated Tasmanian Mail*, February 1929.
495 *Book Lover*, October 1900.
496 *Champion*, 26 December 1896. Coates married Dora Meeson, who designed and carried the flag for London's suffragette march in 1911.
497 *Argus*, 6 August 1932.
498 *Bulletin*, 17 June 1899.
499 *Table Talk*, 30 August 1900.
500 *Age*, 1 September 1900.
501 *Toscin*, 18 October 1900.
502 *Age*, 1 November 1900.
503 *Record*, 16 March 1901.
504 *Table Talk*, 9 January 1902. *Arena*, 21 August 1902. *Bulletin*, 11 October 1902.
505 *Toscin*, 20 November and 18 December 1902.
506 Gould, 1928, p. 279.
507 *Book Lover*, January 1902.

508 *Book Lover*, November 1901.
509 Roe, 2010, p. 95.
510 One of the 'Heroes of Omdurman' in the Sudan in 1898, Arthur Champion married a Sydney girl, Ethel Mary Manning, on 3 June 1905 at the Anglican Holy Trinity Church on Marylebone Road. St John Methuen (his sister's husband) was minister, and a cousin, Major John Hill of 15th Sikhs was best man.
511 *Age*, 11 January 1904.
512 *Table Talk*, 4 August 1904.
513 *Herald*, 25 June 1921.
514 Richards, 1960, pp. 132–33.
515 *Champion*, 14 March 1896.
516 Albinski, 1977, p. 37.
517 Vance and Nettie Palmer's papers show the *Book Lover* operating from Bank Place with the Agency.
518 *Clarion*, 11 October 1907. *Socialist* 16 March 1907.
519 *Socialist*, 14 July 1906.
520 *Clarion*, 21 December 1906.
521 *Socialist*, 22 June 1907 provides a list of delegates.
522 *People*, 29 June 1907.
523 *Socialist*, 18 December 1908.
524 *Socialist*, 27 August 1915.
525 *Woman Voter*, 6 October 1911.
526 *Bendigo Independent*, 10 October 1911. See *Studies in the Psychology of Sex* (third volume). Guido Baracchi bought Havelock's volumes in 1919 (held by National Library of Australia).
527 *Graphic of Australia*, 28 July 1916.
528 Lindsay, 1967, p. 153.
529 Quoted in *Mail*, 13 January 1917.
530 Palmer, 1941, p. 191.
531 *Herald*, 30 June 1917.
532 *Book Lover*, February 1918. Duff's war medals etc went to auction at Sotherby's in July 2006.
533 *Book Lover*, July 1917.
534 *Argus*, 16 August 1918. Henderson, 1973, p. 156. *Herald*, 17 August 1922.
535 Albinski, 1977, p. 37.
536 Quoted in *Age*, 12 October 1940.
537 *Socialist*, 18 June 1920.
538 Miles Franklin papers, MSS364/15.
539 *Australian Worker*, 21 September 1927.
540 *Age*, 15 March 1947.
541 *Herald*, 1 February 1933.

A Guilty Secret:
Katharine Susannah Prichard

542 *Clipper* (Hobart), 12 January 1895.
543 *Herald*, 7 June 1909.
544 Spectator Publishing Company's postal address was 270 Post Office Place, Melbourne, the same box of the Land Insurance and General Agents of E. De Garis for Mildura Investors, as well as the *Champion*, the *Sun: the Society Courier* and the *Book Lover*.
545 At age 19 Edith was a governess. Lancaster Bridges lived in Newbridge near the Lodden River near Bendigo and his son Patton S. Bridge married Katharine's sister Bee.
546 *Argus*, 5 February 1946. *Southerly*, 1968, p. 237.
547 Nettie's translation of Heinrich Heine's poem 'Summer Song' appeared in the *Trident* in January 1909 was followed in April with translations of Catullus and a poem in the *Socialist* in September 1909. She later contributed articles to the *Socialist* between 1912–1920.
548 *Biblionews*, May 1959.
549 *Champion*, 9 January 1897, 13 July 1895.
550 *Socialist*, 26 October 1907.
551 *Socialist*, 13 July 1907.
552 *Sydney Morning Herald*, 29 June 1929. Luffman worked in London

in the 1880s with Clementina Black collecting evidence for the House of Lords Commission on sweating practices in the East End; on the Executive Committee of the National Anti-Sweating League, Black thanked 'my two old friends', Luffman and Champion for their Australian input.
553 Prichard, 1946.
554 *Bulletin*, 17 January 1907.
555 *Sydney Morning Herald*, 14 January 1890.
556 *Book Lover*, March 1901.
557 Throssell, 1975, p. 228. *Argus*, 6 July 1914.
558 *Champion*, 3 October 1896.
559 Prichard Papers, MS6201/13/1. The pamphlet is tucked into a scrapbook.
560 *Meanjin*, 1953, p. 419.
561 Macartney, 1955, p. 19.
562 Letter to Guido Baracchi, 2 January 1969, Baracchi Papers, MS5241/2. 'Lumeah' was a popular boarding house in large grounds with waterfalls, mineral springs and natural fern gullies overlooking Port Phillip Bay. A coach service picked up Melbourne guests from the railway station.
563 *Melbourne Punch*, 4 July 1895.
564 *Argus*, 5 August 1898.
565 Prichard Papers, MS6201/2/1.
566 *Brighton Southern Cross*, 29 June 1907.
567 *Herald*, 16 May 1908.
568 *Weekly Times*, 29 August 1908.
569 *Herald*, 10 October, 26 September 1908. Bertha was also a member of the United Council for Women's Suffrage in 1901.
570 *Socialist*, 10 July 1908.
571 *Socialist*, 16 October 1908.
572 Throssell, 1975, p. 228.
573 *Argus*, 6 March 1909.
574 *Herald*, 17 August 1909.
575 *Bendigo Independent* and *Daily Telegraph*, 27 February 1908. Percy was appointed British Vice-Consul for Umbria and received an MBE in 1923.
576 Miles Franklin Papers, MSS364/15.
577 *Daily News* (Perth), 31 May 1930.
578 *Melbourne Punch*, 11 October 1900.
579 *Herald*, 26 October 1908.
580 *New Idea*, 6 May 1909. *Saturday Review*, 12 March 1870.
581 *Herald*, 7 June 1909. *New Idea*, 6 September 1909.
582 *Daily Telegraph*, 29 September 1900. *Book Lover*, November 1900.
583 *Southerly*, 1968, p. 240.
584 *Herald*, 21 June 1910. *Woman Voter*, 18 November 1915.
585 Fawcett, 1920, p. 166.
586 *Herald*, 10 August 1909, 18 April 1910.
587 *Herald*, 25 July 1911.
588 *Daily Herald* (London), 17 April 1912.
589 *Freewoman*, May 1912.
590 *Herald*, 20 November 1917.
591 *Daily News* (Perth), 6 March 1926.
592 *Worker*, 6 May 1911, reprinted from *Book Lover*.
593 *Socialist*, 5 January 1912.
594 *Herald*, 8 April 1912.
595 *Worker*, 23 May 1912. *Socialist*, 7 June 1912.
596 *Telegraph* (Brisbane), 15 June 1912.
597 *Daily Telegraph* (Sydney), 31 August 1912.
598 Just two years after his step-daughter Vere's death, their ashes were buried together at Swath Fell in the Lake District and the following year Morley published his memories of George Gissing, dedicated to Alice.
599 *Daily News* (London), 14 May 1912. *Daily Telegraph* (Sydney), 31 August 1912.
600 *Daily Herald* (London), 15 May 1912.

601 *Australasian*, 25 March 1916.
602 Neacey, 2012, p. 26.
603 *Daily Herald* (Adelaide), 19 December 1916.
604 *Weekly Times*, 31 January 1914. Frederick Prichard claimed he informed Katharine about Launceston's Christmas scheme and explains her neglect of him in her autobiography. *Examiner* (Launceston), 20 February 1914.
605 *Daily Herald* (Adelaide), 17 July 1915.
606 *Herald*, 12 January 1915. *Weekly Herald*, 17 October 1908.
607 *British Australasian*, 29 April 1915.
608 *Derby Daily Telegraph*, 1 June 1915. Olwen Lloyd George was also stationed there.
609 Letter, 30 March 1915, Palmer Papers, MS1174/1/1425.
610 Also recollected from her stopover in Bombay (Mumbai) in 1909. *Book Lover*, January 1910.
611 Letter, Betty Roland, 27 October 1984.
612 Her sister, mother and fifty journalists/writers attended. Hilda and Louis Esson were in Mallacoota; Vance and Nettie Palmer were in Emerald with their new baby.
613 Prichard Papers, MS6201/2/2. Quotes: 22 February–14 March are from *Notebook: Australia I*.
614 *Fiery Cross*, 25 June 1892.
615 *Age*, 6 December 1890.
616 Parnell and Dilke 'both upset their political apple-carts with a breath of scandal', *Champion*, 17 October 1896. Dilke's notorious divorce case effectively finished his political career, *Book Lover*, February 1911.
617 Brady was away in the city after finishing his commission, *Australia Unlimited*; the Essons had taken a cottage there from January till October 1916.
618 *Australian Worker*, 31 August 1916.
619 *Mail* (Adelaide), 13 January 1917.
620 *Woman Voter*, 10 June 1912, 28 October 1915.
621 *Sunday Times* (Sydney), 15 October, 1916.
622 *Melbourne Punch*, 7 December 1916.
623 *Mail* (Adelaide), 13 January 1917.
624 *Age*, 10 July 1918.
625 *Socialist*, 9 March 1917.
626 Throssell, 1975, pp. 21–22. Throssell, 1989, p. 62.
627 Palmer, 1948, p. 481.
628 Palmer Papers, MS1174/1/1641-2.
629 Betty Roland, letter to Sandra Burchill, 27 October 1984.
630 *Bulletin*, 16 August 1917.
631 Palmer Papers, MS1174/16/3.
632 *Tribune*, 11 April 1956.
633 Throssell, 1975, p. 164.
634 *Herald*, 28 September 1920.
635 *News* (Adelaide), 10 February 1926. *Daily News* (Perth), 2 March 1926.
636 *Bulletin*, 31 March 1927. *Bulletin*, 10 December 1927.
637 Dressed in black mourning after her father's death in 1907, Katharine visited him to submit a story, 'A Modern Pygmalion', to his *Native Companion*. This journal featured a cover by Ruby Lindsay, her three coloured illustration showing dancing native companions under a full moon, an image used later in her stories.
638 Franklin Papers, MSS364/15.
639 *Champion*, 28 September 1895.
640 *Champion*, 30 January 1897.
641 *Australian Woman's Mirror*, 25 September 1928.
642 *Daily Telegraph* (Sydney), 17 June 1905.

643 The novel was commenced in May 1960 after news she was to receive the Joliot medal.
644 Throssell, 1975, p. 215.
645 Prichard Papers, MS6201/10/17.
646 *Southerly*, 1968, p. 243. Prichard Papers, MS6201/13.
647 Throssell 1975, p. 187. Throssell 1984, p. 12.

A Remembrance

648 *Socialist*, 10 July 1908.
649 *Champion*, 20 July 1895.
650 Roberts, 1924, p. 71.
651 *Worker*, 10 February 1906.

Acknowledgements

Original editions of books and journals are from collections in the National Library of Australia and UNSW (Canberra and Sydney) unless otherwise acknowledged. Manuscript material is from the Special Collections of the National Library of Australia, UNSW Canberra and the State Library of New South Wales (Mitchell Library). References to Australian newspaper articles are sourced through National Library of Australia's Trove, www.trove.nla.gov.au and include *Pall Mall Gazette* and *Nineteenth Century* articles that were widely reproduced through Australia in local newspapers. *Book Lover* microfilm is held in the State Library of Victoria and Trove digitized reproduction.

I wish to thank The Society of Authors, as agents of the Bernard Shaw Estate for permission to quote from Bernard Shaw's letters and writings; British Library of Political and Economic Science, London School of Economics for permission to quote from digitised diary entries of Beatrice Potter [Webb]; the National Library of Australia for permission to quote from material held within collections; the UNSW Canberra Academy Library; the British Library Historical Collection; Dr John H. Pollack, Curator, and Eric Dillalogue, Assistant Director of Operations, Research Services in Kislak Center for Special Collections, Rare Book and Manuscripts, Pennsylvania State University for their generous assistance with the Morley Roberts collection. Also for the kind permission given by Meredith F. Creightmore, Karen Throssell, and Francis Clarke. Thank you also to The Salvation Army International Heritage Centre. Professors Nicole Moore and Peter Stanley UNSW Canberra for their advice when the book was first conceived. Finally, to Michael and Matthew for their enthusiasm and interest throughout the project.

A special thanks to Marcus Fielding, Managing Director at Echo Books, Duncan Strachan, Editorial Director at Echo Books, and Katia Ariel, Editor.

Bibliography

Manuscript Collections:

Papers of Hugh Anderson, National Library of Australia, MS6946/15.

Papers of Herbert and Ivy Brookes, National Library of Australia, MS1924/7.

Papers of Miles Franklin, Mitchell Library, MSS364/15.

Papers of Nettie and Vance Palmer, National Library of Australia, MS1174/1; 1174/16.

Papers of Katharine Susannah Prichard, National Library of Australia, MS6201 Series 2, 10, 11, 13 and 18.

Prichard, Katharine Susannah, 'Statement at the Marx School' (12 October 1946), Mitchell Library, A2763.

Morley Roberts Papers, Kislak Center for Special Collections, Rare Books and Manuscripts, Pennsylvania State University, MS726/1/18–19.

Beatrice Webb [Potter] Transcript of Diary 1 January 1889–7 March 1898, London School of Economics Digital Library, <digital.library.lse.ac.uk/objects/ > [accessed 18 May 2016].

Letter, Betty Roland to Sandra Burchill, 27 October 1984 [in possession of the author].

Books:

Albinski, Nan Bowman, *Australian Literary Manuscripts in North American Libraries: A Guide, Australian Scholarly Editions Centre*, University College, UNSW ADFA, 1997.

Barnes, John, *Socialist Champion: Portrait of the Gentleman as Crusader*, Australian Scholarly Publishing, Melbourne, 2005.

Bax, Ernest Belfort, *Reminiscences and Reflexions of a Mid and Late Victorian*, George Allen & Unwin, London, 1918.

Beith, Gilbert (ed.), *Edward Carpenter: In Appreciation*, Routledge, London, 1931.

Benkovitz, Miriam J., *Frederick Rolfe: Baron Corvo*, Putnam, New York, 1977.

Black, Clementina, *An Agitator*, Bliss, Sands and Foster, London, 1894, The British Library Historical Collection (digitized May 2018).

Blainey, Geoffrey, *Centenary History of the University of Melbourne*, Melbourne University Press, Carlton, 1957.

Blatchford, Robert, *My Eighty Years*, Cassell, London, 1931.

Bomford, Janette M., *That Dangerous and Persuasive Woman: Vida Goldstein*, Melbourne University Press, Melbourne, 1993.

Brieux, Eugene, *Damaged Goods*, (trans. John Pollock, preface Bernard Shaw, foreword Mrs Bernard Shaw), Cole's Book Arcade, Melbourne, 1914.

Buchanan, Alfred, *Bubble Reputation: A Story of Modern Life*, 2nd impression, George Robertson & Co, Melbourne, 1906.

Burgess, Joseph, *John Burns: The Rise and Progress of a Right Honourable*, The Reformers Bookstall, Glasgow, 1911.

Burke, Bernard (revised by A.C. Fox-Davies), *A Genealogical and Heraldic History of the Landed Gentry of Ireland*, Harrison & Sons, London, 1912.

Burke, John, *A Genealogical and Heraldic Dictionary of the Landed Gentry of Great Britain & Ireland*, Volume II, Henry Colburn, London, 1846.

Callwell, C. E., *Stray Recollections*, Edward Arnold, London, 1923.

Champion, Henry Hyde, (by 'One of the Middle Class' H.H.C.), *The Facts about the Unemployed: a Warning and an Appeal*, Modern Press, London, 1886.

----, *The Great Dock Strike in London, August, 1889*, E. A. Petherick & Co., Melbourne, 1890.

----, *The Root of the Matter: Being a Series of Dialogues on Social Questions*, E.W. Cole, Melbourne, 1895.

----, [trans. under pseudonym Leslie Orde], Murger, Henri, *Bohemian Life (Scènes de la Vie de Bohème)*, Edmund Downey, London, 1895.

----, [preface] Rosa, S. A., *The truth about the Unemployed Agitation of 1890*, Melbourne: Author, 1890.

Clarke, Patricia, *Pen Portraits: Women Writers and Journalist in Nineteenth Century Australia*, Allen & Unwin, Sydney, 1988.

Clayton, Joseph, *The Rise and Decline of Socialism in Great Britain 1884–1924*, Faber and Gwyer, London, 1926.

Coulthard-Clark, Chris, *Where Australians Fought: the Encyclopaedia of Australia's Battles*, St. Allen & Unwin, Sydney, 1998.

Coustillas, Pierre, *The Heroic Life of George Gissing, Part II: 1888–1897*, Pickering & Chatto, London, 2012.

Croll, Robert Henderson, *I Recall: Collections and Recollections*, Roberson & Mullens, Melbourne, 1939.

Cronwright-Schreiner, S.C. (ed.), *The Letters of Olive Schreiner 1876–1920*, T. Fisher Unwin, London, 1924.

Davitt, Michael, *Life and Progress in Australasia*, Methuen & Co, London, 1898.

Dent, Alan (ed.), *Bernard Shaw and Mrs Patrick Campbell: Their Correspondence*, Alfred Knopf, New York, 1952.

Diack, William, *History of the Trades Council and the Trade Union Movement in Aberdeen*, Aberdeen Trades Council, Aberdeen, 1939.

Draznin, Yaffa Claire (ed.), *My Other Self: The Letters of Olive Schreiner and Havelock Ellis 1884–1920*, Peter Lang, New York, 1992.

Ellis, Havelock, *My Life*, Neville Spearman, London, 1967.

Ellis, Havelock, *Studies in the Psychology of Sex*, Volume 2 (3rd ed.) and Volume 3 (2nd ed.), F. A. Davis, Philadelphia, 1919. [National Library copies are stamped as belonging to Guido Baracchi].

Esson, Louis, *The Southern Cross and Other Plays*, Robertson and Mullens, Melbourne, 1946.

Fawcett, Millicent Garrett, *The Women's Victory—and After: Personal Reminiscences, 1911–1918*, Sidgwick & Jackson, London, 1920.

Gillies, Mary Ann, *The Professional Literary Agent in Britain, 1880–1920*, University of Toronto Press, Toronto, 2007.

Gould, Frederick J., *Hyndman: Prophet of Socialism*, George Allen & Unwin, London, 1928.

A Hand-book for Travellers on the Continent: being a guide through Holland, Belgium, Prussia, and Northern Germany, and along the Rhine, from Holland to Switzerland, 2nd ed John Murray and Sons, London, 1838, www.archive.org/details/handbookfortrav00john/page/n7/mode/2up [accessed 25 May 2021.

Hardie, Keir, *The I.L.P. and all about it*, Independent Labour Party, Manchester, 1908.

Harkness, Margaret [under pseudonym John Law], *A City Girl: A Realistic Story*, Vizetelly, London, 1887.

———, *Imperial* Credit, Vardon and Pritchard, Adelaide, 1899.

———, *George Eastmont: Wanderer*, Burns & Oates, London, 1905 [microfilm State Library of Victoria].

———, *A Curate's Promise: A Story of Three Weeks, September 14–October 5, 1917* Hodder and Stoughton, London, 1921 [free access through The Salvation Army International Heritage Centre, 30 May 2018].

Henderson, Leslie M., *The Goldstein Story*, Stockland Press, Melbourne, 1973.

Holland, Merlin (sel. and ed.), *Oscar Wilde: A Life in Letters*, Fourth Estate, London, 2003.

Holroyd, Michael, *Bernard Shaw: Volume I 1856–1898 The Search for Love*, Penguin, London, 1988.

Humphrey, A. W., *A History of Labour Representation*, Constable & Co, London, 1912.

Hyndman, Henry Mayers, *Further Reminiscences*, Macmillan and Co, London, 1912.

———, *The Record of an Adventurous Life*, London: Macmillan and Co, 1911.

Jameson, Storm, *Morley Roberts: The Last Eminent Victorian*, Unicorn Press, London, 1961.

Kapp, Yvonne, *Eleanor Marx: Volume II, The Crowded Years (1884–1898)*, Lawrence and Wishart, London, 1976.

Kelvin, Norman (ed.), *The Collected Letters of William Morris Volume I 1848–1880*, Princeton University Press, Princeton, 1984.

———, *The Collected Letters of William Morris, Volume II, Part A: 1881–1884* and *Part B: 1885–1888*, Princeton University Press, Princeton, 1987.

———, *The Collected Letters of William Morris, Volume III, 1889–1892*, Princeton University Press, Princeton, 1996.

Kent, William, *John Burns: Labour's Lost Leader*, Williams & Norgat Ltd, London, 1950.

Koss, Stephen E., *Sir John Brunner: Radical Plutocrat, 1842–1919*, Cambridge University Press, Cambridge, 1970.

La Nauze, J. A., *Alfred Deakin: A Biography Volume I*, Melbourne University Press, Melbourne, 1965.

———, *Walter Murdoch: A Biographical Memoir*, Melbourne University Press, Melbourne, 1977.

Laurence, Dan H., (ed.) *Bernard Shaw: Collected Letters, 1874–1897*, (Volume 1), Max Reinhardt, London, 1965.

———, (ed.) *Bernard Shaw: Collected Letters 1898–1910*, (Volume 2), Max Reinhardt, London, 1972.

—, (ed.) *Bernard Shaw: Collected Letters 1911-1925*, (Volume 3), Max Reinhardt, London, 1985.

—, (ed.) *The Bodley Head Bernard Shaw: Collected Plays with Their Prefaces*, Bodley Head Max Reinhardt, London, 1970-74.

Lindsay, Lionel, *Comedy of Life: An Autobiography*, Angus and Robertson, Sydney, 1967.

Lowe, David, *Souvenirs of Scottish Labour*, W. & R. Holmes, Glasgow, 1919.

Mackail, J.W., *The Life of William Morris* (2 volumes), Benjamin Blom, London, 1968.

Macartney, Frederick T., *Furnley Maurice (Frank Wilmot)*, Angus & Robertson, Sydney, 1955.

MacKenzie, Norman (ed.), *The Letters of Sidney and Beatrice Webb, Volume 1 Apprenticeships 1873-1892*, Cambridge University Press, Cambridge, 1978.

MacKenzie, Norman and Jeanne, *The First Fabians*, Weidenfeld and Nicholson, London, 1977.

—, (ed.), *The Diary of Beatrice Webb Volume 1*, Harvard University Press, Cambridge, 1982.

Mann, Tom, *Tom Mann's Memoirs*, Labour Publishing Company Ltd, London, 1923.

Marx and Engels Collected Works: Volume 49, Letters 1890-92, Lawrence & Wishart and Progress Publishers, London, Moscow, 2004.

Mathews, Race, *Australia's First Fabians*, Cambridge University Press, Cambridge, 1993.

Merivale, Herman, *My Experiences in a Lunatic Asylum by a Sane Patient*, Chatto and Windus, London, 1879, <www.gutenberg.org/files/41334/41334-h/41334-h.htm> [accessed 11 December 2019].

Morgan, Emily Kathryn, *'True Types of the London Poor': Adolphe Smith and John Thomson's Street Life in London*, electronic dissertation PhD, University of Arizona, Tucson, 2012 <www.hdl.handle.net/10150/255192> [accessed 3 March 2019].

Morris, May (ed.), *William Morris: Artist, Writer, Socialist*, vol. II, Basil Blackwell, Oxford, 1936.

Morris, William, *Under an Elm-Tree; Or, Thoughts in the Country-side*, James Leatham, Aberdeen, 1891 (printed as a pamphlet from *Commonweal*, 6 July 1889, pp. 212-13).

Naylor, Gillian (ed.), *William Morris by himself: Designs and writings*, Little, Brown and Co., London, 1988.

O'Dowd, Bernard, *Dawnward?* [2nd ed.], Thomas Lothian, Melbourne, 1909.

Palmer, Nettie *Fourteen Years: Extracts from a Private Journal, 1925–1939*, Meanjin Press, Melbourne, 1948.

Palmer, Vance, *National Portraits*, Angus & Robertson, Sydney, 1941.

Pearson, Hesketh, *Bernard Shaw: His Life and Personality*, Collins, London, 1944.

———, *The Life of Oscar Wilde*, Methuen & Co Ltd, London, 1946.

Peile, John, *Biographical Register of Christ's College 1505–1905*, Volume II, Cambridge University Press, Cambridge, 1913.

Prichard, Katharine Susannah, *The Black Opal*, Heinemann, London, 1921.

———, *Child of the Hurricane*, Angus & Robertson, Sydney, 1963 (reprinted 1974).

———, *Golden Miles*, Jonathan Cape in association with Australasian Publishing Co, London, 1948.

———, *Haxby's Circus: The Lightest, Brightest, Little Show on Earth*, Jonathan Cape, London, 1930.

———, *Subtle Flame*, Australasian Book Society, Sydney, 1967.

———, *Winged Seeds*, Australasian Publishing Co in association with Jonathan Cape, Sydney, London, 1950.

———, *The Roaring Nineties*, Jonathan Cape, London, 1946.

———, *The Wild Oats of Han*, Lansdowne, Melbourne, 1968 (revised ed of original 1928).

Richard Rive (ed.), *Olive Schreiner Letters, Volume 1: 1871–1899*, Oxford University Press, Oxford, 1988.

Richards, Grant, *Author Hunting: Memories of Years Spent Mainly in Publishing*, Unicorn Press, London, 1960.

Roberts, Morley, *The Private Life of Henry Maitland*, Hodder and Stoughton, London, 1912.

———, *Selected Stories of Morley Roberts* (ed. with introduction and notes by Markus Neacy, Victorian Secrets, Brighton, 2015.

———, *W. H. Hudson: A Portrait*, Eveleigh Nash & Grayson, London, 1924.

Roe, Jill, *Stella Miles Franklin*, Fourth Estate, Pymble, 2010.

Rolfe, Frederick, *Hadrian the Seventh*, Chatto & Windus, London, 1959.

Serle, Geoffrey, *John Monash: a Biography*, Melbourne University Press, Melbourne, 1982.
Shaw, Bernard, *Cashel Byron's Profession*, Constable & Co, London, 1901, revised 1932.
———, *Pygmalion*, Penguin, Harmondsworth, 1941.
Sladen, Douglas, *Twenty Years of My Life*, E. P. Dutton and Company, New York, 1913.
Smith, H. Llewellyn and Nash, Vaughan, *The Story of the Dockers' Strike: Told by Two East Londoners*, T. Fisher Unwin, London, 1889.
Smith, Warren S. (ed.), *Bernard Shaw's Plays*, WW Norton & Co, New York, 1970.
Spence, W. G., *Australia's Awakening: thirty years in the life of an Australian agitator*, The Worker Trustees, Sydney, 1909.
Tait, Viola, *A Family of Brothers*, Heinemann, Melbourne, 1971.
The Life and Work of Miss Vida Goldstein, Australasian Authors' Agency, Melbourne, 1913.
Throssell, Ric, *My Father's son*, William Heinemann Australia, Richmond, 1989.
———, *Wild Weeds and Wind Flowers: The Life and Letters of Katharine Susannah Prichard*, Angus & Robertson, Sydney, 1975.
Tsuzuki, Chushichi, *H. M. Hyndman and British Socialism*, Oxford University Press, London, 1961 [includes the Strike Committee, Great Dock Labourers' Strike 1889: Manifesto].
———, *Tom Mann, 1856-1941: The Challenges of Labour*, Clarendon Press, Oxford, 1991.
Venn, John and J.A. (ed.), *Alumni Cantabrigienses*, Volume 2, 1752-1900, Cambridge University Press, Cambridge, 1947.
Ward, Mrs Humphry [Mary Augusta], *Marcella*, Macmillan & Co, London, 1894.
———, [under 'A Victorian Lady'], *Echoes of the 'eighties: leaves from the diary of a Victorian lady*, Eveleigh Nash Co. Ltd., London, 1921.
———, *A Writer's Recollections*, W. Collins Sons & Co, London, 1919.
Weintraub, Stanley (ed. & annotated), *Bernard Shaw: The Diaries 1885-1897 Volume I*, Pennsylvania State University Press, London, 1986.
White, Arnold, *The Problems of a Great City*, Remington & Co, London, 1886.

Wilde, W.H. et al (eds), *The Oxford Companion to Australian Literature*, Oxford University Press, Melbourne, 1985.

―――, *Courage a Grace: A Biography of Dame Mary Gilmore*, Melbourne University Press, Melbourne, 1988.

Chapters, Journals, Newspapers:

Albert, Sidney P., '"In More Ways than One": Major Barbara's Debt to Gilbert Murray', *Educational Theatre Journal*, vol. 20, no. 2, May 1968, pp. 123–40, <www.jstor.org/stable/3204896> [accessed 5 April 2016].

'Anecdotal Photograph: Mr Henry Hyde Champion', *Table Talk*, 17 January 1896, pp. 2–3.

Bellamy, Joyce and Kaspar, Beat, 'Harkness, Margaret Elise', in Bellamy, J. M. & Saville, J. *Dictionary of Labour Biography*, vol. VIII, London: Macmillan, 1987, pp. 103–13.

Burchill, Sandra, 'The Early Years of Katharine Susannah Prichard: The Growth of Her Political Conscience', *Westerly*, vol. 33, no. 2, June 1988, pp. 89–100; see also Dissertation UNSW 1989.

'Callan Park', *Sydney Mail*, 12 August 1903, pp. 409–13.

Champion, H. H., 'The Antipodean Repertory Theatre: Ibsen and Some Others', *Pall Mall Gazette*, 13 January 1912, p. 7.

―――, 'The Beginnings of Shaw', *Daily Telegraph*, 31 August 1912, p. 6.

―――, 'Bernard Shaw's Reward', *Socialist*, 23 August 1912, p. 4.

―――, 'Charles Stewart Parnell', *Age*, 6 December 1890, p. 13.

―――, 'The Claims [sic] of Women', *Prahran Chronicle*, 13 April 1895, p. 4.

―――, 'The Crushing Defeat of Trade Unionism in Australia', *Nineteenth Century*, February 1891, pp. 225–37.

―――, 'The Federation of Labour', *New Review*, vol. 2, no. 13, June 1890, pp. 524–33.

―――, 'The Future of Socialism in England', *Common Sense*, 15 September 1887, pp. 65–73; [letter], 'A Personal Matter: To the Editor of Justice', *Common Sense*, 15 October 1887, p. 69. Nineteenth Century Collections Online, tinyurl.galegroup.com/tinyurl/4XeZU2. [accessed 15 March 2017].

―――, 'Henry Edward Manning', *Bulletin*, 14 July 1921, Red page, p. 29.

―――, 'A Labour Inquiry', *Nineteenth Century*, July 1891, pp. 89–99.

―――, 'The Labor Movement in England', *Age*, 28 June 1890; 5 July 1890; 12 July 1890, p. 4.

―――, 'The Labor Movement in Europe', *Age*, 15 June; 18 July; 15 August; 12 September; 19 September; 26 September; 7 November; 14 November; 24 October; 12 December; 26 December 1891.

―――, 'The Labour Platform at the Next Election', *Nineteenth Century*, December 1891, pp. 1036–42.

―――, [Letter to the editor], 'A Lesson in Practical Politics', *Times*, 8 January 1894, p. 6.

―――, [Letter], 'Personal Items', *Bulletin*, 17 February 1921, p. 14.

―――, 'The New Labour Party', *Nineteenth Century*, July 1888, pp. 81–93.

―――, 'The Origin of the Eight Hours System at the Antipodes', *Economic Journal*, vol. 2, no. 5, March 1892, pp. 100–08.

―――, 'Protection as Labour Wants It', *Nineteenth Century*, June 1892, pp. 1027–31.

―――, [as Leslie Orde] 'A Chat with Morley Roberts', *To-Day*, 6 January 1894, p. 14.

Champion, James Hyde and Henrietta, 1895; Arthur Duncan, 1927; Annie Beatrice, 1929; <www.probatesearch.service.gov.uk/#wills>.

Coustillas, Phillip, 'People Gissing Knew: II–H. H. Champion', *The Gissing Newsletter*, vol. XI, no. 3, July 1975, pp. 12–19.

Ellis, Havelock, 'Eleanor Marx', *Modern Monthly*, [renamed *Modern Quarterly*], vol. 9, September 1935, pp. 183–190.

Fitzgerald, John D. 'Mr H.H. Champion on the Australian Strike', *Nineteenth Century*, March 1891, pp. 445–53.

Gross, Alan, 'Some Early Melbourne Booksellers', *Biblionews*, vol. 12, no. 5, May 1959, pp. 17–19.

Harkness, Margaret [under M.E.H.], 'Hospital Nurses', *Leisure Hour*, March 1884, pp. 152–54.

―――, [under Veritas] 'In Western Wilds' (letter to the editor), *Champion*, 21 November 1896, p. 8.

―――, 'Railway Servants' *Leisure Hour*, November 1883, pp. 721–24.

―――, 'Women as Civil Servants', *Nineteenth Century*, September 1881, pp. 369–81.

Harkness, Reverend Robert and Elizabeth 1887, 1916, www.probatesearch. service. gov.uk/#wills.

Howell, David, 'Burgess, Joseph (1853–1934)', in Gildart, Keith & Howell, David (eds), *Dictionary of Labour Biography*, vol. XIV, London: Palgrave Macmillan Press, 2018, pp. 56–72, <www.doi.org/10.1057/978-1-137-45743-1_1> [accessed 6 November 2018].

Kinnell, Don, 'The Langdale Settlement', *New Zealand Journal of History*, vol. 42, no. 1, 2008, pp. 80–100.

Law, John (Margaret Harkness), 'The Gospel of Getting On', *To-Day*, March 1888, pp. 83–84.

———, 'A week on a Labour Settlement', *Fortnightly Review*, new series, no. 56, August 1894, pp. 206–13.

———, [by 'One Who Knows Him'], 'Mr H. H. Champion', *Aberdeen Journal*, 17 June 1891, p. 3.

———, 'Life in an English Convent', *Southern Cross*, 29 June 1900, p. 6.

———, 'Olive Schreiner', *Novel Review*, vol. 1, no. 2, May 1892, pp. 112–15.

———, 'The Fever in Coolgardie', *Cosmos: An Illustrated Australian Magazine*, 29 June 1895, pp. 520–22.

Lonsdale, Margaret, 'Platform Women', *Nineteenth Century*, March 1884, pp. 409–15.

Marx, Eleanor, 'The Woman Question', *Westminster Review*, 9 May 1886, pp. 207–22.

MacKenzie, Norman, 'Percival Chubb and the Founding of the Fabian Society', *Victorian Studies*, vol. 23, no. 1, 1979, pp. 29–55, <www.jstor.org/stable/3827434> [accessed 21 March 2016].

Murdoch, Walter, 'An Open Letter to H. H. Champion', *Trident*, vol. 2, no. 12, April 1909, pp. 239–40.

———, 'Quorum Pars Fui: An Unconventional Autobiography', *Trident*, vol. 2, nos 1–7, May–November 1908.

———, 'Tributes to the Memory of Bernard O'Dowd', *Meanjin*, no. 4, 1953, pp. 407–08.

Neacey, Marcus, 'Morley Roberts's Literary Career in the 1880s and 1890s', *Gissing Journal*, vol. XLVIII, no. 2, April 2012, pp. 1–28, and no. 3, July 2012, pp. 23–40.

Nord, Deborah Epstein, '"Neither Pairs nor Odd": Female Community in Late Nineteenth-Century London', *Signs*, vol. 15, no. 4, 1990, pp. 733–54, <www.jstor.org/stable/3174640> [accessed 10 May 2016].

Pelling, Henry, 'Corvo and Labour Politics', *Times Literary Supplement*, 6 February 1969, p. 137.
Prichard, Katharine Susannah Prichard, 'Some Perceptions and Aspirations', *Southerly* vol. 28, no. 4, December 1968, pp. 235–244.
———, 'Tributes to the Memory of Bernard O'Dowd', *Meanjin*, no. 4, 1953, pp. 418–19.
———, 'Why I am a Communist', *Tribune*, 11 April 1956, pp. 6–7.
Reaney, Geo Sale, 'Outcast London', *Fortnightly Review*, no. 40, December 1886, pp. 687–95.
'Royal Military College', *Hampshire Advertiser*, 23 August 1876, p. 4.
'Salt, Henry S., 'James Leigh Joynes: Some Reminiscences', *Social Democrat*, no. 8, August 1897, pp. 232–38.
Shaw, G. B., 'Mr. Bernard Shaw's Works of Fiction: Reviewed by Himself', *Novel Review*, February 1892, pp. 236–42.
———, [letter to Champion, 31 January 1924], 'Melodius Memories: Pygmalion, A Letter from G.B.S.', *Age*, 12 October 1940, p. 9.
Slade, H. Gordon, 'Craigston Castle, Aberdeenshire', *Proceedings of the Society of Antiquaries of Scotland*, no. 108, 1976–7, pp. 262–99.
'A Story by Miss Clementina Black', *Illustrated London News*, 9 February 1895, p. 174.
Stronach, Alice, 'Socialist Leaders of To-Day', *Windsor Magazine*, vol. 3, January 1896, pp.613–25.
'The Glorified Spinster', *Macmillan's Magazine*, May 1888, pp. 371–76.
Throssell, Ric, 'Katharine Susannah Prichard: A Standard of Value', in John Hay and Brenda Walker eds., *Katharine Susannah Prichard Centenary Essays*, Centre for Studies in Australian Literature, Uni of WA, 1984, pp. 7–12.
———, [Introduction] in *Tribute: Selected Stories of Katharine Susannah Prichard*, St. Lucia: University of Queensland Press, 1988.
Tillett, Benjamin, 'The Dockers' Story', *English Illustrated Magazine*, November 1889, pp. 97–101.
Whitehead, Andrew, 'Champion, Henry Hyde (1859–1928)' in Bellamy, J. M. & Saville, J. (eds), *Dictionary of Labour Biography*, vol. VIII, London: Macmillan, 1987, pp. 24–32.
'Victorian Fiction Research Guides', <www.victorianfictionresearchguides.org> [accessed 30 September 2017].

Index

Page numbers in *italics* indicate illustrations.

A

Aberdeen Trades Council 77, 85, 137, 177
Allender, Leonara 303–4
Anstey, Frank G. 81, 208
Anti-Sweating League 208–9, 210, 235, 237, 277
Arnold, Matthew 149
Atkinson, Rupert 260, 261, 264
Australasian Authors' Agency
　founding of 190, 255–6
　management of 10, 264
　publications 259, 262, 266, 283
Australian Criminology Society 235
Australian Literature Society 241, 320
Australian Volunteer Hospital (Wimereux) 303–4
Australian Woman's Sphere 239, 240, 252
Aveling, Edward ('Alec Nelson')
　and Annie Besant 122
　Champion on 123
　and Eleanor Marx 121, 122–3
　in fiction 122
　and Havelock Ellis 11, 121–2
　and Independent Labour Party 90, 91, 92
　and Maggie Harkness 122
　and SDF 27, 31, 33, 34, 82, 123

B

Baillie, Mrs Gordon 56, 166, 173
Baracchi, Guido 305–6, 309, 313, 315, 316, 317–18, 331
Baracchi, Pietro 242, 244
Barbazon, William 31–2
Barlas, John Evelyn ('Evelyn Douglas')
　and Maggie Harkness 146, 182
　mental health issues 181–4, 235, 278
　police assault on 40, 182

and SDF 46
writing 147, 215–16
Barry, (Michael) Maltman
　and Adolphe Smith 44, 45
　and Independent Labour Party 85, 89, 90, 91, 92
　and James Knowles 180
　at *Labour Elector* 41, 44, 85, 89, 147
Bateman, George 41, 84
Bathurst, Mother Catherine 136–7
Bax, Ernest Belfort
　and Adolphe Smith 43, 45
　and Champion 11, 28, 54, 130
　at International Socialist Workers' Congress 187, 188
　at Modern Press 30
　and SDF 27, 31, 39, 82
　and Socialist League 33
　and Trafalgar Square Riots 56
　writing 64
Beaumont, Lord Allendale Wentworth 181
Bebel, August 11, 31, 137, 187
　Women Under Socialism 258
Bedford, Randolph 244
Beesly, Augustus Henry 17
Bennet, David 70
Bernstein, Eduard 88, 129
　'What Drove Eleanor Marx to Suicide' 123
Besant, Annie
　and Alfred Linnell 105
　and the Avelings 122
　and Beatrice Potter (Webb) 140
　and Bernard Shaw 106
　and Bryant and May factory 41
　and Charles Mowbray 147
　debating society 39
　female peers 120
　in fiction 150
　Friedrich Engels on 122
　and London Dock Strike 62–3
　public speaking 131, 139

publishing activities 96
Theosophy 152, 163, 198
Bevington, Louisa Sarah 105, 121
Black, Clementina
　An Agitator 11, 26, 38, 41, 98, 100–1, 147, 149–50
　and Champion 8, 68, 130, 149, 334–5
　on evening dress 253
　Fabian lecture 41
　female peers 120
　and Independent Labour Party 84
　and Labour Electoral Association 49–50, 72
　and Lewis Lyons 43
　and London Dock Strike 62
　and Maggie Harkness 130
　Sweated Industry and the Minimum Wage 277
　trade union involvement 65, 156
Blackburn (née Hordern), Doris 259
Blackburn, Maurice 258, 259, 298
Bland, Edith *see* Nesbit, Edith
Bland, Hubert 29, 39, 40
Blatchford, Robert 9, 35, 89, 277
bohemian life
　London 118, 185, 303
　Melbourne 176–7, 242, 243–4, 260, 261, 304
　Paris 271, 290
Book Lover
　contributions to 10, 31, 239, 252, 255, 256, 260, 261, 267, 269, 275, 282, 283, 287, 305
　demise of 264, 265, 266
　founding of 240–1
　George Gissing on 251–2
　handwritten submissions 156–7, 303
　postal address 219
　printer 200
　records of 10

INDEX 363

sporadic publication of 264, 314
style changes 249
Book Lovers' Library
  and Champion 233, 246, 264, 299
  Doris Blackburn at 259
  and Elsie Belle Champion 226, 233, 240, 242, 244, 249, 251, 253–4, 255, 259, 266–7, 268, 302, 333
  and Hugh McCrae 260
  and Katharine Susannah Prichard 275
  records of 10, 267
Booth, Charles 22, 59, 145
Booth, William 129, 139, 143, 163, 164, 334
  In Darkest England and the Way Out 138
  see also Salvation Army
Boucicault, Dion 17, 203
Boulevard Cafe (Melbourne) 259–60, 264
Boyd, Martin 256
Bradlaugh, Charles 41, 96
Brady, E.J. 78, 244, 310, 320, 330
Bridge, Patten Smith 305
Brieux, Eugene, *Les Avariés (Damaged Goods)* 264, 310–12, 313, 314, 326
Broadhurst, Henry
  in fiction 147
  and Independent Labour Party 91
  and Joseph Burgess 36, 80
  Maggie Harkness on 140–1, 142
  and Sir John Brunner 42
Broda, Rudolf 257, 276
Brodzky, Leon (Spencer Brodney) 244
Bromby, Charles Henry 22
Bromley, Frederick H. (Fred) 71, 80, 81, 207
Brookes, Herbert
  on Beatrice Webb 146
  and Champion 7, 9, 65, 69, 82, 194, 195–7, 199, 229, 235, 266, 269, 321
  and *Champion* newspaper 200, 201, 205
  on Henry Hyndman 9
  and John Burns 253
  journal articles 283

in mining industry 146, 152, 195–6
tennis playing 222
and Walter Murdoch 266
on William Lane 143
Brookes, Norman 113, 222, 256, 266
Brookesmith, Frank
Browne, T.A. ('Rolf Boldrewood') 282
Browning, Robert 17, 181, 185, 240, 282
  'The Lost Leader' 335
Brunner, Sir John 42, 140
Bryant and May factory 37, 41–2, 60
Bryce, James 80, 87
Buchanan, Alfred John 293
  Bubble Reputation 11, 207–8, 211, 293
Buckden, England 14, 325, 328, 334
Bull, Hilda *see* Esson, Hilda
Burgess, Joseph
  and Champion 80, 94
  and Henry Broadhurst 36, 80
  and Henry Hyndman 32, 36, 57
  and Independent Labour Party 87, 88, 89, 91–2
  memoirs 94
  and Robert William Hudson 36
  and Trafalgar Square Riots 55
Burns, John
  and Alfred Linnell 105
  arrest of 40
  and Beatrice Potter (Webb) 140
  Ben Tillett on 65
  and Champion 8, 9, 49, 65, 68, 73, 94, 136, 233, 253
  cycling interviews 159–60
  and Dorothea Mackellar 253
  and Elsie Belle Champion 267
  in fiction 47, 100–1, 102, 129, 149
  and Henry Hyndman 49, 50–1, 57, 73, 94
  and Herbert Brookes 253
  and Independent Labour Party 88, 91, 92
  and Jack J.D. Fitzgerald 70, 75, 76, 77, 78, 80, 87
  and Juliet Champion 99

and Katharine Susannah Prichard 291
at *Labour Elector* 42, 50, 134
and London Dock Strike 58, 59, 61–2, 63, 64, 66, 74, 133
and Maggie Harkness 138–9, 141, 142
and Miles Franklin 253
portrait *167*
Robert Cunninghame Graham on 62
and SDF 31, 34, 35, 36, 46, 49, 50–1, 57, 82
trade union involvement 65, 67, 69
and Trafalgar Square Riots 54–5, 56–7, 106, 129, 287
and Vida Goldstein 253, 267
and Walter Murdoch 288
William Marcus Thompson on 73–4
writing 180
Burns, Martha 62
Burrows, Herbert 34, 40, 41, 85–6, 105, 198–9

C

Caffyn, Stephen Mannington 177
Callwell, Sir Charles Edward, *Stray Recollections* 18
Carey, Ernest 200, 202
Carpenter, Edward
  and Bernard Shaw 106
  and Champion 109
  in fiction 102
  and Havelock Ellis 11
  and Juliet Champion 99, 109
  and Maggie Harkness 146, 182
  and SDF 30, 33, 39, 181
  Sheffield house guests 124
  Social Science series publication 64
  'The Simplification of Life' 124
Casteau, John Buckley 201, 235
Chamberlain, Joseph 30, 34–5, 55, 56, 57
Champion, Anne (Annie)
  Beatrice (sister)
    birth 14
    and Champion 233, 266, 290, 299, 321
    childhood 15
    and James Hyde Champion 199

Champion, Arthur Duncan
  (brother) 14, 21, 253, 333
Champion, Charles Stuart
  (brother) 14–15
Champion (née Urquhart),
  Elizabeth Herries (paternal
  grandmother) 18
Champion (née Goldstein), Elsie
  Belle
  and Bernard Shaw 267–8
  birth 227, 235
  Book Lovers' Library 226,
    233, 240, 242, 244, 249,
    251, 253–4, 255, 259,
    266–7, 268, 302, 333
  bookplate *172*, 241, 244, 302
  Champion's friendship with
    227, 230–1
  Champion's marriage to 12,
    13, 226, 227, 228–9, 230,
    232, 233, 238, 239–40, 243,
    244, 245, 247, 249, 251,
    253, 259, 264, 265, 266,
    268–9, 298–9, 333, 334
  character 227–8, 244
  Christian Science beliefs 250
  death 268
  education 227, 243
  family background 226, 227
  in fiction 228
  and Hugh McCrae 260–1, 306
  interests and activities 113,
    222, 226, 227, 228, 230,
    253, 254
  and Isabella Goldstein 226,
    235
  and John Burns 267
  and Katharine Susannah
    Prichard 274, 315, 328, 330
  and Miles Franklin 252
  overseas travel 267–8
  and Peter (Roy) Newmarch
    264
  portrait *170*
  school run by 226, 227
  theft from 298
Champion (née Urquhart),
  Henrietta Susan (mother) 14,
  15–16, 18, 99, 199, 231
Champion, Henry Hyde
  bankruptcy 264, 321, 333
  birth 14, 163
  character 7, 8, 9–10, 18, 31,
    32, 44, 49, 52–4, 71, 94–5,
    128, 141–2, 194–5, 232,
    284, 307–8, 329

childhood 11, 14–17
death 10, 224, 321, 326, 333
education 17, 28
health issues 21, 88, 166, 187,
  212, 220, 249–51, 266, 269,
  321, 325, 329
military career 7, 10, 17–18,
  19–21, 23, 36, 56, 197, 248,
  263
personal papers 10, 268
physical appearance 71, 128
portrait *167*
religious faith 333–4
sexuality 96–7
Champion, Henry Hyde, public
  speaking
  Albert Park 109, 247
  Australian tour 67–8, 69, 174
  Fabian Society 39
  'The Future of British
    Democracy' 85
  'Poets of the Revolution' 24
  Social Questions Committee
    256–7
  street corner 99, 257
  'Theosophy in Practical Life'
    197
Champion, Henry Hyde, writing
  'An Aberdeenshire Poet' 147
  'The Age of Gilt' column 156
  agent 255
  'The Antipodean Repertory
    Theatre: Ibsen and Some
    Others' 299
  Australian socialist movement
    column 277
  Bohemian Life (translation of
    Henri Murger's work) 17,
    190, 290
  'A Christmas Meeting' 216
  The Claim of Women 239
  'The Crushing Defeat of Trade
    Unionism in Australia' 79
  on cycling 159, 196, 197
  for David Syme's *Age* 244–6
  The Facts about the Unemployed
    37
  'The Golden Fleece' column
    155
  The Great Dock Strike in London
    59, 64
  'The Labour Platform at the
    Next Election' 87
  'Letters to Revolutionary
    Agents' 30

*The Life and Work of Miss Vida
  Goldstein* 236–7, 256
'The Old Chivalry and the
  New' 198
pseudonyms 17, 30, 88, 145,
  148, 149, 155, 202–3, 215,
  216, 222
'Quorum Pars Fui: An
  Unconventional
  Autobiography' 288
The Root of the Matter 11, 12,
  107–8, 229
'Slough of Despond' 223
'Snick-Snacks' column 222
'Street Fighting' 37
'Victor and Vanquished' 215
'The Yellow Rose: A Memory
  of a Little Girl' 215
Champion, James Hyde (father)
  absence of 11, 14, 15–16
  and Annie Beatrice Champion
    199
  and Champion's military
    career 17–18
  death 199
  estate 10, 199
  financial gift to Champion 25
  marriage 18
  military career 10, 14, 163–4
Champion, John Carey (paternal
  grandfather) 18
Champion (née Bennett), Juliet
  Champion's marriage to 12,
    97–100, 216, 227, 334
  death 99, 100, 106, 124
  employment 98
  in fiction 12, 100–4, 108–13
  see also Shaw, (George)
    Bernard, *Pygmalion*
Champion, Louisa Elizabeth
  (sister) 14, 199
Champion, Mary Leslie (sister)
  14, 126, 148, 199
Champion newspaper 163, 199,
  200–7, 214, 216–18
Chidley, William 256, 278
  The Answer 259
Christian Science 250
Chubb, Percival 29
Churchill, Randolph 84–5, 149,
  262
Churchill, Winston 21, 262
Clarke, Marcus 176
Clarke, William J. 32, 33
Clayton, Joseph, *The Rise and
  Decline of Socialism* 65, 82–3

INDEX

Cole, Elsie 273, 284, 313, 330
Colles, William 189–90
Cosme Colony (New Australia Movement) 143, 151, 158
Courtney, Leonard 128
Cowen, Joseph 24, 56
Craigston Castle, Scotland 18, 19, 102, *167*, 231, 334
Crowley, Aleister 291, 293, 294
Cunninghame Graham, Robert Bontine
  and Alfred Linnell 105
  arrest of 40
  on Ben Tillett 59
  Champion on 127
  dining out 291
  in fiction 129
  and Independent Labour Party 85
  and Jack Fitzgerald 77, 80
  on John Burns 62
  and Keir Hardie 127
  at *Labour Elector* 42
  and London Dock Strike 62
  and Maggie Harkness 127, 141, 161
  and SDF 181
  and Trafalgar Square Riots 129, 182
  and William Morris 28
Currie, Lady Mary Montgomerie ('Violet Fane') 181

D

Daniell, A.C. 23
Davidson, John 184
Davidson, John Morrison 77, 86, 243
Davidson (née Pope), Sarah 278
Davidson, Thomas 29, 86, 100
Davies, Charles and Arthur Llewellyn 17
Davies, John Llewellyn 40
Davitt, Michael 30, 64, 207, 309
  Life and Progress in Australasia 153
Deakin, Alfred
  and Alfred John Buchanan 293
  and Anti-Sweating League 208, 209
  and *Book Lover* 241
  and Champion 68
  citizen-soldier concept 286
  and David Syme 246
  dining out 306

and Edith Prichard 272–3
and Elisha Clement De Garis 201
and Ernest Joske 195
and George Meredith 289
and Henry Bournes Higgins 248
and Katharine Susannah Prichard 289
on Melbourne University Extension Committee 282
newspaper articles 246
residence 273
and Vida Goldstein 242
in Wallaby Club 242
and Walter Murdoch 289
De Garis, Elisha Clement 201
Democratic Federation *see* Social Democratic Federation (SDF) (London) (former Democratic Federation)
Diack, William 53, 87
Downey, Edmund 190
Dreyfus, Irma 272
  The Spring and Summer of French Literature 272
Duff, General Sir Beauchamp 19, 20, 262–3
Dunraven, Lord 43
Dyson, Ambrose 201–2
Dyson, Will 244, 253, 298, 318, 320

E

East London Ropemakers' Union 65, 69
Elder, Alexander Lang 174, 175–6, 215
Elder, Alison 179, 221, 223
Elder, Austin 175–6, 223, 224
Elder, Mary Anne 179–80, 186
Elder, Sir Thomas 175
Elder, Thomas Edward 223
Ellis, Havelock
  and Book Lovers' Library 266
  and Champion 33, 34, 96–7, 109, 111
  and Olive Schreiner 11, 30–1, 121, 125
  and Progressive Association 28–9
  and SDF 29, 30
  Studies in the Psychology of Sex 11, 29, 96–7, 121–2
  and William Chidley 259
Engels, Friedrich

and Adolphe Smith 44, 45
and Annie Besant 122
on *A City Girl* (Harkness) 126
and Eduard Bernstein 88
and Eleanor Marx 63, 65
on Gertrude Guillaume-Schack 122
and Katharine Susannah Prichard 277, 305
Esson (née Bull), Hilda 275, 277, 282, 310, 315, 318, 330
Esson, Louis
  death 330
  dining out 243, 244, 260
  and Katharine Susannah Prichard 310, 320, 330
  residence 315
  and Socialist Party 257
  theatre work 293, 314

F

Fabian Society
  affiliates of 35, 36, 145, 187, 294
  Champion's educational speeches 39
  Clementina Black's lecture 41
  and the clergy 102
  in fiction 148, 150
  founding of 29
  and Henry Hyndman 50
  at International Socialist Workers' Congress 187
  and Jack Fitzgerald 78
  and Katharine Susannah Prichard 294
Fasoli's Restaurant (Melbourne) 243–4, 253, 304
Fellowship of New Life 29, 86, 100, 143
Fennessy, Rodney 189, 190
Fielding, John 33, 34
Fields, Arthur 90, 92, 187
Findley, Edward 80, 81–2, 207, 208, 218, 247
Fitzgerald, J.D. (Jack)
  and Champion 70–1, 75–6, 77–8, 79, 80, 85, 87, 140, 142
  and Fabians 78
  and John Burns 70, 75, 76, 77, 78, 80, 87
  and Keir Hardie 80, 87
  and Robert Cunninghame Graham 77, 80
  and SDF 78

and Tom Mann 80
and William Booth 144
Fletcher, J.S.
  Daniel Quayne 11, 101
  The Quarry Farm 101
Foulger, John C. 24, 25, 28, 30, 114
Franklin, Stella Miles (Miles Franklin) 252–3, 255, 266, 290, 321, 330
  My Brilliant Career 252
Frost, John Dixon 26
Frost, Robert Percival Bodley (Percy)
  and Champion 98, 137, 147, 166, 173, 290
  and *Champion* newspaper 200
  education 17, 174
  and James Leigh Joynes 24
  and Land Reform Union 26
  and Maggie Harkness 165
  and Maritime Strike 68
  marriage 232–3
  at Modern Press 30, 31
  and Mrs Gordon Baillie 56, 166, 173
  and SDF 27, 29, 30, 31
  social consciousness 22

G
Galsworthy, John 254, 267, 287
Garnett, Richard 120, 132
Gas Consumers' League 258–9, 264, 298
Gay, William 202, 204, 213
George, Henry 24, 26, 29, 30, 36
  Progress and Poverty 22–3, 25
Gerrie, George 85, 86–7, 194
Gilmore (née Cameron), Mary 275, 304, 310, 313
Gissing, George 147, 187, 189–90, 251–2, 255
  The Nether World 31
  The Unclassed 185
Gladstone, William E. 180, 181
Gleeson White, Joseph 48–9
Glynn, L.A. 90, 187
Goldstein, Aileen 227, 250, 260, 267, 268, 274
Goldstein, Isabella
  and Champion 212–13, 229, 230, 233, 235
  death 235
  and Elsie Belle Champion 226, 235
  family background 234
financial issues 227
home break-in and theft 298
and Irma Dreyfus 272
as suffragist and social reformer 208, 235, 237, 239
Goldstein, Jacob 235–6
Goldstein, Selwyn 227, 261
Goldstein, Vida
  and Adelaide Hogg 224
  and Adela Pankhurst 260, 292
  and Alfred Deakin 242
  and Bernard Shaw 267–8, 296–7
  and Champion 11, 12, 216, 222, 232, 236–7, 238, 249, 264, 277
  Christian Science beliefs 250
  death 268
  education 272
  election campaigns 233, 234, 236, 238, 253, 256, 259, 295
  and Hugh McCrae 261
  and Ina Higgins 248
  and John Burns 253, 267
  and John Monash 236
  and Katharine Susannah Prichard 274, 295–7, 320
  Les Documents Du Progrès article 276
  The Life and Work of Miss Vida Goldstein 236–7, 256
  and Lilian Locke 298
  overseas travel 267–8
  portrait *171*
  and Rudolf Broda 276
  school run by 226, 227
  'Socialism of To-day: An Australian View' 277
  as suffragist and social reformer 235, 237–8, 239, 240, 295, 296–7, 310, 312, 317
Gordon, Adam Lindsay 161, 176, 178, 204, 260
Gough, Evelyn 234, 238, 278, 320
Gross, Alan 256
Gross, Bertha 264
Guillaume-Schack, Gertrude 122, 147

H
Hackett, John Winthrop 158
Hallward, Cyril R. 28
Hamilton-Smith, Norman 223
Hamlyn, Alice Bruce (Glory)
  and Adelaide Hogg 185–6, 188, 189, 190, 223
  and Champion 229
  and Morley Roberts 156, 185–6, 188–9, 190–1, 232, 299–300, 331, 334
Hancock, John
  and Anti-Sweating League 209
  and Champion 81, 202, 206, 207, 208, 210
  and Maritime Strike 68, 70, 71, 72, 74, 75, 77, 79
  political seat 80
Hardie, Keir
  and Champion 81, 82, 208
  election campaign (1888) 12, 105, 114, 126–7, 134
  extramarital affair 285–6
  in fiction 47
  Henry Hyndman on 94
  and Independent Labour Party 41, 82, 83, 84, 85, 89, 90, 91
  and Jack Fitzgerald 80, 87
  and Maggie Harkness 12, 105, 114, 126–7, 134, 161
  portrait *168*
  and Robert Cunninghame Graham 126
  and SDF 46
  and Tom Mann 105, 126
  and William Morris 28
Harford, Lesbia (Lesbia Keogh) 316, 317
Harkness, Jane 125, 136
Harkness, Margaret (Maggie)
  and Alice Caroline Moon 151
  in Australia 142–4, 146, 147, 150–62
  and the Avelings 122
  and Beatrice Potter (Webb) 114, 115, 116–17, 119–20, 121, 123, 127, 128, 132–3, 134–6, 138, 140–1, 144–6
  and Ben Tillett 133, 136–7, 161
  and Bernard Shaw 130, 145, 147, 148
  and Cardinal H.E. Manning 114, 117, 128, 131–2, 133–4, 135, 145, 162
  Champion's relationship with 12–13, 46, 51, 114, 118, 121, 124–8, 129, 130–3, 137, 139, 141–2, 146, 147, 150, 152,

INDEX

154, 156, 158–9, 161, 165, 198, 211, 216, 227, 280, 333
and Clementina Black 130
on cycling 159
death 164–5
editorial work 146–7, 186
education 116–17
and Edward Carpenter 145, 182
family background 114–15
in fiction 112, 117, 118, 147–8, 149
on Henry Broadhurst 141, 142
in India 163–4
and John Barlas 145, 182
and John Burns 138–9, 141, 142
and Keir Hardie 12, 105, 114, 126–7, 134, 161
and London Dock Strike 12–13, 60, 61, 62, 63–4, 66, 101, 114, 116, 128, 133–4, 162
and Maritime Strike 76, 77
nursing career 117–18, 119, 154
and Olive Schreiner 102, 124, 125, 145, 152, 182
and Percy Frost 165
portrait *172*
residential club 157–8, 160
and Robert Cunninghame Graham 127, 141, 161
and Salvation Army 129, 130, 139, 143, 163, 164, 165
and SDF 105–6, 125, 129, 131
and Sidney Webb 144–6
and Tom Mann 136–7, 139, 141, 142, 161, 286
typing business 155–7
on William Morris 28
Harkness, Margaret (Maggie), writing
agent 255
'An Anarchist's Funeral' 105–6, 146–7
'Called to the Bar' 118, 125, 152–5, 159, 164, 327
Captain Lobe 11, 129, 130–1, 139, 146
'The Children of the Unemployed' 136–7
A City Girl 123, 125–6, 132, 146, 275
'Connie' 147
A Curate's Promise 164

In Darkest London 164
early 118–20
George Eastmont 11, 22, 63–4, 100, 101–4, 106, 108, 109–11, 120, 124–5, 135, 142–3, 151, 162–3, 270, 275, 279, 291, 302–3, 313, 325, 329
'Girl Labour in the City' 130
'The Gospel of Getting On' 101
The Horoscope 164
'Hospital Nurses' 118
'Ideals' 162
Imperial Credit 104, 115–16, 139, 156, 160
Indian Snapshots 164
'John Law' pseudonym 62, 101, 115, 128, 129, 130–2, 144, 146, 147
on labour leaders 141–2
'The Loafer in Germany' 137
A Manchester Shirtmaker 127, 137, 146
newspaper columns 151, 160–1
Novel Review 145, 146, 147
Out of Work 129–30, 132
'Roses and Crucifix' 125, 136, 144
'Some Anglo-Australians I Have Met' 161–2
'Tempted London: young men' 129
'Toilers in London' 129
'Viennese Pauper' 137
Harkness, Robert 115, 117, 125, 164
Hatton Castle, Scotland 14–15, 18, 86, 231, 266, 321
Headlam, Stewart 26, 102
Henry, Alice 238–9, 320
Hervey, Grant 201
Hicks, Amie 31, 33, 34, 65
Higgins, Henry Bournes 108, 194, 237, 241, 242, 248–9, 253
Higgins, Nettie *see* Palmer (née Higgins), Nettie
Higgins, Nina (Ina) 248
Hill, Octavia 123, 140
Hogg, Francis 174
Hogg (née Elder), Adelaide Lashbrooke
affluence 175, 176, 223, 224
and Alice Hamlyn 185–6, 188, 189, 190, 223

birth 224
Champion's affair with 12, 13, 158, 173–4, 178–80, 181, 184, 185, 186–7, 188, 189, 190, 192–4, 196, 197, 198, 199, 203, 207, 209, 210–11, 212–17, 219–22, 224, 227, 229, 230, 269, 274, 280, 287, 308, 314–15, 325, 331, 334
and Champion's second marriage 226
children's holiday program 222
death 224, 225
family background 174, 175
Jemima 174, 275
marriage 174, 186, 190, 192–4, 213, 220, 230
portrait *169*
return to England 220, 221, 223–4
Theosophy 197, 198
and Vida Goldstein 224
Hogg, Henry Roughton
and Champion's affair with wife 174, 178, 179, 186, 189, 190, 192–4, 196, 213, 217, 220, 221, 224, 230, 315
children's holiday program 222
death 224
interests and activities 175, 198
return to England 223, 224
Hogg, Shirley Roughton
childhood 175, 179, 181, 186, 190, 192, 193, 220, 221, 223
and Katharine Susannah Prichard 274
marriage 223
Hogg, William Edward 174
Hope (Hawkins), Anthony 17, 191, 212, 255
Howard, Rosalind (Countess of Carlisle) 149
Hudson, Robert William
and Champion 36, 38, 290
family background 35–6
and Independent Labour Party 83, 88, 89–90, 91
and Joseph Burgess 36
and London Dock Strike 62
move to France 290, 304
as SDF financier 35, 36
Hugo, Victor 21

The Last Day of a Condemned Man 121
The Man Who Laughs 322
Hyndman, Henry Mayer
 and Alfred Linnell 105
 on Bernard Shaw 94
 and Champion 9, 31, 32, 37–8, 39–40, 42–3, 45–6, 49–51, 52, 94, 251
 early activism 24, 25
 and Fabians 50
 in fiction 130
 Herbert Brookes on 9
 and Independent Labour Party 84
 and John Burns 49, 50–1, 57, 73, 94
 and Joseph Burgess 32, 36, 57
 and Juliet Champion 99
 on Keir Hardie 94
 and London Dock Strike 66
 memoirs 94, 123
 portrait *168*
 and SDF 27, 30, 31, 32–3, 34–5, 37–8, 39, 40, 50–1, 78, 128, 199, 263
 and Trafalgar Square Riots 54, 55, 56, 57, 106, 287
Hyndman, Matilda 31, 94

I
Independent Labour Party (ILP)
 founding of 7, 8, 41, 67, 82–95, 128, 308
 at International Socialist Workers' Congress (1893) 90, 187
 Maggie Harkness on 161
International Socialist Workers' Congress (Zurich, 1893) 90, 187–8

J
Jack, Andrew William 142
James, John Stanley '(The Vagabond') 284
Jameson, Storm 188, 334
 The Writer's Situation and Other Essays 331
Jerome, Jerome K. 155, 189, 191
 'Stage-Land' 174
Jollie Smith, Christian 275, 318
Jones, J.P. 256, 257
Joske, Ernest 195
Joynes, James Leigh
 activism 24

Adventures of a Tourist in Ireland 25
 and Champion 28, 216
 and Juliet Champion 99
 at Modern Press 30, 31
 and Percy Frost 24
 and SDF 29, 30, 31, 39, 40

K
Kingsley, Charles 26, 38, 141, 181, 302–3
 'The World of Woman' 303
 The Water Babies 301, 303
Kingsley, Mary ('Lucas Malet') 302
 The Wages of Sin 302
Kipling, Rudyard 20, 279, 291
 Stalky & Co. 17
Knowles, James 79, 146, 180
Kropotkin, Peter 136, 182, 294

L
Labour Elector
 Barry Maltman's role 41, 44, 85, 89, 147
 and *Champion* newspaper 200
 demise of 51, 141
 in fiction 148
 founding of 41, 83
 and social reform 42, 67, 137
 and 'Tory gold' 35, 134
Labour Electoral Association 49–50, 72, 83
Land Reform Union 26, 29
Lane, John 158
Lane, William 143, 158, 161
 The Workingman's Paradise 143
Lawson, Harry 247
Lawson, Henry 204, 205, 255
 In the Days when the World was Wide, and Other Verses 204–5
Lee, H.W. 46, 81, 99, 187, 208
Lenox Simpson, Bertram ('Putnam Weale'), *The Coming Struggle in East Asia* 287
Levy, Amy 120
Lindsay, Daryl 152
Lindsay, Lionel 152, 244, 261
Lindsay, Norman 152, 241–2, 244
Lindsay, Percy 152, 242, 244, 260
Lindsay, Ruby 152, 244
Linnell, Alfred 104–5, 106
Llewellyn, W.R. 23
Locke, Lilian 249, 297–8

Locke, Sumner 249, 297–8, 304, 323
London, Jack 264
London Dock Strike
 Australians' financial support 66, 74
 events of 7, 19, 58–67
 and Maggie Harkness 12–13, 60, 61, 62, 63–4, 66, 101, 114, 116, 128, 133–4, 162
 Strike Committee headquarters 48, 59
Lorimer, W.J. 199, 200
Lowe, Annie 247, 294
Lowe, David 90
Luffman (née Lane), Laura Bogue 43, 277, 311
Lyell, Andrew 71, 72
Lyons, Lewis 34, 43, 45, 46, 130
Lyttelton, Edward 24

M
MacDonald, James (Jem) 23, 24, 25, 30, 63, 99, 333
Macdonald, Louisa 299
MacDonald, Ramsay 93, 267
Mackellar, Dorothea 253, 256
 The Closed Door and Other Verses 256
Mackenzie, W.A. ('A.D. Mack') 189
 'Rowton House Rhymes' 189
Mahon, John 33, 105, 127
Mann, Tom
 and Beatrice Potter (Webb) 140
 and Champion 8, 53, 68, 76, 136, 250–1, 256, 266, 298
 extramarital affair 285, 286
 and Grant Hervey 201
 and Independent Labour Party 67, 84, 92
 and Jack Fitzgerald 80
 and Keir Hardie 105, 127
 at *Labour Elector* 42
 and London Dock Strike 58, 59, 61, 63, 66, 133
 and Maggie Harkness 136–7, 139, 141, 142, 161, 286
 The 'New' Trades Unionism: a reply to George Shipton 301
 on politicians 67
 portrait *168*
 on public speaking 139
 and SDF 33, 34, 37, 46
 and Socialist Party 257

INDEX 369

and Social Questions
  Committee 256–7
 trade union involvement
  65, 69
 *What a Compulsory Eight-Hour
  Day Means* 37, 41
Manning, Cardinal H.E.
 and Champion 68, 73, 334
 in fiction 103
 and Frederick Rolfe 47
 and Henry George 25
 and London Dock Strike 59,
  63–4
 and Maggie Harkness 114,
  117, 128, 131–2, 133–4, 135,
  145, 162
 and Mother Catherine
  Bathurst 136
Maritime Strike, Melbourne
 Champion after 75–82, 177
 Champion's arrival in
  Melbourne 67–8, 173, 174
 events of 69–75
Marsh, William 257, 258
Marshall-Hall, George 244, 283
 Hymns Ancient and Modern 285
Marx, Eleanor
 and Alfred Linnell 105
 on Champion 44
 death 122–3
 and Edward Aveling 121,
  122–3
 female peers 120
 and Friedrich Engels 63, 65
 and Havelock Ellis 11, 121
 at International Socialist
  Workers' Congress 187
 and London Dock Strike 62–3
 at Modern Press 31
 philanthropist committee's
  exclusion of 65
 public speaking 139
 and SDF 27, 31, 32
 and Socialist League 33
 'Sweating in Type-Writing
  Offices' 156
Marx, Karl 18, 23, 44, 45, 63,
 123, 277, 305
Matkin, William 84
Matters, Muriel 294–5
Maudsley, Frederick W. 249
Mauger, Samuel 208
Maurice, Frederick D. 25–6, 102
Maxwell, James Shaw 88, 89,
 90, 187

Maxwell, Maisie (May
 Moorehead) 296, 306
McCrae, Hugh 176, 242, 244,
 260–1, 283, 306, 330
McCubbin, Annie 177, 254, 304,
 320
McCubbin, Frederick 177, 242,
 254, 260, 272, 284, 320
 'The Pioneer' 254, 304
McEacharn, Sir Malcolm 233,
 244
McLean, William 72
McMahon, Gregan 113, 254,
 265, 293, 320
Meadows, Harry 195
Melba, Dame Nellie (Helen
 Mitchell) 176
Melbourne Literary Club 313
Melbourne Literature Society
 282–3
Melbourne Repertory Theatre
 111, 254, 293
Meldrum, Max 201, 244
Meldrum House, Scotland
 18–19, 231, 334
Meredith, George 121, 185, 289
Michel, Louise 105, 147
Modern Press
 and Bernard Shaw 26–7
 and Champion 37, 98, 99
 founding of 25
 and Jack Williams 34
 publications, 1884–5 30–1
 SDF newspaper published by
  29–30, 38
Monash, John 236, 306
Moon, Alice Caroline 151
Moore, Henry Byron 176, 326
Moore, William 244, 253, 293,
 304, 320
Morris, William
 and Alfred Linnell 105
 *Under an Elm-Tree; Or Thoughts
  in the Country-side* 282
 arrest of 34
 and Bernard Shaw 26
 and Champion 28, 38, 53, 98,
  216, 298, 334
 'Chants for Socialists' 30
 character 28
 and Charles Mowbray 147
 as designer 27, 28, 110, 175
 A Dream of John Ball 143
 in fiction 130
 and John Barlas 182
 and Juliet Champion 99

 and Keir Hardie 28
 lectures on 282
 Maggie Harkness on 28
 and parliamentary elections,
  1885 34–5
 'revolutionary' poem 10
 and Robert Cunninghame
  Graham 28
 and Rosalind Howard 148
 and SDF 27, 29, 30, 31, 50,
  82, 181
 socialism, interest in 26
 and Socialist League 28, 32–3,
  34, 56, 105
 on 'Tory gold' 35
 and Trafalgar Square Riots
  55, 56
 'What We Have to Look For'
  334
Mowbray, Charles 34, 105,
 146–7, 188
Muir, Sarah 208
Murdoch, Walter
 and Alfred Deakin 289
 on Bernard O'Dowd 289
 and Bernard Shaw 32, 52,
  253, 288
 and Champion 9–10, 22, 57,
  58, 64–5, 263, 288, 289
 editorial work 283, 288
 and George Meredith 289
 and Herbert Brookes 266
 and John Burns 288
 and Katharine Susannah
  Prichard 282, 288
 lecturing position 282
 in London 288–9
 and Melbourne Literature
  Society 282, 283
Murger, Henri 290
 Scènes de la Vie de Bohème 17,
  190, 290
Murphy, William E. 69, 70, 75,
 80, 210, 243
Murray, Gilbert 112

N

Nash, Vaughan 60, 66, 140
Nesbit, Edith (Edith Bland) 29,
 40, 204
Nesbit, Edward Pariss 204, 278
New Australia Movement
 (Cosme Colony) 143, 151, 158
Newmarch, Peter (Roy) 260, 264
Nightingale, Florence 118, 140,
 292

Novel Review 145, 146, 147

O

O'Dowd, Bernard
Dawnward? 283
dining out 260
journal and newspaper work 201, 288
and Katharine Susannah Prichard 282–3, 330
and Melbourne Literary Club 313
'Poetry Militant' 283
and Socialist Party 257
Walter Murdoch on 289
and William Chidley 259
'Young Democracy' 163
O'Hara, J.B. 204, 273
Olivier, Sydney 187

P

Paine, Thomas, *Common Sense* 38, 79
Palmer (née Higgins), Nettie
and *Book Lover* 241, 275
and Champion 251
Fourteen Years 254
and Katharine Susannah Prichard 275, 282, 304, 315–16, 317
and Melbourne Literature Society 282, 313
and Socialist Party 257
Palmer, Vance
journal contributions 283
and Katharine Susannah Prichard 313, 315, 317–18, 331
military service 262
residence 316
and Socialist Party 257
Pankhurst, Adela 260, 261, 292, 310
Pankhurst, Christabel 292
Pankhurst, Emily 260
Pankhurst, Sylvia 285–6, 292
Parker, Frank Critchley 271, 272
Parkes, Sir Henry 142, 143, 152, 279, 284
Parnell, Charles Stewart 30, 64, 83, 84, 308–9
Paul, Charles Kegan 25
Pease, Edward 29
Pinker, James Brand 255
Pitt, Marie 257, 258, 313
Pitt-Rivers, Emily 113, 265

Playgoers' Club 253
Poole, Stanley Lane 119
Potter, Beatrice *see* Webb (née Potter), Beatrice
Potter, Laurencina 119
Powell, Mrs (Margaret) 277, 294, 297
Prendergast, George Michael
on Bernard Shaw 232
and Champion 81, 194, 195, 206–7, 208, 209, 210, 211–12, 214, 218, 219, 220, 232
in fiction 207–8
and Harry Meadows 195
and Katharine Susannah Prichard 309
political seat 80–1, 194
troubled times of 219–20
Prichard, Alan 274–5, 277, 317, 319
Prichard, Edith
and Alfred Deakin 272–3
and Champion 279, 280
death 319
as governess 275
and Katharine Susannah Prichard 306, 310, 312, 316, 319
marriage 272, 278, 286
Prichard, Frederick 300
Prichard, Katharine Susannah
and Alfred Deakin 289
and Alfred John Buchanan 293
at Australian Volunteer Hospital 303–4
and Bernard O'Dowd 282–3, 330
and Bernard Shaw 291
and Book Lovers' Library 275
Champion's affair with 12, 71, 179, 258, 269, 270–1, 279–82, 284–5, 288, 289–91, 293, 294, 298, 300, 302, 304, 305–9, 312, 313–15, 319, 324, 326, 330–1
Champion's early connection with 274, 276
and Christian Jollie Smith 275, 318
Communism 277, 286, 294, 305, 318, 319
death 330
and Edith Prichard 306, 310, 312, 316, 319

education 272, 273, 275
and E.J. Brady 310, 320, 330
and Elsie Belle Champion 274, 328, 330
and Elsie Cole 284, 330
and Frank Wilmot 283–4, 320, 330
and George Meredith 289
and George Prendergast 309
and Guido Baracchi 305–6, 309, 313, 315, 316, 317–18, 331
health issues 319, 329, 330
and Henry Tate 283, 320, 330
on her writing 331–2
and Hilda Esson 275, 277, 282, 310, 318, 330
and Hugo Throssell 309, 314, 318–19, 330
and John Burns 291
and Lilian Locke 297–8
and Louis Esson 310, 320, 330
and Mary Gilmore 275, 304, 310, 313
and Nettie Palmer 275, 282, 304, 315–16, 317
overseas life 286–8, 289–92, 296–8, 300–5, 323, 325
portrait 172
and Rudolf Broda 276
and Salvation Army 291
and Shirley Roughton Hogg 274
and Sumner Locke 297–8, 304, 323
teaching career 275, 276, 282
and Vance Palmer 313, 315, 317–18, 330
and Vida Goldstein 274, 295–7, 320
and Walter Murdoch 282, 288
and Will Dyson 298, 320
and William Moore 304, 320
Prichard, Katharine Susannah, writing
Bid Me to Love 324–5, 329
The Black Opal 313, 315
'The Bride of Faraway' 327
Brumby Innes 320
The Burglar 297
'Bush Fires' 274
Child of the Hurricane (autobiography) 270, 271, 274, 277–8, 279–82, 283, 287, 293, 295–6, 298, 301,

305, 310, 314, 324, 330, 331, 334
'A City Girl in Central Australia' 275
Clovelly Verses 301
'The Cooboo' 320
Coonardo: The Well in the Shadow 321
Coonardoo 291, 321
'The Cow' 326
'Defence of Australia' 286–7
'Diana of the Inlet' 275, 293–4
The Earth Lover 302, 323
'Exiles' Symposium' 287, 292
'The Farthing Bundle' 303
'Forgotten Child' 303
'For Her Sake' 274
Golden Miles 327
The Great Man 314
'The Grey Horse' 319–20
'Happiness' 320
Haxby's Circus 317, 320, 321–3
Her Place 297
For Instance 295, 297
Intimate Strangers 329
'The Kid' 278
'Lavender' 313, 323–4
Les Documents Du Progrès article 276–7
'Life is Cheap: In Darkest England' 291
'Lips of My Love' 270, 294, 302
'A Night in Slumdom' 291–2
'Our Homes and Altars' 286
The Pioneers 275, 303, 304, 306, 320, 323
pseudonyms 294, 320
The Roaring Nineties 154, 279, 327
'A "Shrieking Sister" at Home' 292
Subtle Flame 11, 228, 317, 327–30
'That Brown Boy' 273–4
'A Wandrin' One' 301
'White Kid Gloves' 326–7
'Why I am a Communist' 277, 294
'Wild Honey' 316–17
The Wild Oats of Han 323–6
Windlestraws 301
Winged Seeds 327
Working Bullocks 277, 320
Prichard, Nigel 274–5, 305, 317, 319
Prichard, Tom 271–2, 273, 274, 275, 277–8, 286
Progressive Association 24, 28–9, 114, 121
Purves, James Liddell 203–4

Q

Quelch, Harry 30, 31, 34, 105, 129

R

Radford, Dollie 120, 123
Reaney, George Sale 25
Reid, (Matthew) Robert 72
Richards, Grant 254–5
Roberts, Frederick 20, 21
Roberts, Morley
and Alice Hamlyn 156, 185–6, 188–9, 190–1, 232, 299–300, 331, 334
Champion's friendship with 88, 92, 147, 184–5, 187, 188, 189, 190–1, 229, 244, 333, 334
Champion's letters to 10, 15, 21, 93, 158, 173, 174, 192, 193, 194, 198, 200, 202, 211, 212, 213, 214–15, 218–19, 220–1, 222–3, 224–5, 226, 227, 228, 230, 232, 233, 240, 243, 245, 246, 247, 251, 264, 268–9, 293, 296, 300, 308, 314–15, 322, 334
in Devon 302
dining out 291
in fiction 229
on literary immortality 331
portrait 172
Roberts, Morley, writing
agent 255
'The Artist' 185, 217
The Circassian 190
Hearts of Women 186, 188
Immortal Youth 185, 269
In Low Relief, A Bohemian Transcript 185
'The Man-Eater' 187
Maurice Quain 11, 191–2
'Mournful Corsica' 187
'Panic' 186
'The Plot of His Story' 192
The Private Life of Henry Maitland 185
'Round the World in a Hurry' 191
A Tramp's Note-Book 187, 188, 191
The Western Avenus 190
Roberts, Tom 284, 320
'The Mailman to Omeo (Snow Shoes)' 196
Robinson, Augustus Frederick 174
Rolfe, Frederick (Baron Corvo) 47, 189, 229, 255, 278
'An Unforgettable Experience' 189
Hadrian the Seventh 9, 11, 46–9
'Toto Tales' 189
Rosa, Samuel 176
The Truth about the Unemployed Agitation of 1890 176
Ross, Robert S. 266, 288
Russell, Sir William Howard 180

S

Salt, Henry S. 24, 29, 39, 99, 181
Salvation Army
farms 198
and John Barlas 182
and Katharine Susannah Prichard 291
and Maggie Harkness 129, 130, 139, 143, 163, 164, 165
and SDF 129, 130
see also Booth, William
Scheu, Andreas 28, 32, 33
Schreiner, Olive
and the Avelings 122, 123
family background 120–1
female peers 120
and Havelock Ellis 11, 30–1, 121, 125
and Maggie Harkness 102, 124, 125, 145, 152, 182
on retreat 124, 136
The Story of an African Farm 121
Undine 121
Scott, Rose 237, 252, 294
Shaw, Charles McMahon 268
Bernard's Brethren 268
Shaw, (George) Bernard
Androcles and the Lion 112
and Annie Besant 106
and Beatrice Potter (Webb) 138
and Champion 10, 26–7, 28, 32, 52–3, 65, 99, 102, 109, 124, 130, 254–5, 265–6, 267–8, 299, 300, 310
on chivalry 300

dining out 287
The Doctor's Dilemma 122
and Edward Carpenter 106
and Elsie Belle Champion 267–8
as Fabian 145, 187, 294
in fiction 150
George Prendergast on 232
Henry Hyndman on 94
and Juliet Champion 99, 109 (see also *Pygmalion* below)
and Katharine Susannah Prichard 291
and Land Reform Union 26
and Maggie Harkness 130, 145, 147, 148
Major Barbara 108, 112, 149
Man and Superman 108
marriage 232
and Miles Franklin 252–3
and Modern Press 26–7
and Muriel Matters 294
and Oscar Wilde 26
personal papers 268
published plays, sale of 254
Pygmalion 12, 22, 103, 106, 107, 108–13, 265, 266
real people as fictional characters 106–7, 112, 122, 149
and SDF 29, 30, 39
on socialism 182
and Socialist League 34
and Trafalgar Square Riots 55
and Vida Goldstein 267–8, 296–7
and Walter Murdoch 32, 52, 253, 288
and William Morris 26
Shelley, Percy Bysshe 22, 188, 282, 328
The Cenci 106, 107
The Revolt of Islam 28
Shelley Society 106, 107, 108
Sherard, Robert H. 182, 183
Sinclaire, Frederick 258, 313
Sladen, Douglas 182, 248
Smillie, Robert 127
Smith, Hubert Llewellyn 59, 60, 66
Smith, Robert Barr 175
Smith (Smith-Headingley), Adolphe 43–6, 47, 48, 49, 130–1, 187
Snodgrass, Evelyn 290

Social Democratic Federation (SDF) (London) (former Democratic Federation)
Champion as secretary 99
Champion's move away from and expulsion 37–8, 39–40, 43–6, 47, 49–51, 81, 82, 127–8, 131, 134
and the clergy 102
early years 27, 181
Edward Aveling's resignation 123
in fiction 131
founding of 7, 257
Henry Hyndman's leadership 27, 30, 31, 32–3, 34–5, 37–8, 39, 40, 50–1, 78, 128, 199, 263
and Independent Labour Party 85
at International Socialist Workers' Congress 187
and Jack Fitzgerald 78
name change 31, 114
newspaper 29–30, 38, 199
and parliamentary elections, 1885 34–5
Robert William Hudson as financier 35, 36
and Salvation Army 129, 130
and Socialist League 32–3
speakers' agreement 34
and 'Tory gold' 9
and Trafalgar Square Riots 54, 55, 56, 57
Social Democratic Federation (SDF) branches
Clerkenwell 31–2
Melbourne 158, 199, 257
Sydney 257–8, 279
Socialist 10, 257, 258, 259, 288, 293, 298, 299
Socialist League
and Bryant and May factory 41
and the clergy 102
and Maritime Strike 72–3, 78
and SDF 32–3
and William Morris 28, 32–3, 34, 56, 105
Socialist Party 92, 93, 256–9, 276, 288, 292, 305
Social Questions Committee (SQC) 256–7
Spectator Publishing Company 200–1

Spence, W.G. 69, 72, 75
Spencer, Baldwin 241
Spencer, Herbert 38, 141, 145, 146
Stanley, John 176
Stawell, Sir William 17, 178
Steele, Thomas 23
Stephens, A.G. 260
Stretch, Theodore 152
Strong, Archibald 229, 259, 288
Strong, Charles 194, 195, 208, 233, 235, 237, 322, 334
Sutherland, Alexander 248
Sutherland, Jane 272, 284
Sutherland, Julia 272
Sweet, Henry 106, 108, 111, 156
Sydney Labor Defence Committee 70, 74
Syme, David 176, 191, 244–6, 248

T
Tate, Henry 283, 284, 313, 318, 320, 330
Taylor, Helen 30
Taylor, Thomas G. 158
Thackeray, William Makepeace 16
The Newcomes 16
The Virginians 16–17, 18
Theosophy 152, 163, 197, 198–9, 294
Thompson, William Marcus 56, 73–4
Thomson, Catherine Hay 234, 238, 278
Threlfall, T.R. 127
Throssell, Hugo 178, 309, 314, 318–19, 330
Tichborne case 15, 112
Tierney, Edward 200
Tillett, Ben
and Champion 8, 65, 68, 76–7, 219
and Independent Labour Party 90
on John Burns 65
at *Labour Elector* 43
and Lewis Lyons 43
and London Dock Strike 58, 59–60, 63, 64, 65–6
and Maggie Harkness 133, 136–7, 161
The 'New' Trades Unionism: a reply to George Shipton 301
portrait *168*

Robert Cunninghame
   Graham on 59
 romantic liaison 285, 286
 trade union involvement 65
Toomey, James 59
'Tory gold' 9, 17, 35, 36, 47, 51,
   88, 91, 134, 155
Toynbee, Arnold J. 112, 149
Trades Hall Council (THC)
 Champion's enemies at 81–2,
   85, 87, 142, 158, 173, 177,
   191, 206–7, 208, 209–10,
   211–12, 218
 Champion's speech at 174
 and Maritime Strike 68, 69,
   70, 71, 73, 74, 75, 78, 79, 177
 members' political seats 80–1
 Ramsay MacDonald at 93
 Rudolf Broda at 257
Trafalgar Square Riots
 Alfred Linnell's death 104–5,
   106
 arrests and trial 56–8, 100,
   106, 124
 events of 54–6, 182, 287
 in fiction 103, 129
 and SDF 34
Trenwith, William 71, 77, 80, 82,
   194, 207
Tucker, T.G. 195
Turner, Ethel 241, 252, 255
Twopenny, Richard 17

U

Urquhart, Beauchamp Colclough
   (8th Laird of Meldrum and
   Byth) 18, 49, 231
Urquhart, Beauchamp Colclough
   (9th Laird of Meldrum and
   Byth) 231
Urquhart, David 18–19, 181
Urquhart, Francis 19
Urquhart, Sir Thomas of
   Cromarty 18, 19
Urquhart, William of
   Craigston 18

Urquhart, William of
   Cromarty 18

V

Vizard, Walter 200, 202, 219

W

Waldstein, Charles 181
Wallaby Club 242, 244, 248
Ward, Mrs Humphry (Mary
   Augusta Arnold)
 and Champion 51, 149
 female peers 120
 Marcella 11, 28, 51, 53, 57,
   66–7, 109, 112, 117, 118,
   141, 147–8, 295, 308–9
 real people as fictional
   characters 112
 Sir George Tressady 92–3, 112,
   149
 and Trafalgar Square Riots 55
Watts, John Hunter 34, 35, 99,
   105, 187
Webb (née Potter), Beatrice
 and Annie Besant 140
 and Bernard Shaw 138
 and Champion 10, 239
 cycling 159
 as Fabian 294
 in fiction 148
 and Havelock Ellis 11
 Herbert Brookes on 146
 and Independent Labour
   Party 91
 and John Burns 140
 and Lewis Lyons 43
 and Maggie Harkness 114,
   115, 116–17, 119–20, 121,
   123, 127, 128, 132–3, 134–6,
   138, 140–1, 144–6
 marriage 138, 145, 155
 and Ramsay MacDonald 267
 and Vaughan Nash 140
 writing 152
Webb, Sidney
 cycling 159
 as Fabian 294

 and Land Reform Union 26
 and Maggie Harkness 144–6
 marriage 138, 145, 155
 and Ramsay MacDonald 267
 writing 64, 152
Wenz, Paul, *Diary of a New Chum*
   254
White, Arnold 25, 43
White, John 247, 248
Wilde, Oscar
 agent 255
 and Bernard Shaw 26
 dining out 291
 and John Barlas 147, 182–4
 and Lady Mary Montgomerie
   Currie 181
 Lady Windermere's Fan 154–5,
   183, 184
 The Picture of Dorian Gray 184
 'The Soul of Man Under
   Socialism' 8, 182, 184
Williams, John Edward (Jack)
 and Champion 25, 28
 early activism 25, 33, 34
 and Juliet Champion 99
 and Modern Press 34
 and SDF 30, 34
 and Trafalgar Square Riots 54,
   56, 57, 106, 287
Wilmot, Frank ('Furnley
   Maurice') 256, 260, 283–4, 313,
   318, 320, 330
 'To God from the Weary
   Nations' 263, 283
Wilmot, Henry 283
Wilson, J. Havelock 69, 91
Wilson-Williams, Lily (Aunt Lil)
   279, 310, 312, 316, 319
Wollstonecraft, Mary,
   *A Vindication of the Rights of
   Women* 12

Y

Yewen, Alfred G. 72, 73
Yorick Club 176–7, 236
Young, Blamire 244, 253, 282

www.ingramcontent.com/pod-product-compliance
Lightning Source LLC
Chambersburg PA
CBHW031313160426
43196CB00007B/507